Hierarchical Linear Modeling

Hierarchical Linear Modeling

Guide and Applications

Editor
G. David Garson

North Carolina State University

Los Angeles | London | New Delhi
Singapore | Washington DC

Los Angeles | London | New Delhi
Singapore | Washington DC

FOR INFORMATION:

SAGE Publications, Inc.
2455 Teller Road
Thousand Oaks, California 91320
E-mail: order@sagepub.com

SAGE Publications Ltd.
1 Oliver's Yard
55 City Road
London EC1Y 1SP
United Kingdom

SAGE Publications India Pvt. Ltd.
B 1/I 1 Mohan Cooperative Industrial Area
Mathura Road, New Delhi 110 044
India

SAGE Publications Asia-Pacific Pte. Ltd.
3 Church Street
#10-04 Samsung Hub
Singapore 049483

Publisher: Vicki Knight
Editorial Assistant: Kalie Koscielak
Production Editor: Brittany Bauhaus
Copy Editor: Teresa Herlinger
Typesetter: C&M Digitals (P) Ltd.
Proofreader: Jeff Bryant
Indexer: Naomi Linzer
Cover Designer: Anupama Krishnan
Marketing Manager: Nicole Elliott
Permissions Editor: Adele Hutchinson

Printed in the United States of America

Library of Congress Cataloging-in-Publication Data

Hierarchical linear modeling: guide and applications / G. David Garson, editor.

p. cm.
Includes bibliographical references and index.

ISBN 978-1-4129-9885-7 (pbk.)

1. Linear models (Statistics) I. Garson, G. David.

QA279.H54 2013003'.74—dc232011051030

This book is printed on acid-free paper.

12 13 14 15 16 10 9 8 7 6 5 4 3 2 1

BRIEF CONTENTS

DETAILED CONTENTS

PREFACE

This book seeks to fill the need for a graduate-level introduction to the concepts, assumptions, and practical implementation procedures involved in common types of projects based on what is called hierarchical linear modeling, multilevel modeling, or linear mixed modeling. As such, it is not intended to replace comprehensive treatments, but rather to serve as a guide, easing the beginning graduate student or researcher into a complex and rapidly evolving field.

The first five chapters constitute the "Guide" portion. Chapter 1 differentiates linear mixed modeling (LMM) from ordinary regression and analysis of variance procedures, discussing why and when the researcher should employ linear mixed modeling. Types of linear mixed models are then presented, followed by a discussion of nonlinear models using generalized linear mixed modeling. LMM is increasingly the preferred procedure for modeling repeated measures, longitudinal, and growth models, and that is treated next. Finally, multivariate models (more than one dependent variable) and cross-classified models are discussed. Chapter 2 discusses the standard intraclass correlation test for assessing whether linear mixed modeling is needed, followed by treatment of the assumptions of linear mixed modeling with regard to estimation options, specification of covariance structure type, and more. An overview is then provided of how the goodness of fit of resulting models is gauged using information theory and likelihood ratio procedures. Chapters 3 through 5 then present for the HLM, SAS, and SPSS statistical packages, respectively, how basic models are implemented, including the null model, random coefficients models, and three-level models. Practical questions are answered, such as "Why do different software packages sometimes give different results for the same model and data?" "What do I do if I get a convergence warning?" "How do I compute effect size measures for linear mixed models?" and many others.

The last 10 chapters of the volume constitute the "Applications" section. These chapters are not reprinted articles, but rather are original essays written for teaching purposes, outlining the steps and rationales for a wide variety of multilevel analyses. The authors present step-by-step instructions using data for real-life examples, going from data entry to analysis of output to reporting of results. Examples are implemented in HLM, SAS, SPSS, and in one essay, Stata. Because different software packages utilize different nomenclature and present results differently, understanding how alternative software packages handle linear mixed models not only helps students read research articles coming from different software perspectives, but it also helps deepen understanding of the procedures involved, just as does reading alternative texts on the same statistical subject.

In the applications section, in Chapter 6, Lane, Nimon, and Roberts present a simple example of a random intercept model focused on interpreting GPA and SAT scores using SPSS. In Chapter 7, Shafto and Adelson present a different random intercept regression model for a math education intervention, using HLM software. Following this, random coefficients models are presented. In Chapter 8, Palardy uses HLM software to model the achievement gap in schools. Another random coefficients model, implemented in SAS for a psychology topic, emotional reactivity to daily stressors, is presented by Neupert in Chapter 9. Following this, three applications involving longitudinal analysis are treated. These include Greenberg and Phillips on modeling growth curve trajectories using HLM software (Chapter 10), Maerten-Rivera on piecewise growth models using HLM (Chapter 11), and Luhmann and Eid on discontinuous change models using HLM (Chapter 12). Next come two applications from cross-classified models: Patterson on natural science College Board scores using SAS (Chapter 13) and Leckie on educational data cross-classified by school and neighborhood (Chapter 14). Chapter 15, by Brant and Sheng, presents a more advanced SAS procedure for predicting future events based on a multivariate longitudinal model.

The editor wishes to thank all the contributors and peer reviewers who helped to shape this volume. It is hoped that the text will help welcome new generations of scholars to an immensely important set of tools that is transforming many disciplines across academia. Intended to supplement works that present a more comprehensive foundation in statistical theory and a wider array of applications and refinements, the present text is analogous to the "quick setup" guides that accompany full-length manuals, which may intimidate the novice software user. While containing information of considerable reference value even for experienced researchers, the hope of this work is to ease the way of graduate students and scholars into what may unnecessarily seem a complex and intimidating topic. If it contributes in some small way to this objective, it has met its intended purpose.

—*G. David Garson*
January 7, 2012

ABOUT THE EDITOR

G. David Garson is full professor of public administration at North Carolina State University, where he teaches courses on advanced research methodology, geographic information systems, information technology, and American government.

Professor Garson is editor of and contributor to the *Handbook of Public Information Systems,* third edition (2010); the *Handbook of Research on Public Information Technology* (2008); *Patriotic Information Systems: Privacy, Access, and Security Issues of Bush Information Policy* (2008), and *Modern Public Information Technology Systems* (2007). He is the author of *Public Information Technology and E-Governance: Managing the Virtual State* (2006); editor of *Public Information Systems: Policy and Management Issues* (2003); coeditor of *Digital Government: Principles and Practices* (2003); coauthor of *Crime Mapping* (2003); author of *Guide to Writing Quantitative Papers, Theses, and Dissertations* (2001); and editor of *Social Dimensions of Information Technology* (2000) and *Information Technology and Computer Applications in Public Administration: Issues and Trends* (1999). He is the author of *Neural Network Analysis for Social Scientists* (1998), *Computer Technology and Social Issues* (1995), and *Geographic Databases and Analytic Mapping* (1992). In addition, Professor Garson is author, coauthor, editor, or coeditor of 18 other books and author or coauthor of over 50 articles. His widely cited online textbook, *Statnotes: Topics in Multivariate Analysis* (2006–2012), is used by over a million people a year. Professor Garson received his undergraduate degree in political science from Princeton University (1965) and his doctoral degree in government from Harvard University (1969). He can be reached by email at David_Garson@ncsu.edu.

ABOUT THE CONTRIBUTORS

Forrest C. Lane is an assistant professor in the Department of Educational Studies and Research at the University of Southern Mississippi. His research focuses on the use of robust quasi-experimental designs, including propensity score analysis and the use of hierarchical linear modeling in educational research. He may be reached at Forrest.Lane@unt.edu.

Kim F. Nimon is an assistant professor in the Department of Learning Technologies at the University of North Texas. Her research agenda focuses on the development of quantitative methodologies to validly assess the outcomes of human resource development interventions. Her work on hierarchical linear modeling has been published in *Exceptional Children* and *Research Methodologies for Conducting Research on Giftedness*. She may be contacted at kim.nimon@unt.edu.

J. Kyle Roberts is an associate professor in the Department of Teaching and Learning at the Simmons School of Education and Human Development at Southern Methodist University. He currently teaches quantitative methods and has conducted numerous training sessions on multilevel analysis at annual meetings of the American Psychological Association, the American Educational Research Association, and the Southwest Educational Research Association. Dr. Roberts has authored two book chapters on multilevel analysis, published articles on the subject, and recently coedited *The Handbook of Advanced Multilevel Analysis* (Hox & Roberts, 2010). He may be reached at kyler@smu.edu.

Carissa L. Shafto, is a PhD candidate in the Department of Psychological and Brain Sciences at the University of Louisville, where she studies language and cognitive development. Carissa has used HLM in her own research and can be reached at carissa.shafto@louisville.edu.

Jill L. Adelson, is an assistant professor in the Educational Psychology, Measurement, and Evaluation program, in the Department of Educational and Counseling Psychology at the University of Louisville. She teaches courses in educational statistics and measurement and can be reached at jill.adelson@louisville.edu.

Gregory J. Palardy is a member of the faculty of the Graduate School of Education at the University of California, Riverside. His research addresses both methodological and substantive issues. Because of their enormous utility in educational research, most of his scholarship involves multilevel and longitudinal modeling, including growth mixture models and cross-classified growth models. The methodology work focuses on extending models for applications in education, while the substantive research addresses issues related to teacher and school effectiveness with an emphasis on equity. He may be reached at gregory .palardy@ucr.edu.

Shevaun D. Neupert is an associate professor in the Department of Psychology at North Carolina State University and may be contacted at shevaun_neupert@ ncsu.edu.

David F. Greenberg received his PhD in physics from the University of Chicago and is professor of sociology at New York University. His interests focus on criminology, sociology of law, deviance and social control, human sexuality, computational linguistics, ancient Near East studies, and quantitative methods. He may be contacted at dg4@nyu.edu.

Julie A. Phillips received her PhD in demography and sociology from the University of Pennsylvania and is associate professor of sociology at Rutgers University. Her research interests center on the demography of lethal violence (homicide and suicide). She may be contacted at jphillips@sociology.rutgers.edu.

Jaime Maerten-Rivera is a research associate in the School of Education, University of Miami, Florida. She researches various educational issues including science achievement, diversity in education, and teacher professional development. Her focus is in the area of applied methodological issues, with a secondary focus on investigating the efficacy of large-scale interventions. She can be contacted at jmaerten-rivera@miami.edu.

Maike Luhmann is currently a postdoctoral scholar in the Department of Psychology at the University of Chicago. She may be contacted at luhmann@ uchicago.edu.

Michael Eid is a full professor of evaluation and methodology at the Department of Psychology, Freie Universität Berlin, Germany. He may be contacted at michael .eid@fu-berlin.de.

Brian F. Patterson is an assistant research scientist in the College Board's Research and Development division, where he has worked since 2005. He may be reached for further questions at bpatterson@collegeboard.org.

George Leckie is a lecturer in Social Statistics at the Centre for Multilevel Modelling (CMM) at the University of Bristol. His main research interests are in applying multilevel modeling methodology to address research questions in social science and educational research that are complicated by complex structured data. His applications of multilevel modeling include highlighting statistical limitations of value-added models for measuring school performance, modeling rater effects in essay scoring, and modeling social and ethnic segregation among schools and neighborhoods. George has taught multilevel modeling workshops in

Bristol, Brussels, Cincinnati, Dublin, Essex, and London. He has authored extensive multilevel modeling Stata and R training materials as part of the highly popular free online multilevel modeling course provided by CMM (www.bristol.ac.uk/cmm/learning/course.html). Finally, George has co-developed the runmlwin Stata command for running the specialised MLwiN multilevel modeling statistical software package from within Stata (www.bristol.ac.uk/cmm/software/runmlwin/). He may be contacted at g.leckie@bristol.ac.uk.

Larry J. Brant is a statistician at the Biomedical Research Center of the Intramural Research Program (IRP) of the National Institute on Aging (NIA) in Baltimore, Maryland. He received his doctorate at the Department of Biostatistics of Johns Hopkins University under the supervision of David B. Duncan. For over 10 years, he taught a course on research analyses in the health services and social sciences in the Department of Health Policy and Management of Johns Hopkins School of Hygiene and Public Health, and he has served as the primary statistician for the IRP of the NIA for over 30 years. He may be contacted at brantl@mail.nih.gov.

Shan L. Sheng is a statistician at the Biomedical Research Center of the Intramural Research Program (IRP) of the National Institute on Aging (NIA) in Baltimore, Maryland. She received her doctorate at the Department of Mathematics and Statistics of McMaster University under the supervision of Narayanaswamy Balakrishnan. She has served as a statistician for the IRP of the NIA for over 10 years, concentrating on statistical computing related to biomedical research. She may be contacted at shengs@mail.nih.gov.

PART I
Guide

Fundamentals of Hierarchical Linear and Multilevel Modeling

G. David Garson

INTRODUCTION

Hierarchical linear models and multilevel models are variant terms for what are broadly called linear mixed models (LMM). These models handle data where observations are not independent, correctly modeling correlated error. Uncorrelated error is an important but often violated assumption of statistical procedures in the general linear model family, which includes analysis of variance, correlation, regression, and factor analysis. Violations occur when error terms are not independent but instead cluster by one or more grouping variables. For instance, predicted student test scores and errors in predicting them may cluster by classroom, school, and municipality. When clustering occurs due to a grouping factor (this is the rule, not the exception), then the standard errors computed for prediction parameters will be wrong (ex., wrong b coefficients in regression). Moreover, as is shown in the application in Chapter 6 in this volume, effects of predictor variables may be misinterpreted, not only in magnitude but even in direction.

Linear mixed modeling, including hierarchical linear modeling, can lead to substantially different conclusions compared to conventional regression analysis. Raudenbush and Bryk (2002), citing their 1988 research on the increase over time of math scores among students in Grades 1 through 3, wrote that with hierarchical linear modeling,

> The results were startling—83% of the variance in growth rates was between schools. In contrast, only about 14% of the variance in initial status was between schools, which is consistent with results typically encountered in cross-sectional studies of school effects. This analysis identified substantial differences among schools that conventional models would not have detected because such analyses do not allow for the partitioning of learning-rate variance into within- and between-school components. (pp. 9–10)

Linear mixed models are a generalization of general linear models to better support analysis of a continuous dependent variable for the following:

1. *Random effects:* For when the set of values of a categorical predictor variable are seen not as the complete set but rather as a random sample of all values (ex., when the variable "product" has values representing only 30 of a possible 142 brands). Random effects modeling allows the researcher to make inferences over a wider population than is possible with regression or other general linear model (GLM) methods.

2. *Hierarchical effects:* For when predictor variables are measured at more than one level (ex., reading achievement scores at the student level and teacher–student ratios at the school level; or sentencing lengths at the offender level, gender of judges at the court level, and budgets of judicial districts at the district level). The researcher can assess the effects of higher levels on the intercepts and coefficients at the lowest level (ex., assess judge-level effects on predictions of sentencing length at the offender level).

3. *Repeated measures:* For when observations are correlated rather than independent (ex., before–after studies, time series data, matched-pairs designs). In repeated measures, the lowest level is the observation level (ex., student test scores on multiple occasions), grouped by observation unit (ex., students) such that each unit (student) has multiple data rows, one for each observation occasion.

The versatility of linear mixed modeling has led to a variety of terms for the models it makes possible. Different disciplines favor one or another label, and different research targets influence the selection of terminology as well. These terms, many of which are discussed later in this chapter, include random intercept modeling, random coefficients modeling, random coefficients regression, random effects modeling, hierarchical linear modeling, multilevel modeling, linear mixed modeling, growth modeling, and longitudinal modeling. Linear mixed models in some disciplines are called "random effects" or "mixed effects" models. In economics, the term "random coefficient regression models" is used. In sociology, "multilevel modeling" is common, alluding to the fact that regression intercepts and slopes at the individual level may be treated as random effects of a higher (ex., organizational) level. And in statistics, the term "covariance components models" is often used, alluding to the fact that in linear mixed models one may decompose the covariance into components attributable to within-groups versus between-groups effects. In spite of many different labels, the commonality is that all adjust observation-level predictions based on the clustering of measures at some higher level or by some grouping variable.

The "linear" in linear mixed modeling has a meaning similar to that in regression: There is an assumption that the predictor terms on the right-hand side of the estimation equation are linearly related to the target term on the left-hand side. Of course, nonlinear terms such as power or log functions may be added to the predictor side (ex., time and time-squared in longitudinal studies). Also, the target variable may be transformed in a nonlinear way (ex., logit link functions). Linear mixed model (LMM) procedures that do the latter are "generalized" linear mixed models.

Just as regression and GLM procedures can be extended to "generalized general linear models" (GZLM), multilevel and other LMM procedures can be extended to "generalized linear mixed models" (GLMM), discussed further below.

Linear mixed models for multilevel analysis address hierarchical data, such as when employee data are at level 1, agency data are at level 2, and department data are at level 3. Hierarchical data usually call for LMM implementation. While most multilevel modeling is univariate (one dependent variable), multivariate multilevel modeling for two or more dependent variables is available also. Likewise, models for cross-classified data exist for data that are not strictly hierarchical (ex., as when schools are a lower level and neighborhoods are a higher level, but schools may serve more than one neighborhood).

The researcher undertaking causal modeling using linear mixed modeling should be guided by multilevel theory. That is, hierarchical linear modeling postulates that there are cross-level causal effects. Just as regression models postulate direct effects of independent variables at level 1 on the dependent variable at level 1, so too, multilevel models specify cross-level interaction effects between variables located at different levels. In doing multilevel modeling, the researcher postulates the existence of mediating mechanisms that cause variables at one level to influence variables at another level (ex., school-level funding may positively affect individual-level student performance by way of recruiting superior teachers, made possible by superior financial incentives).

Multilevel modeling tests multilevel theories statistically, simultaneously modeling variables at different levels without necessary recourse to aggregation or disaggregation.[1] Aggregation and disaggregation as used in regression models run the risk of ecological fallacy: What is true at one level need not be true at another level. For instance, aggregated state-level data on race and literacy greatly overestimate the correlation of African American ethnicity with illiteracy because states with many African Americans tend to have higher illiteracy for all races. Individual-level data shows a low correlation of race and illiteracy.

WHY USE LINEAR MIXED/HIERARCHICAL LINEAR/ MULTILEVEL MODELING?

Why not just stick with tried-and-true regression models for analysis of data? The central reason, noted above, is that linear mixed models handle random effects, including the effects of grouping of observations under higher entities (ex., grouping of employees by agency, students by school, etc.). Clustering of observations within groups leads to correlated error terms, biased estimates of parameter (ex., regression coefficient) standard errors, and possible substantive mistakes when interpreting the importance of one or another predictor variable. Whenever data are sampled, the sampling unit as a grouping variable may well be a random effect. In a study of the federal bureaucracy, for instance, "agency" might be the sampling unit and error terms may cluster by agency, violating ordinary least squares (OLS) assumptions.

Unlike OLS regression, linear mixed models take into account the fact that over many samples, different b coefficients for effects may be computed, one for each group. Conceptually, mixed models treat b coefficients as random effects drawn from a normal distribution of possible b's, whereas OLS regression treats the b parameters as if they were fixed constants (albeit within a confidence interval). Treating "agency" as a random rather than fixed factor will alter and make more accurate the ensuing parameter estimates. Put another way, the misestimation of standard errors in OLS regression inflates Type 1 error (thinking there is relationship when there is not: false positives), whereas mixed models handle this potential problem. In addition, LMM can handle a random sampling variable like "agencies," even when there are too many agencies to make into dummy variables in OLS regression and still expect reliable coefficients.

In summary, OLS regression and GLM assume error terms are independent and have equal error variances, whereas when data are nested or cross-classified by groups, individual-level observations from the same upper-level group will not be independent but rather will be more similar due to such factors as shared group history and group selection processes. While random effects associated with upper-level random factors do not affect lower-level population means, they do affect the covariance structure of the data. Indeed, adjusting for this is a central point of LMM models and is why linear mixed models are used instead of regression and GLM, which assume independence.

It is true that analysis of variance and other GLM methods have been adapted to handle non-independent models also, but these adaptations are problematic. In estimating model parameters when there are random effects, it is necessary to adjust for the covariance structure of the data. The adjustment made by GLM assumes uncorrelated error (that is, it assumes data independence). Lack of data independence is present in multilevel data when the sampling unit (ex., cities, schools, agencies) displays intraclass correlation. LMM does not assume data independence. In addition to handling correlated error, LMM also has the advantage of using maximum likelihood (ML) and restricted maximum likelihood (REML) estimation. GLM produces optimum estimates only for balanced designs (where the groups formed by the factors are equal in size), whereas ML and REML yield asymptotically efficient estimators even for unbalanced designs. ML and REML estimates are normal for large samples (they display asymptotic normality), allowing significance testing of model covariance parameters, something difficult to do in GLM. In contrast, GLM estimates parameters as if they were fixed, calculating variance components based on expected mean squares.

Logistic regression also does not provide for random effects variables, nor (even in the multinomial version) does it support near-continuous dependents (ex., test scores) with a large number of values. Binning such variables into categories, as is sometimes done, loses information and attenuates correlation. However, logistic multilevel models are possible using generalized linear mixed modeling procedures, available in SPSS, SAS, and other statistical packages.

TYPES OF LINEAR MIXED MODELS

Linear mixed modeling supports a very wide variety of models, too extensive to enumerate here. As mentioned above, different disciplines and authors have employed differing labels for specific types of models, adding to the seeming complexity of the subject. In this section, the most common types of models are defined, using the most widely applied labels.

The "types" refer to various combinations of what is being predicted and what is doing the predicting. In ordinary regression, the researcher normally is predicting a level 1 (typically individual subject level) dependent variable such as "employee performance score" from one or more level 1 independent variables (ex., from "employee education"). In the multilevel world of linear mixed modeling, however, there are other possibilities. Let level 2 be defined by the grouping variable "agency" and a level 2 variable such as "mean agency education," with the multilevel theory being that the presence of more highly educated employees in an agency has a synergistic effect at the level of the individual. The level 2 grouping variable may have an effect on the intercept (mean score) at level 1 and/ or on the b coefficient (slope) of education at level 1. Likewise, the level 2 predictor, mean agency education, may have an effect on the level 1 intercept and the level 1 slope. These possibilities give rise to the types of models depicted in Figures 1.1 (see page 10) and 1.2 (see page 11).

There are three broad classes of models: fixed effects, random effects, and mixed. Most models treated in this book are mixed, hence the term "linear mixed modeling."

1. *Fixed effects models.* Linear mixed modeling is mostly about models involving random effects as well as fixed effects. In mixed models, effects that impact the intercept (representing the mean of the dependent variable when other predictors are zero) are modeled as fixed effects. However, purely fixed effects models such as ordinary regression models may be fitted also. These are models with only fixed factors and optional fixed covariates as predictors. An example would be a study of employee performance score by education, controlling for gender. Most models for analysis of variance, regression, and GLM are fixed effects models. These are the most common type of model in social science. Compared to an OLS regression model, a fixed effects model implemented in LMM will generate very similar if not identical estimates with similar (but not identical) output tables.

2. *Random effects models.* Random effects models are those with one or more random factors and optional covariates as predictors. Effects that influence the covariance structure are modeled as random factors. Sampling variables

(ex., state, where individuals are sampled within a sample of states; subject, where a sample of subjects have repeated measures over time) are random factors, as is any grouping variable where the clustering of effects creates correlated error. An example would be a study of employee performance score at level 1 by agency at level 2, controlling for salary level at level 1. Score would be the dependent variable, agency the random factor (assuming only a random sample of agencies were studied), and salary the covariate. The level 1 intercept of score may be modeled as a random effect of agency at level 2. Likewise, the level 1 slope of employee education might be modeled as a random effect of agency. If only the intercept is modeled, it is a random intercept model.[2] If the slope is modeled as well, it is a random coefficients model. Some authors use the term "hierarchical linear model" to refer to random effects models in which both intercepts and slopes are modeled.

3. *Mixed models.* Mixed models, naturally, are ones with both fixed and random effects. A given effect may be both fixed and random if it contributes to both the intercept and the covariance structure for the model. Predictors at any level are typically included as fixed effects. For instance, covariates at level 2 are normally included as fixed effect variables. Slopes of variables at lower levels may be random effects of higher-level variables. Grouping variables (ex., school, agency) at any level are random factors.

Hierarchical linear models (HLM) are a type of mixed model with hierarchical data—that is, where nested data exist at more than one level (ex., student-level data and school-level data, with students nested within schools). In explaining a dependent variable, HLM models focus on differences *between groups* (ex., schools) in relation to differences *within groups* (ex., among students within schools). While it is possible to construct one-level models in linear mixed modeling, most use of LMM can be seen as one or another form of HLM, so the two terms are often used synonymously in spite of nuanced differences.

Random intercept models are models where only the intercept of the level 1 dependent variable is modeled as an effect of the level 2 grouping variable and possibly other level 1 or level 2 (or higher) covariates. *Random coefficients models* are ones where the coefficient(s) of lower-level predictor(s) is/are modeled as well. There are several major types of random intercept and random coefficient models, enumerated below (see Table 1.1).

• The *null model,* also called the "unconditional model" or a "one-way ANOVA with random effects," is a type of random intercept model that predicts the level 1 intercept of the dependent variable as a random effect of the level 2 grouping variable, with no other predictors at level 1 or 2 in a two-level model. For instance, differences in mean performance scores may be analyzed in terms of the random effect of agency at level 2. The researcher is testing to see if there is an agency effect. The null model is used to calculate the intraclass correlation coefficient (ICC), which is a test of the need for mixed modeling as discussed in

Chapter 2. The null model also serves as a "baseline model" for purposes of comparison with later, more complex models. Note that a model is "conditional" by the presence of predictors at level 1 or level 2. Since the researcher almost always employs predictor variables and is not simply interested in the null model, most mixed models are conditional. The central point of LMM often is to assess the difference between the researcher's conditional model and the null model without predictors. The likelihood ratio test (discussed in Chapter 2) can be used to assess this difference.

- *One-way ANCOVA with random effects models.* It is also possible to have a level 1 covariate and still predict the level 1 intercept (but not the slope of the level 1 covariate) as a random effect of the level 2 grouping variable, with no other level 2 predictors. For instance, differences in mean performance scores (the intercepts) may be analyzed as predicted by salary at level 1, predicting only the level 1 intercept of performance scores in terms of the between-groups effect of agency as a grouping variable.

- *Random intercept regression models* are also called "means-as-outcomes regression models." This variant of the random intercept model predicts the level 1 intercept on the basis of the level 2 grouping variable and also on the basis of one or more level 2 random effect predictors. For instance, differences in mean performance scores (the intercepts) may be analyzed, predicting the level 1 intercept in terms of the between-groups effect of agency and the level 2 random effect variable EquipmentBrand (a factor representing a sample of some of many brands of equipment, where different agencies used different brands).

- *Random intercept ANCOVA models* are also called "means-as-outcomes ANCOVA models." This type is simply a random intercept regression model in which there is also a level 1 covariate treated as a fixed effect (slope not predicted by level 2). Some authors would classify this as another type of random intercept regression model.

- *Random coefficients (RC) models,* also called "random coefficient regression models" or "multilevel regression models," are a type of mixed model with hierarchical data. The level 1 dependent is predicted by at least one level 1 covariate. The slope of this covariate and the intercept are predicted by the random effect of the grouping variable at level 2. That is, each group at the higher level (ex., agency level) is assumed to have a different regression slope as well as a different intercept for purposes of predicting a level 1 dependent variable. While this could be visualized by using OLS regression by superimposing the *n* regression lines for the *n* schools, LMM incorporates this variability of regression lines into a single analysis.

- *Full random coefficients models,* also called "intercepts-and-slopes-as-outcomes models," are a type of RC model in which the level 1 slopes and intercepts are modeled not only by the level 2 grouping variable as a random

Figure 1.1 Types of linear mixed models

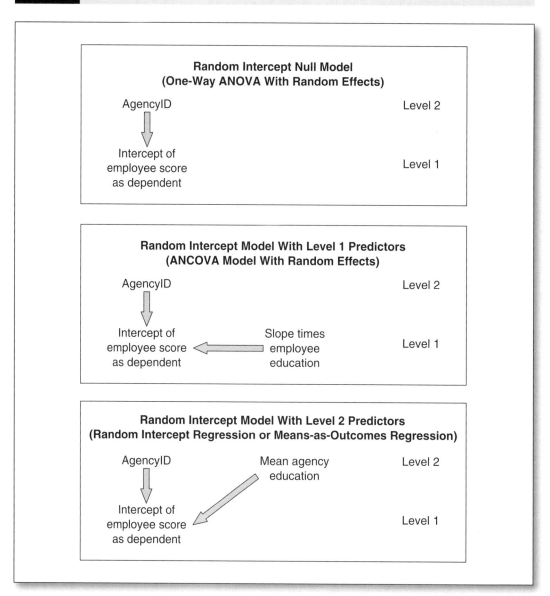

factor, but also by one or more other level 2 variables. For instance, differences in mean performance scores at level 1 may be analyzed, predicting the level 1 intercept and the slope of the level 1 predictor salary in terms of the between-groups effect of agency and the level 2 variable EquipmentBrand.

Figure 1.2   Types of linear mixed models, continued

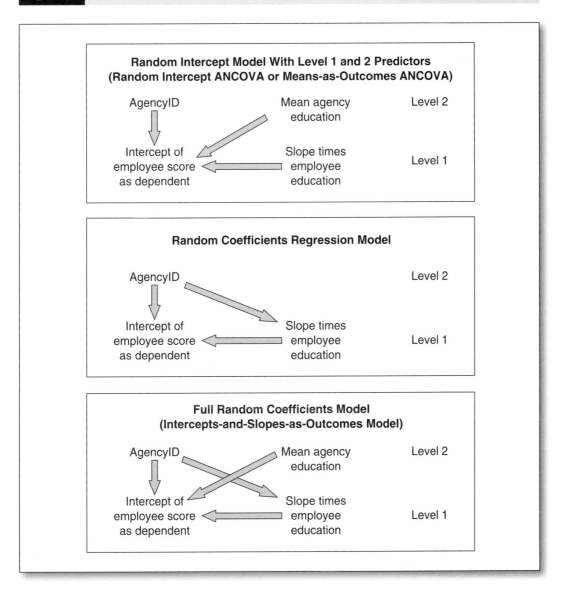

Table 1.1 below summarizes nomenclature for common types of linear mixed models.

Random intercept and random coefficients models are discussed further in Chapters 3, 4, and 5, which treat multilevel modeling using HLM 7, SPSS, and

Table 1.1	Six Common Types of Two-Level Linear Mixed Models

I. Only the intercept is modeled as a random effect.

  A. No level 1 covariates

  1. The null model, also called the unconditional model or one-way ANOVA with random effects

  B. Level 1 covariates only

  2. Random intercept model: ANCOVA with random effects

  C. Level 2 covariates only

  3. Random intercept regression: "means as outcomes regression"

  D. Both level 1 and level 2 covariates

  4. Random intercept ANCOVA: "means as outcomes ANCOVA"

II. One or more level 1 slopes as well as the intercept are modeled.

  A. No level 1 covariates

  Not applicable: A level 1 covariate must exist to have a slope to model!

  B. Level 1 covariates only

  1. Random coefficients regression

  C. Level 2 covariates only

  Not applicable

  D. Both level 1 and level 2 covariates

  2. Full random coefficients model: "intercepts and slopes as outcomes"

SAS software, respectively. In Chapter 6, Forrest C. Lane, Kim F. Nimon, and J. Kyle Roberts further develop the topic in their article, "A Random Intercepts Model of Part-Time Employment and Standardized Testing Using SPSS." In Chapter 7, Carissa L. Shafto and Jill L. Adelson present "A Random Intercept Regression Model Using HLM: Cohort Analysis of a Mathematics Curriculum for Mathematically Promising Students." Then, in Chapter 8, Gregory J. Palardy presents "Random Coefficients Modeling With HLM: Assessment Practices and the Achievement Gap." Finally, in Chapter 9, Shevaun Neupert presents "Emotional Reactivity to Daily Stressors Using a Random Coefficients Model With SAS PROC MIXED: A Repeated Measures Analysis."

GENERALIZED LINEAR MIXED MODELS

Generalized linear mixed models serve similar purposes to the models already discussed except that the "generalized" label means that new algorithms have been added to support a variety of link functions. *Link functions,* of course, are transforms of the dependent variable similar to that found, for instance, in binary logistic regression, where what is predicted is not the dependent variable itself (using the identity link function of OLS regression) but instead is the logit (the natural log of the odds that the dependent equals 1) of the dependent variable. Although the predictor side of the equation must be linearly related to the link function of the dependent, the original values of the predictor variables may be nonlinearly related to the original values of the dependent variable. A large number of link functions are possible, only some of which are currently supported by statistical packages for hierarchical linear modeling. Of fundamental importance is that generalized linear mixed modeling supports dependent variables that are not continuous and not normally distributed, as is required by ordinary regression and other general linear model procedures.

Although GLMM is not the focus of this book, it is important that the researcher be aware of the possibilities supported by generalized linear mixed modeling and be assured that the data at hand are best modeled by the LMM models described in this volume rather than by GLMM methods. Nonetheless, even if GLMM is selected due to the nature of the researcher's dependent variable, nearly all of the LMM considerations discussed in the present volume still apply.

Figure 1.3   HLM 7 "Basic Settings" dialog

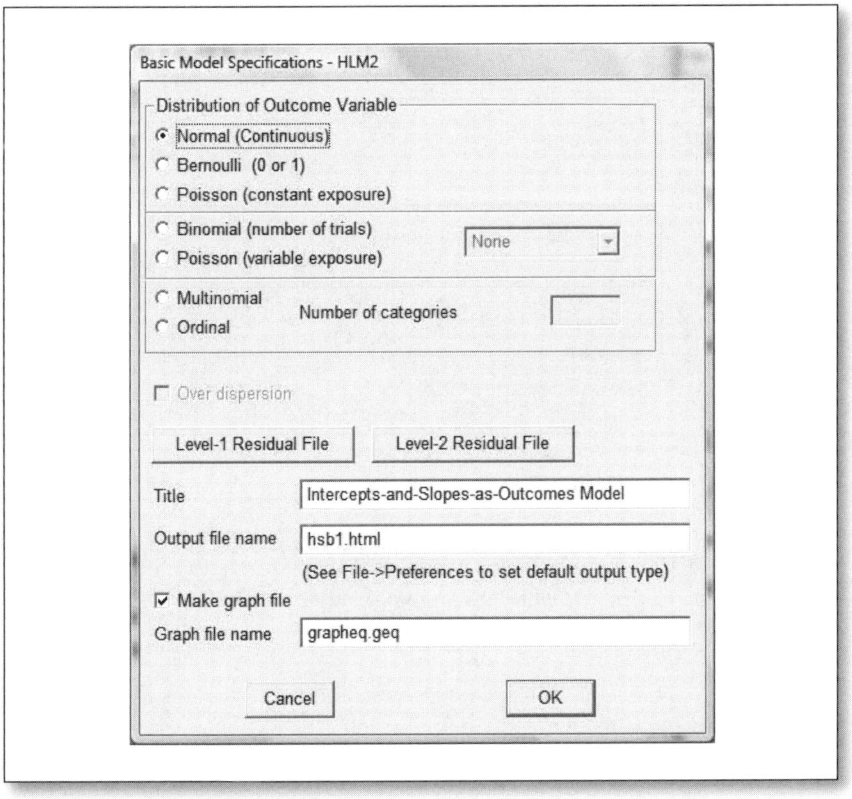

In HLM 7 software, generalized linear mixed models are integrated into the main user interface in the Basic Settings menu choice, as illustrated in Figure 1.3 above. In SPSS (starting with SPSS 19), GLMM is obtained in the GENLINMIXED procedure obtained by selecting Analyze, Mixed Models, Generalized Linear from the menu system, then going to the Target pane of the Fixed Effects tab, as illustrated in Figure 1.4 below. In SAS, GLMM is mainly associated with PROC GLIMMIX.

Figure 1.4   SPSS 19 generalized linear mixed models "Target" dialog

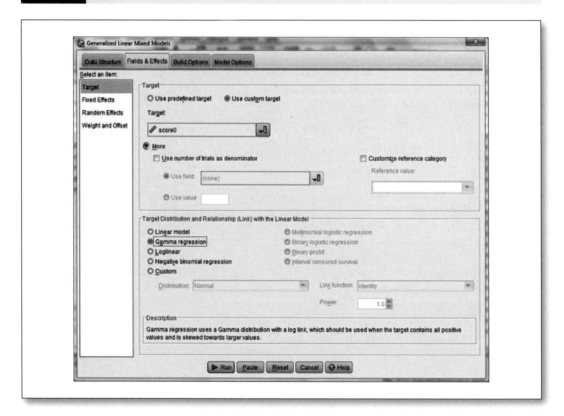

At the core of analysis with generalized linear mixed models is selecting the type of data distribution and link function that corresponds to the nature of the researcher's dependent variable. As shown in Figure 1.3, HLM 7 offers seven GLMM possibilities[3]:

1. *Normal (continuous).* This alternative assumes a normal distribution of the dependent variable with an identity link function. The outcome variable at level 1

may have any value on a continuous scale (ex., employee-level performance scores). This option creates the same models as for ordinary linear mixed modeling.

2. *Bernoulli.* This alternative assumes a Bernouilli distribution, which is a special case of the binomial distribution, employing a logit link function. In a Bernouilli model, the outcome variable at level 1 (ex., employee-level retirement status) has only two outcomes (ex., not retired = 0, retired = 1).

3. *Binomial (number of trials).* This alternative assumes a dependent variable with a binomial distribution and a logit link function, corresponding to binary logistic regression.

4. *Poisson (constant exposure).* This alternative assumes a dependent variable reflecting count data (hence non-negative integer values) with a log link function. The "constant exposure" term, also called "equal exposure," means each level 1 subject had the same chance to accumulate the count (ex., the same time interval).

5. *Poisson (variable exposure).* An example of this type would be a count of people displaying some trait in multiple cities of differing populations. The "exposure" varies since, all other things equal, larger cities might be expected to have a larger count. Like Poisson-constant exposure models, this alternative also assumes Poisson distribution of count data with a log link function, but the Poisson variance is weighted by the exposure variable.

6. *Multinomial.* This alternative assumes a multinomial distribution of the dependent variable, with a generalized logit link function. Multinomial data are categorical, such as "career choice" with values 1 = administrative, 2 = clerical, 3 = other. The coding values are arbitrary. A multinomial model is an extension of the Bernouilli model for dependents with more than two categories.

7. *Ordinal.* This alternative also assumes the dependent variable has a categorical distribution, but the categories are ordered—for example, ordered from "strongly agree" to "strongly disagree." The link function is cumulative logit.

SPSS 19 offers eight link alternatives plus a "Custom" alternative. In addition, there is a checkbox for "Use number of trials as denominator," which can convert the dependent variable into a ratio (ex., number of successes divided by number of trials, transforming a count into a rate). For categorical dependent variables, the SPSS "TARGET" pane also allows the researcher to set the reference category to something other than the default, which is the highest-coded category.

1. *Linear model.* Used with an identity link function when the dependent is continuous and normal. This is the same as the "Normal" selection in HLM 7.

2. *Gamma regression.* Used for dependents whose values are skewed toward larger values, this alternative assumes a gamma distribution with a log link.

3. *Loglinear.* Used for count data over a fixed time period, this alternative assumes a dependent with a Poisson distribution with a log link. It corresponds to the "Poisson-constant exposure" option in HLM 7.

4. *Negative binomial regression.* This option specifies a negative binomial distribution with a log link. It is used for data on number of trials required to observe k successes.

5. *Multinomial logistic regression.* This is the same option as for the "Multinomial" alternative in HLM 7, with a multinomial distribution and generalized logit link.

6. *Binary logistic regression.* This is the same logistic regression model as for the "Binomial" option in HLM 7, with a binomial distribution and logit link.

7. *Binary probit.* This option assumes the dependent exhibits a binomial distribution with a probit link, which in turn assumes the binary values reflect an underlying normal distribution.

8. *Interval censored survival.* This option assumes a dependent with a binomial distribution using a complementary log-log link. This option is used with survival and event history data, which include right-censored observations (where some cases do not experience the event of interest by the time the measurement period ends).

9. *Custom.* The Custom alternative allows any permissible combination of dependent variable distribution and link function. Multinomial distributions must use the logit link. Binomial distributions are the only other type that may use the logit link. The identity, power, and log links may be used with any distribution other than multinomial. The CLOGLOG (log complement) link, the negative log-log link, and the probit link are only used with a binomial distribution. Apart from these restrictions, the combinations that the researcher may select are reflected in options listed in the SPSS syntax for the Target clause:

```
/TARGET_OPTIONS]
    [REFERENCE = value]
    [DISTRIBUTION = NORMAL | BINOMIAL | MULTINOMIAL |
    GAMMA|INVERSE_GAUSSIAN | NEGATIVE_BINOMIAL |
    POISSON]
    [LINK = IDENTITY | CLOGLOG | LOG | LOGC | LOGIT |
    NLOGLOG | PROBIT | POWER]
    [LINK_PARAMETER = number]
```

SAS 9.2 PROC GLIMMIX contains a DIST= statement with these options:

BETA, defaulting to a logit link function

BINARY, defaulting to a logit link function

BINOMIAL, defaulting to a logit link function

EXPONENTIAL, defaulting to a log link function

GAMMA, defaulting to a log link function

GAUSSIAN|NORMAL, defaulting to an identity link function

GEOMETRIC, defaulting to a logit link function

INVGAUSS, defaulting to an inverse squared link function

LOGNORMAL, defaulting to an identity link function

MULTINOMIAL, defaulting to a cumulative logit link function

NEGBINOMIAL, defaulting to a log link function

POISSON, defaulting to a log link function Poisson

TCENTRAL, defaulting to an identity link function

In SAS 9.2, the LINK = keyword in PROC GLIMMIX syntax supports the following link functions:

CUMCLL (cumulative, complementary log-log)

CUMLOGIT or CLOGIT (cumulative logit)

CUMLOGLOG (cumulative log-log)

CUMPROBIT (cumulative probit)

CLOGLOG (complementary log-log)

GLOGIT (generalized logit)

IDENTITY (identity)

LOG (log)

LOGIT (logit)

LOGLOG (log-log)

PROBIT (probit)

POWER() (power with exponent within the parentheses)

POWERMINUS2 (power with exponent −2)

RECIPROCAL or INVERSE (reciprocal)

While the number of combinations of dependent variable distributions and associated link functions is very large, the most common pairings are

(1) normal distribution with identity link, which is the linear regression or ANOVA model;

(2) inverse Gaussian (a.k.a. inverse normal) with an inverse squared link function, which models positively skewed, positively valued dependents;

(3) gamma distribution with a log link, also used for skewed dependents in gamma regression;

(4) multinomial distribution with a generalized or cumulative logit link, used for categorical or ordinal dependents in multinomial or ordinal regression;

(5) binomial distribution with a logit link, for binary logistic regression models;

(6) Poisson distribution with a log link, for count of events per fixed number of time periods in Poisson regression; and

(7) negative binomial distribution, used instead of Poisson for count data with overdispersion (when the variance is greater than the mean).

REPEATED MEASURES, LONGITUDINAL AND GROWTH MODELS

Increasingly, linear mixed modeling is the preferred approach when analyzing longitudinal data.[4] Studies in this category carry a variety of labels, including repeated measures designs, longitudinal analysis, and growth models. The common thread is the need to address the autocorrelation problem: Repeated observations for the same unit (ex., same employee with repeated performance score measures) exhibit clustering. Just as linear mixed models address the problem of clustering of measures and correlation of error by grouping or level variable, LMM addresses the problem of clustering by observation unit. Put another way, longitudinal data in LMM may be modeled by treating the multiple measures (ex., performance scores) as level 1 and the observation units (ex., employees) as level 2. Of course, level 2 units may still be nested within or cross-classified by levels 3 and 4 (ex., agency and department).

Repeated Measures

The object of repeated measures designs is to model within-subject variance. What is "within" a subject is, of course, the series of measurements taken over time for a given unit of analysis (typically an individual subject). Each subject will have multiple rows of data corresponding to multiple observation times. In terms of multilevel analysis, level 1 is within-subjects (for the variance among repeated measures for given individuals, on the average) and level 2 is between-subjects, with the observation unit (usually the individual) being a grouping variable for the measures. The grouping (subjects) variable can be used to assess the between-subjects random effect on a level 1 variable, such as employee performance test score. In a random intercepts model where there are level 1 covariates (predictors), this is done by creating one regression for each subject, generating multiple intercepts, where the true intercept is estimated as a random function of the intercepts of all the regressions. Random slopes may be generated in the same way to obtain a random coefficients model.

Longitudinal and Growth Models

Growth models are a common type of repeated measures linear mixed model in which time is modeled as a fixed and as a random effect on some measurement about the individual (ex., employee performance score). Visualized graphically, a "growth curve" for each employee can be charted in which time is the X-axis and the dependent variable, such as performance score, forms the Y-axis. Growth curves will vary by individual, depending on time-invariant and time-variant variables such as IQ or training workshop hours, respectively.

The object of growth modeling is not merely to see if there is a trend in score over time, but also to discover if the grouping variable has an effect on the trend (ex., if there is an employee effect) and if there is a pattern to the change in intercepts or coefficients over time. Assuming the time variable is measured in equal metric intervals, the time variable is a covariate and the growth pattern may be analyzed to see, for instance, if on average it increases linearly in steps, grows quadratically, or grows according to some other function of time.

Many different types of linear mixed models can be constructed in which time is a variable. To take one example, that of predicting a metric time series of employee performance scores at level 1 grouped by employee at level 2, the purpose of longitudinal analysis may be to see if and how the linear correlation of score and time is influenced by employee-specific effects. Time may be modeled as a fixed effect to capture the linear correlation, and in the fixed effects output, the b coefficient for time indicates how much, on average, each employee increases or decreases in score per measurement period. Time can also be modeled as a random effect to capture the effect of time nested within employees on the coefficient of time at level 1. (A regression is fitted for each employee, and a standard error is computed for the b coefficient of time in these regressions.)

If an unstructured covariance structure (see Chapter 2) is assumed, one will get covariance parameters for the intercept, for the b coefficient of the level 1 predictor, and for the covariance of the two. The larger the parameter for the intercept, the greater the variance of score among employees when time = 0, which is the start time. The larger the parameter for time as a random effect nested within employees, the greater (and more likely to be significant) the between-employees variability of the time coefficient. If there are level 2 (employee-level) covariates, these are treated as additional fixed factors. For instance, if education is such a covariate, fixed factors include time, education, and time*education. Time is also a random effect. The covariance parameter for the residua! reflects the within-subjects variance, which is the variance of test scores across time for any given employee after controlling for other variables in the model (time, education, and the time*education interaction), and as such is the unexplained variance in the model.

There are many types of random coefficients growth models, some of which are illustrated in Chapters 3, 4, and 5. These provide an introductory guide to multilevel modeling using HLM 7, SPSS, and SAS software, respectively.

Chapter 10, by David F. Greenberg and Julie A. Phillips, treats "Hierarchical Linear Modeling of Growth Curve Trajectories Using HLM," dealing with a standard form of growth modeling. Chapter 11, by Jaime Lynn Maerten-Rivera, presents "A Piecewise Growth Model Using HLM7 to Examine Change in Teaching Practices Following a Science Teacher Professional Development Intervention," where piecewise growth models are ones where growth trajectories are divided and modeled separately. And in Chapter 12, Maike Luhmann and Michel Eid treat "Studying Reaction to Repeated Life Events With Discontinuous Change Models Using HLM," where discontinuous change models handle data where the individual growth trajectory is divided into discrete segments punctuated by discontinuities such as life events.

MULTIVARIATE MODELS

Multivariate linear mixed modeling (MLMM) is to LMM what multiple analysis of variance (MANOVA) and covariance (MANCOVA) are to general linear models (GLM): Each enables simultaneous analysis of multiple dependent variables defined at level 1 in a multilevel model. MLMM also goes under the label "hierarchical multivariate linear modeling" (HMLM).

In addition, nonlinear link functions can be added using multivariate generalized linear mixed modeling (MGLMM), extending what is possible with generalized linear mixed modeling (GLMM) of dependent variables considered singly.

MLMM and MGLMM are often used in analysis of latent variables, where the multiple level 1 dependents are seen as indicators for an underlying latent construct. This is the "multilevel latent outcome model." For instance, measures of six specific skills, skill1 through skill6, may be seen as indicators for the latent variable "performance." As another example, Sammel, Lin, and Ryan (1999), in a study of several teratogenic (birth defect–inducing) agents, used MLMM to model the latent variable "teratogenic exposure" based on multiple indicators associated with the different agents.[5]

In a second application, MLMM and MGLMM may be used for joint analysis of what would otherwise be separate repeated measures analyses of different outcome variables. This is the "multilevel model for correlated outcomes" or "repeated measures multivariate linear mixed model" (see Molenberghs, 2007). In a third usage, MLMM and MGLMM may be used where skill1 through skill6 measure the same skill, but at different times; output1 through output6 measure objective productivity at different times; and the research focus is on testing a "parallel growth model." MLMM can also be employed as a form of cluster analysis, based on longitudinal data on individuals' behavior over time, classifying individuals according to differences in growth curves (Villarroel, 2009). A fifth type of usage of MLMM and MGLMM centers on analysis where the multiple dependents are members of an exponential family, such as score, score-squared, and other exponential functions (see Gueorguieva, 2001). Multivariate modeling is discussed further in Chapter 15, by Larry J. Brant and Shan L. Sheng, in their article, "Predicting Future Events From Longitudinal Data With Multivariate Hierarchical Models and Bayes' Theorem Using SAS." For more on MLMM in HLM 7, see Raudenbush, Bryk, Cheong, Congdon, and Du Toit (2011). For more on MLMM in SPSS, see Heck, Thomas, and Tabata (2010, Ch. 7). For more on MLMM in SAS, see Wright (1998).

CROSS-CLASSIFIED MODELS

Cross-classified models handle data that do not meet the nesting assumptions of hierarchical models. Above, an example of assumed test scores are grouped by individual employee, with employees nested within agencies and agencies within departments. However, what if the data include employees who are employed by multiple agencies? In educational research, what if students are members of multiple classrooms rather than each student belonging to just one classroom? As another example, in repeated measures studies involving interviews of subjects, the same subject may be interviewed by more than one interviewer, and therefore the subject is cross-classified on the interviewer effect. Such data, illustrated in Figure 1.5 below, are cross-classified and require cross-classified random effects modeling (see Beretvas, Meyers, & Rodriguez, 2005). Exclusively hierarchical data are less common than cross-classified data, and thus cross-classified linear mixed modeling (CCLMM; also called cross-classified multilevel measurement modeling [CCMMM], and cross-classified random effects modeling [CCREM]) is an important tool within the LMM family.

Applying hierarchical linear mixed modeling to cross-classified data can seriously bias variance component estimates as well as bias the estimation of the standard errors of the regression coefficients. Meyers and Beretvas (2006) found that such misspecification did not significantly affect parameter estimates for fixed effects, but did bias estimates for standard errors, and also biased estimates of variance components of the random effects, inflating Type 1 error. Luo and Kwok (2009), using simulation studies, likewise found that "ignoring a crossed factor causes overestimation of the variance components of adjacent levels and underestimation of the variance component of the remaining crossed factor" (p. 182). In the present volume, George Leckie (Chapter 14) similarly notes that ignoring cross-classification effects leads to overestimation of level 1 (ex., student) and level 2 (ex., school) effects using conventional hierarchical linear modeling. Moreover,

> ignoring a crossed factor at the kth level causes underestimation of the standard error of the regression coefficient of the predictor associated with the ignored factor and overestimation of the standard error of the regression coefficient of the predictor at the (k-1)th level. (Luo & Kwok, 2009, p. 182)

Figure 1.5 Hierarchical vs. cross-classified data

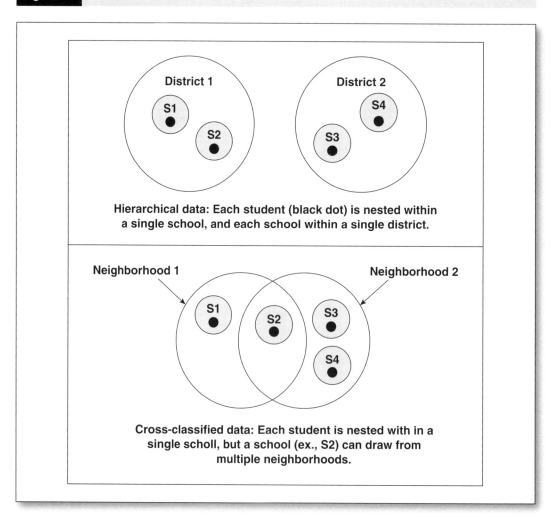

Hierarchical data: Each student (black dot) is nested within a single school, and each school within a single district.

Cross-classified data: Each student is nested with in a single scholl, but a school (ex., S2) can draw from multiple neighborhoods.

This type of misspecification bias can be great and is greater the less the two cross-classified factors are related,[6] the greater the variance of the factor modeled incorrectly, and the larger the design effect (reflected in larger per-cluster sample sizes) (Meyers & Beretvas, 2006).

In Chapter 13 of this volume, Brian F. Patterson illustrates cross-classified models further in his article, "A Cross-Classified Multilevel Model for First-Year College Natural Science Performance Using SAS." Then, in Chapter 14, George Leckie discusses "Cross-Classified Multilevel Models Using Stata: How Important Are Schools and Neighborhoods for Students' Educational

Attainment?" For more on cross-classified models in HLM 7, see Raudenbush et al. (2011). For more on cross-classified models in SPSS, see Heck, Thomas, and Tabata (2010, Ch. 8). For more on cross-classified models in SAS, see Beretvas (2008). All three packages support two- and three-level CCLMM models.

SUMMARY

Multilevel and hierarchical modeling through various types of linear mixed models has rapidly become a required asset in the statistical toolkit of researchers worldwide. By correctly modeling correlated error, which arises from the clustering of data at the group level, LMM models address a major shortcoming of regression, ANOVA, and other general linear model analyses. Failure to take correlated error into account can easily affect the researcher's substantive conclusions. Whether used to model random effects, hierarchical effects, or repeated measures effects, linear mixed modeling is a versatile tool, applicable to a broad range of common research problems. Generalized linear mixed modeling incorporates nonlinear link functions of the dependent variable. Multivariate linear mixed modeling incorporates analysis of multiple dependent variables. Cross-classified linear mixed modeling handles crossed factors that depart from strictly hierarchical structure. All variants handle cross-level interaction terms as well as cross-level main effects, and all variants test multi-level theories without necessity to aggregate or disaggregate data — a commonly flawed practice in ordinary regression modeling. With this versatility and power, it is small wonder that courses on hierarchical linear modeling, multilevel modeling, and linear mixed modeling now pervade doctoral research programs.

After evaluating the research design and after screening data to meet the assumptions of LMM (to be discussed in Chapter 2), the researcher must select the type of model to explore. This depends on the research question. If the research interest is confined to understanding why mean values of the dependent variable vary, then a random intercept model may suffice. If, however, the research interest is in exploring the relative effects of predictor variables, a random coefficients model is ordinarily selected. If there are multiple dependent variables to be treated as a set, multivariate models are required. If data are not nested in a strictly hierarchical manner, cross-classified models will be needed. Models also vary by number of levels of data involved, though in practice nearly all linear mixed modeling is confined to analysis of two to four levels.

Within these broad categories, there are many variations on type of model. The null model models the dependent variable without predictors apart from the grouping variable(s). One-way random effects ANCOVA models predict the level 1 dependent as a fixed effect of level 1 covariates and a random effect of higher-level grouping variables. Random intercept regression models (means-as-outcomes regression models) add higher-level random effect predictors.

Random intercept ANCOVA models (means-as-outcomes ANCOVA) are a type of random intercept regression in which there are also level 1 fixed effect predictors. Random coefficients (RC) models predict level 1 slopes as well as intercepts. Full random coefficients models (intercepts-and-slopes-as-outcomes models) model level 1 slopes and intercepts as functions of higher-level grouping factors and higher-level covariates. With any model, data for repeated measurements may be present, in which case some type of longitudinal or growth model may be undertaken.

In summary, linear mixed modeling is a versatile procedure that supports an extremely large number of variations of type of model, only some of which are mentioned in this chapter. Generalized linear mixed modeling (GLMM) supports still more types, covering nonlinear link functions for a variety of data distributions of the dependent variable. In this way, GLMM supports linear mixed modeling for binary, ordinal, and multinomial logistic models; probit, gamma, and negative binomial regression models; Poisson regression models and models for interval-censored survival data such as used in event history analysis, to name a few.

Looking ahead, Chapter 2 presents considerations preliminary to multilevel analysis, focusing on meeting the assumptions of linear mixed modeling and on understanding how models are evaluated. Then, in the following three chapters, the details of implementing a number of types of basic linear mixed models are presented. Chapters 3 through 5 present the same models as implemented in HLM 7, SPSS 19, and SAS 9.2, respectively. The remaining 10 chapters of this volume, written by authors from diverse fields, present further applications based on these statistical packages (plus one application illustrated for Stata), all following a standard format emphasizing how to implement and report data analysis for linear mixed models.

NOTES

1. It should be noted, though, that in practice some variables may represent aggregated scores.

2. Some authors use the term "hierarchical linear model" to refer to random effects models in which both intercepts and slopes are modeled.

3. Different options are offered in HLM 7 for multivariate generalized linear mixed models.

4. For a discussion comparing repeated measures ANOVA and event history approaches, see Schulz and Maas (2010).

5. This article also contains a useful comparison of GLMM methods with factor analysis and structural equation modeling as alternative approaches to modeling latent variables.

6. This may seem anomalous, but if factors are correlated, then modeling one of them in a hierarchical design will reduce some of the bias that otherwise would occur.

REFERENCES

Beretvas, S. N. (2008). Cross-classified random effects models. In A. A. O'Connell & D. B. McCoach (Eds.), *Multilevel modeling of educational data* (pp. 161–197). Charlotte, NC: Information Age Publishing.

Beretvas, S. N., Meyers, J. L., & Rodriguez, R. A. (2005). The cross-classified multilevel measurement model: An explanation and demonstration. *Journal of Applied Measurement, 6*(3), 322–341.

Gueorguieva, R (2001). A multivariate generalized linear mixed model for joint modelling of clustered outcomes in the exponential family. *Statistical modeling, 1*(3), 177–193.

Heck, R. H., Thomas, S. L., & Tabata, L. N. (2010). *Multilevel and longitudinal modeling with IBM SPSS.* New York: Routledge.

Luo, W., & Kwok, O. M. (2009). The impacts of ignoring a crossed factor in analyzing cross-classified data. *Multivariate Behavioral Research, 44*(2), 182–212.

Meyers, J. L., & Beretvas, S. N. (2006). The impact of inappropriate modeling of cross-classified data structures. *Multivariate Behavioral Research, 41*(4), 473–497.

Molenberghs, G. (2007). Random-effects models for multivariate repeated measures. *Statistical Methods in Medical Research, 16*(5), 387–397.

Raudenbush, S. W., & Bryk, A. S. (2002). *Hierarchical linear models: Applications and data analysis methods* (2nd ed.) (Advanced Quantitative Techniques in the Social Sciences Series, No. 1). Thousand Oaks, CA: Sage.

Raudenbush, S. W., Bryk, A. S., Cheong, Y. F., Congdon, R., & Du Toit, M. (2011). *HLM 7: Hierarchical linear and nonlinear modeling.* Lincolnwood, IL: Scientific Software International.

Sammel, M., Lin, X., & Ryan, L. (1999). Multivariate linear mixed models for multiple outcomes. *Statistics in Medicine, 18*(17–18), 2479–2492.

Schulz, W., & Maas, I. (2010). Studying historical occupational careers with multilevel growth models. *Demographic Research, 23*(24), 669–696. Retrieved March 13, 2011, from http://www.demographic-research.org/volumes/vol23/24/23-24.pdf

Villarroel, L. (2009). Cluster analysis using multivariate mixed effects models. *Statistics in Medicine, 28*(20), 2552–2565.

Wright, S. P. (1998). *Multivariate analysis using the MIXED procedure.* Paper presented at the Twenty-Third Annual Meeting of SAS Users' Group International, Nashville, TN (Paper 229). Retrieved March 14, 2011, from http://www2.sas.com/proceedings/sugi23/Stats/p229.pdf

Preparing to Analyze Multilevel Data

G. David Garson

2

TESTING IF LINEAR MIXED MODELING IS NEEDED FOR ONE'S DATA

When the researcher asks if it is necessary to use linear mixed modeling (LMM) or generalized linear mixed modeling (GLMM) methods, the question is whether there is a level or grouping variable (ex., schools in a study of student-level test scores), and if so, whether the dependent variable exhibits a clustering effect with respect to that level or grouping variable (ex., do scores cluster by schools, giving rise to correlated error, which violates the assumptions of ordinary regression models?). The usual statistic that tests if there is a grouping-level clustering effect is ICC, the intraclass correlation coefficient.[1] ICC is computed as statistical output when analyzing the null model using LMM, as explained below.

A significant ICC means there is significant clustering by group of individual-level values of the target variable. Intraclass correlation thus measures the extent to which observations are not independent of a grouping variable (ex., if student scores are not independent of schools). Put another way, when ICC is significant, there are significant differences on the mean value of the dependent variable between the groups that form the higher levels of the model. If ICC approaches zero, there is no between-groups effect. If there is no between-groups effect, there is no need to model individual-level regression parameters as random effects of a higher or grouping level. That is, in random intercept models, the lower the ICC, the less difference will exist between hierarchical linear modeling or linear mixed modeling estimates compared to traditional regression techniques. HLM is not appropriate for random intercept models when ICC is non-significant. Note, however, that a non-significant ICC does not rule out the need for a random coefficients model since ICC just tests group differences in intercepts of the dependent variable, not differences in slopes of the predictors.

The intraclass correlation is the between-groups effect divided by the total effect for the null model. The null model in linear mixed models is the one in which there is only the dependent variable at level 1 and only the grouping variable itself at level 2 (ex., performance score at level 1 and agency at level 2; student verbal score at level 1 and school at level 2). The null model is also called the intercept-only model, the unconditional model, or the one-way ANOVA model with random effects.

The computation of ICC using HLM, SPSS, and SAS software is treated in Chapters 3 through 5, respectively. In general, however, the software generates an ANOVA table showing the residual effect (representing a within-group variance component) and an effect of the grouping variable on the intercept (representing the between-groups variance component). In a variance components model,[2] the ICC is the between-groups component divided by the sum of both components. That is, ICC is the grouping effect's percentage of the total of both within- and between-groups effects. A non-significant ICC means the grouping effect is insignificant. When there is no grouping effect, error may be assumed to be uncorrelated and ordinary regression methods may be applied in lieu of linear mixed modeling procedures, if all other assumptions are met. However, pursuing OLS regression anyway in the face of a significant ICC, which signals lack of independence and lack of homoscedastic error variance, will mean that significance tests will not be accurate. Significance tests (and standard errors and confidence limits) in ordinary regression are not at all robust when the assumption of independence is violated, which is the case when ICC is significant.

TYPES OF ESTIMATION

The researcher should be aware of the type of estimation algorithm used to calculate parameter estimates in LMM. Software packages for linear mixed modeling differ in their default methods of estimation and also in the estimation options they make available to the researcher. These differences in estimation can lead to substantively different results depending on the software package and options selected. However, the great majority of time the researcher accepts the default, which is restricted maximum likelihood (REML) in HLM 7, SPSS, SAS, and most statistical programs, and will come to the same substantive conclusions though not necessarily with the same exact coefficients.

The major alternative methods of estimation are maximum likelihood (ML, offered by SPSS and SAS); full information maximum likelihood (FIML, offered by HLM 7 (Specify Other Settings, Estimation Settings, Full Maximum Likelihood); and restricted maximum likelihood estimation (REML, offered by all three statistical packages). However, invoking the same default (REML) does not necessarily mean one will arrive at the same coefficients, because there are differences in how each statistical package updates its estimates of the restricted log likelihood between iterations (see West, Welch, & Galecki, 2007, p. 29).

While log likelihood values and variance components will usually be very close across statistical packages, sometimes the differences are significant. Among the reasons why HLM 7, SAS 9.2, and SPSS 19 may differ on computed values of coefficients are these:

• HLM software uses an expectation maximization (EM) algorithm with Fisher scoring used for every fifth iteration.[3] SAS uses a ridge-stabilized Newton-Raphson (N-R) algorithm by default, but Fisher scoring is available and in some circumstances may solve failure-to-converge problems. SPSS uses Fisher scoring for the first iteration by default (this can be overridden in the Estimation Settings window) and the N-R algorithm thereafter, provided the Hessian matrix is non-negative definite and the step 1 log-likelihood increment is 1.0 or less. The practical result is that the computed deviance statistic (−2LL) may differ between packages, with the EM algorithm used by HLM tending toward more optimistic (lower) estimates of model fit as well as being slower but more likely to converge. Variance components of model random effects may also differ between packages.

- Software packages differ in the starting values each employs at the outset of applying their respective estimation algorithms. HLM 7 uses the average of the OLS estimates for starting values, whereas many other programs simply start at 0.0.[4] The more variables in the model, the more difference the various starting points may make in convergence.

- Software packages apply different constraints on estimation. HLM 7 constrains the correlation of random effects to be no greater than absolute 0.997 at maximum, whereas SPSS allows correlation greater than absolute 1.0. (This largely accounts, for instance, for the differences in variance components in models discussed in Chapters 3, 4, and 5.) SPSS and SAS support a variety of covariance types as constraints on the solution. In particular, the variance component (VC) type is the default in SPSS and SAS, which requires covariances among random effects to be zero, whereas by default HLM 7 estimates all coefficients in the variance–covariance matrix, akin to the unstructured covariance type in SPSS and SAS. Table 2.1 below illustrates SPSS output for a two-level full random coefficients model (to be discussed in Chapters 3–5) under variance components versus unstructured covariance type constraints, with zero covariances in the former and all coefficients freely estimated in the latter.

Table 2.1 Random Effect Covariance Structures for the Same Two-Level Full Rc Model Under Variance Components vs. Unstructured Covariance Type Constraints (SPSS 19 output)

When type is variance components:

Random Effects Covariance Structures (G)

Intercept [subject = Agency]

	Intercept	Agency
Intercept	Agency	111.064924

Variance Components

(Continued)

Table 2.1	(Continued)

	YrsExpr [subject = Agency]
	*YrsExpr	Agency*
YrsExpr	Agency	57.952831

Variance Components

Note. There are additional similar tables for each modeled random effect.

When type is unstructured:

Random Effect Covariance Structure (G)[a]

	*Intercept	Agency*	*YrsExpr	Agency*	*AgcyPCCtrd	Agency*	*YrsExpr * AgcyPCCtrd	Agency*
Intercept	Agency	1004.810566	61.844827	−80.283014	−845.965018
YrsExpr	Agency	61.844827	958.588318	245.501431	−53.230816
AgcyPCCtrd	Agency	−80.283014	245.501431	1316.220303	−454.595263
YrsExpr * AgcyPCCtrd	Agency	−845.965018	−53.230816	−454.595263	931.240069

Unstructured

The HLM 7 default can be overridden by checking the "Diagonalize tau" radio button in its "Estimation" window, causing all covariances to be zero as in diagonal and variance components models. For unstructured solutions, convergence under the EM estimation algorithm in HLM 7 is far less apt to be a problem than in the algorithms used by SPSS or SAS, where Hessian and convergence warnings are not uncommon when an unstructured solution is requested.[5]

• Software packages differ in the models they support. SPSS and SAS support a wider variety of types of constraint on the solution for the estimated variance–covariance matrix, with many more options than a variance components or an unstructured solution.[6] How the covariances are constrained sometimes leads to significant differences in estimates. Also, HLM 7 easily supports the modeling of heterogeneous residual variance, which in turn yields different deviance values for what is otherwise the same model. This is discussed in Chapter 3.

- For estimating the significance of fixed effects, software packages differ in the algorithms used to calculate degrees of freedom, which can lead to differences when inferring which fixed effects are significant.[7]

- The simpler the model, the smaller the differences between packages. Coefficients will be closest for the null model, which has only one random effect (the intercept) and covariance of random effects is moot. As the model becomes more complex, small differences can compound into larger differences.

Among statisticians, each approach to estimation has its advocates. That computed $-2LL$ differs between estimation methods is mitigated by the fact that the deviance is not used in absolute terms but in comparing the $-2LL$ coefficients of a model and one nested within it. As long as the same method is used to obtain the two coefficients, the likelihood ratio test will almost always return the same substantive result. Likewise, variance components are not interpreted in absolute terms but relative to one another, so similar mitigation applies.

- Restricted maximum likelihood estimation (REML) has better bias characteristics (Diggle, 1988) than ML, handles high correlations more effectively, and is less sensitive to outliers. Compared to REML estimates, ML estimates are downwardly biased (Giesbrecht & Burns, 1985). REML is "restricted" in the sense that the likelihood function includes only variance components, not regression coefficients as does ML. REML estimates will be the same as ML estimates for large samples, but when the number of level 2 groups is small, REML is less biased than ML. Therefore, REML is commonly recommended when sample size is relatively small.

However, REML estimates of fixed effects cannot be used for model comparison, as noted below in the section on likelihood ratio tests. By the same token, REML is not appropriate when models are to be compared using the Akaike information criterion (AIC) or other information criteria measures of goodness of fit. Specifically, REML log-likelihood functions are comparable only for models with the same mean structure, which implies models with the same fixed effects (see, for ex., Greven & Kneib, 2010; Verbeke & Molenberghs, 2000). When fixed effects differ, as they do when different models have different predictors, ML or FIML estimation should be used instead in order to properly employ information criteria comparisons using measures like AIC. (Yafune, Funatogawa, & Ishiguro, 2005, have proposed an REML-compatible information criteria measure, the extended information criterion, EIC, which is a bootstrap-based extension of AIC, but it is not yet widely implemented by statistical packages.) While not used for fixed effects comparisons, REML is appropriate when comparing random effects (variance components).

• Maximum likelihood (ML) estimation finds the parameter estimates that maximize the probability of arriving at estimates of the dependent variable equal to the observed values. ML estimates ignore the degrees of freedom used up by fixed effects in mixed models, leading to underestimation of variance components and parameter estimates, especially for small samples. However, ML may nonetheless be preferred when comparing two models with different parameterizations of the same effect (ex., simple variable vs. quadratically transformed version of the variable) because ML is invariant to different parameterizations of a fixed effect, whereas REML will treat different parameterizations as different models and compute different likelihood ratios. ML should be used if the research purpose is to compare fixed effect regression coefficients as well as variance components for a set of nested models, or if one wishes to compare model fit across models differing in fixed effects.

• Full information maximum likelihood (FIML). The REML and ML estimation methods used by LMM give asymptotically efficient estimates for unbalanced as well as balanced designs (that is, for large samples). In contrast, the ANOVA methods in GLM are optimum only for balanced designs. Especially for smaller samples, when sample sizes within groups are unbalanced, tests of parameter estimates and of overall fit will have inflated Type I error (Hox & Maas, 2001) using REML or ML. FIML estimators are more robust for and should be used for such unbalanced designs (du Toit & du Toit, 2008). Also, FIML is more robust for and is recommended for datasets with missing values.

• Other estimation methods may be used for binary, Poisson, and other forms of generalized linear mixed modeling (GLMM). HLM 7, for instance, offers penalized quasi-likelihood (PQL) estimation for modeling dichotomous, multinomial, and ordinal outcomes when ML is not available. Likewise, HLM 7 offers LaPlace and adaptive Gauss-Hermite quadrature (AGQ) estimation for other generalized linear mixed models (ex., binomial and Poisson count models). SAS also offers AGQ. SPSS does not offer estimation method choices within its GLMM dialog but reportedly uses PQL. See software documentation for further discussion of these alternative estimation methods.

To summarize, the software default for estimation method for HLM, SAS, and SPSS software is REML. It is the default because it is less biased than ML, resulting in more accurate parameter estimates. For small samples with relatively equal-sized groups (balanced designs), REML is particularly recommended. However, REML is not appropriate when the purpose is to conduct likelihood ratio tests or use information criteria (ex., AIC, BIC [Bayesian information criterion]) to compare model fit between models with different fixed effects (different predictors). As that is a common research purpose, a common practice is to routinely replace the REML default with ML estimation unless the research purpose is restricted to testing random effects or obtaining parameter estimates. However, for large samples, REML and ML estimates are different only to a negligible degree (see Snijders & Bosker, 1999), which is why some statistical packages see the choice between REML and ML as "a matter of personal taste" (StataCorp, 2005, p. 188), and some textbooks sanction use of either for likelihood ratio tests (Kleinbaum, Kupper, Nizam, & Muller, 2007, p. 716).

CONVERGING ON A SOLUTION IN LINEAR MIXED MODELING

One of the most basic assumptions of linear mixed modeling is that in the iterative algorithms by which linear mixed model estimates are calculated, the algorithm is able to converge on a solution. The fact that statistical software packages will generate output in the absence of convergence can and does tempt researchers to ignore convergence warnings and interpret output anyway. However, such output may well reflect a suboptimal solution, and interpretations made on the basis of such output may be substantively wrong.

In addition to the fact that the iterative algorithm used in maximum likelihood estimation may fail to converge on a solution, there is also the possibility that convergence may be achieved but the algorithm cannot invert the Hessian, which is a matrix used to compute standard errors for the covariance parameters. If variances equal to zero or negative variances appear on the diagonal of the Hessian, it cannot be inverted to compute the needed standard errors. One of the following warnings shown in Figure 2.1 may appear (shown for SPSS output).

Figure 2.1 Convergence warnings in SPSS

Warnings

Iteration was terminated but convergence has not been achieved. The MIXED procedure continues despite this warning. Subsequent results produced are based on the last iteration. Validity of the model fit is uncertain.

Warnings

The final Hessian matrix is not positive definite although all convergence criteria are satisfied. The MIXED procedure continues despite this warning. Validity of subsequent results cannot be ascertained.

If either of these warnings appears, there are three recourses for the researcher:

1. Re-specify the model or adjust estimation parameters. This recourse should be taken before considering either of the next two. Several remedial actions may be possible by changing the design of the study or by changing constraints on the estimation process. Changes from default estimation settings should be reported.

2. Stop and throw out the model. This strategy is the technically correct one, since without convergence, parameter estimates may be suboptimal, and without an invertible Hessian, the computed standard errors may be erroneous.

3. Proceed on an exploratory basis. Convergence and non-positive definite Hessian warnings are similar to other violations of the assumptions of a procedure. The calculated results cannot be interpreted to mean exactly what they are supposed to mean. The researcher does not know how different the printed estimates and standard errors are from the ones that should have been the output. However, in most cases the direction and general magnitude (weak, moderate, strong) of effects will not differ, and in many cases differences will prove to be minor, justifying proceeding with analysis on a purely exploratory basis.

One or more of the following steps may eliminate convergence-related warnings:

- Model Specification and Design Changes

1. Estimation problems may reflect multicollinearity. Check for and remove any redundant variables. In some cases, footnotes to output tables may flag redundant variables. Running a regression to check for variables with high variance inflation factor (VIF) coefficients is another method. A third method is to print out the complete iteration history (SPSS has a Print iteration history option, for instance) and look for any covariance parameter that is constant across all iterations, signaling it may very well be redundant.

2. Specifying a simpler covariance type for random effects, including the grouping effect, may avoid warnings. For instance, the "Unstructured" type is the most complex, having the most parameters, and one may consider instead specifying a "Diagonal" or other type. Covariance types are discussed below.

3. If the estimate for a slope/intercept covariance for a random effect approaches zero, the researcher may make the slope variable a fixed effect only. In general, lack of convergence can result from trying to estimate random coefficients that are close to or equal to zero.

4. Consider a simpler model with fewer variables.

5. Increase the sample size if small.

6. There cannot be fewer observations than parameters

- Estimation Parameter Changes

Model specification and research design changes should be considered before considering changing estimation parameter defaults. As depicted in Figure 2.2, SPSS software provides for the researcher making any of a variety of changes to parameters for the estimation algorithm, and other software packages provide similar options if they apply to the algorithms used by that package.

Figure 2.2 Estimation options dialog in SPSS

1. Increase the maximum iterations above the default (ex., above 100) so that the algorithm searches longer for a convergent solution.

2. Increase step-halvings above the default (ex., above 5), causing step sizes to be smaller and hence more precise. When step-halvings are increased, the maximum number of iterations is also increased. The Newton-Raphson algorithm used by SAS and SPSS (but not HLM) employs a default step size of 1 for each iteration. Halving the step size at each iteration is an effort to check that the likelihood does not decrease (indicating better fit) between iterations. In SPSS, the maximum number of step-halvings is 10. Increasing this default allows finer and finer checking between iterations for lower likelihood, which may be useful when the default settings fail to lead to convergence. For further description of the Newton-Raphson algorithm, see Ypma (1995).

3. Increase the parameter convergence value to be larger than the default (ex., greater than .000001). The algorithm considers convergence achieved when change between successive iterations in an estimated parameter is less than the specified parameter convergence value. Increasing it makes it easier to achieve convergence because one has defined convergence to be less demanding. While this may be appropriate for exploratory research, it is not customary in confirmatory research.

4. Change the values for "Log-likelihood Convergence" and for "Hessian Convergence." In SPSS, these are set to 0 by default, which means these convergence criteria are not used. However, setting either to a non-negative value will

invoke these alternative criteria. Likewise, setting the parameter convergence criterion to 0, as above, disables that default convergence criterion in SPSS.

5. Increase the singularity tolerance value. The SPSS drop-down estimation choices for this allow successively larger tolerances by factors of 10. However, larger singularity tolerances increase the likelihood of accepting an ill-conditioned matrix (one in which rows or columns approach collinearity). While larger tolerance values do indeed improve the chance of convergence, it may be convergence on a solution that is unstable (small changes in the data lead to large changes in the fixed effect estimates). Indeed, erratic shifts in these estimates suggest an ill-conditioned matrix. Thoroughly check for multicollinearity before considering this adjustment.

6. Increase the number of scoring steps above the default (ex., above 1 up to about 5). If 5 is entered, for instance, Fisher scoring is used for the first 5 iterations of estimation, rather than the default of reverting to Newton-Raphson at iteration 2. This has the effect of counteracting a possible bad starting value and may lead to convergence.

MEETING OTHER ASSUMPTIONS OF LINEAR MIXED MODELING

Being able to converge on a solution and to compute standard errors for the solution is only one assumption of linear mixed modeling. In this section, others are presented.

• *Proper model specification.* As is true in GLM, the researcher's model must be properly specified. Adding or deleting critical predictors (or highly correlated spurious ones) can substantially change and even reverse the direction of parameter estimates. In spite of a review of the literature, the researcher may not be aware of all critical predictors. One recommended strategy is to forego trying to "validate the model," and instead make the research objective one of showing that Model A is more consistent with the data than is Model B, where both models emerge from the literature or where Model B is a revision of Model A proposed by the researcher. Models should be selected based on theory, not a blunt force approach testing a large number of models on a data-driven basis.[8]

• *Homogeneity of variance of residuals.* Error variance is not necessarily assumed to be constant across groups, unlike in OLS regression. However, homogeneity of error variance is the default, and different models must be requested explicitly when error variances are heterogeneous. This critical assumption is discussed further in Chapter 3 in the section on full random coefficients models, where HLM 7's test for homogeneity is illustrated. A finding of heterogeneity may signal improper model specification. SAS supports heterogeneous variance models by employing the variable associated with heterogeneity as a repeated measure in the REPEATED clause of PROC MIXED (see Hedeker & Mermelstein, 2007).

Similarly, SPSS's REGWGT option in its mixed modeling module is a form of weighted least squares method for adjusting the residual covariance matrix when unequal error variance is present.

- *Random sampling.* As true for other procedures, significance tests assume that for levels above the bottom (individual) level, the groups (ex., schools, where students are the bottom level) are representative. This means they must be a random sample of all such groups (ex., all schools) or an enumeration of all groups.[9] This is a critical assumption in multilevel modeling. For convenience samples and other types of nonrandom sampling, unknown bias is introduced into significance testing, although standard errors can be estimated by data-driven approaches such as bootstrapping.[10]

- *Adequate sample size.* The efficiency and power of multilevel tests rest on pooled data across the units comprising two or more levels, which implies large datasets. The restricted expected maximum likelihood (REML) and maximum likelihood (ML) estimation methods used by linear mixed modeling give asymptotically efficient estimates, meaning efficiency depends on large samples. For purposes of improving power and precision of parameter estimates, increasing the number of level 2 groups is more important than increasing the number of level 1 individuals. For instance, simulation studies by Kreft (1996) found there was adequate statistical power with 30 groups of 30 observations each, 60 groups with 25 observations each, and 150 groups with 5 observations each. More recently Maas and Hox (2005), based on simulation studies, concluded, "The standard errors of the second-level variances are estimated too small when the number of groups is substantially lower than 100. With 30 groups, the standard errors are estimated about 15% too small" (p. 90). In view of this, Maas and Hox suggest that with small samples (as small as 10), bootstrapping be used to estimate standard errors. Bootstrapping, however, is not available in all statistical packages for multilevel modeling and is a data-driven approach that may fail to yield replicable results, especially if not cross-validated. Cheung and Au (2005) used resampling to test sample size effects and found that sample size "can be as small as 50, yet the results are still comparable with other larger sample size conditions" (pp. 91–92). Unbalanced individual-level samples within groups (that is, when group sizes vary) may require larger group samples. Cheung and Au's experiments also disconfirmed the assertion of some that larger individual-level samples could compensate for small group-level samples.

In summary, there is a rapid fall-off in statistical power as the number of groups/observations falls below the threshold needed. With less than adequate power, there is an unacceptable risk of not detecting cross-level interactions (ex., between schools and students). Both adequate number of individual observations and adequate number of groups are needed. Power for individual-level estimates depends on the number of individuals observed, and power for second-level estimates depends on the number of groups. Selecting Bayesian estimation rather than REML or ML estimation is one approach to research on smaller samples. That is, when Bayesian estimation is selected, smaller level 2 samples may be tolerated (Raudenbush & Bryk, 2002, p. 14).

- If there is a level 3, it too must meet minimum sample size requirements. When this requirement is not met, the researcher may enter the level 3 grouping variable as a set of level 2 dummy variables. In this volume, for instance, Shafto and Adelson (Chapter 7) do this by entering the would-be level 3 variable, School, as a set of nine level 2 dummy variables, thereby accounting for school differences at level 2 since a sample size of 10 schools did not suffice to create a three-level model.

- *Similar group sizes.* The default REML estimation method, as well as ML estimation, is an efficient estimator for larger samples with similar or different group sizes (that is, with balanced as well as unbalanced designs). Nonetheless, when sample sizes within groups are unbalanced, tests of parameter estimates and of overall fit will have inflated Type I error. However, especially for smaller samples, as discussed in the section on estimation, full information maximum likelihood (FIML) estimators are more robust for unbalanced designs and should be employed when group sizes differ significantly.

- *Dropped cases due to missing values* should be less than 5% of the total sample unless such cases can be shown to be randomly missing. As with any form of analysis, a substantial number of nonrandom missing cases can bias analysis severely.

- *Continuous outcome variables.* Linear mixed modeling, including HLM modeling, assumes the dependent variable is continuous. Binary, multinomial, and even ordinal dependent variables should not be employed with the default ML and REML estimation methods, but ordinal data may be used with Bayesian estimation. However, generalized linear mixed modeling *does* allow binary, multinomial, and ordinal outcome variables.

- *Centered data.* It is customary to center data prior to running a linear mixed model. Grand mean centering is by far the most usual type,[11] and is based on subtracting the grand mean from all raw data values, making the new mean zero. This often improves the interpretability of coefficients and may reduce multicollinearity. After centering, the phrase "controlling for other variables in the model" becomes equivalent to "holding other variables in the model at their mean." Note, however, that binary variables normally are not centered.[12] For the binary variable "sex," coded 0 = male and 1 = female, the phrase "holding sex constant" is equivalent to "holding sex at 0," which is equivalent to "for males."

- *Rescaling start time to zero.* In studies where time is a variable, start time should be set to 0. For instance, if "year" as a variable were coded 2011, 2012, 2013, etc., and was not rescaled, then controlling time would be controlling time at the traditional year of Christ's birth, far outside the range of study data.

- *Linearity.* Linear mixed models assume linearity between the independent and the dependent variables. However, like ordinary regression, nonlinear terms may be added (ex., time-squared as well as time). In generalized linear mixed modeling (GLMM), nonlinear link functions (ex., logistic rather than linear [identity] linking of the dependent variable) are supported. GLMM rather than LMM is required when nonlinearity persists even after adding nonlinear terms to the predictor side of the equation, and even then, it is not assured that linearity in the link function can be achieved.

- *Multicollinearity.* As with other forms of regression, high multicollinearity will make parameter estimates inefficient.

- *Normal distribution of variables.* REML and ML estimates may be assumed to display asymptotic normality for large samples, making normality not a critical assumption for linear mixed modeling. However, when Bayesian estimation is employed, as it often is for ordinal dependent variables, normality is assumed. Extensions have been developed for non-normal data (Goldstein, 1991; Morris, 1995; Wong & Mason, 1985).

- *Normal distribution of residuals.* Residual normality is required to properly define significance tests (for ex., to define the alpha region = .05) unless bootstrap methods are applied. This can be tested in any statistical package by saving the residuals, then requesting a Q-Q plot: The more points lie on a straight line in this plot, the more residuals are normally distributed. This is done, for instance, in Chapter 10 of this volume. When there is violation of normality, robust standard errors are used.

- *Outliers.* As with other forms of regression, presence of outliers will bias parameter estimates. Outliers may be tested using Mahalanobis distance, leverage, and Cook's D. In some statistical packages, including SPSS, it is necessary to get these coefficients by running the regression procedure.

- *Properly specified covariance structures.* Linear mixed model solutions are iterative and require starting from researcher-supplied parameters, including specifying the type of covariance structure to be assumed for the repeated and random effects. While often not making a substantive difference, changing the specified covariance structure will change the covariance parameter estimates and tests of fixed effects, and in some cases may lead to different substantive conclusions. Covariance structure is discussed later in this chapter.

- *Independent blocks.* While observations are not assumed to be independent, the groups (blocks) formed by the subject variable(s) are assumed to be independent and to have the same covariance structures, for models that involve random effects or repeated measures.

- *Repeated measures designs*, if not adjusted by specifying repeated measures in LMM, involve autocorrelation, which will inflate the F and t tests as well as the R-squared value.

- *Independent observations are not assumed*, which is why multilevel modeling is recommended when intraclass correlation exists.

In a survey of journal articles, Dedrick et al. (2009) found that in many studies, the researcher failed to report sufficient information to determine if the assumptions of linear mixed modeling were met. The authors provide sound reporting guidelines. In general, the researcher should err on the side of completeness in discussion of the assumptions listed above.

COVARIANCE STRUCTURE TYPES

Linear mixed modeling uses an iterative algorithm to estimate coefficients. Estimates will be more reliable if the algorithm uses as a starting point an accurate assumption about the nature of the variance–covariance matrix for the variables in the model. For REML, FIML, or ML estimation algorithms, the covariance structure type must be specified by the researcher whenever there are random effects or repeated measures in the model. Assuming a too-simple covariance structure will increase Type I errors, while assuming a too-complex structure will increase Type II errors when interpreting variance components for random effects in the output of linear mixed modeling software. Although the selection of a covariance type frequently makes little difference in estimates for some data, in some instances it is entirely possible that misselection could lead to substantive error in analysis.

Setting the covariance structure type also sets corresponding constraints on the solution. A variance components (VC) type, for instance, constrains the estimated variance–covariance matrix to have zeros on the off-diagonal, signifying that variance components have zero covariance. Selecting an "Unstructured" covariance type imposes no constraints but by the same token is the most complex model for the matrix. Other covariance-type assumptions may yield coefficients not significantly different but reflecting a simpler model, which may be preferred on parsimony grounds.

There are two domains for types of covariance structure assumptions. The first domain is for random effects, which specify the random effects "G" variance/covariance matrix. This is the basis for estimating between-subjects effects. The second domain is for repeated measures, which specifies the repeated measures "R" variance/covariance matrix. This is the basis for estimating within-subjects effects. The covariance structure specified for random effects need not be the same as that specified for repeated measures. Note also that while ordinarily there will be just one random effects model and just one covariance type specified for it, it is possible in SPSS and other packages to run multiple independent random effects models, each with its own specified covariance structure and each referring to a different combination of grouping variables.

Variance components structure type. The covariance structure matrix is one table per random effect, in which both rows and columns are levels of the random effect factor (ex., certified = 0, certified = 1). Diagonal cell entries represent variances of residuals (error terms), and off-diagonal cell entries represent the covariances of the residuals when predicting the dependent variable for the row unit and the column unit. For instance, consider Figure 2.3, which illustrates the "Variance Components" (VC) covariance structure matrix type for a study in which "City" is the random factor. The VC type is also called "simple structure" or "the independence model." This is the default covariance structure type for random effects models. In the example, each city has the same variance of residuals (error terms) as each other element city. The covariance of residuals between different cities is assumed to be 0. That is, residuals are uncorrelated and independent. Because of independence, random effects will be additive: The ratio of effect covariance estimates to residual covariance estimates is the ratio of the importance of between-subject effects to within-subject effects in accounting for the variance of the dependent variable.

Diagonal structure type. The VC covariance structure type is not available for repeated measures because in repeated measures designs, level 1 is the repeated measurements and the grouping variable is the subject being measured. In a repeated measures study, there are multiple measurement occasions (a time variable). Rows and columns in the R matrix would be the levels of the time variable (time = 1, time = 2, etc.). In a diagonal structure, it is assumed that the off-diagonal covariances would still be zero, as in VC structure, meaning that residual covariances between times are assumed independent. Unlike VC structure, it is assumed each time has different variances of residuals. This is the "diagonal structure," which is the default for repeated measures, shown in Figure 2.4.

Unstructured covariance structure type. This is a completely general type in which each element in the matrix can assume a different value. Unstructured, while not the default, is a common assumption for random coefficients models

Figure 2.3   Variance components covariance structure

Random Effect Covariance Structure (G)[a]			
	[City=1]	*[City=2]*	*[City=3]*
[City=1]	3.8131E7	0	0
[City=2]	0	3.8181E7	0
[City=3]	0	0	3.8181E7
Variance Components			

a. Dependent Variable: Price.

| Figure 2.4 | Diagonal covariance structure. |

Random Effect Covariance Structure (R)[a]			
	[Time=1]	[Time=2]	[Time=3]
[Time=1]	6.8820E7	0	0
[Time=2]	0	.000000	0
[Time=3]	0	0	2.5922E7
Diagonal			

a. Dependent Variable: Price.

(regression models where slopes as well as intercepts are modeled by LMM). In unstructured models, the intercept, slope, and intercept*slope covariance are all modeled. This choice is appropriate when the researcher has no basis for knowing what the covariance structure is. Unstructured models are the assumption in GLM MANOVA. The presence of non-zero off-diagonal elements in the variance–covariance matrix means that unlike VC models, in unconstrained models, variance components are not additive. Unconstrained models are unparsimonious, requiring the computation of many parameters. Lack of parsimony means a greater risk of incurring convergence errors and also means that parsimony-based goodness-of-fit measures (ex., BIC) will penalize unstructured models. One strategy is to choose the unstructured covariance type initially, but to request output of a matrix of covariances of residuals to discern possible patterns that would warrant re-running the model with a simpler covariance type assumption. Sometimes dropping outliers may make such a pattern more discernable. When slope coefficients or slope-intercept covariances are very small, an unstructured solution may not be possible, and an error message will be generated. In such situations, it is common to try a diagonal covariance structure, discussed above.

Autoregressive covariance structure types. The "first-order autoregressive structure with homogenous variances" (AR(1)) is commonly assumed for time series data that display a common trend, such as where the correlation of any pair of repeated measurements is assumed to decrease exponentially according to how far apart they are in time, measured at equally spaced intervals. The larger the time lag, the lower the correlation of residuals. In the residual covariance matrix, the diagonal variances will be roughly equal, and the off-diagonal covariances will show a pattern, normally decreasing over time. On-diagonal residual variances are assumed to be equal. A related autoregressive type is "AR(1): Heterogeneous," which is the same but assumes the diagonal elements may differ. A third autoregressive type is "ARMA(1,1)," which refers to a first-order autoregressive moving average structure. As with AR(1), variances are homogenous, but the diminishing of correlations is a function of moving average parameters as well as time. The "Toeplitz" type is a generalization of the AR(1) type that assumes the pattern sequence for off-diagonal covariances does not have to step by some common multiple but may step by some unique multiple associated with that time step. It assumes homogenous variances and heterogeneous correlations between elements. There is also a "Toeplitz: Heterogeneous" type that assumes heterogeneous variances and heterogeneous correlations between elements.

Compound symmetry. Also called "Exchangeable" structure, this is a common alternative for repeated measures. It assumes that if elements are time periods, the correlation of residuals for measurements nearby in time should be the same as for measurements far apart in time. That is, residuals have the same covariance for any pair of time periods (repeated measures) or cities (random effects). The variances on the diagonal are assumed to be the same for any time period or city, and the covariances on the off-diagonal are also assumed to be roughly the same. This is the type assumed in univariate ANOVA models and is the classical approach to repeated measures. The assumption of compound symmetry is more likely to be met with classical experimental data than with longitudinal data, where autoregressive or Toeplitz assumptions may be more appropriate. A related type is "Compound Symmetry: Correlation Metric," which is assumed to have homogenous variances and homogenous correlations (not covariances) between elements. The "Compound Symmetry: Heterogeneous" type assumes heterogeneous variances but constant correlation between elements.

Other covariance structure types. Among the many other covariance structure types are these: "Ante-Dependence: First Order, AD(1)" assumes heterogeneous variances and heterogeneous correlations between adjacent elements such that the correlation between two nonadjacent elements is the product of the correlations between the elements that lie between the elements of interest. The "Factor Analytic: First Order" covariance structure type assumes that the covariance between any two elements in the matrix is the square root of the product of their heterogeneous variance terms. The "Factor Analytic: First Order, Heterogeneous" type assumes the covariance between any two elements is the square root of the product of the first of their heterogeneous variance terms. The "Huynh-Feldt" type assumes a "circular" matrix in which the covariance between any two elements is equal to the average of their variances minus a constant. "Scaled Identity" is a type that assumes no correlation between any elements (for example, scaled identity is a common assumption when modeling the interaction of a random factor with a fixed grouping factor, where it is assumed that the interaction effect is normally distributed around a mean of zero, with unknown variance to be estimated).

Selecting the Best Covariance Structure Assumption

Goodness-of-fit statistics (AIC, AICC, BIC—discussed below in the section on goodness of fit) can be used to select the best covariance structure type to assume. Simulation studies by Ehlers (2004) suggest BIC is preferred generally (compared to AIC, BIC penalizes for lack of parsimony), but AICC is better for sample sizes < 20 and when there is only one group. Usually, however, this is a moot question because these information criteria measures will agree in most cases. The model with the lowest value on BIC (or other chosen fit criterion) is the one with the best-fitting covariance structure assumption.[13] It is also possible to run a likelihood ratio test (LR test, discussed below) on the difference between two models, one under a given covariance structure assumption and another model under a different assumption. Note, however, that both the information criteria and the LR test methods are data-driven and thus prone to over-fitting, particularly if cross-validation is not part of the design. Covariance structure assumptions should start with theoretical selection based on covariance expectations.

COMPARING MODEL GOODNESS OF FIT WITH INFORMATION THEORY MEASURES

Once analysis is complete, how are alternative models compared for goodness of fit? A common method is to use information theory goodness-of-fit measures, which are output by many statistical packages for linear mixed modeling. These measures are appropriate when comparing models that have been estimated using REML when fixed effects are the same or when only random effects are modeled, or maximum likelihood (ML) when these conditions are not met. Specifically, these measures are based on adjusting the computed likelihood statistic (−2LL, a.k.a. model chi-square or deviance). While the absolute values of such measures do not carry an easily expressed intrinsic meaning (they are not "percent of variance explained," for example), the model with the lower value displays the better fit to the data when comparing models. This approach assumes models are selected based on theory and are not so numerous as to threaten over-fitting of the data, leading to spurious confirmation. As with all methodologies, false or misleading findings are apt to result if the true model or an approximation of it is not in the model set being compared. Data are assumed to be fixed across models, and information theory measures are not to be used to compare models derived from different datasets. Information theory measures do not have significance tests, as there is no known distribution of the difference in such measures between models.

HLM 7 does not report information theory measures, though it does report deviance, from which such measures may be computed easily on a manual basis.[14] SPSS LMM reports AIC, AICC, CAIC, and BIC. SPSS GLMM reports AICC and BIC. SAS MIXED reports AIC, AICC, and BIC. SAS GLIMMIX reports AIC, AICC, BIC, CAIC, and HQIC. These measures are explained below.

- AIC is the Akaike information criterion. This goodness-of-fit measure adjusts –2 log likelihood to penalize for model complexity. It may be used to compare non-hierarchical as well as hierarchical (nested) models based on the same dataset, whereas likelihood ratio tests discussed in the next section are used only for nested models. Lower AIC reflects a better-fitting model. In model development, the researcher stops modifying the model when AIC fails to drop appreciably or starts rising. In this volume, Patterson (Chapter 13), for instance, uses the criterion that when comparing models, AIC should be reduced by twice the difference in number of parameters (ex., by 4 if two parameters are added). Manually, given deviance (–2LL, minus 2 log likelihood), AIC = –2LL + 2p, where p is the number of estimated parameters.

- AICC is AIC corrected for small sample size. Anderson and Burnham (2002) recommend use of AICC when sample size or the number of estimable parameters ≤ 40 for the model in the set with the largest number of parameters. AICC is then used for all the models in the set of models being compared. Manually, AICC = AIC + [(2p(p + 1))/(n – p – 1)].

- BIC is the Bayesian information Criterion, also known as Akaike's Bayesian information criterion (ABIC) and the Schwarz Bayesian criterion (SBC). BIC penalizes for additional model parameters more severely than does AIC. In general, BIC has a conservative bias tending toward Type II error (thinking there is poor model fit when the relationship is real). Put another way, BIC favors parsimonious models with fewer parameters. BIC is recommended when sample size is large or the number of parameters in the model is small. Note that a model with large sample size but having small variance in its variables and/or highly collinear independents may yield misleading model fit using BIC.

- CAIC is consistent AIC, an alternative to AICC that also penalizes for sample size as well as model complexity (lack of parsimony). The penalty is greater than for AIC but less than for BIC.

- HQIC is the Hannan and Quinn information criterion. It also penalizes for model complexity (over-parameterization). HQIC can be seen as a compromise between AIC's relative leniency toward adding parameters to the model and BIC's relative harshness.

In a time series analysis study seeking to predict appropriate time period lags for autoregressive models, Mikusheva (2007) found HQIC to be consistent and BIC to be strongly consistent, but found AIC to be biased toward overestimating the number of lags asymptotically.

COMPARING MODELS WITH LIKELIHOOD RATIO TESTS

In all software packages for linear mixed modeling, nested models can be compared using a likelihood ratio test, also called a model chi-square difference test. Likelihood ratio tests evaluate which of two nested models has better fit to the data. A nested model has only variables and terms found in the parent model but is missing one or more. The null model is always a nested model. Comparison of nested models is a form of hierarchical analysis. Other measures of fit, such as AIC or BIC, may be used for non-hierarchical comparisons. Note that a problem with the likelihood ratio test is that it, like the chi-square, is sensitive to sample size. In large samples, differences of trivial size will be found to be significant, whereas in small samples even sizable differences may test as non-significant.

Be warned that Monte Carlo simulations by Yuan and Bentler (2004) have demonstrated that the likelihood ratio test can lead to erroneous inferences when the base model has been misspecified. One way to misspecify the base model is to assume an inappropriate covariance structure type. For this reason, the researcher may wish to start with an unstructured (UN) type, then demonstrate non-significance of difference in deviance values with a more constrained type (ex., variance components) as a basis for selecting the more constrained covariance structure type. HLM 7 defaults to an unstructured model, whereas SAS and SPSS do not. Direct selection of a covariance type without this sort of testing may represent misspecification of the base model.

To determine which of two nested models has better fit to the data, a model is run with and without one or more random effects, and the difference is taken between the two model chi-square values, which are the -2 log likelihood ($-2LL$) coefficients, also called the deviance. For this model chi-square difference, the degrees of freedom are the difference in the number of model parameters (the df for the larger model minus the df for the smaller model), usually corresponding to the number of terms dropped in the smaller model (often 1). Given the chi-square value and the degrees of freedom, the significance of the model fit difference can be looked up in a chi-square table, though most software packages will return the p significance level automatically. If the computed probability is greater than .05, meaning the difference is non-significant, then the two models have equivalent fit and on parsimony grounds, the smaller model is preferred.

The likelihood ratio test may also be used when the researcher is considering dropping a fixed effect from the model. Whereas the likelihood ratio test for model covariance parameters may be used under either ML or REML estimation, the likelihood ratio test for fixed effects assumes ML estimation. A computed probability greater than .05 means the population coefficient for the fixed factor cannot be assumed to be different from 0, and the researcher proceeds with dropping the fixed factor.

The Wald test is an alternative to the likelihood ratio test when determining which terms to drop from a model. Parameters for which the Wald test has a non-significant probability are ones that are candidates for dropping. As such, the Wald test is analogous to backward stepwise regression. However, when considering whether to drop a term from the model, the likelihood ratio test is preferred over the Wald test because the Wald test tends to report inflated standard errors for large effect sizes, thus leading to Type II errors.

EFFECT SIZE IN LINEAR MIXED MODELING

The concepts of "effect size" and "percent of variance explained" are problematic in linear mixed modeling, so much so that some authors avoid reporting effect size measures. In multilevel modeling, there is unexplained variance at multiple levels, not just level 1. Variance explained at lower levels is dependent on higher levels. In fact, residual variance could be attributed to any level, including any that were omitted from the model. In random coefficients models, where lower-level slopes are modeled by higher-level random effects, the random slope reflects one regression per group, and "explained variance" is not uniquely defined, but rather is a mean, subject to the problems of means as measures of central tendency. Adding certain variables may affect the variance of the level 1 intercept, and therefore the percent of variance accounted for when slopes and intercepts are correlated. (Group mean centering may eliminate the correlation, but this also changes the meaning of the variable in question as noted elsewhere in this volume.) Add to this the fact that in some linear mixed models, random effects may be allowed to exhibit covariance and groups may overlap as well as be nested, the problem of assessing effect size can become even more complex. Nonetheless, some of the most common approaches are summarized below.

A. *Percent of between-group variance explained by effects added in a more complex model, defined as the percent reduction in the effect of the level 2 grouping variable on the dependent variable*

This definition is most appropriate for making judgments about adding level 2 predictors (Raudenbush & Bryk, 2002, p. 111). It is interpreted as the proportion of variance explained for the level 2 model. For models estimated by ML rather than REML, let Model 1 be the reduced model (often the null model) and Model 2 be one with additional effects.[15] Model 1 is nested within Model 2, which is the research model of interest. Raudenbush and Bryk defined "proportion of variance explained" as the intercept effect (p. 74). For the example of a level 2 school effect on test scores at level 1, the intercept effect is measured as the difference between Model 1 and Model 2 school effects divided by the Model 1 school effect, where "school effect" refers to the school intercept variance component (the school mean component). The result is the percent of between-group (here, between-school) variance in the dependent variable accounted for effects added in Model 2. Note that the school effect is a conditional effect controlling for other predictors added in Model 2 (in Raudenbush and Bryk, for ex., adding school mean socioeconomic status as a fixed effect).

B. *Percent of within-group variance explained by effects added in a more complex model, defined as percent reduction in within-group (residual) variance on the dependent variable*

This definition is most appropriate for making judgments about adding level 1 predictors. It is interpreted as the proportion of variance explained for the level 1 model. It must be recognized, however, that residual variance (which is within-group variance in the level 1 dependent variable) may be attributed to any level, not just level 1. The overall model effect is the difference between Model 1 and Model 2 residual variance components, that quantity divided by the residual variance component in Model 1. The result is the percent of Model 1 residual variance in the dependent variable explained by additional effects added in Model 2. As compared to the null model with no predictors, adding predictors at level 1 may reduce unexplained variance not only at level 1, but also at higher levels. In unusual circumstances (adding a suppressor variable), it may even increase residual variance in the research model compared to the reduced model, thereby yielding negative variance explained estimates. Approaches A and B are illustrated, for instance, in Chapter 11 of this volume.

C. *Partition of variance associated with random effects*

Variance partition is used to compare random effects. For a model that constrains the covariance of random effects to zero (ex., variance components or diagonal models), the sum of estimated variance components is the total variance associated with the dependent variable at level 1. The residual component divided by the total gives the percent of that variance attributable to within-group effects, controlling for other random effects in the model. Dividing the intercept component by the total gives the percent of total variance associated with the level 2 grouping variable, controlling for other random effects in the model (ex., the school effect, where level 1 is student test scores and level 2 refers to the schools they attend; for the null model with no predictors, this is the intraclass correlation coefficient, the ICC). Some authors call this the variance partition coefficient, or VPC. Dividing any other component by the total gives the percentage of total variance attributable to that random effect, controlling for other random effects in the model.

A number of other methods of assessing effect sizes have been proposed and even used, including Cohen's d and standardized parameter estimates for fixed effects, but a review of the literature suggests these are not widely adopted within the HLM community. Measuring effect size and variance explained in a multilevel model raises many issues, and there is as yet no consensus among statisticians on this matter. For further discussion, see Snijders and Bosker (1994), Xu (2003), Edwards et al. (2008), and Hassjer (2008).

SUMMARY

Not all multilevel data require multilevel analysis. Rather, the criterion is whether the grouping (level) factor is correlated with the dependent variable. The most-used test statistic is the intraclass correlation coefficient (ICC), computed on the null model (one with no other predictors apart from the group-ing variable).[16] ICC is zero when observations are distributed randomly by group, and it is 1.0 when there are significant differences on the mean value of the dependent variable between the groups but total uniformity of score on the dependent variable within each group. A non-significant ICC means there is no between-groups effect and no need for linear mixed modeling in random inter-cept models. Random coefficients models, which analyze a grouping effect on slopes as well as on means, require a more complex test to rule out the need for LMM, but the presence of a significant ICC means mixed modeling is needed even for random coefficients models.

Not all linear mixed models have a solution. That is, estimates may fail to converge, or if they converge, the Hessian matrix associated with the estimates may not be invertible. While statistical software packages generate output in spite of such problems, software also generates warnings that should be heeded since such output reflects a solution that is suboptimal to an unknown degree. Bluntly put, ensuing interpretations may be substantively wrong. When convergence or Hessian warnings are given, the model must be re-specified, or the estimation parameters must be adjusted in ways described earlier.

Likewise, it is important to meet the other assumptions of linear mixed model-ing. Prime among these is the assumption that groups formed at level 2 or higher are representative, meaning that they are randomly sampled or an enumeration of all groups. If the sample of groups is biased, so will be the estimates of random effects. Moreover, the sample size at level 2 and higher must be large. While bootstrapped estimates can be requested for nonrandom and small samples in some statistical packages, bootstrapping is not a panacea. Full information maxi-mum likelihood (FIML) estimates should be requested when group sizes differ substantially. Generalized linear mixed models should be used for binomial, ordinal, and multinomial outcome variables. Data should be centered to enhance interpretability of estimates. The predictors should be linearly related to the dependent variable in ordinary LMM, and linearly related to the link function of the dependent variable in generalized LMM. As with general linear models, high multicollinearity makes parameter estimates inefficient. Presence of outliers, presence of many missing values, and non-normal distribution of residuals all violate assumptions of linear mixed modeling. Above all, as with general linear models, the model must be properly specified. Adding or deleting critical predic-tors (or highly correlated spurious ones) can substantially change and even reverse the direction of parameter estimates.

Regardless of type, linear mixed models using maximum likelihood methods generate goodness-of-fit measures, which may be used to compare models. Common likelihood-based measures of fit are Akaike's information criterion (AIC) and the Bayesian information criterion (BIC). The model with the lower AIC or BIC better fits the data. For nested models, a likelihood ratio test may be employed based on the difference of −2 log likelihoods (−2LL, also called the deviance) between models and difference of degrees of freedom between mod-els. The −2LL difference follows a chi-square distribution for large samples, therefore likelihood ratio tests are also called model chi-square tests. When the chi-square difference is non-significant, the nested model is preferred on model parsimony grounds.

In the next three chapters, common types of linear mixed models are presented, including hierarchical linear models. Chapter 3 deals with models using HLM 7 software. Chapter 4 deals with models using SPSS 19 software. Chapter 5 deals with models developed using SAS 9.2 software. While these chapters examine the same dataset in parallel models, different observations about the linear mixed modeling process occur in each, making it worthwhile for the users of one statistical package also to read chapters describing other packages. The remaining 10 chapters present additional, often more complex applications using these three software packages, plus one chapter using the software package Stata. The applications chapters emphasize how to construct a given type of model, how to interpret output, and how to report results.

NOTES

1. In an alternative to check for lack of independence, meaning some form of mixed modeling and repeated measures analysis is needed, the researcher can run an OLS regression and save the residuals. An ANOVA of residuals by group (ex., agency, where agency is the level 2 grouping for level 1 individual data) can be run. If the ANOVA F-test is significant, the researcher rejects the null hypothesis that residuals are independent by group. That is, a significant F means data are correlated, not independent, and LMM should be used instead of OLS.

2. A variance components model is one in which a variance components covariance structure is specified, as treated in a later section of this chapter.

3. Fisher scoring can stray outside parameter space, allowing correlations of random effects greater than 1.0. In such cases, HLM 7 discards Fisher scoring for that iteration and uses EM.

4. Private email from Mathilda du Toit, Scientific Software International, April 19, 2011.

5. The HLM manual recommends diagonalizing tau as an alternative that may lead to convergence when the default unstructured solution does not converge.

6. HLM 7 does support a wider variety of covariance types, such as auto-regressive, in its HMLM2 module.

7. HLM 7 uses the Kenward-Roger (KR) method of determining degrees of freedom for the denominator when calculating standard errors for fixed effects. The KR method has been found to be more reliable for a wider range of research problems. Schaalje, McBride, and Fellingham (2001) conclude, "The KR (Kenward-Roger) method works reasonably well with more complicated covariance structures when sample sizes are moderate to small and the design is reasonably balanced. . . . [But] When the covariance structure is complex and the sample size is small, the KR method produces inflated Type I error rates" (p. 4). SPSS uses a modified Satterthwaite (SAT) method. SAS, which allows the user to set the method, defaults to the containment (CON) method when RANDOM statements are specified and to the between-within (BW) method when REPEATED statements are used without RANDOM statements. The BW method was utilized in the early influential article by Singer (1998), but the more recent KR method is now often preferred. Schaalje

et al. (2001) note, "The BW (between-within) method should only be considered to give exact ddf values for balanced repeated measures designs with the compound symmetry covariance structure (type=cs) for which levels of the within-subjects effect are not replicated within any of the subjects. In other cases, the method is at best approximate, and can be unpredictable" (p. 2).

8. At a minimum, the researcher should report number of models tested.

9. For enumerations, all effects are significant since chance of sampling is ruled out. Significance tests are customarily reported anyway for inference purposes. For enumerations, proportions associated with variance components are not biased.

10. In all data-driven approaches, cross-validation of results from the model development dataset with a holdout validation dataset is recommended.

11. Group mean centering, in contrast, changes the meaning of coefficients in complex ways that make coefficients hard to interpret, since different mean values are subtracted from different sets of raw scores. In essence, one is dealing with a different variable after group mean centering. Grand mean–centered income, for instance, will yield different slopes but the same deviance and residual errors as uncentered raw data. Group mean–centered income will not. Group mean–centered income is no longer simple income but rather measures income deviation from group means.

12. Under some circumstances, binary variables may be centered. See Enders and Tofighi (2007).

13. Note that if one or more fixed effects is dropped from the model, BIC (or other fit criteria) must be reestimated and reevaluated. Also note that this method of selection of covariance structure assumptions is data-driven. See endnote 2 above.

14. For instance, given deviance ($-2LL$), the common formula, used by HLM, SPSS, and SAS, for AIC is $AIC = -2LL + 2p$, where p is the number of estimated parameters. Stata and R compute AIC as $-2LL + 2*(p + f)$, where f is the number of fixed effects (West, Welch, & Galecki, 2007, p. 92). The common formula for BIC is: $BIC = -2LL + p*\ln(n)$, where n is the level 1 sample size.

15. The null model need not be the basis of comparison. It may be of little interest, for example, in studies focused on variance components associated with slopes rather than intercepts. See Chapter 8 of this volume for further discussion.

16. Though HLM 7 defaults to full estimation of the entire variance–covariance matrix, akin to the unstructured covariance type in SPSS or SAS, identical coefficients will result for the null model under this default as under a diagonal covariance type model (invoked by selecting "Diagonalize tau" in the HLM 7 "Estimation" window). This is because covariance of random effects is moot when there is only one random effect component (the intercept) other than the residual, as is the case in a null model.

REFERENCES

Anderson, D. R., & Burnham, K. P. (2002). Avoiding pitfalls when using information-theoretic methods. *Journal of Wildlife Management, 66*(3), 912–918.

Cheung, M. W.-L., & Au, K. (2005). Applications of multilevel structural equation modeling to cross-cultural research. *Structural Equation Modeling, 12*(4), 598–619.

Dedrick, R., Ferron, J., Hess, M., Hogarty, K., Kromrey, J., Lang, T., et al. (2009). Multilevel modeling: A review of methodological issues and applications. *Review of Educational Research, 79*(1), 69–102.

Diggle, P. J. (1988). An approach to the analysis of repeated measurements. *Biometrics, 44,* 959–971.

du Toit, S. H. C., & du Toit, M. (2008). Multilevel structural equation modeling. In J. de Leeuw & I. G. G. Kreft (Eds.), *The analysis of multilevel models.* London: Springer-Verlag.

Edwards, L. J., Muller, K. E., Wolfinger, R. D., Qaqish, B. F., & Schabenberger, O. (2008). An R^2 statistic for fixed effects in the linear mixed model. *Statistics in Medicine, 27,* 6137–6157.

Ehlers, M. (2004). *Assessment of covariance selection strategies with repeated measures data.* Paper presented at the 34th Annual Meeting of the South Carolina American Statistical Association (SCASA), Columbia. Retrieved April 23, 2007, from http://www.stat.sc.edu/scasa/Apr04t.html

Enders, C. K., & Tofighi, D. (2007). Centering predictor variables in cross-sectional multilevel models: A new look at an old issue. *Psychological Methods, 12*(2), 121–138.

Giesbrecht, F. G., & Burns, J. C. (1985). Two-stage analysis based on a mixed model: Large-sample asymptotic theory and small-sample simulation results. *Biometrics, 41,* 477–486.

Goldstein, H. (1991). Nonlinear multilevel models with an application to discrete response data. *Biometrika, 78,* 45–51.

Greven, S., & Kneib, T. (2010). On the behaviour of marginal and conditional AIC in linear mixed models. *Biometrika, 97*(4), 773–789.

Hassjer, O. (2008). On the coefficient of determination for mixed regression models. *Journal of Statistical Planning and Inference, 138,* 3022–3038.

Hedeker, D., & Mermelstein, R. J. (2007). Mixed-effects regression models with heterogeneous variance: Analyzing ecological momentary assessment data of smoking. In T. D. Little, J. A. Bovaird, & N. A. Card (Eds.), *Modeling contextual effects in longitudinal studies* (pp. 183–206). Mahwah, NJ: Erlbaum.

Hox, J. J., & Maas, C. J. M. (2001). The accuracy of multilevel structural equation modeling with pseudobalanced groups and small samples. *Structural Equation Modeling, 8,* 157–174.

Kleinbaum, D. G., Kupper, L. L., Nizam, A., & Muller, K. E. (2007). *Applied regression analysis and multivariable methods* (4th ed.). Belmont, CA: Duxbury Press.,

Kreft, I. G. G. (1996). *Are multilevel techniques necessary? An overview, including simulation studies.* Unpublished manuscript, California State University, Los Angeles.

Maas, C. J. M., & Hox, J. J. (2005) Sufficient sample sizes for multilevel modeling. *Methodology, 1*(3), 86–92.

Mikusheva, A. (2007). *Spectrum estimation and information criteria.* Retrieved March 9, 2011, from http://ocw.mit.edu/courses/economics/14-384-time-series-analysis-fall-2008/lecture-notes/lec5.pdf

Morris, C. (1995). Hierarchical models for educational data—an overview. *Journal of Educational and Behavioral Statistics, 20*(2).

Raudenbush, S. W., & Bryk, A. S. (2002). *Hierarchical linear models: Applications and data analysis methods* (2nd ed.) (Advanced Quantitative Techniques in the Social Sciences Series, No. 1). Thousand Oaks, CA: Sage.

SAS. (2010). *SAS/STAT (R) 9.2 user's guide* (2nd ed.). Retrieved December 11, 2011, from http://support.sas.com/documentation/cdl/en/statug/63033/HTML/default/viewer.htm#statug_mixed_sect015.htm

Schaalje, G. B., McBride, J. B., & Fellingham, G. W. (2001, April 22–25). *Approximations to distributions of test statistics in complex mixed linear models using SAS® Proc*

MIXED. Proceeding of the SUGI 26 Conference, Long Beach, CA. Retrieved December 11, 2011, from http://www2.sas.com/proceedings/sugi26/p262-26.pdf

Singer, J. (1998). Using SAS PROC MIXED to fit multilevel models, hierarchical models, and individual growth models. *Journal of Educational and Behavioral Statistics, 24*(4), 323–355.

Snijders, T. A. B., & Bosker, R. J. (1994). Modeled variance in two-level models. *Sociological Methods & Research, 22*(3), 342.

Snijders, T. A. B. & Bosker, R. J. (1999). *Multilevel analysis: An introduction to basic and advanced multilevel modeling.* Thousand Oaks, CA: Sage.

StataCorp. (2005). *Stata longitudinal/panel data reference manual, release 9.* College Station, TX: StataCorp LP.

Verbeke, G., & Molenberghs, G. (2000). *Linear mixed models for longitudinal data.* New York: Springer.

West, B. T., Welch, K. B., & Galecki, A. T. (2007). *Linear mixed models: A practical guide using statistical software*. Boca Raton, FL: Chapman & Hall.

Wong, G., & Mason, W. (1985). The hierarchical logistic regression model for multilevel analysis. *Journal of the American Statistical Association, 80,* 513–524.

Xu, R. (2003). Measuring explained variation in linear mixed effects models. *Statistics in Medicine, 22,* 3527–3541.

Yafune, A., Funatogawa, T., & Ishiguro, M. (2005). Extended information criterion (EIC) approach for linear mixed effects models under restricted maximum likelihood (REML) estimation. *Statistics in Medicine, 24,* 3417–3429.

Ypma, T. J. (1995). Historical development of the Newton-Raphson method. *SIAM Review* (Society for Industrial and Applied Mathematics), *37*(4), 531–551. Retrieved December 11, 2011, from http://www.jstor.org/stable/2132904

Yuan, K. H., & Bentler, P. M. (2004). On chi-square difference and z tests in mean and covariance structure analysis when the base model is misspecified. *Educational and Psychological Measurement, 64*(5), 737–757.

Introductory Guide to HLM With HLM 7 Software

3

G. David Garson

H LM software has been one of the leading statistical packages for hierarchical linear modeling due to the pioneering work of Stephen Raudenbush and Anthony Bryk, who created the software and authored the leading text on hierarchical linear and nonlinear modeling (Bryk & Raudenbush, 1992; Raudenbush & Bryk, 2002). Though differences among software packages' capabilities have diminished over time, HLM 7 offers a number of appealing advantages and capabilities. Among these are what many consider to be a more intuitive model specification environment, greater ease in creating three- and four-level models, its wide choice of estimation options, integrated likelihood ratio hypothesis testing, graphics options, and the ability easily to handle heterogeneous hierarchical linear models (where the dependent is thought to have different error variances for different levels of some grouping variable such as Agency).

HLM SOFTWARE

Scientific Software International (SSI) distributes HLM 7. A free student edition of HLM 7 is available.[1] The student edition is full-featured, including examples, but is limited in the size and complexity of models (though it will work with all example files provided with the software). HLM 7 software operates through several modules, each designed for a different type of HLM model, only some of which can be illustrated here due to space constraints:

HLM2. For two-level linear and nonlinear models with one dependent variable.

HLM3 and HLM4. For three-level and four-level models with one dependent variable.

HGLM. For generalized linear models for distributions other than normal and link functions other than identity, handling binary, count, multinomial, and ordinal outcome variables in Bernoulli, binomial, Poisson, multinomial, and ordinal models.

HMLM. For multivariate normal models with more than one outcome variable, including when the level 1 covariance structure is homogenous, heterogeneous, loglinear, or AR(1) (first-order autoregressive).

HMLM2. For two-level HMLM models where level 1 is nested within level 2.

HCM2. For models where level 1 units are cross-classified by two level 2 units.

HCM3. For three-level cross-classified models.

HLMHCM. For two- and three-level hierarchical linear models with cross-classified random effects (ex., repeated test scores nested within students who are cross-classified by schools and neighborhoods).

In summary, HLM 7 is a versatile and full-featured environment for many linear and generalized linear mixed models.

ENTERING DATA INTO HLM 7

HLM software stores data in its own multivariate data matrix (MDM) format, which may be created from raw data or from data files imported from SPSS, SAS, Stata, SYSTAT, or other packages. MDM format files come in flavors keyed to the several types of HLM modules noted above. File creation options are accessed from the HLM File menu, illustrated in Figure 3.1 below. The example below illustrates data entry from an SPSS .sav file for models of type HLM2, but similar procedures are followed for other model types.

"Stat package input," depicted above, is the most common method of creating .mdm data files. Further, not only are data commonly prepared using statistical or data packages outside HLM 7, but as an additional preprocessing step, the researcher also should rule out multicollinearity among the level 2 (or higher) predictors. Having done this, there are two methods of importing files into HLM 7 from other statistical packages.

Input Method 1: Separate Files for Each Level

This method results in faster processing but requires more time to set up the data. It requires that separate files be created outside of HLM 7 for each level of HLM analysis. For SPSS, these are .sav files. For SAS, these are SAS 5 transport files. Separate SYSTAT and Stata files are also acceptable. For instance, HLM 7 software comes with example files from the Singer (1998) "High School and Beyond" study. The SPSS files for this example include HSB1.SAV, which contains the level 2 link field (ID is school ID) and any student-level variables. There are multiple rows per school, one row per student. It is critical that the level 1 file is sorted such that all students for a given school ID are adjacent.

| Figure 3.1 | HLM 7 file menu |

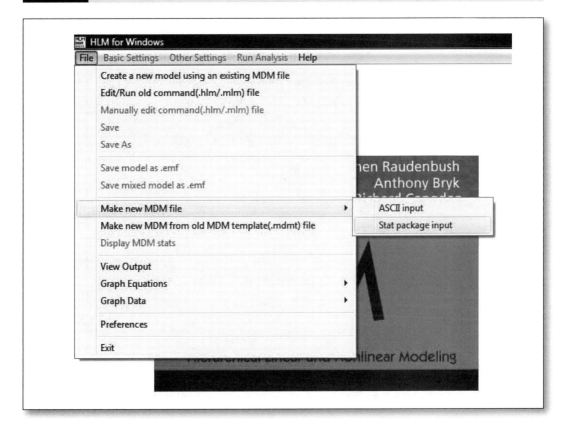

Likewise, the school-level (level 2) file, HSB2.SAV, contains the same level 2 link field and any school-level variables.

Input Method 2: Using a Single Statistics Program Data File

This method[2] is easier in terms of data management and is the one illustrated in this chapter. The same statistics package file formats as for Method 1 may be used. For the example, the single data file must be sorted such that all students for a given school ID are adjacent.

Making the MDM File

The next step is to create the .mdm file, which is HLM software's native data format. After it is created, the input data files are not needed. After creating the

Figure 3.2 HLM 7 select MDM type window

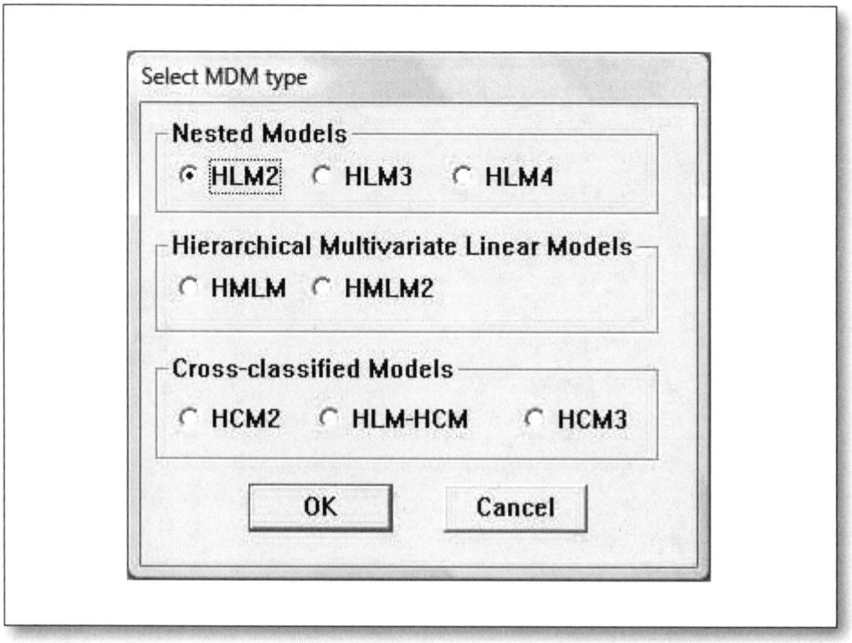

input data file in SPSS, SAS, or another package, HLM 7 is run and "Stat package input" is selected. This causes the "Select MDM type" window illustrated above to appear.

The researcher chooses the HLM model type wanted. For instance, for a simple two-level hierarchical linear model, the selection would be HLM2.

After selecting HLM2, the "Make MDM - HLM2" dialog box appears, illustrated in Figure 3.3.

Here, the following steps are necessary:

Set the "Input File Type" to "SPSS/Windows" (or another statistical package format).

In the level 1 specification area, click the "Browse" button and browse to the input file for level 1. Then, as illustrated at the top of Figure 3.4, click the "Choose variables" button, click the checkbox indicating the level 2 link variable (id in the example), and click the checkboxes of any other level 1 variables in the analysis.

In the level 2 specification area, click the "Browse" button and browse to the input file for level 2. This may be the same file as for level 1 (following Method 2 above). Again click the "Choose variables" button, click the checkbox indicating the level 2 link variable (agency), and click the checkboxes of any other level 2 variables in the analysis, as indicated in the lower half of Figure 3.4.

| Figure 3.3 | Make MDM - HLM 2 window in HLM 7 |

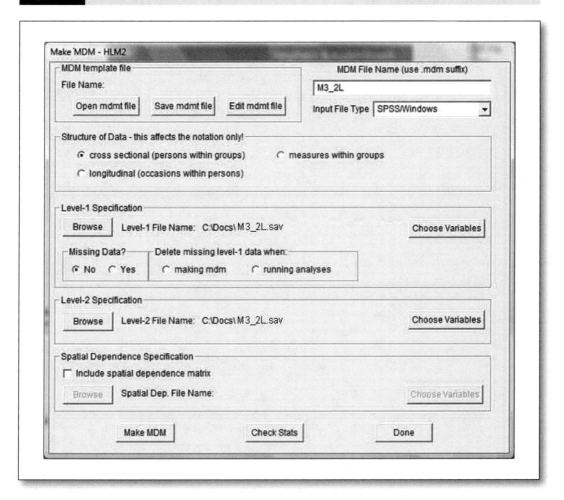

Save the MDM template file by clicking the "Save mdmt file" button, making sure the file location window points to the desired folder and giving a filename (add the .mdmt extension), then clicking the "Save" button.

To complete the process, the researcher clicks the "Make MDM" button, giving a filename (here, M3_L2.mdm, standing for mixed linear model Chapter 3, 2-level). The .mdm file is created, and the descriptive statistics module runs. Alternatively, one may click the "Check Stats" button. This output, shown in Figure 3.5, should be examined to verify the results. For instance, it is prudent to examine the reported sample size, which, if low, flags that the researcher has not sorted the Level 1 file to assure that individual rows for the same level 2 ID (AGENCY in this example) are adjacent.

Figure 3.4 Choose variables windows in HLM 7

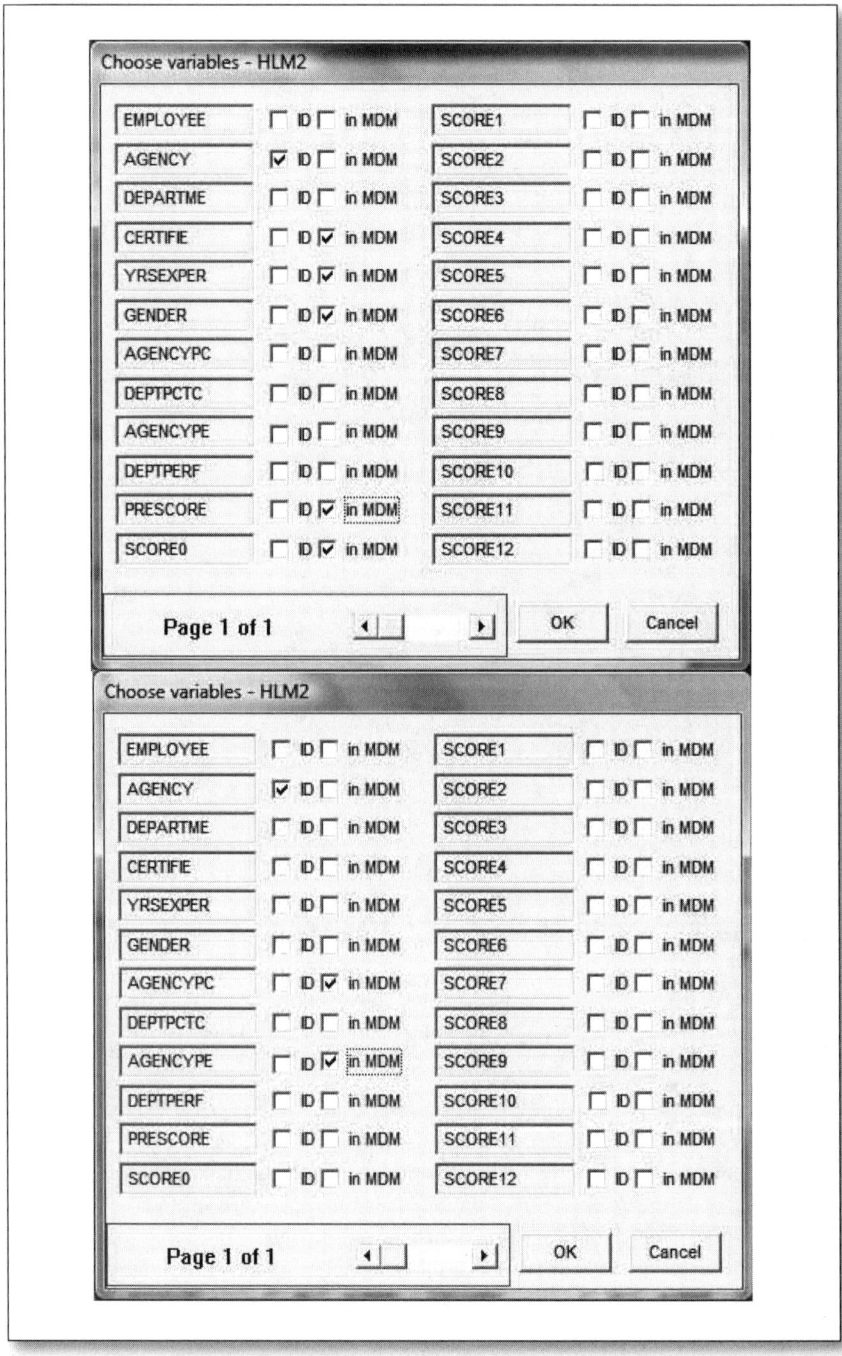

Figure 3.5	"Check Stats" button output in HLM 7

```
HLM2MDM.STS - Notepad
File  Edit  Format  View  Help

                 LEVEL-1 DESCRIPTIVE STATISTICS

VARIABLE NAME      N       MEAN      SD       MINIMUM    MAXIMUM
  CERTIFIE        3495     0.70     0.46       0.00       1.00
  YRSEXPER        3495    -0.00     0.36      -0.79       0.56
  GENDER          3495     0.50     0.50       0.00       1.00
  PRESCORE        3495    42.97     9.78      14.48      77.36
  SCORE0          3495    58.81    18.43       7.17     100.00


                 LEVEL-2 DESCRIPTIVE STATISTICS

VARIABLE NAME      N       MEAN      SD       MINIMUM    MAXIMUM
  AGENCYPC         132     0.66     0.19       0.11       1.00
  AGENCYPE         132     0.00     0.09      -0.35       0.06

MDM template:  C:\DOCS\M3_2L.mdmt
MDM file name: M3_2L.mdm
Date:          Apr 1, 2011
Time:          15:18:42
```

Click the "Done" button to exit to the WHLM model construction screen discussed below. At this point, the researcher will have saved three files to the disk: the newly created HLM-compatible data file, H3_L2.mdm in this example; the default template creatmdm.mdmt (the researcher may override the default name); and the output file above, HLM2MDM.STS (if desired, use File, Save As, to save output under a different name, as this default file may get reused with new content if there are multiple runs).

THE NULL MODEL IN HLM 7

After data are entered, the next step is to create the model. Typically, the first model created is the null model. The null model serves two purposes: (1) It is the basis for calculating the intraclass correlation coefficient (ICC), which is the usual test of whether multilevel modeling is needed; and (2) it outputs the deviance statistic (−2LL) and other coefficients used as a baseline for comparing later, more complex models. For the current example, the null model addresses the question, "Is there a (level 2) agency effect on the (level 1) intercept of performance score, which represents the mean score?" If there is an agency effect, then ordinary regression methods will suffer from correlated error, and some form of linear mixed modeling is required.

The null model, like all two-level hierarchical models in HLM 7, is created in the WHLM modeling dialog, illustrated in Figure 3.6. This dialog is reached either on clicking "Done" in the "MAKE MDM" dialog or, if the MDM file was

Figure 3.6 WHLM modeling window in HLM 7: Null model

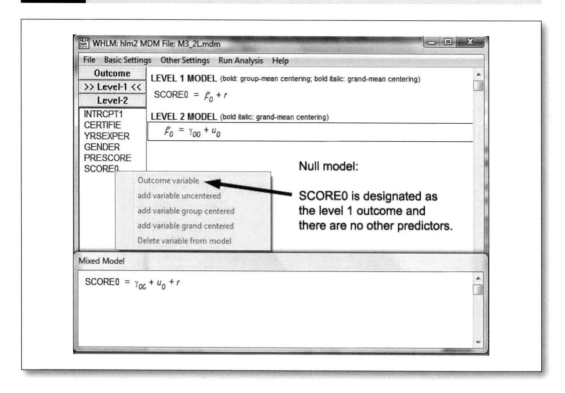

previously saved, from the HLM menu by selecting File, "Create a new model using an existing MDM file," and then opening the appropriate .mdm file.

In the WHLM modeling dialog illustrated in Figure 3.6, the employee level (level 1) dependent variable performance score (SCORE0) is designated as the outcome variable. No other predictors are added. HLM 7 already knows "Agency" is the level 2 grouping variable and automatically assumes it is a predictor of the level 1 intercept of SCORE0.

When SCORE0 is designated as the outcome variable, HLM 7 constructs and displays the model, in this case the null model (also called the intercept-only model or the one-way ANOVA model with random effects). The null model is shown in Table 3.1 below. Clicking the "Mixed" button at the bottom of the WHLM dialog creates the combined HLM equation shown at the bottom of the figure: The two separate equations shown in the upper main window are mathematically equivalent to the single combined mixed model equation. For learning purposes, it is easier to examine the equations

Table 3.1 Summary of the Null Model

Level 1 Model

$$SCORE0_{ij} = \beta_{0j} + r_{ij}$$

Level 2 Model

$$\beta_{0j} = \gamma_{00} + u_{0j}$$

Mixed Model

$$SCORE0_{ij} = \gamma_{00} + u_{0j} + r_{ij}$$

at each level. At level 1, SCORE0 is predicted by an intercept term and a random term. The symbol for the intercept term varies depending on the distribution specified for the outcome variable (this is done in the "Basic Settings" window, described below) and is expressed equivalently but differently in output.

The level 1 intercept term, expressed as β_{0j} in output, is a function of a random intercept term at level 2 (γ_{00}) and a level 1 residual error term (r_{ij}). The level 1 intercept, in turn, is a function of the grand mean (γ_{00}) across level 2 units, which are agencies in this example, plus a random error term (u_{0j}), signifying the intercept is modeled as a random effect. Substituting the right-hand side of the level 2 equation into the level 1 equation gives the mixed model equation for the null random intercept model. HLM 7 will create one level 1 regression for each agency, and then will utilize the variance in these intercepts when estimating parameters and standard errors at level 1. This is what makes the process different from ordinary regression, where a single overall intercept is estimated.

Before calculating estimates, the researcher may specify the distribution of the outcome variable by selecting "Basic Settings" from the main menu bar, yielding the window shown in Figure 3.7. The normal distribution, used in this example, is the default. Other available specifications support Bernoulli, Poisson, multinomial, and ordinal distributions. Selecting "Bernoulli" for a binary outcome variable applies a logistic link function, and in the ensuing multilevel logistic regression, interpretations are in terms of the log odds of the outcome rather than in terms of the raw outcome itself. Selecting "Multinomial" creates a multilevel multinomial regression using a logit link. "Ordinal" supports multilevel ordinal regression models. Multilevel Poisson regression models employ a Poisson log link and require an exposure variable (time, for example). In this window, one may also specify the name and location of the output statistics file and the output graphics file.

It is also possible to modify model estimation settings prior to running the model by selecting "Other Settings" from the main menu bar, then "Estimation Settings," as illustrated in Figure 3.8. Estimation settings were discussed in Chapter 2. For the null model, we use the default setting, restricted maximum likelihood estimation. There is also an "Iterations Settings" window, also from the "Other Settings" menu. Though not illustrated here, it provides options discussed in Chapter 2 with regard to estimation settings.

One may also select "Other Settings" from the main menu bar, then "Output Settings" to obtain the window shown in Figure 3.9. For this model, one may choose to print out variance–covariance matrices or to restrict output to the main results. The default is restricted output and no matrices.

To run the null model, the researcher simply selects "Run Analysis" from the main menu bar. Output is sent to the file location and a name is specified in the "Basic Model Specifications" window (Figure 3.7). To view the output, select File, View Output, from the main menu bar. For this example, the critical output of the null model looks as shown in Table 3.2.

The phrase "Number of estimated parameters = 2" refers to the fact that in a null model, estimates are made for the level 1 intercept and the level 2 intercept. In the

Figure 3.7 Basic Model Specifications window from Basic Settings menu in HLM 7

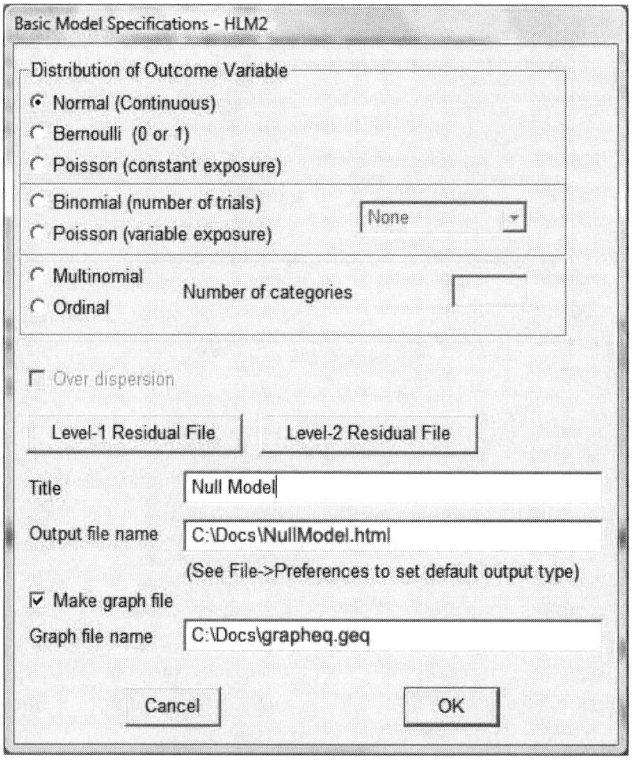

final variance components table, the fact that the component for the intercept (161.94, which HLM labels tau, τ) is significant means that the intercept of the outcome variable, SCORE0, is significantly affected by its predictors, which in this example is the level 2 effect of agency. A non-significant intercept in the variance components table term (not the case here) would mean that after other variables in the model are controlled, there would be no residual between-groups variance in the level 1 dependent variable (Score0). The agency effect is smaller than the residual variance component (212.69, which HLM also labels sigma-squared, σ^2), indicating that there is still considerable residual variation in Score0 yet to be explained and that a model with additional predictors may be needed.

The fact that the intercept component is significant means that the intraclass correlation coefficient, ICC, is also significant, indicating that a multilevel model is appropriate and needed. ICC varies from +1.0 when group means differ but within any group there is no variation, to $-1/(n-1)$ when group means are all the same but within-group variation is very large. At the extreme, when ICC

| Figure 3.8 | Estimation Settings window from Other Settings menu in HLM 7 |

| Figure 3.9 | Output Settings window for HLM2 |

| Table 3.2 | Final Estimation of Variance Components for the Two-Level Null Model |

Random effect	Standard deviation	Variance component	d.f.	χ^2	p-value
INTRCPT1, u_0	12.72558	161.94029	131	2391.61810	<0.001
level-1, r	14.58375	212.68575			
Statistics for current covariance components model					
Deviance = 29028.420032					
Number of estimated parameters = 2					

approaches 0 or is negative, hierarchical modeling is not appropriate. For this example, the magnitude of ICC may be calculated as the intercept variance component in the null model divided by the total of variance components. That is, ICC = 161.94/(161.94 + 212.69) = .43.

The fixed effect tables are of lesser interest in a null model but are presented in Table 3.3. Mean performance score (the intercept at level 1) is estimated to be 55.60 for this example, when the level 2 grouping variable, agency, is the only effect modeled. Confidence limits around the mean, of course, are approximately plus or minus two standard errors. The lower table, "with robust standard errors," produces the same estimate but has a slightly different standard error. Robust standard errors are recommended when it is possible the researcher has specified the wrong distribution of the dependent variable. Significant differences between the ordinary and robust estimates of the standard error may flag a problem with the distribution specified by the researcher. This is not the case in this example, which specified a normal distribution (which is the default).

The "Deviance" value of 29028.42 in Table 3.2 is the basis of model fit measures. While not used at this point, for the null model it is the baseline model fit. More complex models are assessed in part by how greatly they reduce deviance (which is also called -2 log likelihood, $-2LL$, and model chi-square). These tests of the difference in deviance values between models are likelihood ratio tests, requested in HLM 7 by selecting "Other Settings" from the main menu bar, then "Hypothesis Testing," as discussed later in this chapter. In summary, at the end of analysis of the null model we have demonstrated that there is a significant agency effect on employee performance scores; that therefore multilevel modeling is

Table 3.3 Fixed Effects Tables for the Null Model

Final estimation of fixed effects

Fixed effect	Coefficient	Standard error	t-ratio	Approx.d.f.	p-value
For INTRCPT1, β_0					
INTRCPT2, γ_{00}	55.598248	1.145778	48.524	131	<0.001

Final estimation of fixed effects (with robust standard errors)

Fixed effect	Coefficient	Standard error	t-ratio	Approx. d.f.	p-value
For INTRCPT1, β_0					
INTRCPT2, γ_{00}	55.598248	1.141423	48.710	131	<0.001

needed; and that additional, more complex models with more predictors should reduce significantly the baseline deviance value of 29028.42.

A RANDOM COEFFICIENTS REGRESSION MODEL IN HLM 7

Given level 1 representing employees, with performance score as an outcome (dependent) variable, and level 2 representing agencies, a random coefficients regression model is one with one or more level 1 predictors such as gender, years of experience, or a binary indicator for whether the employee is certified or not. The level 2 grouping variable (Agency) remains a random factor, but there are no other level 2 predictors. The "coefficients" term in the label means that the agency effect is used not only to model the level 1 intercept of SCORE0 as an outcome, but also to model the regression coefficients of the level 1 predictors.

As an example of random coefficients (RC) regression, employee performance score (score0) at level 1 is predicted from the level 1 covariates years of experience (YrsExper) and sex (Gender, where 0 = male, 1 = female). Note that HLM 7 enters binary variables like Gender as covariates by default. There are no predictors at level 2, but Agency is the subjects variable under which employees are grouped. The intercept of score0 at level 1 and the b coefficient of YrsExper at level 1 are both modeled as random effects of Agency. Gender is treated as a simple level 1 fixed effect. This model explores whether the Agency effect discovered in the null model may be attributed in part to some agencies having more experienced employees than others. The model also explores whether the demographic variable, Gender, modifies the relationship of years of experience to performance score.

Figure 3.10 illustrates this RC regression model. An often-cited advantage of HLM software is how its user interface clearly separates regression models at different levels. Here, at level 1, score0 is predicted from YrsExper and Gender, plus an intercept term β_{0j} and an error term r_{ij}:

$$\text{SCORE0}_{ij} = \beta_{0j} + \beta_{1j}*(\text{YRSEXPER}_{ij}) + \beta_{2j}*(\text{GENDER}_{ij}) + r_{ij}$$

At level 2, there are no predictors. However, the level 1 intercept is predicted by the level 2 mean (γ_{00}) of score0 plus a level 2 error term (u_{0j}). The level 2 error term represents the random effect of agency on score0 at level 1. Also, the level 1 regression coefficient (slope) of YrsExper (β_{1j}) is predicted by the mean of agency regression coefficients where this mean is based on the 132 agencies in the sample, plus a level 2 error term (u_{1j}) representing the random effect of Agency on the level 1 regression of score0 on YrsExper. HLM 7 output represents the level 2 equations as below:

$$\beta_{0j} = \gamma_{00} + u_{0j}$$
$$\beta_{1j} = \gamma_{10} + u_{1j}$$
$$\beta_{2j} = \gamma_{20}$$

The level 1 and level 2 equations can be combined, through substitution, into the single mixed model equation below:

$$\text{SCORE0}_{ij} = \gamma_{00} + \gamma_{10}*\text{YRSEXPER}_{ij} + \gamma_{20}*\text{GENDER}_{ij} + u_{0j} + u_{1j}*\text{YRSEXPER}_{ij} + r_{ij}$$

Figure 3.10   A two-level random coefficients regression model in HLM 7

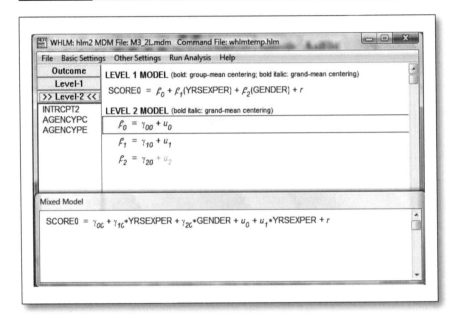

As explained in Chapter 1, by designating a level 2 subjects variable, Agency, one is requesting that regressions be created separately for each agency so that the variance in intercepts and coefficients can be calculated and used in subsequent estimates of fixed and random effects. If full rather than reduced output is requested from the Other Settings, Output Settings menu selection, HLM 7 will print the OLS regression coefficients for the first 10 agencies (the default of 10 can be overridden by the researcher to get all coefficients), as shown in Table 3.4. Using these intercepts and slopes, one can create a plot of multiple different regression lines across agencies, graphically illustrating the nature of random intercepts and random slopes for the given data.

The likelihood ratio test, discussed in Chapter 2, can be used as an overall test of whether the RC regression model with predictors is a significantly better fit than the intercept-only (null) model without predictors. In HLM 7, this is done from the main menu by selecting Other Settings, Hypothesis Testing, leading to the "Hypothesis Testing" window shown in Figure 3.11. In this window, one

Table 3.4 OLS Coefficients for the First 10 Agencies in the RC Regression Model

Level-1 OLS Regressions

Level 2 Unit	INTRCPT1	YRSEXPER slope
1	26.91987	−8.59458
2	33.31829	2.13703
3	−190.35526	−308.72487
4	32.08813	−3.68785
5	31.26302	−4.19888
6	29.55992	−1.72763
7	31.67209	1.19479
8	36.08018	5.47836
9	48.24087	27.07489
10	37.73941	2.49587

The average OLS level 1 coefficient for INTRCPT1 = 56.98519

The average OLS level 1 coefficient for YRSEXPER = 11.88690

Figure 3.11 Hypothesis Testing window in HLM 7

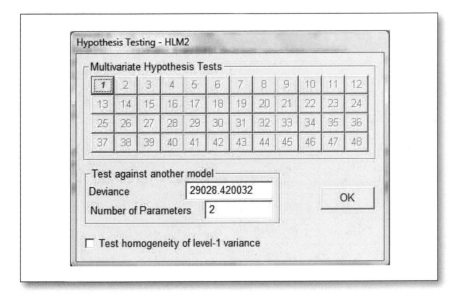

Table 3.5	HLM 7 Likelihood Ratio Test for the RC Regression Model Compared to the Null Model

Deviance

Deviance = 28201.160055

Number of estimated parameters = 4

Variance-Covariance components test

χ^2 statistic = 827.25998

Degrees of freedom = 2

p-value = <0.001

manually enters the deviance value and number of estimated parameters from the null model. The greater the drop in the deviance ($-2LL$), the more likely the fit is to be significantly better. For this example, deviance dropped from 29028.42 in the null model to 28201.16 in the RC regression model. The likelihood ratio test, shown in HLM 7 output in Table 3.5, shows this difference to be significant at better than the .001 level. Later, the likelihood ratio test can be used to compare any two models if one is nested within the other, as the null model is nested within the RC regression model.[3]

Another way to assess improvement in model fit is to examine the residual variance component in the "Final Estimation of Variance Components" table (Table 3.6). The residual variance component is variance associated with the within-agency variation in score0 not accounted for by the random effects of Agency on the intercept of score0 and on the slope of YrsExper. As the random effects explain more, the residual component will drop. HLM 7 lists the residual variance component as "level-1, r." For these data, the residual component drops from 212.69 in the null model to 163.77 in the RC regression model. Since both were models in which the off-diagonal covariances were constrained to zero,[4] we can calculate that residual variance was $163.774/(163.774 + 130.569 + 63.299) = 46\%$ of total variance in the RC regression model compared by similar calculation to 57% in the null model.

In the same manner, in Table 3.6 we can calculate that the random effect of Agency on mean performance scores by agency (the "INTRCPT1, u_0" effect) is 37% of total effects. This means that there is a significant, moderately strong

Table 3.6	Variance Components Table for the RC Regression Model

Final estimation of variance components

Random effect	Standard deviation	Variance component	d.f.	χ^2	p-value
INTRCPT1, u_0	11.42668	130.56897	131	1910.92848	<0.001
YRSEXPER slope, u_1	7.95609	63.29930	131	299.94754	<0.001
level-1, r	12.79742	163.77400			

tendency for some agencies to have higher mean scores than others. The random effect of Agency on slopes of YrsExper (the "YRSEXPER slope, u_1," effect) is 18% of total effects. This means that there is a significant but weaker tendency for YrsExper to have a stronger effect on performance score in some agencies than others.

Table 3.7 shows the fixed effects table for the RC regression model. HLM 7 prints two fixed effects tables, one using robust standard errors and one not. Robust standard errors should be used when it is possible that the distribution of the dependent variable was misspecified, though for this example the coefficients are identical. For these data, score0 is normally distributed, as specified (for example, skew and kurtosis were both within +/− 1.0), and coefficients and the probability levels are identical between the two versions of the fixed effects table. From Table 3.7, we conclude that both YrsExper and Gender are significant predictors of employee performance scores (score0). YrsExper was centered (mean = 0) and for Gender "male" was coded 0. Therefore, a male with mean years of experience could be expected to score 59.4 points on the performance test. The fact that the slope of Gender was negative means that being female (Gender = 1) was associated with scoring 6.5 points less, controlling for other variables in the model. The t-ratios are the regression coefficients divided by their standard errors. The fact that the absolute t-ratios for YrsExper and Gender are similar indicates similarity in effect size. (Note that a 1-year increase in years of experience does *not* predict an increase of score of 16.25 points because YrsExper was not only centered but was also transformed to decimal form, ranging from −.79 to +.56: That is, the units were no longer raw years.)

Table 3.7 The Fixed Effects Table for the RC Regression Model

Final estimation of fixed effects (with robust standard errors)

Fixed effect	Coefficient	Standard error	t-ratio	Approx. d.f.	p-value
For INTRCPT1, β_0					
INTRCPT2, γ_{00}	59.390114	1.035557	57.351	131	<0.001
For YRSEXPER slope, β_1					
INTRCPT2, γ_{10}	16.252170	1.058662	15.352	131	<0.001
For GENDER slope, β_2					
INTRCPT2, γ_{20}	−6.482774	0.434132	−14.933	3230	<0.001

HOMOGENOUS AND HETEROGENEOUS FULL
RANDOM COEFFICIENTS MODELS

Also called an "intercepts-and-slopes-as-outcomes" model, the full random coefficients model is a type of hierarchical linear model in which, for two levels, there are predictors at both levels, and both the level 1 intercept and the level 1 slopes are predicted as random effects. As shown in Figure 3.12 below, the level 1 model for this example remains similar to the previous model.

The essential features of the model are these:

- At level 1, Score0 is predicted by YrsExper and Gender.
- Agency remains the grouping variable defining level 2, which means that as many level 1 regressions are run as there are agencies in the sample, yielding an estimate of the variability of level 1 slopes and intercepts.
- The intercept at level 1 is predicted as a random effect of Agency and of the level 2 predictor AgencyPC, which is a newly added covariate measuring percent of employees certified in an agency.
- The slope of YrsExper at level 1 is predicted as a random effect of Agency. In a subsequent example later in this section, a different model will illustrate modeling the slope of YrsExper as a random effect of both Agency and AgencyPC at level 2. The current model tests the proposition that the mean (intercept) for Score0 is a random effect of Agency and of AgencyPC at level 2, and that the strength of relationship (slope) of YrsExper to Score0 is a function of Agency but not of AgencyPC.
- The slope of Gender is not predicted as a random effect, as signified by its random error term (u2) being grayed out in Figure 3.12.

Figure 3.12   A two-level random coefficients model in HLM 7

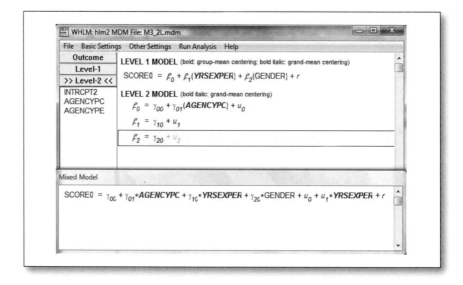

Though not illustrated, we click "Other Settings" to obtain a window similar to that shown in Figure 3.11 above. We enter the deviance (28201.16) and number of parameters (4) from the previous RC regression model without the level 2 agency percent certified variable. This requests a likelihood ratio test of the model fit difference, to be discussed below, between the current model and the previous one. In a second run, a likelihood test was also requested comparing the current model with the null model. In addition, the "Test level-1 homogeneity of variance" checkbox, also illustrated in Figure 3.11 above, was checked. (Figure 3.11 also shows the HLM 7 option for "Multivariate Hypotheses Tests," as illustrated, for example, in Chapter 12.)

The overall test of the model that is reflected in the likelihood ratio test of the difference in deviance ($-2LL$) between models is shown in Table 3.8. While deviance declined another 40.39 points compared to the RC regression model and reflects significantly better fit than the null model, the difference between the current model and the RC regression model is not significant (p-value = >.500). That is, agency percent certified as a level 2 covariate in the current model reduced deviance by a non-significant amount. On parsimony grounds, the researcher would prefer the RC regression model. Nonetheless, for instructional purposes, the remaining HLM 7 output is examined below.

Table 3.8	HLM 7 Likelihood Ratio Test for the Two-Level Homogenous Full RC Model

Statistics for current covariance components model

Deviance = 28160.766143

Number of estimated parameters = 4

Variance-Covariance components test (compared to RC regression model)

χ^2 statistic = 40.39391

Degrees of freedom = 0

p-value = >.500

The "Test level-1 homogeneity of variance" output, not previously discussed, is shown in Table 3.9. Although not invoking this test is the default in HLM 7, it is sufficiently critical that Raudenbush and Bryk (2002) state, "investigators generally will wish to begin with this assumption" (p. 263). This test refers to the assumption that when the model is run for each of the 132 agencies in the current example, the residual variances are homogenous. Optionally, the researcher may override the default and test this assumption. For the example data, the test p-value is 0.000. This finding of sig-

Table 3.9	Test of Homogeneity of Level 1 Variance

Test of homogeneity of level 1 variance

χ^2 statistic = 271.67767

Degrees of freedom = 131

p-value = 0.000

nificance means that residual variances do differ significantly for these data across agencies. Raudenbush and Bryk (p. 263) note that heterogeneity of error variance is a serious problem if variances are not random but are a function of level 1 or level 2 predictors. Heterogeneity may indicate one of four problems in the research design:

1. Model misspecification. One or more level 1 predictors have been omitted from the model, where the variables in question are distributed with unequal variance across groups. This is the most likely cause of heterogeneity, making this test a form of screening for model misspecification.

2. A level 1 predictor has been modeled as a fixed effect when in fact it is a random effect.

3. One or more level 1 predictors are non-normal (for example, kurtotic with heavy tails), causing the significance test statistic for homogeneity of residual variance, which assumes normality, to report lack of homogeneity. Transformation of the predictor, as in OLS regression, may mitigate non-normality. Likewise, use of a link function other than identity in a generalized linear mixed model may also moderate the effects of non-normality.

4. Coding or other data entry errors, or presence of outliers, may cause heterogeneous error variance in some groups.

It is possible to visually inspect residual variance by level 2 groups (agencies for this example) in a variety of ways (see Raudenbush & Bryk, 2002, pp. 263–267; Raudenbush et al., 2011, pp. 274–278). For instance, within HLM 7 one may select File, Graph Equations, "Level 1 residual versus predicted value" to obtain a plot where points represent agencies. A more complex graphical method is to use a combination of HLM 7, SPSS, and Excel, yielding a plot of residual variances by agency, as shown in Figure 3.13. The process is described in the endnotes to this chapter.[5] The steeper the trend line and the more outliers in this chart, the less homogenous residual variance is. Sometimes it may be possible to obtain a non-significant test of homogeneity by identifying outliers, such as Agency 48 in Figure 3.13, and removing them from the sample for separate analysis. However, if the trend line is steep, the researcher may need to create a heterogeneous model. Endnote 5 describes how to obtain a table of the correlations of Agency residual variance with the predictor variables, showing for these data that such variance is correlated with years of experience though not with gender.

To deal with the problem of heterogeneous residual variance, the four possibilities above need to be explored first. Ultimately, however, it may be necessary to create a heterogeneous variance model. This is done in HLM 7 by selecting Other Settings, Estimation Settings, giving the window shown in Figure 3.8 above. Clicking the "Heterogeneous sigma^2" button leads to the dialog screen of the same name, shown in Figure 3.14. Here, one must enter a level 1 variable, which may account for heterogeneous residual variance. The variable may be one not otherwise used in the model.

Figure 3.13 Residual variance by agency for the two-level random coefficients model

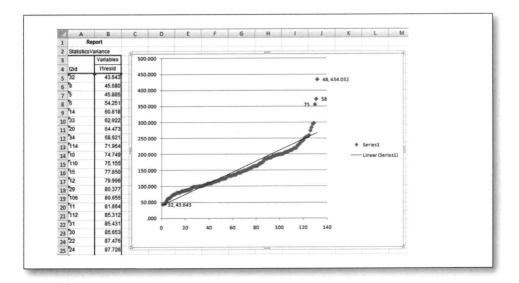

Figure 3.14 Modeling heterogeneity in HLM 7

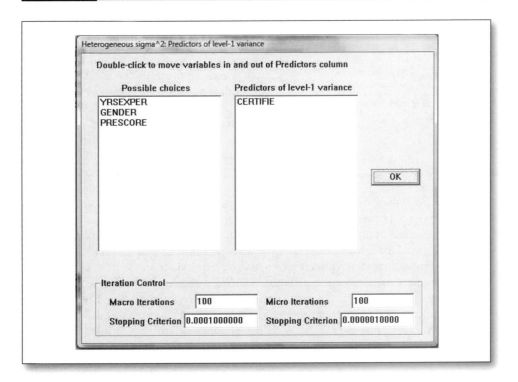

Determining which variable to use as the predictor of level 1 residual variance can be explored using a statistical package to view the variances of the OLS residuals by candidate variables. In this example, in SPSS, select Analyze, Regression, Linear; set the dependent to Score0. Set the independents to YrsExper and Gender, as in the current model. Set the Selection variable to be Certified (coded 0 = not certified, 1 = certified). Set the Rule to be Certified = 0 in a first run and Certified = 1 in a second run. In the ANOVA table output, residual sum of squares for not certified is 57,488.9 and for certified is 668,407.4. The larger the difference, the better the selection variable is as a candidate predictor to be specified in Figure 3.14 when creating a heterogeneous variance model.

Table 3.10	Likelihood Ratio Test and Homogeneity of Residual Variance Test for the Heterogeneous Full Random Coefficients Model

Statistics for the current model

Deviance = 27686.815423

Number of estimated parameters = 9

Model comparison test

χ^2 statistic = 514.34458

Degrees of freedom = 5

p-value = <0.001

Test of homogeneity of level 1 variance

χ^2 statistic = 136.59649

Degrees of freedom = 131

p-value = 0.351

Having determined that the level 1 variable Certified is a good candidate to predict residual variance, Certified could be incorporated in the model in one of three ways: (1) It could be added as a level 1 variable not modeled as a random effect of level 2; (2) it could be added and also modeled as a random effect; or (3) it could be used as the predictor of level 1 residual variance by using a heterogeneous residual variance model. For these data, option (1) would yield results that fail the test of level 1 homogeneity of variance and that fail to show significantly better fit than the previous RC regression model. Option (2) would drop the deviance value enough to show significantly better fit but would also fail the test of level 1 homogeneity of residual variance. As shown in Table 3.10, option 3, the heterogeneous model, yields results that pass the homogeneity test (the homogeneity p-value is non-significant) and that also show significantly better fit than the RC regression model discussed earlier (the model comparison likelihood ratio test p-value is significant).

As shown in Figure 3.15, the heterogeneous model is identical to that shown in Figure 3.12 except that at level 1, terms are added that model residual variance as a function of the predictor variable Certified.

Fixed effects of the heterogeneous model are shown in Table 3.11. HLM prints out two fixed effects tables, one with robust standard errors and one with ordinary standard errors. Robust standard errors are advisable when there is misspecification of the distribution of the dependent variable. Therefore, significant differences between the ordinary and robust estimates of the standard error may flag a problem with the distribution specified by the researcher (normal is default). This does not appear to be a problem for this example, and

Figure 3.15 The heterogeneous random coefficients model in HLM 7

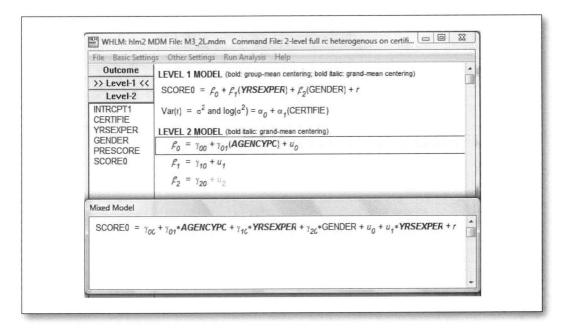

Table 3.11 Fixed Effects for the Heterogeneous Full Random Coefficients Model

Final estimation of fixed effects (with robust standard errors)

Fixed effect	Coefficient	Standard error	t-ratio	Approx. d.f.	p-value
For INTRCPT1, β_0					
INTRCPT2, γ_{00}	56.525630	0.820256	68.912	130	<0.001
AGENCYPC, γ_{01}	19.826460	2.563049	7.735	130	<0.001
For YRSEXPER slope, β_1					
INTRCPT2, γ_{10}	17.868835	0.817503	21.858	131	<0.001
For GENDER slope, β_2					
INTRCPT2, γ_{20}	−4.786541	0.426161	−11.232	3230	<0.001

one arrives at the same statistical inferences either way. For this example, all fixed effects are significant:

- The level 1 intercept of 56.5 gives the mean performance score across all agencies when other variables in the model are controlled at zero. Since YrsExper and

AgencyPC were centered, controlling means when both are at their mean values. Since Gender was coded such that 0 = male, controlling means "for men." That is, men with mean years of experience working in agencies with a mean percent of certified employees are predicted to have performance scores, on the average, of 56.5.

- The level 2 predictor AgencyPC (percent certified for a given agency) is significant. This variable, which ranged from .11 to 1.0, was centered when used in the HLM model. Its coefficient is positive, meaning that the higher the percent certified in an agency, the higher the intercept (hence the higher the mean performance score) for employees of the agency. Its slope, 19.8, means that when the percent certified goes up by 1 percent (which is .01 units on a scale from .11 to 1.0), mean performance scores are expected to rise by .198 units.

- The slope of the level 1 predictor variable Gender is significant and negative. Since Gender was coded 0 = male, 1 = female, a 1-unit increase means being female. That is, being female lowered the expected performance score by 4.79 points, on the average, controlling for other variables in the model.

- The slope of the level 1 predictor YrsExper was significant and positive. This variable was centered on its mean and expressed in standardized units ranging from −.79 to +.56 (not in raw years). The fact that it is positive means the more years experience, the higher the predicted performance score, controlling other variables in the model. That its t-ratio in absolute terms is about twice that for Gender means YrsExper has a greater effect on performance score than does Gender.

Table 3.12 shows the random effects components in the heterogeneous random coefficients model, of which there are two. Because residual variance is being modeled in a heterogeneous model, there is no residual variance component as, for instance, shown in Table 3.6 for a related homogenous model. The Intrcpt1 component is the effect on mean performance scores at level 1 due to Agency as a random factor at level 2. The YrsExper slope component is the effect on the slope of YrsExper and level 1 due to Agency as a random factor at level 2. Both effects are significant. Thus, both mean performance score and the regression coefficients for YrsExper vary significantly by Agency, confirming that multilevel analysis is required to properly model employee performance score at level 1. Coefficients in the fixed effects table discussed above will be more reliable than coefficients from the equivalent model in OLS regression due to the existence of these significant random effects. That the intercept component

Table 3.12 Random Effects for the Heterogeneous Random Coefficients Model

Final estimation of variance components

Random effect	Standard deviation	Variance component	d.f.	χ^2	p-value
INTRCPT1, u_0	8.89447	79.11164	130	1283.08288	<0.001
YRSEXPER slope, u_1	6.64525	44.15935	131	330.23181	<0.001

is significant even controlling for other variables in the model means that there remains significant variation, which might be explained by adding additional predictors to the model.

As a final example in this section, Figure 3.16 illustrates a full random coefficients model in HLM otherwise paralleling the foregoing one, but now with the level 2 predictor, centered agency percent certified (AgencyPC), used to model the level 1 slope of years of experience (YrsExper) as well as the level 1 intercept. As can be seen in Figure 3.16, this is simply a matter of adding AgencyPC to the level 2 equation that models the level 1 slope of YrsExper. In the level 2 equation, $\beta_{1j} = \gamma_{10} + \gamma_{11}*(AGENCYPC_j) + u_{1j}$, the u_{1j} term is the Agency effect on the slope of YrsExper and the $\gamma_{11}*(AGENCYPC_j)$ term is the AgencyPC effect on the slope.

Table 3.13 shows the deviance model fit statistic for this model. It is very close to the homogenous RC model in which AgencyPC modeled only the level 1 intercept and not the slope (Table 3.8). This strongly hints at the finding shown below in the fixed effects table, which shows the AgencyPC effect on the slope of YrsExper to be non-significant (Table 3.14). We conclude that agency percent certified at level 2 does not account for a significant portion of the variance in the strengths (slopes) of the relation of YrsExper with performance scores across

Figure 3.16	A full random coefficients model with a level 2 covariate modeling level 1 slope and intercept

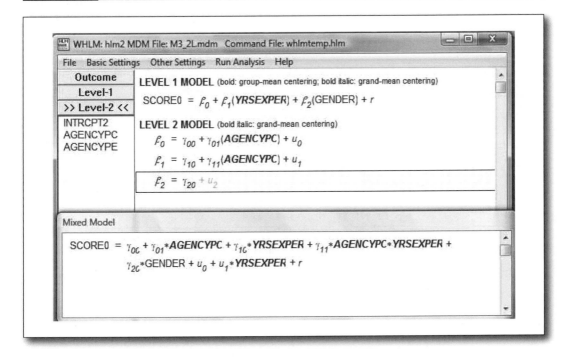

| Table 3.13 | Deviance and Likelihood Ratio Test of the Homogenous RC Model With Agency Modeling Both Slope and Intercept, Compared to the RC Regression Model |

Statistics for current covariance components model

Deviance = 28156.789317

Number of estimated parameters = 4

Variance-Covariance components test

χ^2 statistic = 44.37074

Degrees of freedom = 0

p-value = >.500

agencies. Neither of these homogenous models has as good a fit as did the heterogeneous model just discussed. The likelihood ratio tests compare the full homogenous RC model (Table 3.8), the full heterogeneous RC model (Table 3.10), and the full homogenous RC model with agency percent certified modeling slope as well as intercept. (Table 3.13 shows only the heterogeneous model to be better fitting than the RC regression model with no level 2 predictors.)

Because the interpretation parallels that of full RC models discussed above, the variance components table for the homogenous RC model with agency percent certified modeling slope as well as intercept is not presented. Also, though not presented in table form, it may be noted that this homogenous full RC model just discussed fails the test of homogeneity of level 1 variance, as did the earlier homogenous full RC model. However, for pedagogic reasons and because SAS and SPSS cannot easily compute models for heterogeneous error variance, this is the model reproduced in SAS 9.2 in Chapter 4 and in SPSS 19 in Chapter 5. It should be noted that such testing for homogeneity of error variance routinely returns a finding of heterogeneity, yet it is common practice to execute homogenous models anyway, in part because the same substantive

| Table 3.14 | Fixed Effects for the Homogenous RC Model With AGENCYPC Modeling Both Slope and Intercept |

Final estimation of fixed effects (with robust standard errors)

Fixed effect	Coefficient	Standard error	t-ratio	Approx. d.f.	p-value
For INTRCPT1, β_0					
INTRCPT2, γ_{00}	59.360637	0.952706	62.307	130	< 0.001
AGENCYPC, γ_{01}	30.975071	5.264133	5.884	130	< 0.001
For YRSEXPER slope, β_1					
INTRCPT2, γ_{10}	15.505130	1.077111	14.395	130	< 0.001
AGENCYPC, γ_{11}	−3.500075	6.720186	−0.521	130	0.603
For GENDER slope, β_2					
INTRCPT2, γ_{20}	−6.491174	0.433456	−14.975	3230	< 0.001

conclusions are often arrived at. Also, even if error variance is heterogeneous, it may not be correlated with predictor variables (though it is correlated with YrsExper for these data). How to check is discussed in the endnotes.[6]

| Figure 3.17 | Correlations of residual error variance with level 1 predictors |

Correlations

		ResidVar	yrsexper_mean_1	gender_mean
ResidVar	Pearson Correlation	1	.462**	-.043
	Sig. (2-tailed)		.000	.626
	N	132	132	132
yrsexper_mean_1	Pearson Correlation	.462**	1	-.074
	Sig. (2-tailed)	.000		.401
	N	132	132	132
gender_mean	Pearson Correlation	-.043	-.074	1
	Sig. (2-tailed)	.626	.401	
	N	132	132	132

**. Correlation is significant at the 0.01 level (2-tailed).

THREE-LEVEL HIERARCHICAL LINEAR MODELS

Three-level problems occur frequently in real-world data: cross-sectional studies of students nested within classrooms nested within schools, for instance, or longitudinal studies of yearly tests nested within students nested within schools. To create a basic, cross-sectional three-level hierarchical linear model, we will use the same SPSS data file, mixed3level.sav, which had within it a previously undiscussed field for the third level: Department (Employees are nested within Agencies, and Agencies within Departments, with Department being the department ID variable) and two department-level covariates to serve as potential level 3 predictors. As HLM 7 has only minimal data management capabilities, like most HLM users, we initially create the dataset in another statistical package, in this case SPSS 19. SAS may also be used for this purpose, as HLM 7 reads both SPSS and SAS formats directly. While separate data files might be created for levels 1, 2, and 3, this is not necessary and was not done for the example data.

The first step is to import the data from SPSS .sav format and to create the HLM 7 multivariate data matrix file (.mdm format) and data template file (.mdmt format). This assumes that the data are previously sorted in a nested order: employees within agencies within departments. The .mdm file will be incorrect if data are not sorted properly in SPSS or other statistical packages used for data management. Three-level cross-sectional models are created in the HLM3 module. When HLM 7 opens, select File, Make new MDM file, Stat package input. A "Select MDM Type" window opens. Check the HLM3 radio button and click OK to arrive at the "Make MDM HLM3" window shown in Figure 3.18.

Figure 3.18   HLM 7 setup for three-level cross-sectional models (HLM3)

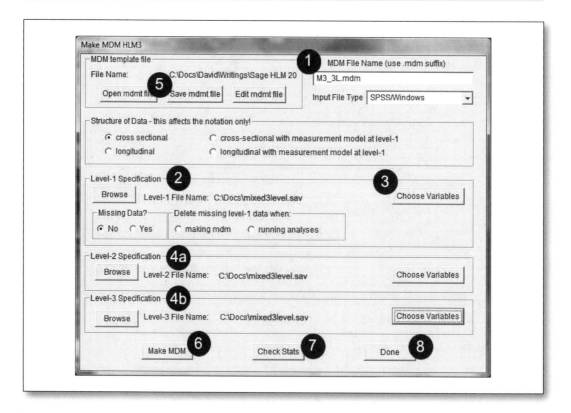

1. In the "Make MDM HLM3" window, follow these steps:

2. In the upper right, first enter the desired filename for the data matrix file. Here, it is M3_3L.mdm.

3. In the "Level-1 Specification" area, click the Browse button and browse to the SPSS .sav file and enter it. Also click the appropriate radio buttons regarding how to handle missing data, if any.

4a. Click the Choose Variables button to enter level 1 variables as shown in Figure 3.19. For level 1, enter all three ID variables (Department, Agency, and Employee)

Figure 3.19 Variable selection for three-level models in HLM 7

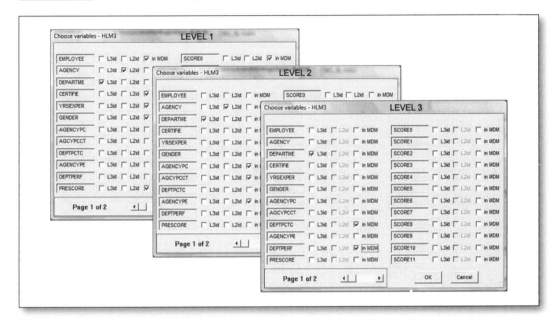

as shown, as well as entering any level 1 covariates and the level 1 dependent variable in "in MDM" checkboxes. For level 2, enter just Department and Agency, plus any level 2 predictors. For level 3, enter just Department, plus any level 3 predictors.

4b. Repeat for levels 2 and 3.

5. Save the template file.

6. Make (and save) the data matrix file.

7. Click "Check Statistics" to get a window showing the count of cases and descriptive statistics (mean, standard deviation, minimum, maximum) at each level. While this is an optional step, it is wise to check to see if data are being imported as expected.

8. Click "Done" to finish, and exit to the "WHLM: hlm3File" window, from which one may select options and run a three-level model. Alternatively, one may close and later run HLM 7, then select File, Create a new model from an existing .mdm file.

After the .mdm file is created, any of a variety of different cross-sectional three-level models may be created. With any model, the first analysis step is to specify the distribution of the dependent variable. For the example data, the dependent is employee performance score (Score0), which is normally distributed. This is the default selection, shown earlier in Figure 3.7. In the same "Basic

Model Specifications" window, the researcher should also specify the file location for the output and the title for the given run of the model.

Model A

Figure 3.20 shows the three-level null model in HLM 7 (compare to the two-level null model in Figure 3.6). For the null model, there are no predictors at any level. However, the intercept of performance score at level 1 is modeled for the Agency grouping effect at level 2 (signified by the r_0 random effects term in the level 2 equation). There is also a Department grouping effect at level 3 (signified by the u_{00} random effects term). The key element of the output is that the deviance is 28880.49, a value that can be compared with later models with predictors. Also, both the level 2 and level 3 intercepts were significant, confirming the existence of both a level 2 Agency effect and a level 3 Department effect. Finally, the residual within-group variance component was 212.40, a baseline value that will decrease as predictors are added to the model.

Figure 3.20   The three-level null model in HLM 7 (Model A)

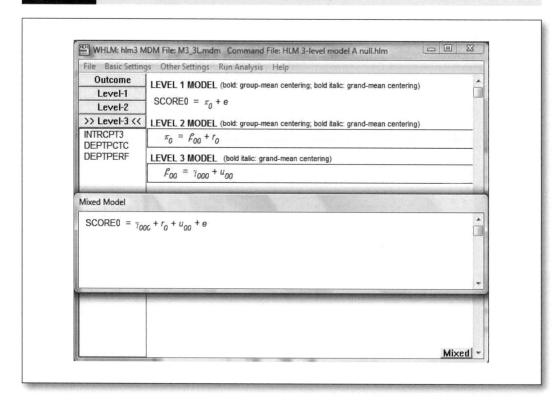

Model B

Figure 3.21 displays the three-level random intercepts model, but one that adds a Department effect at level 3 to further model the level 1 intercept of performance score. At level 1, performance score is still predicted from years of experience and gender. The intercept of performance score is also still modeled as a random effect of Agency at level 2 and of Department at level 3. This is done by modeling the intercept of the level 2 Agency effect on the level 1 intercept, as a function of Department at level 3, as shown in the figure below.

Table 3.15 presents model fit and random effects output for this model. The deviance is now 28102.81, some 777.67 points lower in the direction of better model fit. The likelihood ratio (model comparison) test comparing the null model confirms the current model is a significantly better fit. This is also reflected in the fact that the within-Agencies residual variance component has dropped from 212.40 in the null model to 170.99 in the random intercepts model (Model B), since its effects explain some of the previously unexplained within-groups variance.

The variance components shown in the random effects tables have to do with partitioning the variance in performance scores at level 1. These components are

| Figure 3.21 | A three-level random intercepts model in HLM 7 (Model B) |

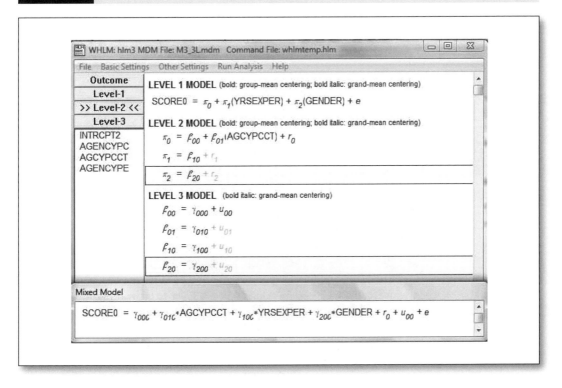

Table 3.15 Random Effects and Model Fit for the Three-Level Random Intercepts Model (Model B)

Final estimation of level 1 and level 2 variance components

Random effect	Standard deviation	Variance component	d.f.	χ^2	p-value
INTRCPT1,r_0	1.42285	2.02449	71	91.84951	0.049
level-1, e	13.07647	170.99418			

Final estimation of level 3 variance components

Random Effect	Standard deviation	Variance component	d.f.	χ^2	p-value
INTRCPT1/INTRCPT2,u_{00}	8.95949	80.27238	61	1325.17420	<0.001

Statistics for the current model

Deviance = 28102.809960

Number of estimated parameters = 7

Model comparison test

χ^2 statistic = 777.67997

Degrees of freedom = 3

p-value = <0.001

not to be interpreted in the fashion discussed below of estimates of fixed effects, which have an interpretation similar to regression. The Department effect on the level 1 intercept (which reflects mean performance score) is large (80.27) and highly significant (p = <.001). The Agency effect on the intercept, however, is small (2.02) and only barely significant (p = 0.049). Though we conclude there is both an Agency and a Department effect on performance score, the latter dominates the former. That the within-group residual variance is large (170.99) means that there is considerable within-Agency variation in performance scores as yet unexplained by modeled effects, suggesting the need to add additional effects and predictors to the model.

Table 3.16 shows the fixed effects in the three-level random intercepts model. These effects are interpreted similarly to regression. There are four fixed effects, all significant. The uppermost one (61.74, p < 0.001) is the estimate of the intercept, which is the mean performance score at level 1, controlling for other variables in the model. In descending order, the next (7.89, p = 0.043) is the effect of the level 2 predictor, centered agency percent certified (AGCYPCCT), on the level 1 intercept. This variable ranged from −.59 to +.30. A 0.1 increase in centered agency percent certified increases mean performance score by 0.79 points.

Table 3.16 Fixed Effects for the Three-Level Random Intercepts Model (Model B)

Final estimation of fixed effects (with robust standard errors)

Fixed effect	Coefficient	Standard error	t-ratio	Approx. d.f.	p-value
For INTRCPT1, π_0					
For INTRCPT2, β_{00}					
INTRCPT3, γ_{000}	61.740246	1.143603	53.987	61	<0.001
For AGCYPCCT, β_{01}					
INTRCPT3, γ_{010}	7.893035	3.822309	2.065	71	0.043
For YRSEXPER slope, π_1					
For INTRCPT2, β_{10}					
INTRCPT3, γ_{100}	16.316538	1.630712	10.006	3297	<0.001
For GENDER slope, π_2					
For INTRCPT2, β_{20}					
INTRCPT3, γ_{200}	−6.635115	0.403094	−16.460	3297	<0.001

The next coefficient is the estimate of the slope of years of experience at level 1 (16.32, p < 0.001). This centered variable ranged from −.79 to + .56. A 0.1 increase in years of experience as coded increases mean performance score by 1.63 points. The t-ratios suggest that the level 1 effect of years of experience is stronger than that of agency percent certified at level 2. Finally, the Gender effect at level 1 is −6.35. Gender was coded 0 = male, 1 = female. A 1-unit increase in Gender (in other words, being female) is associated with a 6.35 drop in performance score below the mean of 61.74, controlling for other variables in the model. The t-ratios suggest that the Gender effect is somewhat stronger than the YrsExper effect, controlling for other variables in the model.

Model C

As a final three-level model illustration, we now create a random coefficients model, shown in Figure 3.22, where centered agency percent certified at level 2 is used as a random factor with respect to a random effect not only on the level 1 intercept of performance score, but also on the slope of years of experience at level 1 (compare to the two-level model in Figure 3.16, as well as the previous three-level random intercepts model in Figure 3.21).

The effect added in Model C is reflected in the second of the level 2 equations shown in Figure 3.22. Each equation is a potential random effect and hence associated with a variance component, but Model C invokes only three of the eight possible random effects. The variance components (random effects) table will

| Figure 3.22 | A three-level random coefficients model in HLM 7 (Model C) |

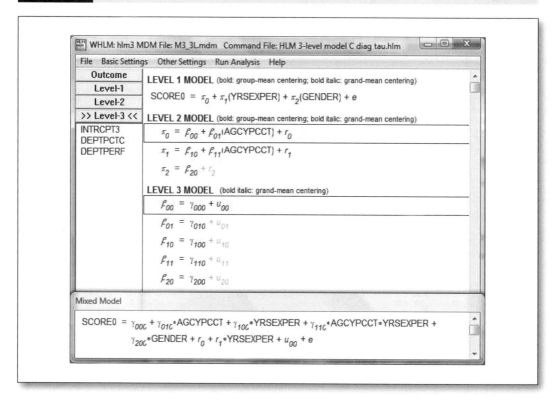

have four estimates: the three shown as active (by virtue of their random error terms being toggled on and not grayed out) plus the within-groups residual effect. At level 2 (the Agency level), Model C invokes the first two random effects, which are the Agency effect on the level 1 intercept (mean performance score) and the Agency effect on the level 1 slope of the predictor YrsExper. The third potential level 1 random effect, the Agency effect on the slope of Gender, is not activated. At level 3, only the first potential random effect is activated: the Department effect on the level 1 intercept (created by way of an effect on the level 2 intercept for the equation representing the Agency effect on the level 1 intercept of performance score). The remaining four level 3 potential effects, not activated, are in descending order. They are all Department effects on (a) the slope of AGCYPCCT as a level 2 predictor of the level 1 intercept of performance score; (b) on the slope of YrsExper, by way of the level 2 equation for the Agency effect on this slope; (c) on the slope of AGCYPCCT as a level 2 predictor of the slope of YrsExper at level 1; and (d) on the slope of Gender, by way of the level 2 equation for the Agency effect on this slope. This recitation highlights the obvious fact that mixed models can quickly become very complex as levels and effects are added. It also highlights the usefulness of the HLM 7 user interface in tracking just what is being modeled more easily than other packages.

While this three-level model may seem only slightly different from the two-level model, adding Department effects, there is now a very important difference: There will now be two random effects (the random effects on the intercept and on the slope of YrsExper). Because there is now more than one between-groups effect (not counting the residual within-groups effect), the researcher must confront the issue of covariance of random effects. As discussed in Chapter 2, the default in HLM 7 approaches this issue quite differently from the default in SPSS or SAS, with the consequence that estimated coefficients may be significantly different. By default, HLM 7 estimates each coefficient in the entire covariance matrix, whereas by default SPSS and SAS impose a variance components (VC) constraint, which requires zero covariance among random effects. The advantage of the unstructured approach of HLM is that it may be more realistic to expect and allow non-zero covariances on the off-diagonal and heterogeneous variances on the diagonal (VC models constrain solutions to have zeros on the off-diagonal and homogenous variances on the diagonal.). The advantage of the VC approach is that it may result in equally good model fit even though a simpler model, and that the model may converge more quickly and with fewer problems. Refer back to Chapter 2 for a discussion of selecting an appropriate covariance type.

Different packages offer different covariance type models, which is to say, different types of constraints on the variance–covariance matrix. For two- and three-level cross-sectional models of the type discussed in this chapter, HLM 7 offers only the default unstructured type and a diagonal type (invoked from the "Estimation" window shown in Figure 3.8 by checking the "Diagonalize tau" radio button). The diagonal model constrains the solution to one with covariances of 0 (like VC) but allows heterogeneous variances (unlike VC). SPSS and SAS also support the DIAG covariance type, though the default VC type results are often very similar or identical. When there is the possibility of covarying random effects, HLM 7 results often will be closest to those in SAS and SPSS if the comparison is between (a) an HLM 7 model with diagonalized tau vs. an SPSS or SAS model with DIAG or VC covariance type, or (b) a default HLM 7 model versus an SPSS or SAS model with UN (unstructured) type. For reasons given in Chapter 2, such as differences in estimation algorithms, estimates may still vary between packages.

Not shown here, the model in Figure 3.21 was run on the default (unstructured) basis in HLM 7 and on a diagonalized basis. A likelihood ratio test was run to compare the two models. While the unstructured approach did yield a lower deviance (lower is better model fit), it was not enough lower to be significant. Therefore, the simpler, diagonalized model is discussed below. The SAS and SPSS parallel examples in Chapters 4 and 5, respectively, illustrate the default variance components model, but for these data, the VC and DIAG models generate very similar estimates.

Table 3.17 shows model fit and random effects for the final three-level random coefficients model, with the slope of years of experience modeled as a random

Table 3.17 Random Effects and Model Fit for the Final Three-Level Random Coefficients Model (Model C)

Final estimation of level 1 and level 2 variance components

Random effect	Standard deviation	Variance component	d.f.	χ^2	p-value
INTRCPT1,r_0	1.58976	2.52733	70	125.63509	<0.001
YRSEXPER slope, r_1	7.84488	61.54207	131	301.72408	<0.001
level 1, e	12.80223	163.89697			

Note. The chi-square statistics reported above are based on only 133 of 134 units that had sufficient data for computation. Fixed effects and variance components are based on all the data.

Final estimation of level 3 variance components

Random effect	Standard deviation	Variance component	d.f.	χ^2	p-value
INTRCPT1/INTRCPT2,u_{00}	9.34926	87.40861	61	1258.08679	<0.001

Statistics for the current model

Deviance = 28055.839714

Number of estimated parameters = 10

Model comparison test

χ^2 statistic = 47.05989

Degrees of freedom = 3

p-value = <0.001

effect of Agency, and AGCYPCCT. The likelihood ratio test for model comparison with the previous model (Model B) shows a reduction in deviance of 47.06, an amount significant at p < 0.001. Likewise, we see that the within-Agency residual variance component has dropped further, from 170.99 in the previous model (B) compared to 163.89 in this model (C). This suggests that the changes made in Model C compared to Model B were significant.

There are three other variance components beyond the residual, which HLM 7 labels "level-1, e" and which reflects as-yet unexplained within-agency variation in performance scores. All other components reflect between-group (in this example, between-agency and between-department) variance. In the "Final estimation of level 1 and level 2 variance components" section of Table 3.17, the "INTRCPT1" term is variance associated with the Agency effect. Agency as the level 2 subjects (grouping) variable has a small (2.53) but significant (p < 0.001) effect on mean performance score (the intercept). The "YRSEXPER slope" term is variance associated with random effects on the slope of years of experience as a predictor of level 1 performance scores. This random effect, which was modeled as a function of both Agency and AGCYPCCT at level 2, is moderately large (61.54) and significant (p < 0.001). In the lower, "Final estimation of level-3 variance components" portion of Table 3.17, the single intercept term reflects variance associated with the Department effect on the intercept of performance score. It is large (87.41) and significant (p < 0.001).

Table 3.18 displays the fixed effects for Model C. There are now five fixed effects: all those for the previous model (see Table 3.16) plus a new one for the random effect of agency percent certified centered (AGCYPCCT) at level 2 on the slope of YrsExper at level 1. This added effect has the lowest t-ratio and is the least significant, though it is significant by the usual .05 alpha criterion.

In Table 3.18, the uppermost coefficient is the estimate (61.74) of the intercept or mean value of performance score, controlling for other variables in the model.

Table 3.18   Fixed Effects for the Final Three-Level Random Coefficients Model (Model C)

Final estimation of fixed effects (with robust standard errors)

Fixed effect	Coefficient	Standard error	t-ratio	Approx. d.f.	p-value
For INTRCPT1, π_0					
For INTRCPT2, β_{00}					
INTRCPT3, γ_{000}	61.742258	1.241603	49.728	61	<0.001
For AGCYPCCT, β_{01}					
INTRCPT3, γ_{010}	10.517761	4.065604	2.587	69	0.012
For YRSEXPER slope, π_1					
For INTRCPT2, β_{10}					
INTRCPT3, γ_{100}	15.571292	1.360052	11.449	69	<0.001
For AGCYPCCT, β_{11}					
INTRCPT3, γ_{110}	2.641930	9.479845	0.279	69	0.781
For GENDER slope, π_2					
For INTRCPT2, β_{20}					
INTRCPT3, γ_{200}	−6.579907	0.409705	−16.060	3164	<0.001

It is virtually identical to that in Model B (Table 3.16). In descending order, the next coefficient (10.52) is the effect of agency percent certified centered (AGCYPCCT) on the level 1 intercept, now estimated to be larger than in Model B but interpreted similarly. Next is the estimate of the slope of years of experience at level 1 (15.57), quite close to that in Model B and also interpreted similarly. The fourth coefficient down in Table 3.18 is the AGCYPCCT effect on the slope of YrsExper as a level 1 predictor of performance score. This effect is non-significant. Finally, the Gender effect at level 1 is −6.58, little changed from the previous model.

We conclude that there is both a Department and an Agency effect in explaining variance in mean performance score, with the Department effect being much greater than the Agency effect. There is also an Agency-level effect on the variance in the strength of relationship (slope) of YrsExper as a predictor of performance scores. At level 1, YrsExper and Gender are both significant predictors of performance score. We also conclude that while agency percent certified has a significant effect on mean employee performance score, it does not have a significant effect on the strength of relationship between years of experience and score. The model could be revised by dropping this non-significant effect. The remaining large residual variance component also indicates that additional effects and variables may be needed to fully explain the variance in employee-level performance scores.

GRAPHICS IN HLM 7

Before closing this chapter, it should be noted that HLM 7 also offers a variety of graphics options useful for analysis and diagnostics. These options are described in Chapter 18 of the HLM 7 manual by Raudenbush et al. (2011). Options are also illustrated in the present volume, in Chapters 8 and 10. To illustrate briefly here, Figure 3.23 below shows level 1 equation graphing for the two-level full random coefficients model described earlier in this chapter. Recall that linear mixed modeling computes separate regressions for each level 2 group (agencies for this example). Figure 3.23 shows the regression lines for 25% of the 132 agencies, predicting Score0 from YrsExper. Although it is true for all agencies that scores increase as experience increases, Figure 3.23 shows graphically that (a) intercepts differ by group, with some agencies scoring higher than other agencies at all levels of experience; and (b) slopes differ by group, with the steepness of the regression lines showing that within some agencies, experience is more related to score than for other agencies.

Figure 3.23 was obtained from the HLM 7 menu by selecting File, Graph equations, Level 1 equation graphing; then, in the "Level 1 Equation Graphing" dialog, the x-focus was made to be YrsExper and the number of groups set to "random Sample" with a probability of .25; and in the same dialog, under "Range/Titles/Color," the graph title was set.

Figure 3.23	Score0 by YrsExper for 25% of the groups in the two-level full random coefficients model

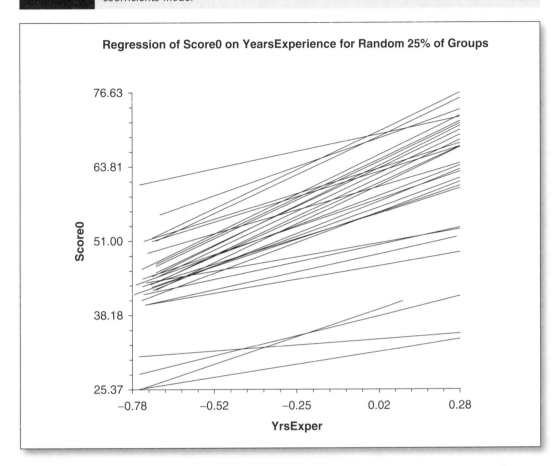

As a second illustration, Figure 3.24 displays the relationship of Gender to Score0 for the first 10 groups in the same study. With men coded 0 and women coded 1, the graphs show that men tend to score higher than women, though this tendency is more pronounced in some groups than others. This figure was obtained from the HLM 7 menu by selecting File, Graph Data, "Line plots, scatter plots"; then, the number of groups was set to "First 10 groups."

Other HLM 7 graphing options support plots of residuals versus predicted values, residual box-whisker plots, coefficient confidence intervals, and more. For all figures, in the figure display window one may select File, Save As, and save the figure in either extended metafile format (.emf, compatible with Microsoft Word's Insert, Picture command and with Microsoft PowerPoint) or Windows metafile format (.wmf, compatible with Microsoft Office and with Adobe Illustrator).

Figure 3.24 Score0 by Gender for first 10 groups in the two-level full random coefficients model

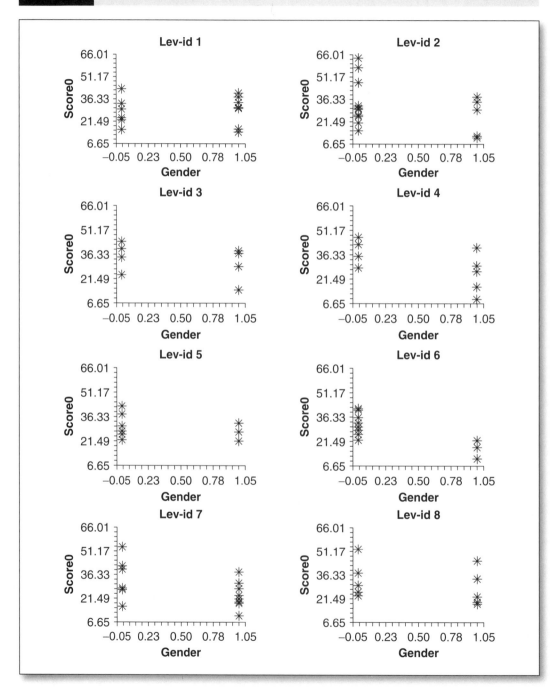

SUMMARY

As this is intentionally an introductory guide and due to space limitations, this chapter has sought to present only some of the most important types of linear mixed models that may be implemented with HLM 7 software. Multilevel modeling supports a far, far richer array of models and variations, some of which are treated in subsequent application chapters in this volume. These include cohort models, longitudinal and growth models, and cross-classified models not discussed in this chapter, to name a few. Moreover, generalized linear mixed modeling software extends many of these models to ones using nonlinear link functions where the outcome variable is not a normally distributed continuous variable (ex., to binomial, multinomial, ordinal, or Poisson distributions, implemented in GLMM in SPSS, GLIMMIX in SAS, and built into HLM 7). Additional types of models are presented in comprehensive texts on multilevel modeling, which this work is intended to introduce and for which it may serve as a supplement. While only the surface of what is possible with linear mixed modeling is presented in this volume, the basic principles concerning types of effects, model assumptions, and inference logic apply to all types and hopefully serve as a stepping stone toward more advanced work.

NOTES

1. At this writing, the student version is available at http://www.ssicentral.com/hlm/downloads/HLM7StudentSetup.exe.

2. Method 2 is supported for HLM 6 and higher.

3. For pedagogical reasons, the default REML output has been illustrated. However, keep in mind the admonitions in Chapter 2 that model fit comparisons using likelihood ratio tests or information criteria measures when models differ in fixed effects require ML estimation.

4. For reasons of comparability to parallel SPSS and SAS output, output for this and subsequent examples (except the heterogeneous model) is obtained based on a diagonalized tau constraint, explained later in this chapter.

5. To create Figure 3.14, in HLM 7, select Basic Settings, which opens the "Basic Model Specifications" window. Click the "Level 1 Residual File" to save residuals. (The default filename will be resfil1.sav if SPSS format is desired. SAS, Stata, and ASCII alternatives are available.) In the .sav file, the agency id field is saved as l2id, signifying it is the variable designating level 2 units. The residual values for each employee are saved as l1resid, signifying level 1 residuals. In SPSS, to aggregate the residuals by agency and compute the variance, select Analyze, Compare Means, and in the "Means" window, let l1resid be the dependent and l2id the independent; and under the Options button, let variance be the only statistic. In SPSS syntax, the command is as follows: MEANS TABLES=l1resid BY l2id / CELLS VAR. The resulting report lists residual variances by agency id. This is copied into Excel, where the table is sorted in ascending order by l1resid. Block out the sorted column and select Insert, and in the Chart Layouts block, select Scatter as the chart type. Click on a point to select all points, and then right-click and select "Add trend line." To label outlier points, block both the l2id and l1resid columns; double-click on a point to select it, and then

right click and choose "Add data label. Then re-select the point, right click, select "Format data label," and set the contents field and label alignment.

6. In SPSS, with the residual file () discussed previously in this chapter as the active dataset, select Data, Aggregate, and let Agency be the "Break Variable"; move the predictor variables and the residual variable (l1resid by default) into the "Aggregated Variables" area, and then click on the "Functions" button to let the statistic for the residual variable be the standard deviation (variance is not an option). The other predictor variable statistics will default to means. Choose to save the aggregated file under a different filename. After running the Aggregate function, open the file (aggr.sav by default) and use Transform, Compute Variable, to create a new residual variance variable based on the residual standard deviation. Then select Analyze, Correlate, to obtain the correlations of residual variance by Agency with the predictor variables. For the example data, output is shown in Figure 3.17.

REFERENCES

Bryk, A. S., & Raudenbush, S. W. (1992). *Hierarchical linear models in social and behavioral research: Applications and data analysis methods* (1st ed.). Newbury Park, CA: Sage.

Raudenbush, S. W., & Bryk, A. S. (2002). *Hierarchical linear models* (2nd ed.). Thousand Oaks, CA: Sage.

Raudenbush, S. W., Bryk, A. S., Cheong, A. S., Fai, Y. F., Congdon, R. T., & du Toit, M. (2011). *HLM 7: Hierarchical linear and nonlinear modeling.* Lincolnwood, IL: Scientific Software International.

Singer, J. D. (1998). Using SAS PROC MIXED to fit multilevel models, hierarchical models, and individual growth models. *Journal of Educational and Behavioral Statistics, 23*(4), 323–355.

Introductory Guide to HLM With SAS Software

4

G. David Garson

S AS is a full-featured statistical and data management suite of tools, which, among many other things, supports hierarchical linear and multilevel modeling. Its two main modules for doing this are PROC MIXED and PROC GLIMMIX, which are respectively the modules for linear mixed modeling and generalized linear mixed modeling. Where PROC GLM (general linear model) in SAS is used when there are only fixed effects in a regression or analysis of variance model, PROC MIXED is required for correct solutions when there are random effects. In this chapter, PROC MIXED is used to run several of the common types of linear mixed models described in Chapter 1 and already implemented in HLM 7 software in Chapter 3.

ENTERING DATA INTO SAS

SAS has several methods of entering data, described below.

Direct Data Entry Using VIEWTABLE

It is possible to enter data directly into a SAS table by selecting Tools, Table Editor, as illustrated in Figure 4.1. SAS "tables" are synonymous with SAS "datasets." In the VIEWTABLE window that opens, the columns will be variables and the rows will be observations. Double-click the heading (not row 1) of the first column, and enter the name of the first variable, then tab to repeat for additional columns and variables. After the variable names are entered, enter the first observation's data in row 1. SAS uses row 1 to determine automatically whether a variable is of numeric or string (character) type. Additional observations, of course, are entered in subsequent rows.

When finished, temporarily save the data by selecting File, Save As, from the main menu. The "Save As" window, shown in Figure 4.2, organizes data files into "libraries," also called directories or folders. The library called "Work" is used for the temporary working data file in memory. Enter the desired filename of the dataset in the "Member Name" textbox at the bottom of the Save As window. The data

Figure 4.1   SAS VIEWTABLE window

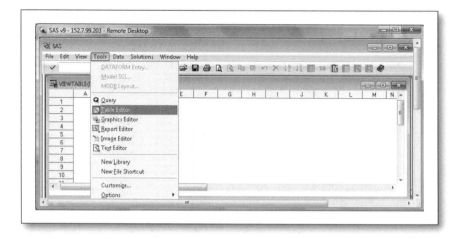

Figure 4.2   SAS Save As window

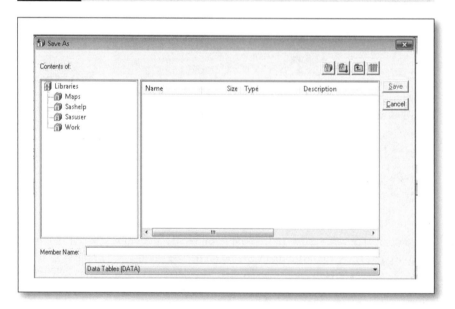

will be saved (but only for the duration of the current SAS session) with a prefix (ex., Work.MyData1). The "Work" prefix indicates the data file is temporary.

To save data permanently, go to the Save As window, with the desired dataset open, and click the "Create new library" icon (the file drawer icon at the upper right), shown in Figure 4.3. This will cause the "New Library" window (not shown) to open, where one can enter the new library name and browse to the

Figure 4.3 The "Create new library" icon in SAS

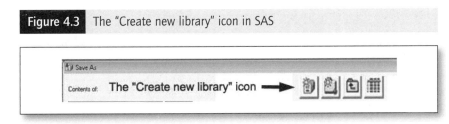

desired file location path. The filename will be saved with the filename shown in the VIEWTABLE window, but in its permanent file version by default it will have the extension ".sas7bdat." SPSS, as well as SAS, reads files with this extension, but one can save to other formats as well.

Data Entry Using the SAS Import Wizard

A second method of entering data into SAS, assuming the researcher already has data in some common format such as .sav for SPSS or .xls for Microsoft Excel, is to select File, Import Data, from the SAS main menu, thereby invoking the SAS import wizard shown in Figure 4.4. The import wizard is capable of importing many file formats, including SPSS .sav files, but not HLM .mdm files. Subsequent screens (not shown) of the import wizard are self-explanatory, asking the user to browse to the location of the file to be imported and to assign a name for the temporary SAS work file to be created or to designate a member name in a library other than WORK, which is the default.

Figure 4.4 The SAS Import Wizard initial screen

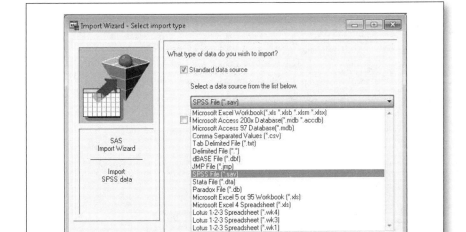

Data Entry Using SAS Commands

Traditionally, SAS has been a command-driven package. In spite of it now having a menu system, direct entry of SAS code is still the easiest method of getting one's data into SAS. The code shown in Table 4.1 is typed into the SAS editor window, and then the code is run by selecting Run, Submit, as shown in Figure 4.5.

Table 4.1 Commented SAS Code to Import a Data File

```
PROC IMPORT OUT= WORK.M3_2L
    DATAFILE= "C\Docs\mixed3level.sav"
       DBMS=SPSS REPLACE;
* PROC IMPORT imports the file in the DATAFILE clause;
* The OUT=  term assigns the imported data to a table called M3_L2 in
the WORK directory;
* The DBMS clause designates SPSS files as the type to import;
* It then creates a working data file called M3_2L;
* This does not change the .sav file nor create a new file on disk;
RUN;
```

Figure 4.5 Importing data into a SAS workfile

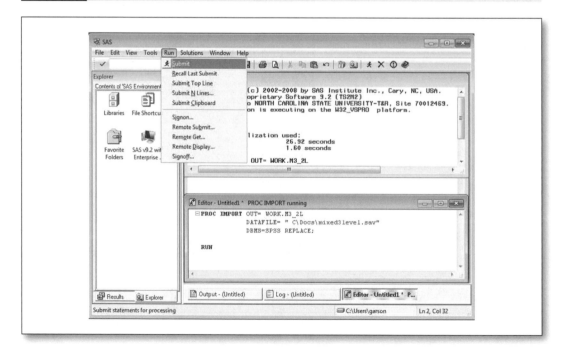

For this example, the temporary work file M3_2L is created, containing the SPSS .sav format data previously used in Chapter 3 on employee performance scores grouped by agency. The first step by custom often is to create the baseline null model, discussed next.

THE NULL MODEL IN SAS PROC MIXED

Table 4.2 displays the commented SAS command code needed to run the null model on the same data as used for the null model in Chapter 3. As before, lines beginning with asterisks and ending in semicolons are explanatory comments, not actually needed to run the model.

The model is run as shown in Figure 4.6, which displays the log window, the program editor window, and the output window. Note that because a null model has no predictors, the MODEL statement designates only the dependent variable,

Table 4.2 Commented SAS Code to Run the Null Model

```
* Null model;
PROC MIXED DATA=M3_2L COVTEST;
    * PROC MIXED includes an intercept by default;
    * DATA invokes the imported dataset (see Table 4-1);
    * COVTEST asks for printing of covariance components of random
effects;
    * No METHOD statement implies restricted maximum likelihood
estimation, the default;
    * METHOD=ml would have asked for maximum likelihood estimation;
CLASS agency;
    * CLASS identifies agency as a categorical variable;
MODEL score0 = /SOLUTION;
    *MODEL sets score0 as the dependent/outcome variable;
    */SOLUTION outputs estimates of fixed effects;
    *In later models, fixed effects are listed in the MODEL
statement;
RANDOM intercept / SUBJECT=agency TYPE=VC;
    * RANDOM makes the level 1 intercept a random effect of agency at
level 2;
    *SUBJECT defines the level 2 grouping variable, agency;
    *TYPE sets the covariance structure assumption as variance
components;
    *In later models, random effects are listed in the RANDOM
statement;
TITLE 'Null (Baseline) Model';
run;
```

Figure 4.6   Running the null model in SAS 9.2

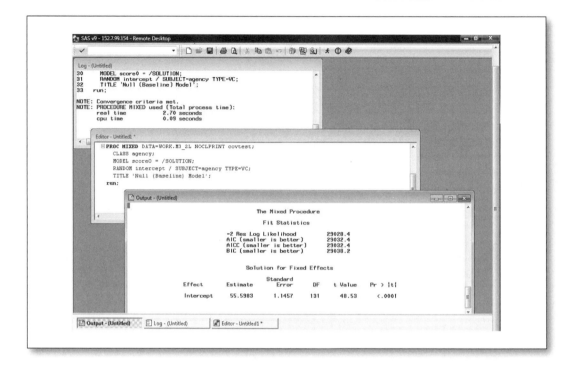

which is employee performance score (score0), and no fixed effects. The RANDOM statement models the level 1 intercept of score0 as a random effect of the subject variable agency at level 2 (employees are grouped within a random sample of agencies). The TYPE term in the RANDOM statement specifies a variance components covariance structure, used when computing the intraclass correlation (ICC) as discussed in previous chapters.

After some preliminary model information and data on iterations prior to convergence, and without issuing any convergence warnings, SAS outputs the "Covariance Parameters Estimates" table as shown in Table 4.3. The covariance parameter estimates are identical (after rounding) to those produced by HLM 7. Agency as a random factor has a between-agency variance component of 161.92, while the residual within-agency variance component is 212.69. The agency effect is shown to be significant at better than the .0001 level, which means that the ICC will be significant. This in turn means that general linear model methods like OLS regression and ANOVA will not return correct estimates and standard errors, but instead multilevel modeling is needed.[1]

The next table in SAS output is the fit statistics table, shown in Table 4.4. The value listed as "−2 Res Log Likelihood" is identical, after rounding, to the "deviance" reported by HLM 7 in Table 3.2. Unlike HLM 7 but like SPSS 19, SAS 9.2

Table 4.3	The Covariance Parameter Estimates Table for the Null Model

```
              Covariance Parameter Estimates

                                    Standard        Z
Cov Parm    Subject    Estimate       Error      Value     Pr > Z

Intercept   Agency      161.92      21.7108       7.46     <.0001
Residual                212.69       5.1896      40.98     <.0001
```

Table 4.4	The Fit Statistics Table for the Null Model

```
                  Fit Statistics

       -2 Res Log Likelihood          29028.4
       AIC (smaller is better)        29032.4
       AICC (smaller is better)       29032.4
       BIC (smaller is better)        29038.2
```

reports the information theory measures AIC, AICC, and BIC. All four measures are baseline values, which may be used later to compare models, with lower values reflecting better fit.[2]

Finally, SAS outputs the fixed effects table shown in Table 4.5. The null model models the level 1 intercept of performance score both as a random effect of agency at level 2, and also as a fixed effect at level 1. The estimate, 55.5983, is virtually identical to HLM 7 (see Table 3.3) and SPSS 19 output (see Table 5.3). It represents the grand mean of score0 when there are no predictors in the model. On the average, an employee can be expected to score 55.6 on performance.

Table 4.5	The Fixed Effects Table for the Null Model

```
              Solution for Fixed Effects

                         Standard
Effect       Estimate      Error       DF    t Value    Pr > |t|

Intercept     55.5983     1.1457      131      48.53      <.0001
```

A RANDOM COEFFICIENTS REGRESSION MODEL IN SAS 9.2

Paralleling Chapter 3, a random coefficients (RC) regression model is next computed. This model has Gender and YrsExper as predictors of Score0 (employee performance score) at level 1. Like in the null model, Agency is the level 2 random factor (grouping variable). There are no other level 2 predictors. Agency is used to model both the level 1 intercept of employee test scores (score0, the dependent) and the regression coefficients of YrsExper at level 1.

In comparison with the null model, Figure 4.7 displays essentially the same SAS interface but with the SAS code for the RC regression model. This code is displayed in Table 4.6, also below. As before, the CLASS statement defines the level 2 grouping variable, Agency. The MODEL statement declares the dependent variable, score0, and the level 1 fixed effects. The RANDOM statement specifies that both the level 1 intercept of score0 and the slope of YrsExper are to be modeled as random effects of Agency.

In SAS output, "−2 Res Log Likelihood" is the deviance, here 28201.2 compared to 29028.4 in the null model—a drop of 827.2 points, reflecting better fit. Other information theory measures (AIC, AICC, BIC) are also lower, again reflecting better fit. Knowing YrsExper and Gender, and also modeling YrsExper as a random effect of Agency at level 2, improves predictions in estimating employee performance scores compared to predictions based on knowing only how scores cluster by agency.

Figure 4.7 Running the random coefficients regression model in SAS 9.2

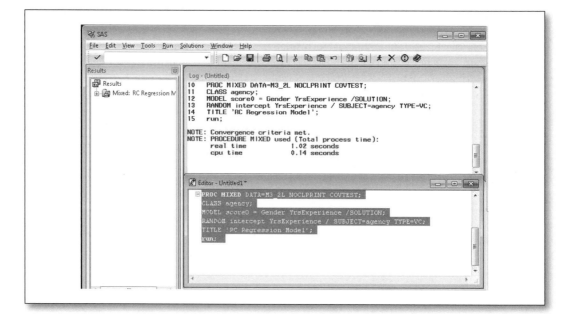

Table 4.6 SAS Code for the Random Coefficients Regression Model

```
* RC regression model;
PROC MIXED DATA=M3_2L COVTEST;
* In Table 4-1, M3_2L is defined as the SAS working file;
CLASS agency;
MODEL score0 = Gender YrsExper /SOLUTION;
RANDOM intercept YrsExper / SUBJECT=agency TYPE=VC;
TITLE 'RC Regression Model';
run;
```

Table 4.7 The Fit Statistics Table for the RC Regression Model

```
                    Fit Statistics

        -2 Res Log Likelihood          28201.2
        AIC (smaller is better)        28207.2
        AICC (smaller is better)       28207.2
        BIC (smaller is better)        28215.8
```

Table 4.8 presents the fixed effects in the model, which were the level 1 effects of Gender and YrsExper on Score0. Both level 1 predictors are shown to be significant. The t-ratio values, which are the estimates divided by their standard errors, show that Gender and YrsExper have a similar absolute level of effect in predicting performance score (score0).

Model random effects are shown in Table 4.9. The three random effects are for the intercept of Score0, the slope of YrsExper, and the residual random effect. The residual reflects the within-Agency variation in Score0 unaccounted for by other terms in the model. It is significant and higher than other variance components, meaning that there is significant within-Agency variation remaining to be explained. However, the RC regression model has reduced its percentage of the total of all variance components from 56.8% in the null model (see Table 4.5: 212.69/(212.69+161.92)) to 43.6% (163.78/(163.78 + 130.55 + 63.09)) in the RC regression, shown in Figure 4.9 below. The variance component for the intercept random effect has also dropped, from 161.92 in the null model to 130.55. The new random effect, that of Agency on the slope of YrsExper, is the smallest variance component (63.09), but it shows there is a significant tendency for the strength of the relation of YrsExper to Score0 to be stronger in some agencies than others. The drop in the variance components for the residual and intercept components is an indicator of the effect size of the YrsExper random effect.

Table 4.8 Fixed Effects Tables for the Random Coefficients Regression Model

```
                    Solution for Fixed Effects

                                Standard
    Effect             Estimate    Error      DF      t Value     Pr > |t|

    Intercept          59.3901     1.0559     131      56.24       <.0001
    Gender             -6.4829     0.4466     3230    -14.52       <.0001
    YrsExper           16.2529     1.0507     131      15.47       <.0001


                 Type 3 Tests of Fixed Effects

                        Num       Den
        Effect           DF        DF     F Value     Pr > F

        Gender            1       3230    210.74      <.0001
        YrsExper          1        131    239.28      <.0001
```

Table 4.9 Covariance Parameter Estimates Table for the Random Coefficients Regression Model

```
                 Covariance Parameter Estimates

                                      Standard        Z
    Cov Parm        Subject  Estimate   Error       Value     Pr > Z

    Intercept       Agency    130.55   17.8281       7.32      <.0001
    YrsExper        Agency    63.0943  15.8277       3.99      <.0001
    Residual                  163.78    4.0748      40.19      <.0001
```

A FULL RANDOM COEFFICIENTS MODEL

In the next model to be discussed, called a full random coefficients model or an "intercepts-and-slopes-as-outcomes" model, there are predictors at both levels. Moreover, both level 1 intercepts and level 1 slopes are predicted as random effects not only by the level 2 grouping variable, but also by one or more level 2 predictors. Specifically, performance score (Score0) at level 1 is predicted by years of experience (YrsExper) and gender (Gender), also at level 1. The intercept of Score0 is modeled as a random effect of Agency and as an effect of the level 2 predictor, Agency percent certified (AgcyPCCtrd). YrsExper is coded on a centered basis. For Agency percent certified, a new, centered variable was created (AgcyPCCtrd), as SAS lacks HLM's ability to center predictors on the fly. The slope of YrsExper at level 1 was modeled as a random effect of Agency at level 2 and as an effect of AgcyPCCtrd. The SAS syntax for this model is shown in Table 4.10.

In this code, the IC parameter is added to the PROC MIXED statement, requesting output of the "Information Criteria" table, which provides fuller output than the default "Fit Statistics" table, as shown in Table 4.11. As before, the CLASS statement defines the level 2 groups as being those associated with Agency. Performance score (Score0) at level 1 is defined as the dependent by virtue of being on the left-hand side of the MODEL statement equation, while the terms on the right-hand side are predictors. Gender and YrsExper are level 1 predictors, and AgcyPCCtrd (centered agency percent certified) is a level 2 predictor for which every subject in a given agency has the same value. The YrsExperi*AgcyPCCtrd interaction is used to assess the effect of agency percent certified at level 2 on the slope of YrsExper at level 1. The RANDOM statement requests that the SUBJECT variable (Agency) be used as a random factor to model the level 1 intercept and also the slope of YrsExper as random effects. The TYPE parameter requests the default variance components (VC) covariance structure assumption, discussed in Chapter 2.

The "Fit Statistics" table and the "Information Criteria" table for this model, shown in Table 4.11, yield a deviance value ($-2RLL$) of 28156.79 and an AIC of 28162.79. These values are identical to those in SPSS in Chapter 5 and close to the value of deviance output by HLM 7. Differences arise for reasons given in Chapter 2 in the discussion of difference in estimation methods. Also, these values are somewhat lower and therefore a better fit than the corresponding values for the previous random coefficients regression model shown in Table 4.7.[3]

Table 4.12 shows the fixed effects output for the full random coefficients model. The "Solution for Fixed Effects" table shows the regression estimates and their standard errors, along with a t-test of significance. A companion "Type 3

Table 4.10 SAS Syntax for the Full Random Coefficients Regression Model

```
* RC full rc regression model;
PROC MIXED DATA=M3_2L COVTEST IC;
CLASS agency;
MODEL score0 = Gender YrsExper AgcyPCCtrd YrsExper*AgcyPCCtrd/SOLUTION;
RANDOM intercept YrsExper / SUBJECT=agency TYPE=VC;
TITLE 'Full RC Model in SAS 9.2';
run;
```

| Table 4.11 | Model Fit Statistics for the Full Random Coefficients Model in SAS 9.2* |

```
                    Fit Statistics

        -2 Res Log Likelihood          28156.8
        AIC (smaller is better)        28162.8
        AICC (smaller is better)       28162.8
        BIC (smaller is better)        28171.4


                 Information Criteria

Neg2LogLike    Parms      AIC      AICC      HQIC       BIC       CAIC

   28156.8        3    28162.8   28162.8   28166.3   28171.4   28174.4


* The Fit Statistics table is part of default output. The Information
Criteria table is output if the IC parameter is added to the PROC MIXED
statement as shown in Table 4.10.
```

Tests of Fixed Effects" provides F-tests of the hypothesis that the given fixed effect differs from zero. Inferences for these data are identical. The major inferences are these:

1. Knowing an agency's percent of certified employees does not predict the strength of the relationship (slope) of years of experience as a predictor of employee performance score. This is shown by the term YrsExper*AgcyPCCtrd being non-significant.

2. YrsExper is positively and significantly associated with performance score, controlling for other variables in the model. As this variable was centered on its mean and expressed in standardized units ranging from −.79 to +.56 (not in raw years), a 0.1 unit increase in YrsExper is associated with a 1.54 unit increase in performance scores when other variables in the model are controlled at 0. AgcyPCCtrd is a centered variable. The other significant predictor is gender, with 0 = Male, the phrase "when other variables are controlled" is equivalent to "for men when agency percent certified is at its mean."

3. Gender is negatively and significantly associated with performance score, controlling for other variables. As Gender was coded 0 = Male, 1 = Female, the phrase "a unit increase" transmutes to "being female." One may say that on the average, being female reduces the estimated performance score by 6.5 points controlling for other variables in the model. YrsExper is centered, so 0 corresponds

to mean years of experience. Likewise, AgcyPCCtrd is also centered. Therefore "controlling for other variables" equates to "when years of experience and agency percent certified are at their means."

4. The percent certified in an agency (AgcyPCCtrd) at level 2 is a positive and significant predictor of performance score at level 1. A 0.1 (10%) increase in agency percent certified is associated with a 3.1 point increase in employee performance score when other variables in the model are controlled, which means for men when years of experience is at its mean.

The random effects estimates in SAS 9.2 are given in the "Covariance Parameter Estimates" table, shown in Table 4.13 below. The three random effects are Agency on the intercept of Score0, Agency on the slope of YrsExper, and the residual effect. The estimates are those of the between-agency variances in fixed effects means for the level 1 intercept, the between-agency variances in fixed effects means for the slope, and the residual within-agency variance in performance scores. The residual variance component is 49.6% of the total of variance components, indicating that a substantial amount of within-agency variation remains unexplained.

The "Intercept" effect is the Agency effect and is 30.7% of the total of variance components, a substantial and significant proportion, confirming that performance

Table 4.12   Fixed Effects Tables for the Full Random Coefficients Model in SAS 9.2

```
                         Solution for Fixed Effects

                                   Standard
Effect                  Estimate     Error       DF     t Value    Pr > |t|

Intercept                60.4432    0.9636       130      62.72      <.0001
Gender                   -6.4912    0.4463      3230     -14.54      <.0001
YrsExper                 15.3834    1.1545       130      13.32      <.0001
AgcyPCCtrd               30.9730    5.1454      3230       6.02      <.0001
YrsExperi*AgcyPCCtrd     -3.4985    6.2628      3230      -0.56      0.5765


                       Type 3 Tests of Fixed Effects

                            Num      Den
            Effect           DF       DF     F Value     Pr > F

            Gender            1      3230     211.56      <.0001
            YrsExper          1       130     177.55      <.0001
            AgcyPCCtrd        1      3230      36.23      <.0001
            YrsExperi*AgcyPCCtrd   1  3230      0.31      0.5765
```

| Table 4.13 | Random Effects Table for the Full Random Coefficients Model in SAS 9.2 |

```
                          Covariance Parameter Estimates

                                          Standard          Z
Cov Parm            Subject     Estimate     Error      Value      Pr > Z

Intercept           Agency       101.37    13.9878       7.25      <.0001
YrsExper            Agency       64.7705   16.2645       3.98      <.0001
Residual                         163.64     4.0707      40.20      <.0001
```

scores at level 1 do cluster by Agency even when controlling for agency percent certified. Adding AgcyPCCtrd as a level 2 covariate reduces (from 130.6 to 101.4) the Agency effect, confirming that agency percent certified does explain some of the Agency effect seen in the previous model. That the Agency effect on the level 1 intercept is still significant means there is variation that might be explained by inclusion of additional level 2 predictors. This is discussed further in the parallel section of Chapter 5.

The YrsExper effect is 19.6%. This component, while smaller than the Agency effect on the level 1 intercept, is still sizable and significant, indicating that YrsExper at level 1 also clusters by Agency, and demonstrating the importance of modeling its slope and its standard error as a random effect of Agency at level 2. The slopes of YrsExper vary significantly across agencies, meaning the strength of relationship of years of experience to performance scores at level 1 is significantly different for different agencies.

In summary, in this model, agency percent certified at level 2, agency was shown to be a significant predictor of employee performance score at level 1, though not significantly related to the strength of relation (slope) of years of experience as a level 1 predictor. The random effects table confirmed the need for multilevel analysis in computation of slopes as well as intercepts at level 1. That is, a random coefficients model, not just a random intercepts model, is appropriate.

THREE-LEVEL HIERARCHICAL LINEAR MODELS

We now turn to cross-sectional three-level hierarchical linear models, importing in the same manner the same SPSS data file, mixed3level.sav. (SAS code to import a file was shown in Table 4.1.) In this file is a subject ID code for Department as level 3, such that employees are nested within agencies, and agencies within departments. Data rows should be sorted in this nested manner. We discuss three models: (a) the three-level null model, (b) a three-level random intercepts model, and (c) a three-level random coefficients model.

Model A

Table 4.14 shows the SAS code for the three-level null model in SAS 9.2 (compare to the two-level null model in Table 4.2). The null model has no predictors at any level, but the intercept of performance score at level 1 is modeled by the Agency effect at level 2 (signified by the first RANDOM statement, with Agency*Department as the subject).[4] There is also a Department grouping effect at level 3 (signified by the second RANDOM statement, with Department as subject). In the PROC MIXED command, COVTEST asks for tests of random effects, and IC asks for information criteria measures of model fit, such as AIC and BIC. The MODEL statement identifies score0 as the dependent variable. Note that neither the MODEL nor the RANDOM statements specify any predictor variables.

The key element of the output shown in the "Fit Statistics" and repeated in the "Information Criteria" table is what HLM 7 labeled deviance but SAS labels −2 Res Log Likelihood ("Res" because restricted) or Neg2LogLike. As shown below in Table 4.15, it is 28887.9, a value that can be compared with later models to which predictors are added.

Table 4.14 SAS Code for Three-Level Linear Mixed Model A (the null model)

```
* Three-level hlm model;
PROC MIXED DATA=M3_2L COVTEST IC;
CLASS agency;
MODEL score0 = /SOLUTION;
RANDOM intercept  / SUBJECT= Agency*Department TYPE=VC;
RANDOM intercept / SUBJECT= Department TYPE=VC;
TITLE 'Three-level HLM model A (null) in SAS 9.2';
run;
```

Table 4.15 Goodness-of-Fit Measures for Model A (the three-level null model)

```
                          Fit Statistics

             -2 Res Log Likelihood        28877.9
             AIC (smaller is better)      28883.9
             AICC (smaller is better)     28883.9
             BIC (smaller is better)      28890.3
```

Neg2LogLike	Parms	AIC	AICC	HQIC	BIC	CAIC
		Information Criteria				
28877.9	3	28883.9	28883.9	28886.4	28890.3	28893.3

Also, in the "Covariance Parameter Estimates" table shown in Table 4.16, both the level 2 and level 3 intercepts were significant, confirming that both the level 2 Agency effect and a far larger level 3 Department effect differed from zero. The residual within-group variance component was 212.4; little changed from the two-level null model in Table 4.3. The residual component reflects unexplained within-group variance and serves as a baseline value that will decrease as predictors are added to the model.

Model B

Table 4.17 displays the SAS code for a three-level random intercepts model with a Department as well as Agency effect modeling the level 1 intercept of performance score. At level 1, in the MODEL statement, performance score is still predicted from years of experience and gender, but now is also modeled as a fixed effect of AgcyPCCtrd at level 2. Table 4.18 shows deviance, labeled "−2 Res Log Likelihood," as 28094.9. This is significantly lower than deviance in the null model, which was 28877.9. Likewise, all the information criteria measures, such as AIC and BIC, are also lower (in the direction of better fit).

Table 4.16 Covariance Parameter Estimates For Model A (the three-level null model)

		Covariance Parameter Estimates			
Cov Parm	Subject	Estimate	Standard Error	Z Value	Pr > Z
Intercept	Department*Agency	4.0577	2.2717	1.79	0.0370
Intercept	Department	122.86	23.4824	5.23	<.0001
Residual		212.41	5.1738	41.05	<.0001

Table 4.17 SAS Code for Three-Level Model B (the random intercepts model)

```
* Three-level model B;
PROC MIXED DATA=M3_2L COVTEST IC;
CLASS agency;
MODEL score0 = YrsExper Gender AgcyPCCtrd /SOLUTION;
RANDOM intercept / SUBJECT= Agency*Department TYPE=VC;
RANDOM intercept / SUBJECT= Department TYPE=VC;
TITLE 'Three-level HLM model B in SAS 9.2';
run;
```

Table 4.18   Goodness-of-Fit Measures for Model B (the three-level random intercepts model)

```
                          Fit Statistics

              -2 Res Log Likelihood        28094.9
              AIC (smaller is better)      28100.9
              AICC (smaller is better)     28100.9
              BIC (smaller is better)      28107.2


                     Information Criteria

Neg2LogLike    Parms      AIC       AICC      HQIC        BIC       CAIC

   28094.9        3    28100.9    28100.9    28103.4    28107.2    28110.2
```

Table 4.19 displays the random effects for the three-level random intercepts model. As only intercepts are being modeled, there are only three random effects: the Agency effect, the Department effect, and the within-groups residual effect. The Department effect on the level 1 intercept (which reflects mean performance score) is large (82.09) and highly significant (p < .001). The Agency effect on the intercept, however, is small (2.09) and not significant (p = 0.11). We conclude there is a Department effect on performance score, which dominates the Agency effect. (Note that this is an instance where different algorithms of different packages can yield different substantive conclusions, as HLM 7 estimated the Agency effect to be significant, albeit barely so.) The fact that the residual variance component has dropped from 212.41 in the null model to 171.11 in the random intercepts model (Model B) indicates that the added random effect of Department explains some of the previously unexplained within-groups residual variance. The fact that it is large (171.11) means

Table 4.19   Covariance Parameter Estimates for Model B (the three-level random intercepts model)

```
                    Covariance Parameter Estimates

                                         Standard        Z
Cov Parm      Subject          Estimate     Error     Value     Pr > Z

Intercept     Department*Agency   2.0869    1.6938     1.23     0.1090
Intercept     Department         82.0855   16.3698     5.01     <.0001
Residual                         171.11     4.1727    41.01     <.0001
```

there is considerable within-Agency variation in performance scores as yet unexplained by modeled effects, suggesting the need to add additional effects and predictors to the model.

Table 4.20 displays fixed effects for Model B. These effects are interpreted similarly to regression. There are four fixed effects, all significant. The upper-most one (61.74, p < 0.001 in HLM 7 but not estimated by SAS due to differ-ences in algorithms) is the estimate of the intercept, which is the mean performance score at level 1, controlling for other variables in the model. In descending order, next is the estimate of the slope of years of experience at level 1 (16.31, p < 0.001). Centered with a range from −.79 to +.56, a 0.1 increase in years of experience as coded increases mean performance score by 1.63 points. Next is the Gender effect: A one-unit increase in Gender (in other words, being female) is associated with a 6.64 drop in performance score below the mean of 61.74, controlling for other variables in the model. Last listed is the effect of the level 2 predictor, centered agency percent certified (AGCYPCCT), on the level 1 intercept, significant at the 0.34 level. This vari-able ranged from −.59 to +.30. A 0.1 increase in centered agency percent certi-fied increases mean performance score by 0.78 points. The t-ratios suggest that the level 1 effect of years of experience is stronger than that of either gender at level 1 or agency percent certified at level 2, controlling for other variables in the model.

Table 4.20   Fixed Effects for Model B (the three-level random intercepts model)

Solution for Fixed Effects

Effect	Estimate	Standard Error	DF	t Value	Pr > |t|
Intercept	61.7391	1.2100	0	51.02	.
YrsExper	16.3149	0.7006	3358	23.29	<.0001
Gender	-6.6355	0.4496	3358	-14.76	<.0001
AgcyPCCtrd	7.7966	3.6820	3358	2.12	0.0343

Type 3 Tests of Fixed Effects

Effect	Num DF	Den DF	F Value	Pr > F
YrsExper	1	3358	542.27	<.0001
Gender	1	3358	217.83	<.0001
AgcyPCCtrd	1	3358	4.48	0.0343

Model C

Table 4.21 displays SAS code for a three-level random coefficients model. For this example, employee performance score is still predicted as a fixed effect (in the MODEL statement) of YrsExper and Gender at level 1 and of AgcyPCCtrd (agency percent certified centered) at level 2. Both level 2 Agency and level 3 Department random effects on the intercept of score are also still modeled in the RANDOM statements. What is new is that the slope of the level 1 predictor, YrsExper, is now also modeled in the first RANDOM statement as a random effect of Agency at level 2, controlling for the level 2 effect of AgcyPCCtrd on the slope, modeled by the YrsExper*AgcyPCCtrd term in the MODEL statement.

As noted in the parallel section of Chapter 3, Model C is critically different from Model B by virtue of being a random coefficients model. In Model C, there will now be two random effects (the random effects on the intercept and on the slope of YrsExper). Because there is now more than one between-groups effect (not counting the residual within-groups effect), random effects may covary. It becomes important to specify the covariance structure type, which is both a starting point that, if good, will accelerate convergence of the iterative algorithm, and it is also a constraint on the solution. Covariance structure types were discussed in Chapter 2, where it was noted that the default in SAS (and SPSS) is quite different from that of HLM 7. By default, SAS imposes a variance components (VC) constraint that assumes zero covariances on the off-diagonal of the variance–covariance matrix, while HLM 7 estimates each coefficient in the entire covariance matrix. While the unstructured approach of HLM 7 may be more realistic, the VC approach may result in equally good model fit, even though reflecting a simpler (and therefore more parsimonious) model. SAS users may prefer to start by specifying an unstructured covariance type, and then use likelihood ratio tests to determine if simpler models like the variance components model yield significantly different model fit as measured by deviance (−2LL). For this example, the default VC model assuming zero covariance of random effects is presented.

Table 4.22 presents SAS 9.2 model fit statistics for Model C. Deviance ("−2 Res Log Likelihood") has dropped from 28094.9 in model B to 28041.5 in Model C.

Table 4.21   SAS Code for Three-Level Model C (the random intercepts model)

```
* Three-level hlm model;
PROC MIXED DATA=M3_2L COVTEST IC;
CLASS agency;
MODEL score0 = YrsExper Gender AgcyPCCtrd YrsExper*AgcyPCCtrd/SOLUTION;
RANDOM intercept YrsExper / SUBJECT= Agency*Department TYPE=VC;
RANDOM intercept / SUBJECT= Department TYPE=VC;
TITLE 'Three-level HLM model C in SAS 9.2';
run;
```

Table 4.22 Goodness-of-Fit Measures for Model C (the three-level random coefficients model)

```
                            Fit Statistics

                  -2 Res Log Likelihood         28041.5
                  AIC (smaller is better)       28049.5
                  AICC (smaller is better)      28049.5
                  BIC (smaller is better)       28058.0


                        Information Criteria

Neg2LogLike    Parms       AIC       AICC      HQIC        BIC       CAIC

   28041.5        4    28049.5    28049.5    28052.8    28058.0    28062.0
```

This is a reduction of 53.4, an amount significant at $p < 0.001$.[5] Likewise, in Table 4.23, the within-Agency residual variance component has dropped further, from 171.11 in Model B compared to 163.96 in Model C. This also suggests that the changes made in Model C reduced previously unexplained variance in performance scores at level 1.

In Table 4.23, there are three variance components other than the residual. These components reflect between-group variance in performance scores. The "Intercept" for the "Subject" = "Department*Agency" term is variance associated with the Agency effect, which has a small (2.52) and non-significant ($p = 0.094$) effect on mean performance score (the intercept).

In contrast, the Department effect ("Intercept" for "Subject" = "Department") is large (89.55) and significant ($p < .001$), showing that when the Department effect at level 3 is in the model, the Agency effect at level 2 is dominated. The "YrsExper"

Table 4.23 Covariance Parameter Estimates for Model C (the three-level random coefficients model)

```
                   Covariance Parameter Estimates

                                           Standard         Z
Cov Parm          Subject        Estimate     Error     Value    Pr > Z

Intercept    Department*Agency     2.5191    1.9133      1.32    0.0940
YrsExper     Department*Agency    63.7436   16.0678      3.97    <.0001
Intercept    Department           89.5501   17.7792      5.04    <.0001
Residual                          163.96     4.0766     40.22    <.0001
```

for the "Subject" = "Department*Agency" term is variance associated with the effect of Agency at level 2 on the slope of YrsExper at level 1. This random effect is moderately large (63.74) and significant (p < 0.001). That is, while Agency is not accounting for variance in mean performance score (the intercept), Agency is accounting for a significant variance component in the strength of relationship of YrsExper with score0 (the slope).

Table 4.24 displays fixed effects for Model C. There are now five fixed effects: all those for the previous model (see Table 3.16), plus a new one for the random effect of agency percent certified centered at level 2 on the slope of YrsExper at level 1. This added effect, YrsExper*AgcyPCCtrd, has the lowest t-ratio and is not significant. That is, Model C shows there is a significant random effect on the slope of YrsExper from Agency but not from AgcyPCCtrd at level 2. The "Intercept" is 61.74, indicating this is the mean performance score for the sample, controlling for all effects in the model. "YrsExper" is the estimate of the slope (15.55), quite close to that in Model B and interpreted similarly. Likewise, the "Gender" estimate is the level 1 slope of Gender. At −6.58, it is little changed from Model B. The "AgcyPCCtrd" estimate is the level 2 slope of agency percent certified centered (10.46) and as such represents the effect of that variable on the level 1 intercept.

We conclude that there is a Department but not an Agency effect in explaining variance in mean performance score. That is, with the Department effect in the

Table 4.24 Fixed Effects for Model C (the three-level random coefficients model)

Solution for Fixed Effects

Effect	Estimate	Standard Error	DF	t Value	Pr > |t|
Intercept	61.7440	1.2654	0	48.79	.
YrsExper	15.5530	1.1361	132	13.69	<.0001
Gender	-6.5796	0.4438	3225	-14.83	<.0001
AgcyPCCtrd	10.4630	3.9829	3225	2.63	0.0087
YrsExperi*AgcyPCCtrd	2.6426	5.9046	3225	0.45	0.6545

Type 3 Tests of Fixed Effects

Effect	Num DF	Den DF	F Value	Pr > F
YrsExper	1	132	187.40	<.0001
Gender	1	3225	219.84	<.0001
AgcyPCCtrd	1	3225	6.90	0.0087
YrsExperi*AgcyPCCtrd	1	3225	0.20	0.6545

model, there is no Agency effect on mean performance score. There is, however, an Agency effect on the variance in the strength of relationship (slope) of YrsExper as a predictor of performance scores. At level 1, YrsExper and Gender are both significant predictors of performance score. We also conclude that while agency percent certified has a significant fixed effect on mean employee performance score, it does not have a significant effect on the strength of relationship between years of experience and score. The model could be revised by dropping this non-significant effect. The remaining large residual variance component also indicates that additional effects and variables may be needed to fully explain the variance in employee-level performance scores.

SUMMARY

As this is intentionally an introductory guide and due to space limitations, this chapter has sought to present only some of the most important types of linear mixed models that may be implemented with SAS software. Multilevel modeling supports a vastly richer array of models and variations, some of which are treated in subsequent application chapters in this volume. These include cohort models, longitudinal and growth models, and cross-classified models not discussed in this chapter, to name a few. Moreover, generalized linear mixed modeling software extends many of these models to ones using nonlinear link functions where the outcome variable is not a normally distributed continuous variable (ex., to binomial, multinomial, ordinal, or Poisson distributions, implemented in GLMM in SPSS, in GLIMMIX in SAS, and built into HLM 7). Additional types of models are presented in comprehensive texts on multilevel modeling, which this work is intended to introduce and for which it may serve as a supplement. While only the surface of what is possible with linear mixed modeling is presented in this volume, the basic principles concerning types of effects, model assumptions, and inference logic apply to all types and hopefully serve as a stepping stone to more advanced work.

NOTES

1. ICC, as explained in Chapter 2, is the between-subjects variance component divided by the total of variance components in a VC null model. That ICC is significant in this example, which means that error is not independent, as required in OLS regression models, due to the clustering of scores within agencies.

2. For pedagogical reasons, the default REML output has been illustrated. However, keep in mind the admonitions ion Chapter 2 that model fit comparisons using likelihood ratio tests or information criteria measures when models differ in fixed effects require ML estimation.

3. Unlike HLM 7, SAS 9.2 does not provide a convenient likelihood ratio test of difference, but one may use the difference in −2RLL values shown in the SAS "Model Fit"

tables and for degrees of freedom, the difference in number of model parameters shown in the SAS "Information Criteria" tables, to determine the significance using a chi-square table. SAS code for providing likelihood ratio tests of difference is found at http://support .sas.com/kb/24/addl/fusion24447_1_contrasts.sas.txt.

4. SAS supports alternative syntaxes to achieve the same statistical output for Models A, B, and C discussed in this section. The RANDOM statement may express the department effect in a nested manner: Agency(Department) rather than as Agency*Department. However, since one cannot nest within continuous variables, first Agency and Department must be declared categorical in the CLASS statement. Also, if the Agency*Department term is used in the RANDOM statement, Department is not necessary in the CLASS statement. Leaving out the CLASS statement altogether also yields almost the same result: Covariance parameter estimates and standard errors are identical, fixed effect estimates, and standard errors are identical in large samples (since the loss of 1 degree of freedom does not affect results in a sample as large as that in the example); fit statistics except BIC (in this example, BIC is lower) will be the same also.

5. The likelihood ratio test follows a chi-square distribution for a value equal to the difference in −2LL between a model and a nested model, using degrees of freedom equal to the difference in the number of covariance parameters (shown in the default "Dimensions" table output in SAS 9.2). Let M3_2L be the name of the working dataset, Bdev and Cdev be the deviances for Models B and C, and df be the difference in number of covariance parameters between the two models. The SAS code for computing the likelihood ratio test is as follows:

```
DATA M3_2L;
Bdev = 28094.9;
Cdev = 28041.5;
df = 1
chi = Bdev-Cdev;
p = 1-probchi(chi,df);
RUN;
PROC PRINT data=M3_2L; run;
```

Introductory Guide to HLM With SPSS Software

G. David Garson

5

SPSS 19 frames multilevel analysis in terms of linear mixed modeling and offers two modules for its implementation: linear mixed modeling (LMM) and generalized linear mixed modeling (GLMM), for outcome variables with a normal distribution or for other distributions, respectively (though GLMM can also implement LMM models). These modules are chosen from the SPSS main menu bar by selecting Analyze, Mixed Models, and then either Linear or Generalized Linear. In this chapter, examples are given using the LMM module, which in SPSS syntax is the MIXED procedure. In the sections that follow, model explanations that are redundant with what is given in Chapter 3 (models in HLM 7) and Chapter 4 (models in SAS 9.2) are omitted. The reader may wish to refer to these earlier chapters, which cover the same models in the same order, yielding the same results using the same example, in which employee performance scores at level 1 are grouped by agency at level 2.

THE NULL MODEL IN SPSS

Recall that the purposes of the null model are to determine if there is an agency effect on mean employee performance scores, to determine if there is significant intraclass correlation (thereby showing that multilevel modeling is needed), and to compute baseline goodness-of-fit coefficients to be used later when comparing models. To do this, a model is constructed in which the intercept of scores (the mean of SCORE0) at level 1 is a random function of the grouping variable, Agency, at level 2. SPSS calls a grouping variable a "Subjects" variable.

The subjects variable, Agency (which carries agency id numbers), is entered in the opening "Specify Subjects and Repeated" window after selecting Analyze, Mixed models, Linear mixed from the SPSS menu bar. This window is shown in Figure 5.1. The researcher simply moves Agency into the Subjects area. If Agency is not entered as a subject here, it will not be available to enter as a random factor in the Random Effects window described below. As there are no repeated measurements

Figure 5.1 LMM Specify Subjects and Repeated window in SPSS 19

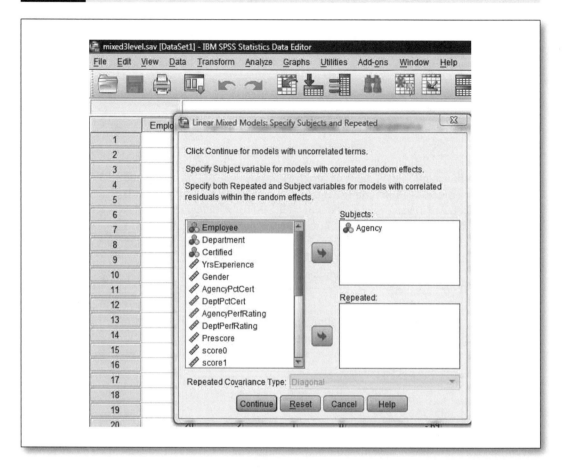

of performance score over time, nothing is placed in the "Repeated" area, and there is no need to specify a repeated measures covariance structure.

On clicking the Continue button shown in Figure 5.1, one is placed in the main LMM window shown in Figure 5.2. Here, one moves the outcome variable (score0) into the "Dependent Variable" text box. As a null model has no other predictors, there are no factors or covariates.

From the main LMM window, one may click the Fixed button to access the Fixed Effects window shown in Figure 5.3. As there are no predictors at either level in a null model, the only thing to do in this window is to make sure that the "Include intercept" checkbox is checked, as a null model does estimate the level 1 intercept. In more complex models having factors, in the multivariate cross-tabulation of all factors, if some cells have an empty count, thereby violating an

Figure 5.2   Linear Mixed Models window for the null model

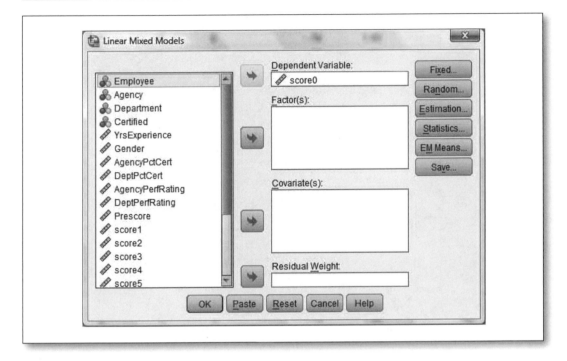

assumption of linear mixed modeling, it would be appropriate in this window to correct by selecting Type IV sums of squares. Click the Continue button to close the Fixed Effects window.

From the main LMM window, click the Random button to access the LMM Random Effects window shown in Figure 5.4. Here, one moves the grouping/ subjects variable Agency into the "Subjects/Combinations" area, indicating it is a random factor that may have an effect on the intercept of the outcome variable at level 1. Also, one checks the "Include intercept" checkbox to indicate that a level 2 intercept should be estimated. The covariance structure type is set to "Variance Components" in a null model, as VC models create additive variance components in the output described below for the random effect on level 1 intercepts of Agency as a subjects variable at level 2. Additivity allows the intraclass correlation (ICC) to be computed.

Before calculating estimates for the null model, it is possible to click the Estimates button in the main LMM window. This was discussed and illustrated in Chapter 2 in Figure 2.2. However, as noted there, this is rarely done if the researcher's model is able to converge on a solution. For this example, the defaults are accepted.

Figure 5.3   LMM Fixed Effects window for the null model

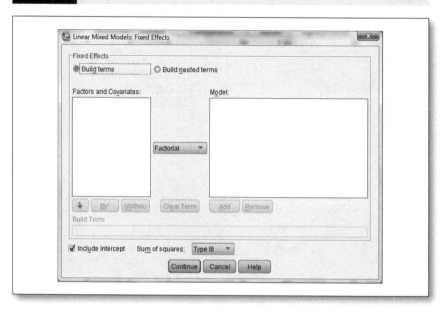

Figure 5.4   LMM Random Effects window in SPSS 19

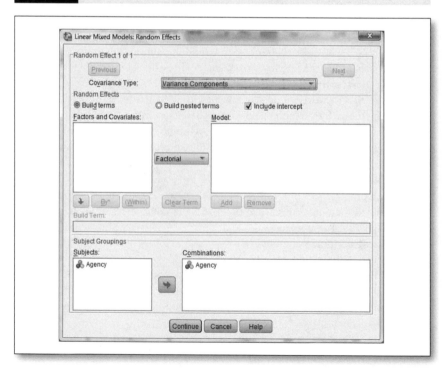

Finally, before running the null model, the researcher selects the output desired by clicking the Statistics button in the main LMM window and selecting the desired output, as shown for this example in Figure 5.5. If nothing is requested, the default is to print four tables: (1) Model Dimensions, showing two parameters to be estimated (the Fixed Effects level 1 intercept and the Random Effects level 2 intercept); (2) Information Criteria, showing the deviance and other fit measures discussed below; (3) Type III Tests of Fixed Effects, testing the level 1 intercept; and (4) Estimates of Covariance Parameters, giving the values or variance components associated with random effects at level 2. In addition, if "Descriptive statistics" are requested, one will get a table of the same name showing the count, mean, standard deviation, and coefficient of variation for score0 for each Agency id. This is useful for spotting outlier agencies. If Case Processing Summary is requested, this table shows just the count and marginal percentage for each level (id) of agency. If Parameter Estimates are requested, then for fixed effects one gets not only

Figure 5.5 LMM Statistics window in SPSS 19

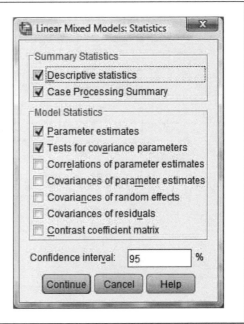

significance tests of fixed effects, but also the actual parameter estimates (in this example, the estimated level 1 intercept). If Tests for Covariance Parameters are requested, one gets not only the estimates of variance components for random effects, but also the corresponding significance tests.

SPSS transforms menu choices into syntax code, which may be viewed (and saved) by clicking the Paste button. The syntax for the selections described here for the null model is shown in Table 5.1 below.

Table 5.1 SPSS 19 Syntax for the Null Model

```
MIXED score0
/CRITERIA=CIN(95) MXITER(100) MXSTEP(10) SCORING(1) SINGULAR(0.000000000001)
HCONVERGE(0,
ABSOLUTE) LCONVERGE(0, ABSOLUTE) PCONVERGE(0.000001, ABSOLUTE)
/FIXED=| SSTYPE(3)
/METHOD=REML
/PRINT=CPS DESCRIPTIVES SOLUTION TESTCOV
/RANDOM=INTERCEPT | SUBJECT(Agency) COVTYPE(VC).
```

Clicking the OK button in the main Linear Mixed Models window runs the model. After running, the output window opens. Below the Case Processing, Descriptive Statistics, and Model Dimensions tables described above, the first output table is the Information Criteria table shown in Table 5.2.

Table 5.2 Information Criteria Table for the Null Model

Information Criteria[a]	
−2 Restricted Log Likelihood	29028.420
Akaike's Information Criterion (AIC)	29032.420
Hurvich and Tsai's Criterion (AICC)	29032.423
Bozdogan's Criterion (CAIC)	29046.738
Schwarz's Bayesian Criterion (BIC)	29044.738

Note. The information criteria are displayed in smaller-is-better forms.

a. Dependent variable: score0.

The "−2 restricted log likelihood" coefficient is identical to the deviance coefficient computed by HLM 7. As mentioned in Chapter 3, this value, also called −2LL, is used as a baseline when comparing other models in likelihood ratio tests to be described later in this chapter. However, SPSS 19 also gives four other goodness-of-fit coefficients, including one (CAIC) not reported by SAS 9.2. Later, when comparing models, the model with the lower coefficient will be considered as having better fit to the data. However, better fit is weighed against model complexity since for models with similar fit, the less complex (more parsimonious, with fewer parameters) model is usually preferred. The difference among fit coefficients partly reflects different ways of penalizing for lack of model parsimony. Information theory fit measures were discussed and compared in Chapter 2.

The next two tables in SPSS 19 output for the null model concern fixed effects, as shown in Table 5.3 below. The Type III Tests of Fixed Effects table contains an F-test of the model as a whole, which is significant for this example. The Estimates of Fixed Effects table shows the actual estimated level 1 intercept, representing the mean of employee performance score (score0) as modeled by Agency as a level 2 random factor. The intercept, representing mean score, is 55.60, identical to that in HLM 7 software.

Table 5.4 shows the output for variance components associated with Agency as a random factor. This is the heart of null model output. The variance components estimates are identical to those for HLM 7 software. Though SPSS 19 prints significance tests based on the Wald statistic and HLM 7 uses chi-square tests, the significance levels of the variance components are identical in substantive interpretation.[1] As discussed in Chapter 3, the fact that the variance component for the level 2 intercept is significant means that there is an agency effect. It also means the intraclass correlation (ICC) is significant, necessitating multilevel rather than ordinary regression modeling. Computation of the ICC, which turns out to be .43, is the same as discussed in Chapter 3.

Table 5.3 Fixed Effects for the Null Model

Type III Tests of Fixed Effects[a]

Source	Numerator df	Denominator df	F	Sig.
Intercept	1	126.946	2354.619	.000

a. Dependent variable: score0.

Estimates of Fixed Effects[a]

Parameter	Estimate	Std. Error	df	t	Sig.	95% Confidence Interval	
						Lower Bound	Upper Bound
Intercept	55.598248	1.145779	126.946	48.524	.000	53.330949	57.865547

a. Dependent variable: score0.

Table 5.4 Covariance Parameters for Random Effects in the Null Model

Estimates of Covariance Parameters[a]

Parameter	Estimate	Std. Error	Wald Z	Sig.
Residual	212.685750	5.189536	40.984	.000
Intercept [subject = Agency] Variance	161.940337	21.715530	7.457	.000

a. Dependent variable: score0.

Estimates of Covariance Parameters[a]

Parameter	95% Confidence Interval	
	Lower Bound	Upper Bound
Residual	202.753827	223.104190
Intercept [subject = Agency] Variance	124.512349	210.619049

a. Dependent variable: score0.

In summary, the SPSS analysis of the null model reaches identical conclusions to those of HLM and SAS. There is a significant agency effect on employee performance scores, signaling the need for multilevel modeling. Later models with additional predictors will need to improve upon the $-2LL$ value of 29028.42 and other fit measures for the null model, which serves as a baseline for comparison.

A RANDOM COEFFICIENTS REGRESSION MODEL IN SPSS 19

Next, as in Chapter 3 and 4, a random coefficients regression model is computed. This predicts performance score (score0) from level 1 predictors gender (coded 0 = male, 1 = female) and years of experience, entered as covariates. At level 2, there is still an agency effect as in the null model, but there are no other level 2 predictors. Agency as a random level 2 subject variable is used to model both the level 1 intercept of employee test scores (score0) and also the regression coefficients of the level 1 predictors. As in Chapters 3 and 4, this model explores whether the Agency effect discovered in the null model may be attributed in part to some agencies having more experienced employees than others, and whether the Gender effect modifies the relationship of experience with performance score.

To construct the model in SPSS, Agency is entered on the initial screen as a subjects variable, as previously shown in Figure 5.1. Next, in the main "Linear Mixed Models" screen, where in the null model only the dependent variable was entered, now the two additional covariates are also entered, as shown in Figure 5.6.

Figure 5.6   Linear Mixed Models window for the random coefficients regression model

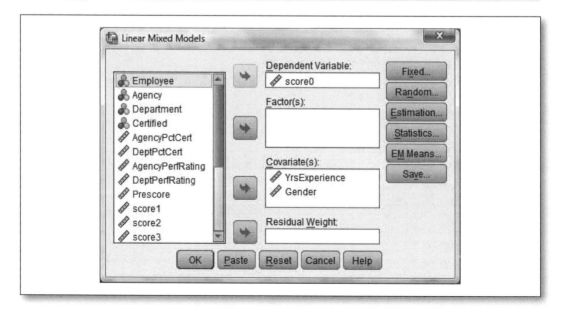

The Fixed button is clicked and, as shown in Figure 5.7, both covariates are entered as fixed effects. Level 1 intercepts are requested by default. Click Continue to return to the main LMM dialog.

Figure 5.7   LMM Fixed Effects window for the random coefficients regression model

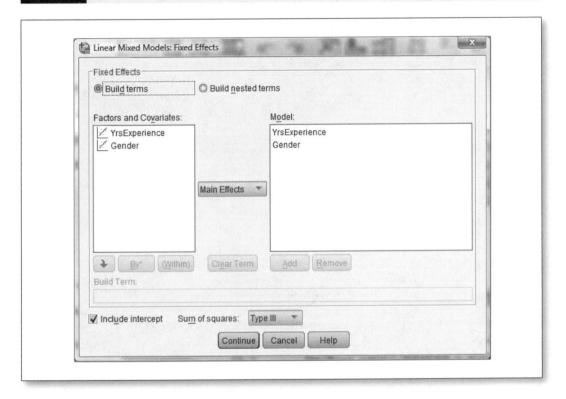

Next the Random button is pressed and Agency is entered as the Subjects/ Combinations variable as shown in the lower portion of Figure 5.8. By entering a level 1 variable in the upper portion of the window, it signifies that the regression coefficient for that variable should be modeled as a random effect of the subjects variable. In this example, only the b coefficient of YrsExper is modeled as a random effect of Agency. The "Include intercepts" checkbox is checked (not the default), requesting level 2 intercepts. Click Continue to return to the main LMM dialog.

In this example, settings listed under the "Estimation" button are the defaults, shown in Chapter 2, Figure 2.2. Also, the "Statistics" output settings are the same as for the null model, shown in Figure 5.5 above. Click "OK" in the main LMM window to run the model.

Figure 5.8 LMM Random Effects window for the random coefficients regression model

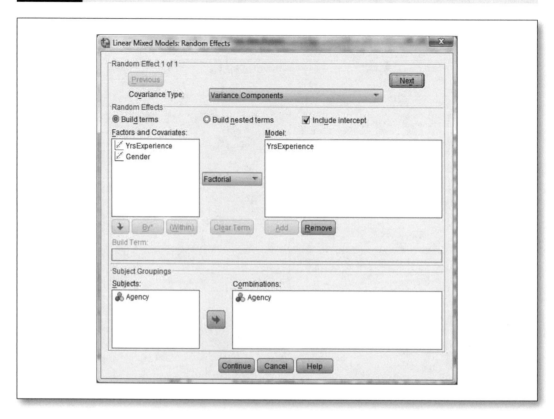

The SPSS syntax code for this model, created automatically through the menu choices above, is viewed by clicking the Paste button. The syntax for the random coefficients regression model described here is shown in Table 5.5 below.

Table 5.5 SPSS 19 Syntax for the Random Coefficients Regression Model

```
MIXED score0 WITH YrsExper Gender
/CRITERIA=CIN(95) MXITER(100) MXSTEP(10) SCORING(1) SINGULAR(0.000000000001)
HCONVERGE(0, ABSOLUTE) LCONVERGE(0, ABSOLUTE) PCONVERGE(0.000001, ABSOLUTE)
/FIXED=YrsExper Gender | SSTYPE(3)
/METHOD=REML
/PRINT=SOLUTION TESTCOV
/RANDOM=INTERCEPT YrsExper | SUBJECT(Agency) COVTYPE(VC).
```

As with the null model, SPSS 19 output leads with the "Information Criteria" table shown in Table 5.6. This contains the deviance (−2 restricted log likelihood), AIC, BIC, and related measures of goodness of fit, where lower is better. Deviance has fallen from 29028.42 in the null model to 28201.16 in the RC regression model. SPSS 19 does not provide a convenient likelihood ratio test, but the difference of 827.26 is significant when looked up in a table of the chi-square distribution.[2]

Table 5.6 Information Criteria table for the Random Coefficients Regression Model

Information Criteria[a]	
−2 Restricted Log Likelihood	28201.160
Akaike's Information Criterion (AIC)	28207.160
Hurvich and Tsai's Criterion (AICC)	28207.167
Bozdogan's Criterion (CAIC)	28228.635
Schwarz's Bayesian Criterion (BIC)	28225.635

Note. The information criteria are displayed in smaller-is-better forms.

a. Dependent variable: score0.

Table 5.7 shows the fixed effects output from SPSS 19 for the random coefficients regression model. Whereas the only fixed effect in the null model was the level 1 intercept, here there are three: the intercept, YrsExper, and Gender. All three are shown to be significant. The t-ratio values in the "Estimates of Fixed Effects" table show the two level 1 predictors (YrsExper and Gender) to be of roughly equal importance in predicting employee performance score.

Table 5.7 Fixed Effects Tables for the Random Coefficients Regression Model

Type III Tests of Fixed Effects[a]

Source	Numerator df	Denominator df	F	Sig.
Intercept	1	135.354	3163.219	.000
YrsExper	1	113.942	238.953	.000
Gender	1	3325.949	210.743	.000

a. Dependent variable: score0.

(Continued)

Table 5.7 (Continued)

Estimates of Fixed Effects[a]

Parameter	Estimate	Std. Error	df	t	Sig.
Intercept	59.390129	1.055965	135.354	56.243	.000
YrsExper	16.252392	1.051384	113.942	15.458	.000
Gender	−6.482813	.446567	3325.949	−14.517	.000

a. Dependent variable: score0.

Estimates of Fixed Effects[a]

Parameter	95% Confidence Interval	
	Lower Bound	Upper Bound
Intercept	57.301804	61.478454
YrsExper	14.169597	18.335187
Gender	−7.358386	−5.607239

a. Dependent variable: score0.

Table 5.8 displays the corresponding random effects tables for the random coefficients regression model. The residual component, representing within-agency variation in score0 not explained by the model, dropped from 212.69 in the null model to 163.78 in the RC regression model. This corresponds to a drop from 57% of the total of variance components to 46%. The RC regression model thus reduced the residual variance component by 11%, a drop of 19%. The Agency effect (component = 130.56) was much greater than that of YrsExper as a random effect (component = 63.25). All random effects were significant. That the residual component is significant means there is a significant amount of within-agency variation in performance scores unaccounted for by the model. That the agency effect is significant means the clustering of scores by agency accounts for a significant percentage (37%) of total effects. By a significant margin, some agencies have higher mean performance scores than others. That the random effect of Agency on slopes of YrsExper is 18% of total effects means there is a significant but weaker tendency for YrsExper to have a stronger effect on score0 in some agencies than others.

Table 5.8	Random Effects Tables for the Random Coefficients Regression Model

Estimates of Covariance Parameters[a]

Parameter	Estimate	Std. Error	Wald Z	Sig.
Residual	163.775537	4.074633	40.194	.000
Intercept [subject = Agency] Variance	130.561814	17.828167	7.323	.000
YrsExper [subject = Agency] Variance	63.253467	15.873108	3.985	.000

a. Dependent Variable: score0.

Estimates of Covariance Parameters[a]

Parameter	95% Confidence Interval	
	Lower Bound	Upper Bound
Residual	155.980988	171.959588
Intercept [subject = Agency] Variance	99.904470	170.626873
YrsExper [subject = Agency] Variance	38.679425	103.440035

a. Dependent Variable: score0.

A FULL RANDOM COEFFICIENTS MODEL

The full random coefficients model, also called the "intercepts-and-slopes-as-outcomes" model, has predictors at both levels in a two-level model. Both level 1 intercepts and level 1 slopes are predicted as random effects. In terms of the example, performance score (Score0) at level 1 is predicted by years of experience (YrsExper) and gender (Gender), also at level 1. The intercept of Score0 is also predicted as a random effect of Agency as the level 2 grouping variable and as effect of Agency percent certified (AgcyPctCert), a level 2 covariate. YrsExper was coded on a centered basis. For Agency percent certified, a new, centered variable was created (AgcyPCCtrd), as SPSS lacks HLM's ability to center predictors on the fly. The slope of YrsExper at level 1 was modeled as a random effect of Agency at level 2, and as an effect of AgcyPCCtrd. The SPSS syntax for this model is shown in Table 5.9.

Thus, the full RC model has the following settings:

1. On the initial "Linear Mixed Models: Specify Subjects and Repeated" screen, Agency is entered as the "Subjects" variable, as in Figure 5.1. This makes Agency available for selection as the "Subjects-Combinations" variable later on the "Random Effects" page. The subjects-combinations variable is the grouping variable defining level 2.

2. On the next "Linear Mixed Models" screen, Score0 is entered as dependent, and both level 1 and level 2 predictor variables (YrsExper and Gender from

level 1, and AgcyPCCtrd from level 2), are entered as covariates, similar to what is shown in Figure 5.6.

3. On the Fixed Effects page, all three predictors are entered (YrsExper, Gender, and AgcyPCCtrd) to model fixed effects similar to an OLS regression model. However, the interaction of AgcyPCCtrd with YrsExper is also entered (YrsExper*AgcyPCCtrd), to represent the effect of AgcyPCCtrd at level 2 on the slope of YrsExper at level 1. All employees in a given agency must have been assigned the same values on level 2 predictors (in this case, the AgcyPCCtrd score). Note that the intercept is requested, meaning the level 1 intercept.

4. On the Random Effects page, Agency is made the Subjects-Combinations variable and YrsExper is moved into the "Model" area, meaning the slope of YrsExper is to be a random effect of Agency. Note that the intercept is requested, meaning the level 2 intercept.

5. In output for this mode, the Information Criteria table, shown in Table 5.10, shows a deviance value (−2RLL) of 28156.79 and an AIC of 28162.79. This is somewhat lower and therefore a better fit than the corresponding values for the previous random coefficients regression model shown in Table 5.6.[3]

Table 5.9 SPSS 19 Syntax for the Full Random Coefficients Regression Model

```
MIXED score0 WITH YrsExper Gender AgcyPCCtrd
/CRITERIA=CIN(95) MXITER(100) MXSTEP(10) SCORING(1) SINGULAR(0.000000000001)
HCONVERGE(0, ABSOLUTE) LCONVERGE(0, ABSOLUTE) PCONVERGE(0.000001, ABSOLUTE)
/FIXED=YrsExper Gender AgcyPCCtrd YrsExper*AgcyPCCtrd | SSTYPE(3)
/METHOD=REML
/PRINT=CPS CORB G SOLUTION TESTCOV
/RANDOM=INTERCEPT YrsExper | SUBJECT(Agency) COVTYPE(VC).
```

Table 5.10 Model Fit Measures for the Full Random Coefficients Model

Information Criteria[a]	
−2 Restricted Log Likelihood	28156.792
Akaike's Information Criterion (AIC)	28162.792
Hurvich and Tsai's Criterion (AICC)	28162.799
Bozdogan's Criterion (CAIC)	28184.265
Schwarz's Bayesian Criterion (BIC)	28181.265

Note. The information criteria are displayed in smaller-is-better forms.

a. Dependent variable: score0.

The SPSS 19 "Estimates of Fixed Effects" table presents the main regression results (see Table 5.11), which are identical to those in SAS 9.2. The major inferences from this table are these:

- Modeling the slope of YrsExper at level 1 as an effect of the level 2 covariate AgcyPCCtrd does not significantly affect the slope of YrsExper, as shown by the term YrsExper*AgcyPCCtrd being non-significant. That is, an agency's percent of certified employees does not affect the strength of the relationship of years of experience to employee performance score.
- YrsExper is positively and significantly associated with performance score, controlling for other variables in the model. As the coefficients are identical to those in SAS, see Chapter 4 for further discussion of this point.
- Gender is negatively and significantly associated with performance score, controlling for other variables. Again, see further discussion of the identical coefficients in Chapter 4, which covers SAS.
- The percent certified in an agency (AgcyPCCtrd) at level 2 is a positive and significant predictor of performance score at level 1. Further discussion is found in the parallel section of Chapter 4.

Table 5.11 Fixed Effects for the Full Random Coefficients Model in SPSS 19

Estimates of Fixed Effects[a]

Parameter	Estimate	Std. Error	df	t	Sig.	95% Confidence Interval	
						Lower Bound	Upper Bound
Intercept	60.443214	.963634	141.843	62.724	.000	58.538274	62.348154
YrsExper	15.383420	1.154488	129.085	13.325	.000	13.099252	17.667589
Gender	−6.491237	.446287	3331.496	−14.545	.000	−7.366260	−5.616213
AgcyPCCtrd	30.973053	5.145435	142.078	6.020	.000	20.801549	41.144557
YrsExper * AgcyPCCtrd	−3.498515	6.262809	138.453	−.559	.577	−15.881630	8.884601

a. Dependent variable: score0.

The random effects table for the model is shown in Table 5.12. There are three covariance components: the YrsExper effect, the Agency effect, and the residual effect. The estimates are estimates of the variances of individual employees. The major inferences are these:

- The residual component is almost half the total of variance components, meaning that considerable within-agency variation in performance scores remains and the need for additional predictors is indicated.

- The "Intercept[subject=Agency]" parameter is the Agency effect on the level 1 intercept (mean score) after controlling for agency percent certified. That this component is significant means there remains considerable between-agency variation in performance scores, which might be explained by adding additional predictors. The mean intercept from the fixed effects table was a score of 60.4. The variance estimate from the random effects table is 101.4, equating to a standard deviation of 10.1. Controlling for predictors presently in the model, we expect that about 95% of agencies will have mean scores within plus or minus 2*10.1 = 20.2 points of 60.4.

- Compared to the previous random coefficients model, the present one, which adds AgcyPCCtrd as a level 2 predictor, reduces neither the residual component nor the years experience component. However, it does reduce appreciably the Agency effect (from 130.6 to 101.4), meaning the agency percent certified does explain some of the Agency effect, as one would expect.

- The "YrsExper[subject=Agency] component, while not as large as the Agency effect, is substantial and significant, indicating that YrsExper at level 1 also clusters by Agency, confirming the need to estimate its slope and its standard error as a random effect of Agency at level 2.

In sum, the full random coefficients regression model introduced a level 2 predictor, agency percent certified, which was found to be a significant predictor of employee performance score at level 1, though not significantly related to the strength of relation (slope) of the level 1 predictor, years of experience, with the dependent, employee performance score. The need for multilevel analysis in computation of slopes as well as intercepts at level 1 was confirmed (that is, a random coefficients model, not just a random intercepts model, is called for).

Table 5.12 Random Effects for the Full Random Coefficients Model

Estimates of Covariance Parameters[a]

Parameter	Estimate	Std. Error	Wald Z	Sig.	95% Confidence Interval	
					Lower Bound	Upper Bound
Residual	163.644388	4.070669	40.201	.000	155.857392	171.820441
Intercept Variance [subject = Agency]	101.366707	13.987790	7.247	.000	77.345735	132.847781
YrsExper Variance [subject = Agency]	64.771376	16.264732	3.982	.000	39.594787	105.956654

a. Dependent variable: score0.

THREE-LEVEL HIERARCHICAL LINEAR MODELS

This section presents a cross-sectional three-level hierarchical linear model based on the same SPSS data file, mixed3level.sav. The file contains a previously unused subject id code for Department as level 3, such that employees are nested within agencies, and agencies within departments. Data rows are sorted in this nested manner. We discuss three models: (A) the three-level null model, (B) a three-level random intercepts model, and (C) a three-level random coefficients model.

Model A

Table 5.13 shows SPSS syntax for the three-level null model in SPSS 19 (compare to the two-level null model in Table 5.1). In the null model, there are no predictors at any level, but the intercept of performance score at level 1 is modeled by the Agency effect at level 2 (signified by the second RANDOM statement, with Agency*Department as the subject). There is also a Department grouping effect at level 3 (signified by the first RANDOM statement, with Department as subject). As there are no predictors, the FIXED statement lists no variables. The MIXED command line identifies score0 as the dependent variable. The CRITERIA clause lists the default estimation settings. The METHOD statement indicates that the default estimation method, restricted maximum likelihood, has been selected. (REML and other estimation methods were discussed in Chapter 2.)[4]

Creating this SPSS syntax may be done directly in the syntax window or through the menu system illustrated in previous figures. If the latter, the id variables Agency and Department are entered as subject variables in the linear mixed models screen, which opens upon selecting Analyze, Mixed Models, Linear from the SPSS menu. For this example, click Continue and then enter Score0 as the dependent variable in the "Linear Mixed Models" dialog. For the null model, no variables are entered as factors or covariates. As there are no predictors, the Fixed button is ignored (though the "Include intercept" checkbox should be checked, which it is the default). Click the Random button and enter Agency and Department in the Subjects-Combinations area for Random Effect 1 of 2; also check the "Include intercept" checkbox to ask for the level 2 intercept; finally, accept Variance Components as the default covariance type, or select another. Then, click the Next button to repeat the process for Random Effect 2 of 2, this time entering only Department in the Subjects-Combinations area. Click Continue. Back on the LMM dialog screen, click the Statistics button and check the output wanted, including "Parameter estimates" and "Tests of covariance parameters." Then, click Continue. For this example, the Estimation button is not selected, thereby setting REML estimation as the default. Click "OK" to run the model.

The "Information Criteria" table presents key baseline measures against which later models to which predictors are added may be compared. The "−2 Restricted Log Likelihood" figure (28887.9) is what HLM 7 labeled deviance. It is "Restricted" because REML estimation was used. Other information criteria measures

Table 5.13	SPSS 19 Syntax for Model A (the three-level null model)

MIXED score0

/CRITERIA=CIN(95) MXITER(100) MXSTEP(10) SCORING(1) SINGULAR(0.000000000001)
HCONVERGE(0, ABSOLUTE) LCONVERGE(0, ABSOLUTE) PCONVERGE(0.000001, ABSOLUTE)

/FIXED=| SSTYPE(3)

/METHOD=REML

/PRINT=SOLUTION TESTCOV

/RANDOM=INTERCEPT | SUBJECT(Agency*Department) COVTYPE(VC)

/RANDOM=INTERCEPT | SUBJECT(Department) COVTYPE(VC).

Table 5.14	Model Fit Measures for Model A (the three-level null model)

Information Criteria[a]	
−2 Restricted Log Likelihood	28877.915
Akaike's Information Criterion (AIC)	28883.915
Hurvich and Tsai's Criterion (AICC)	28883.922
Bozdogan's Criterion (CAIC)	28905.391
Schwarz's Bayesian Criterion (BIC)	28902.391

Note. The information criteria are displayed in smaller-is-better forms.

a. Dependent variable: score0.

(discussed in Chapter 2) represent various ways to penalize for lack of parsimony (that is, for adding parameters) in the model. They serve a similar function as measures of goodness of fit, with lower being a better fit.

In the "Estimates of Covariance Parameters" table shown in Table 5.15, the residual component is little changed from that in the two-level null model in Table 5.4. However, the Agency component shrinks to a non-significant level once the Department component is added in the three-level model. (Note that this is an example where small differences between SPSS and SAS estimates lead to different substantive conclusions, since the Agency effect was still significant in the SAS model in Table 4.16.) The Department component accounts for over half of the total variance in performance scores at level 1. The residual within-group variance component is 212.41, a substantial quantity that reflects as-yet unexplained within-group variance. This is a baseline value that will decrease as predictors are added to the model.

Table 5.15   Variance Components for Model A (the three-level null model)

Estimates of Covariance Parameters[a]

Parameter	Estimate	Std. Error	Wald Z	Sig.	95% Confidence Interval	
					Lower Bound	Upper Bound
Residual	212.407129	5.173827	41.054	.000	202.504866	222.793602
Intercept [subject = Variance Agency * Department]	4.058242	2.271941	1.786	.074	1.354586	12.158200
Intercept [subject = Variance Department]	122.858865	23.482356	5.232	.000	84.472236	178.689491

a. Dependent variable: score0.

Model B

Table 5.16 shows SPSS syntax for the three-level random intercepts model in SPSS 19 (compare to the three-level null model in Table 5.13). The RANDOM statements for the Agency (level 2) and Department (level 3) random effects remain the same, as do all other statements except the MODEL command line and the FIXED statement, both of which list YrsExper and Gender at level 1 and AgcyPCCtrd (agency percent centered) at level 2 as predictors.

Creating the SPSS syntax for Model B follows the same steps as described above for Model A (the null model), except the three predictor variables are entered as covariates on the main "Linear Mixed Models" screen. The Fixed button is selected, all three predictors are entered as main effects in the "Model"

Table 5.16   SPSS Syntax for Model B (the three-level random intercepts model)

```
MIXED score0 WITH YrsExper Gender AgcyPCCtrd
/CRITERIA=CIN(95) MXITER(100) MXSTEP(10) SCORING(1) SINGULAR(0.000000000001)
HCONVERGE(0,
ABSOLUTE) LCONVERGE(0, ABSOLUTE) PCONVERGE(0.000001, ABSOLUTE)
/FIXED=YrsExper Gender AgcyPCCtrd | SSTYPE(3)
/METHOD=REML
/PRINT=SOLUTION TESTCOV
/RANDOM=INTERCEPT | SUBJECT(Department) COVTYPE(VC)
/RANDOM=INTERCEPT | SUBJECT(Agency*Department) COVTYPE(VC).
```

area, and the "Include intercept" checkbox remains checked. Entries under the Random button remain the same, as do those under the Statistics and Estimation buttons. Click "OK" to run the model.

Table 5.17 presents goodness-of-fit measures for Model B. Deviance is reported as "−2 Restricted Log Likelihood" and is lower (in the direction of better fit) compared to that in the null model. Specifically, deviance has dropped 783.06 points, from 28877.92 in the null model to 28094.86 in the random intercepts model. This is a significant difference, indicating that at least one of the added predictors is accounting for additional variance in employee performance score (see footnotes 2 to 4 for conducting the likelihood ratio test of difference in deviances). Likewise, information criteria measures such as AIC and BIC are also lower, in the direction of better fit.

Table 5.18 displays variance components (the random effects) for Model B. In a three-level random intercepts model, there are only three random effects: the between-groups Agency effect, the between-groups Department effect, and the within-groups residual effect. Of these, only the Department and Residual variance components are significant. The Department effect on the level 1 intercept (which reflects mean performance score) is large (82.08) and highly significant ($p = <.001$) but still represents only about a third of total variance. The Agency effect on the intercept, however, is small (2.09) and not significant ($p = 0.22$).

We conclude that there is a Department effect on performance score that dominates the Agency effect. (Note that HLM 7 estimated the Agency effect to be significant, albeit barely so.) The fact that the residual variance component has dropped from 212.41 in the null model to 171.10 in the random intercepts model (Model B) indicates that the added random effect of Department explains some of the previously unexplained within-groups residual variance. The fact that it is large (171.11) means that there is considerable within-Agency variation in performance scores as yet unexplained by modeled effects, even after controlling for

Table 5.17   Information Criteria for Model B (the three-level random intercepts model)

Information Criteria[a]	
−2 Restricted Log Likelihood	28094.862
Akaike's Information Criterion (AIC)	28100.862
Hurvich and Tsai's Criterion (AICC)	28100.869
Bozdogan's Criterion (CAIC)	28122.336
Schwarz's Bayesian Criterion (BIC)	28119.336

Note. The information criteria are displayed in smaller-is-better forms.

a. Dependent variable: score0.

Table 5.18 Variance Components for Model B (the three-level random intercepts model)

Estimates of Covariance Parameters[a]

Parameter	Estimate	Std. Error	Wald Z	Sig.	95% Confidence Interval	
					Lower Bound	Upper Bound
Residual	171.104130	4.172663	41.006	.000	163.118233	179.480999
Intercept [subject = Variance Agency * Department]	2.092675	1.696091	1.234	.217	.427378	10.246879
Intercept [subject = Variance Department]	82.081076	16.369624	5.014	.000	55.524658	121.338937

a. Dependent variable: score0.

AgcyPCCtrd as a level 2 predictor, suggesting the need to add additional effects and predictors to the model.

Table 5.19 displays Model B fixed effects. There are four fixed effects, all significant. The uppermost one (61.74, Sig. = .000) is the estimate of the intercept, which is the mean performance score at level 1, controlling for other variables in the model. In descending order, next is the estimate of the slope of years of experience at level 1 (16.31, Sig. = .000) Centered with a range from −.79 to +.56, a 0.1 increase in years of experience, as coded increases mean performance score by 1.63 points. Next is the Gender effect: a 1-unit increase in Gender (in other words, being female) is associated with a 6.64 drop in performance score below the mean of 61.74, controlling for other variables in the model. Last listed is the effect of the level 2 predictor, centered agency percent certified (AGCYPCCT), on the level 1 intercept, significant at the 0.36 level. This variable ranged from −.59 to +.30. A 0.1 increase in centered agency percent certified increases mean performance score by 0.78 points. The t-ratios suggest that the level 1 effect of years of experience is stronger than that of either gender at level 1 or agency percent certified at level 2, controlling for other variables in the model.

Model C

Table 5.20 displays SPSS syntax for a three-level random coefficients model. In this model, employee performance score is still predicted as a fixed effect (in the MIXED command and FIXED statement) of YrsExper and Gender at level 1 and of AgcyPCCtrd (agency percent certified centered) at level 2. Both level 2 Agency and level 3 Department random effects on the intercept of score are also still modeled in the RANDOM statements. What is new is that the slope of the level 1 predictor, YrsExper, is now also modeled in the first RANDOM statement

Table 5.19 Fixed Effects for Model B (the three-level random intercepts model)

Type III Tests of Fixed Effects[a]

Source	Numerator df	Denominator df	F	Sig.
Intercept	1	61.384	2603.321	.000
YrsExper	1	3429.040	542.272	.000
Gender	1	3430.662	217.829	.000
AgcyPCCtrd	1	146.153	4.483	.036

a. Dependent variable: score0.

Estimates of Fixed Effects[a]

Parameter	Estimate	Std. Error	df	t	Sig.	95% Confidence Interval	
						Lower Bound	Upper Bound
Intercept	61.738996	1.210029	61.384	51.023	.000	59.319700	64.158292
YrsExper	16.314897	.700609	3429.040	23.287	.000	14.941244	17.688550
Gender	−6.635448	.449585	3430.662	−14.759	.000	−7.516930	−5.753966
AgcyPCCtrd	7.797763	3.682726	146.153	2.117	.036	.519488	15.076038

a. Dependent variable: score0.

Table 5.20 SPSS Syntax for Model C (the three-level random coefficients model)

```
MIXED score0 WITH YrsExper Gender AgcyPCCtrd
/CRITERIA=CIN(95) MXITER(100) MXSTEP(10) SCORING(1) SINGULAR(0.000000000001)
HCONVERGE(0,
ABSOLUTE) LCONVERGE(0, ABSOLUTE) PCONVERGE(0.000001, ABSOLUTE)
/FIXED=YrsExper Gender AgcyPCCtrd YrsExper*AgcyPCCtrd | SSTYPE(3)
/METHOD=REML
/PRINT=SOLUTION TESTCOV
/RANDOM=INTERCEPT YrsExper | SUBJECT(Agency*Department) COVTYPE(VC)
/RANDOM=INTERCEPT | SUBJECT(Department) COVTYPE(VC).
```

as a random effect of Agency at level 2, controlling for the level 2 effect of AgcyPCCtrd on the slope, modeled by the YrsExper*AgcyPCCtrd term in the FIXED statement.

Again, creating the SPSS syntax for Model C follows the same steps as described above for Models A and B. What is new is that the interaction term YrsExper*AgcyPCCtrd is entered under the Fixed button to model the effect of AgcyPCCtrd on the slope of YrsExper. Also, under the Random button, for Random Effect 1 of 2 (the Agency effect), YrsExper is entered in the "Model" area, to model the Agency effect on the slope of YrsExper, controlling for other variables in the model. Click "OK" to run the model.

As noted in the corresponding sections of Chapters 3 and 4, Model C is critically different from Model B: There are now two between-group random effects (the random effects on the level 1 intercept of Score0 and on the slope of YrsExper). Random effects may now covary, making it important to specify the covariance structure type (see discussion of covariance structure types in Chapter 2). By default, SPSS imposes a variance components (VC) constraint that assumes zero covariances on the off-diagonal of the variance–covariance matrix, similar to SAS. However, HLM 7 estimates each coefficient in the entire covariance matrix. The unstructured approach of HLM 7 is often more realistic, but the VC approach may result in equally good model fit, even though it reflects a simpler (and therefore more parsimonious) model. SPSS users may prefer to start by specifying an unstructured covariance type, and then use likelihood ratio tests to determine if simpler models like the VC model yield significantly different model fit as measured by deviance (−2LL). For this example, the SPSS default VC model assuming zero covariance of random effects is presented.

Table 5.21 presents SPSS 19 model fit statistics for Model C. In the "Information Criteria" table, deviance ("−2 Restricted Log Likelihood") has dropped from 28094.9 in Model B to 28041.5 in Model C. This is a reduction of 53.4, an amount significant at $p < 0.001$. Likewise, in Table 5.22, the within-Agency residual

Table 5.21   Information Criteria for Model C (the three-level random coefficients model)

Information Criteria[a]	
−2 Restricted Log Likelihood	28041.493
Akaike's Information Criterion (AIC)	28049.493
Hurvich and Tsai's Criterion (AICC)	28049.505
Bozdogan's Criterion (CAIC)	28078.124
Schwarz's Bayesian Criterion (BIC)	28074.124

Note. The information criteria are displayed in smaller-is-better forms.

a. Dependent variable: score0.

variance component has dropped further, from 171.10 in Model B to 163.96 in Model C. This also indicates that the changes made in Model C reduced previously unexplained variance in performance scores at level 1.

In Table 5.22, there are three between-groups variance components (the Residual is within-groups), reflecting the between-group variance in performance scores. The "Intercept[Subject = Agency*Department]" term is the variance component associated with the Agency effect, which has a small (2.52) and non-significant (Sig. = .188) effect on mean performance score (the intercept). In contrast, the Department effect ("Intercept[Subject = Department]" is large (89.55) and significant (Sig. = .000), showing that when the Department effect at level 3 is in the model, the Agency effect at level 2 is dominated. That the Department-level (level 3) intercept is significant suggests that there may be level 3 predictors still unspecified, which would account for this Department effect. The "YrsExper[Subject = Agency*Department]" term is variance associated with the effect of Agency at level 2 on the slope of YrsExper at level 1. This random effect is moderately large (63.74) and significant (Sig. = .000). That is, while Agency is not accounting for variance in mean performance score (the intercept), Agency is accounting for a significant variance component in the strength of relationship of YrsExper with score0 (the slope), even controlling for AgcyPCCtrd (agency percent certified centered) at level 2.

Table 5.23 displays Model C fixed effects, of which there are five: all those for the previous model plus a new one for the random effect of AgcyPCCtrd at level 2 on the slope of YrsExper at level 1. This effect, added as YrsExperi*AgcyPCCtrd, has the lowest t-ratio and is not significant. That is, Model C demonstrates that there is a significant random effect on the slope of YrsExper from Agency but not

Table 5.22 Variance Components for Model C (the three-level random coefficients model)

Estimates of Covariance Parameters[a]

Parameter	Estimate	Std. Error	Wald Z	Sig.	95% Confidence Interval	
					Lower Bound	Upper Bound
Residual	163.963994	4.076614	40.221	.000	156.165532	172.151889
Intercept [subject = Agency * Department]	Variance 2.519141	1.913263	1.317	.188	.568556	11.161739
YrsExper [subject = Agency * Department]	Variance 63.744621	16.068125	3.967	.000	38.893849	104.473505
Intercept [subject = Department]	Variance 89.550123	17.779147	5.037	.000	60.683401	132.148567

a. Dependent variable: score0.

| Table 5.23 | Fixed Effects for Model C (the three-level random coefficients model) |

Type III Tests of Fixed Effects[a]

Source	Numerator df	Denominator df	F	Sig.
Intercept	1	62.180	2380.891	.000
YrsExper	1	132.281	187.400	.000
Gender	1	3382.038	219.844	.000
AgcyPCCtrd	1	128.919	6.901	.010
YrsExper * AgcyPCCtrd	1	133.655	.200	.655

a. Dependent variable: score0.

Estimates of Fixed Effects[a]

Parameter	Estimate	Std. Error	df	t	Sig.	95% Confidence Interval	
						Lower Bound	Upper Bound
Intercept	61.744035	1.265393	62.180	48.794	.000	59.214697	64.273373
YrsExper	15.552956	1.136130	132.281	13.689	.000	13.305623	17.800289
Gender	−6.579556	.443751	3382.038	−14.827	.000	−7.449603	−5.709509
AgcyPCCtrd	10.463015	3.982923	128.919	2.627	.010	2.582657	18.343373
YrsExper * AgcyPCCtrd	2.642591	5.904591	133.655	.448	.655	−9.035935	14.321117

a. Dependent variable: score0.

from the level 2 predictor, AgcyPCCtrd. The "Intercept" is 61.74, representing the mean performance score for the sample, controlling for all effects in the model. "YrsExper" is the estimate of the slope (15.55), quite close to that in Model B and interpreted similarly. Likewise, the "Gender" estimate is the level 1 slope of Gender. At −6.58, it is little changed from Model B. The "AgcyPCCtrd" estimate is the level 2 slope of agency percent certified centered (10.46) and represents the effect of that variable on the level 1 intercept.

From the three three-level models we can conclude that there is a Department but not an Agency effect in explaining between-group variance in mean performance score. That is, with the Department effect in the model, there is no Agency effect on mean performance score. There is, however, an Agency effect on the variance in the strength of relationship (slope) of YearsExperience as a predictor of performance scores. At level 1, YrsExper and Gender are both significant predictors of performance score. Also, while agency percent certified has a significant fixed effect on mean employee performance score (the level 1 intercept), it does not have a significant effect on the strength of relationship between years of experience and score (the slope of YrsExper at level 1). The model could be revised by dropping this non-significant effect. The remaining large residual variance component also indicates that additional effects and variables may be needed to fully explain the variance in within-group employee-level performance scores at level 1.

SUMMARY

As this is intentionally an introductory guide and due to space limitations, this chapter has sought to present only some of the most important types of linear mixed models that may be implemented with SPSS software. Multilevel modeling supports a far, far richer array of models and variations, some of which are treated in subsequent application chapters in this volume. These include cohort models, longitudinal and growth models, and cross-classified models not discussed in this chapter, to name a few. Moreover, generalized linear mixed modeling software extends many of these models to ones using nonlinear link functions where the outcome variable is not a normally distributed continuous variable (ex., to binomial, multinomial, ordinal, or Poisson distributions, implemented in GLMM in SPSS, GLIMMIX in SAS, and built into HLM 7). Additional types of models are presented in comprehensive texts on multilevel modeling, which this work is intended to introduce and for which it may serve as a supplement. While only the surface of what is possible with linear mixed modeling is presented in this volume, the basic principles concerning types of effects, model assumptions, and inference logic apply to all types and hopefully serve as a stepping stone to more advanced work.

NOTES

1. HLM reports standard deviations of the variance components, which are simply the square roots of the variance components. SPSS reports standard errors of the variance components, which are needed for the Wald tests since the Wald Z value is the covariance parameter estimate divided by its standard error. Confidence limits on the covariance parameter estimate are approximately the estimate plus or minus 1.96 standard errors.

2. The "Model Dimensions" table shows six parameters for the RC regression model and three for the null model, the difference giving the degrees of freedom for the chi-square table.

3. Unlike HLM 7, SPSS 19 does not provide a convenient likelihood ratio test of difference, but one may use the difference in −2RLL values shown in the SPSS "Information Criteria" tables and for degrees of freedom, the difference in number of model parameters shown in the SPSS "Model Dimensions" tables to determine the significance using a chi-square table.

4. For pedagogical reasons, the default REML output has been illustrated. However, keep in mind the admonitions in Chapter 2 that model fit comparisons using likelihood ratio tests or information criteria measures when models differ in fixed effects require ML estimation.

PART II

Introductory and Intermediate Applications

A Random Intercepts Model of Part-Time Employment and Standardized Testing Using SPSS

6

Forrest C. Lane

Kim F. Nimon

J. Kyle Roberts

The value of higher education has become more evident over recent decades, as those with a college degree earn nearly double the annual salary of those who do not (Zhan & Sherraden, 2011). However, rising costs of higher education have also made the affordability of such pursuits increasingly difficult. For example, the average annual cost of tuition at a 4-year public institution has risen 36%, from $10,463 in 2000 to $14,060 in 2009 (U.S. Department of Education, National Center for Education Statistics, 2010). This has generated mounting concerns regarding the impact of fiscal pressures for students. It has been reported that as many as 74% of undergraduates work an average of 25.5 hours per week while in school (Dundes & Marx, 2006). And as Riggert, Boyle, Petrosko, Ash, and Rude-Parkins (2006) suggest, "student employment is no longer an isolated phenomenon; it is an educational fact of life" (p. 64).

Given the preponderance of student employment in school, the question then for educational researchers is, how does part-time employment affect student academic performance? A number of recent studies have investigated this question, but the interpretation from these findings is generally mixed. For example, Astin (1993) suggested that working both full- and part-time has uniformly negative effects on the satisfaction of one's academic experience. However, others suggest that those who are employed but work less than 15 hours a week are more likely to graduate in 4 years (King, 2002) and demonstrate increased academic achievement compared to those who do not work at all (DeSimone, 2008). Dundes and Marx (2006) also found part-time work to be related to an increase in time spent studying and a higher GPA.

A potential problem in these and other similar studies is that systematic differences among these identified relationships across participants may exist as a result of nested data structures and can confound the interpretation of these relationships.

Many studies use ordinary least squares analyses, which assume error terms of independent variables are uncorrelated (i.e., the independence of observation assumption). In other words, differences in the outcome are believed to be independent of the institution from which they were drawn. If observations are independent, then error terms should be random and hence uncorrelated. In reality, variability explained at the individual or student level may be affected by environmental factors at each higher level of the data structure (e.g., students within schools, within districts, within states). Statistical models that ignore this hierarchical structure in the data may underestimate standard errors (Roberts, 2004). Failure to recognize these systematic differences may also result in the misinterpretation of effects because relationships across higher levels of the data can change not just in relative magnitude, but also in direction.

Linear mixed modeling (LMM) is a statistical approach that allows the researcher to examine hierarchical data without violating the independence of observation assumption. As such, it allows the researcher to correctly model correlated error. Furthermore, LMM provides for an efficient comparison of regression models across level 2 units because traditional OLS approaches would require the researcher to estimate and plot separate regressions for each level 2 unit (e.g., teachers, schools, states). Finally, LMM assumes a general linear model and can perform multiple types of analyses such as ANCOVA, regression (OLS), repeated measures, and multivariate analyses. This ensures that information is not lost through the analysis but instead the complexity of the relationships within the data is utilized by the researcher's statistical procedure.

Linear mixed modeling utilizes a model-building strategy so that meaningful comparisons can be made as predictors are added to the model. Although all models are relevant in LMM, we present a brief overview of only the simplest linear mixed models in this chapter. This includes a null model and one-way ANCOVA with random effects where students are nested within schools. In addition, we demonstrate the estimation of level 2 variance in the model through the calculation of the intraclass correlation coefficient (ICC). Finally, we use heuristic data to illustrate these methods and the differences in interpretation when compared to traditional OLS approaches (e.g., regression).

THE NULL LINEAR MIXED MODEL

Linear mixed modeling typically begins with a one-way ANOVA model, testing the influence of the level 2 grouping variable (e.g., school) on the dependent variable mean (e.g., test score mean). This is also sometimes referred to as the "benchmark model" because it will become the yardstick by which we will evaluate subsequent models. From this benchmark, the researcher builds more complicated models by adding one parameter at a time and evaluating the subsequent change in the model characteristics, determining which model specifications are warranted and which are of no benefit.

Given that LMM are evaluated at both the individual (e.g., level 1) and nested level (e.g., level 2), it is important to define the parameters at both levels in the analysis. The level 1 model equation is identical to a simple linear regression equation and represents the variance within the linear mixed model at the individual level. This equation is defined as follows:

$$Y_{ij} = \beta_{0j} + e_{ij} , \qquad (6.1)$$

where Y_{ij} represents the outcome for an individual student (i) within a school or other level 2 unit (j). Given that the null model is a baseline model and has no predictors, the outcome is identified by the intercept only, β_{0j} plus a random error component e_{ij} defined as residual (or individual) variation.

The intercept in the null model, β_{0j}, also represents the mean outcome for each level 2 unit and can be expressed as

$$\beta_{0j} = \gamma_{00} + u_{0j} , \qquad (6.2)$$

where γ_{00} is the grand mean and u_{0j} is the effect for each level 2 unit (e.g., random effect). These equations are generally written separately but can be combined to represent a full null model expressed as

$$Y_{ij} = \gamma_{00} + u_{0j} + e_{ij} , \qquad (6.3)$$

where u_{0j} is the group-level effect (level 2) and e_{ij} is the individual-level effect (level 1). The null model is a useful tool in its ability to provide both a point estimate and confidence interval around the grand mean.

INTERCLASS CORRELATION COEFFICIENT (ICC)

Having estimated the null model, one should examine the systematic variance as a function of the nested structure of the data. As such, the interclass correlation coefficient (ICC) provides an estimate of the proportion of the total variance that lies between groups in the outcome variable. The ICC (ρ) for a two-level model is defined as the proportion of group-level variance from the total variance, where τ_{00} represents the variance at level 2 and σ_e^2 represents the variance at level 1:

$$\rho = \frac{\tau_{00}}{\tau_{00} + \sigma_e^2} \qquad (6.4)$$

This is easily calculated by dividing the variance at the highest level (e.g., level 2 or τ_{00}) by the sum of the variances at the lowest and highest level (σ_e^2), which can be obtained from the information provided from the null model.

The intraclass correlation coefficient (ICC) may be important to the LMM evaluation process because, as noted by Kreft and de Leeuw (1998), a significant ICC demonstrates a violation of the assumption of independent observations (and hence of uncorrelated error). This violation indicates that OLS methods, which assume independence, should not be used. Lee (2000) suggested ICC greater than .10 as a cutoff criterion for this determination. However, Roberts (2002) argued that the absence of a significant ICC does not indicate that the assumption of independence has not been violated. For a more thorough discussion of the issue with using only ICC in determining the appropriateness of LMM, see Roberts, Monaco, Stovall, and Foster (2011).

ONE-WAY ANCOVA WITH RANDOM EFFECTS

Following the specification of the null model and assuming a sufficient level of variability present in the outcome at level 2, we begin a process of adding level 1 predictors (or parameters) to the model. Typically, only one variable (e.g., Variable X in the equation below) is added at a time.

$$Y_{ij} = \gamma_{00} + \gamma_{10}X_{ij} + u_{0j} + e_{ij} \qquad (6.5)$$

The result of this process is a set of coefficient estimates that are then interpreted somewhat like the results from OLS but with additional estimates of the variances and covariances that reflect the hierarchical structure within the data. From these estimates, the variability explained by the new predictor in the model (i.e., effect size) can be calculated by dividing the difference between the null (σ_{null}^2) and conditional model ($\sigma_{conditional}^2$) variances by the null model variance, as indicated by Snijders and Bosker (1999).

$$\sigma_{explained}^2 = \frac{\sigma_{null}^2 - \sigma_{conditional}^2}{\sigma_{null}^2} \qquad (6.6)$$

SAMPLE

To illustrate the null model and a one-way ANCOVA with random effects, we suppose that an educational agency is interested in the effect of part-time employment on student academic performance based on corresponding literature (Astin, 1993; Dundes & Marx, 2006; Pascarella & Terenzini, 2005; Riggert et al., 2006). For the purposes of illustration, a heuristic dataset was constructed from parameters discussed below to illustrate both OLS and LMM approaches.

This dataset contains scores from a total of 220 students within 22 schools on two variables, a standardized college entrance exam variable (Exam) and a variable indicating the average number of hours worked per week in a part-time job (Hrs). The design was fully nested with 10 students selected from each school, and all continuous variables were normally distributed.

The standardized college entrance exam (Exam) variable served as the dependent variable, and the number of hours worked (Hrs) served as the independent variable. Because part-time employment is generally considered less than 30 hours per week, students working less than this amount were sampled from the simulated population data, resulting in a mean of approximately 15 hours per week $(\bar{x}=15.05, SD = 6.93)$. In addition, students with below-average exam scores were sampled from the population data given that the literature suggests part-time employment may have an adverse effect on exam score performance. This resulted in a mean exam score of 1,050 out of a possible 2,400 $(SD = 209.40)$.

SOFTWARE AND PROCEDURE

A variety of statistical software programs are available for LMM, including HLM, MPlus, R, SAS, Stata, and SuperMIX. However, researchers and graduate students often use SPSS for many types of statistical analyses. Therefore, we demonstrate how SPSS can be used to conduct LMM using the MIXED module. This module is a default package available in most current versions of this statistical software. Linear mixed models can be estimated in SPSS with command language alone using the syntax editor. However, point-and-click methods are also available for those less familiar with this language or those who may not have access to the syntax feature through graduate versions of the software. We illustrate how SPSS syntax is generated through point-and-click methods to estimate fixed and random effects of the null and random intercepts model.

ANALYZING THE DATA

In order to use the MIXED module in SPSS, we selected ANALYZE → MIXED MODELS → LINEAR in the SPSS data editor (Figure 6.1). This opens a separate window from which the clustering or nesting structure within the data can be identified. Although more than two levels are possible with LMM, we illustrate only the two-level model.

The first step is to identify the nesting variable (e.g., school), which should be selected from the variable list and placed within the "subjects" line. This allows the MIXED module to identify the clustering effect within the data. In our example, individual-level data are nested within 22 different schools. Therefore, "school" is the clustering variable and should be selected so that the MIXED module will estimate variance at both the individual and school levels. Once the nesting variable has been identified, select "continue."

Figure 6.1   Illustration of the Mixed Module in SPSS

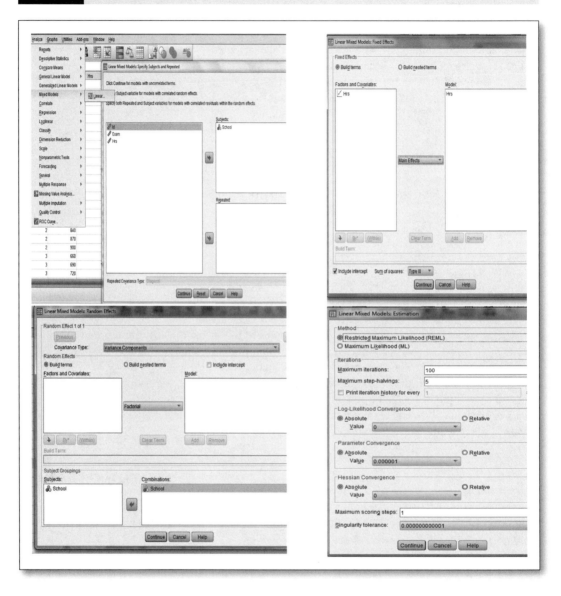

The identification of the cluster variable leads to a main screen for parameter estimation within the MIXED module. At this point, it is necessary to specify independent and dependent variables as well as variable parameters (e.g., fixed, random, estimation, statistics). These variables can be selected from the variable list on the left-hand side of the linear mixed models window and moved into the "dependent variable" and/or "covariates" lines. This generates syntax for estimating the LMM (MIXED), which is followed by the researcher's independent variables. If no independent variable is specified, as in the one-way ANCOVA with random effects, only the dependent variable is listed in the syntax. The command line is as follows:

MIXED Exam WITH Hrs

Once independent and dependent variables have been identified, fixed and random effects must be specified. The order in which these effects are specified is arbitrary in SPSS. In this example, we began by specifying FIXED effects. The number of hours a student works per week (Hrs) was selected as a possible predictor of standardized tests scores. Note that the default of "factorial" should also be changed to "main effects" under the drop-down box. The following fixed effects syntax is generated:

/FIXED = Hrs | SSTYPE (3)

Next, we can specify the random effects (i.e., variance components) by clicking the "Random" tab. It is not necessary to explicitly specify the level 1 residual variance because this component is estimated by default. However, it is necessary to specify the level 2 identification variable (i.e., school). In the random intercepts model, the only random effects are the intercepts (u_{0j}) themselves, estimated by the regression equation of each school. Therefore, we select "include intercepts" only in this window. In addition, the nesting variable (e.g., school) should be selected and moved to the "Combinations" line; then click "Continue." This step generates the following RANDOM effects syntax:

/RANDOM INTERCEPT | SUBJECT (School) COVTYPE (VC)

Following the specification of fixed and random effects, it is important to determine the estimation method used in the LMM. The most common estimations methods within LMM include maximum likelihood (ML) and restricted maximum likelihood (REML), both of which are available in SPSS. The primary difference between the two estimation methods is that ML does not adjust for the uncertainty in fixed effects and can lead to small variance estimates and liberal statistical tests. However, Raudenbush and Bryk (2002) suggest that the two methods will generally produce similar results as the number of groups at level 2 increases. Readers are directed to Ferron et al. (2008) or Raudenbush and Bryk for a more detailed discussion of these estimation methods. For the purposes of this chapter, maximum likelihood estimation with 100 iterations was selected in this example so that the Akaike information criterion (AIC) and Bayesian information criterion (BIC), as discussed in Chapter 2, can be compared directly. However, the number of iterations for both methods can be increased if the estimation process does not converge. This step will generate the following syntax:

/METHOD = ML

/CRITERIA = CIN(95) MXITER (100) MXSTEP(5)

SCORING(1)

Lastly, the statistics tab should be selected to obtain the fixed effects estimates, standard errors, and tests for the variances of the random effects. These can be obtained by selecting "parameter estimates" and "tests for covariance parameters" under the model statistics and produces the following syntax:

/PRINT = SOLUTION TESTCOV

OUTPUT AND ANALYSIS

Traditional Ordinary Least Squares (OLS) Approach

The primary research question in this heuristic example is, how does part-time employment affect student academic performance, as measured by individual scores on a standardized college exam score (e.g., SAT)? Given this question, we first illustrate the traditional OLS approach (e.g., regression) to evaluate the statistical and practical significance of this relationship. For later comparison purposes, one intercept and one weight (e.g., b) for each independent variable or exam score would be computed and evaluated across all students. As such, exam scores would be modeled as a linear equation of hours worked per week (Hrs) plus a random error component:

$$Exam = \beta_0 + \beta_1 * (Hrs)_i + e_i \qquad (6.7)$$

In this equation, β_0 is the exam score for a student who works zero hours per week (intercept), β_1 is the rate of change in the exam score for every 1 additional hour worked, and e_i is the unique error variance associated with an individual i. As such, the following syntax was specified in SPSS to evaluate this relationship:

REGRESSION

/MISSING LISTWISE

/STATISTICS COEFF OUTS R ANOVA

/CRITERIA= PIN (.05) POUT (.10)

/NOORIGIN

/DEPENDENT Exam

/METHOD=ENTER Hrs./

The result of this OLS analysis suggests the number of part-time hours a student is employed explains approximately 49% of the variability of exam scores ($R^2 = .486$). This finding was statistically significant ($p < .001$) and would likely be characterized as strong by most social science researchers. Given the model significance, the unstandardized coefficient (b) for the slope of hours worked revealed that exam scores increased approximately 21 points for each additional part-time hour of work per week (Table 6.1). The results from Table 6.1 and Figure 6.2 also reveal coefficients with low standard errors. This would suggest that the relationship between exam scores and hours worked is positive, meaning that when students are employed in part-time jobs requiring more hours, they tend to do better on standardized college exams. This may lead the uninformed researcher to conclude that the results from these data support prior findings in the literature (DeSimone, 2008; King, 2002). However, this interpretation would be incorrect if the hierarchical structure of the data was ignored. A best fit least squares regression line to the data illustrates this point (Figure 6.2).

The potential problem of the OLS regression model is that only one error term is generated to describe the variability of the students' actual test score from their predicted test score. This can underestimate standard error and may not be appropriate given the between-student differences in test scores within schools. As such, the interpretation of results for these data is confounded in the nested structure of the data. Therefore, the data are refit into an LMM and contrasted to the results produced through OLS regression.

Figure 6.2   Raw data compared to group regression

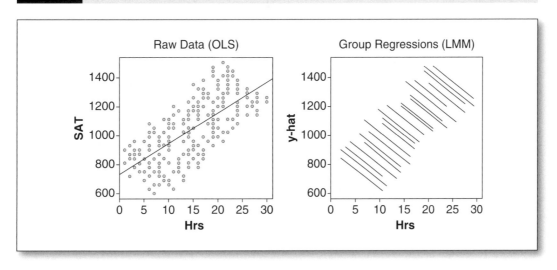

| Table 6.1 | OLS Regression Results for Heuristic Data |

	SS	df	MS	F	p	Multiple R^2
Regression	4664379.185	1	4664379.185	205.894	<.001	.486
Residual	4938620.815	218	22654.224			
Total	9603000.000	219				
	b	Error	β	t	p	
Intercept	733.156	24.301		30.169	<.001	
Hrs	21.059	1.468	.697	14.349	<.001	

LINEAR MIXED MODEL (LMM) APPROACH

We begin the LMM by specifying a null model or benchmark model (M_0) with only the nesting variable identified and no predictors.

$$Exam_{ij} = \gamma_{00} + u_{0j} + e_{ij} \tag{6.8}$$

The following SPSS syntax was used in the estimation of level 1 and level 2 variance in the model:

MIXED Exam

/CRITERIA = CIN(95) MXITER (100) MXSTEP(5) SCORING(1)

/FIXED= | SSTYPE (3)

/METHOD = ML

/PRINT= SOLUTION TESTCOV

/RANDOM = INTERCEPT | SUBJECT (School) COVTYPE (VC).

From the output, we see that the intercept of the null model taken from the estimates of fixed effects is 1050.00 (Figure 6.3). This value is interpreted as the grand mean of the dependent variable "Exam," and the standard deviation of all of the individual group means around this grand mean is 188.15 (i.e., variance estimate or $\sqrt{35400}$). Note that in our example, the intercept of the null model is the same as the mean of the dependent variable. However, such values will not exactly match when group sizes differ since LMM effects are estimated via an empirical Bayes (EB) estimation procedure (Roberts, 2004). In the EB algorithm, estimates that are far away from the mean will be "shrunk" so as to downplay their influence on the entire dataset.

Figure 6.3	SPSS output for LMM null model with no predictors

Fixed Effects

Information Criteria[a]

−2 Log Likelihood	2.691E3	chi-square
Akaike's Information Criterion (AIC)	2.697E3	
Hurvich and Tsai's Criterion (AICC)	2.698E3	
Bozdogan's Criterion (CAIC)	2.711E3	Grand Mean β_{01}
Schwarz's Bayesian Criterion (BIC)	2.708E3	

a. Dependent Variable: Exam.

Estimates of Fixed Effects[a]

Parameter	Estimate	Std. Error	df	t	Sig.	95% Confidence Interval	
						Lower Bound	Upper Bound
Intercept	1050.00	40.578207	22	25.876	.000	965.845949	1134.154051

a. Dependent Variable: Exam.

Level 1 Variance Estimate τ_{00}

Covariance Parameters

Level 2 Variance Estimate σ^2

Estimates of Covariance Parameters[a]

Parameter	Estimate	Std. Error	Wald Z	Sig.	95% Confidence Interval	
					Lower Bound	Upper Bound
Residual	8250.00	829.156198	9.950	.000	6774.932531	1.004623E4
Intercept Variance [subject = School]	35400.00	1.092256E4	3.241	.001	1.933604E4	6.480954E4

a. Dependent Variable: Exam.

In this example, we see from this null model M_0 that the ICC (ρ) is large ($\rho = .811$), indicating a school effect.

$$\rho = \frac{\tau_{00}}{\tau_{00} + \sigma_{e0}^2} = \frac{35400}{(35400 + 8250)} = .811 \qquad (6.7)$$

Having built our null model, we add our one predictor (Hrs) to the model (M_1) in order to estimate the fixed effect for the "Hrs" variable. In doing so, we have produced the linear mixed model expressed as

$$Exam_{ij} = \gamma_{00} + \gamma_{10}Hrs_{ij} + u_{0j} + e_{ij} \qquad (6.8)$$

where γ_{00} is the grand mean, γ_{10} is the rate of change in exam scores per the number of hours worked, u_{0j} is the group-level effect (level 2), and e_{ij} is the individual-level effect (level 1).

The following syntax was specified in SPSS to model this additional parameter:

MIXED Exam WITH Hrs

/CRITERIA = CIN(95) MXITER (100) MXSTEP(5) SCORING(1)

/FIXED= Hrs| SSTYPE (3)

/METHOD = ML

/PRINT= SOLUTION TESTCOV

/RANDOM = INTERCEPT | SUBJECT (School) COVTYPE (VC).

The estimate for the intercept (or average intercept) has now changed from 1050.00 to 1432.726 with an SD of 351.08, and the slope for the "Hrs" predictor variable is –25.438 (Figure 6.4). This change is a result of examining the regression equation for each school rather than as one equation for all individuals. If we had just the results from the OLS regression, we would have been led to believe that as students work more hours in part-time jobs, they tend to do better on standardized college exams. The results of the multilevel model illustrate exactly the opposite. Students decrease about 25 points in their exam scores for each additional part-time hour worked.

This relationship, as illustrated earlier in Figure 6.2, shows the predicted regression lines for each of the 22 schools. Because the variable "Hrs" was modeled as a fixed effect, with no random effects, all of the slope coefficients remain the same for each group or school (parallel lines). The only random effect included is the random effect for the intercept. Interpretation of this model is relatively straightforward. It simply states that as students work more hours,

Figure 6.4 SPSS output for LMM random intercepts model with level 1 predictor

Fixed Effects

Information Criteria[a]

chi-square

-2 Log Likelihood	2.486E3
Akaike's Information Criterion (AIC)	2.494E3
Hurvich and Tsai's Criterion (AICC)	2.494E3
Bozdogan's Criterion (CAIC)	2.511E3
Schwarz's Bayesian Criterion (BIC)	2.507E3

Slope of Hrs, β_{01}

a. Dependent Variable: Exam.

Estimates of Fixed Effects[a]

Parameter	Estimate	Std. Error	df	t	Sig.	95% Confidence Interval	
						Lower Bound	Upper Bound
Intercept	1432.726	77.179367	24.193	18.564	.000	1273.502828	1591.948930
Hrs	-25.437	1.229866	201.742	-20.684	.000	-27.863014	-23.012933

a. Dependent Variable: Exam.

Level 1 Variance Estimate τ_{00}

Covariance Parameters

Level 2 Variance Estimate σ^2

Estimates of Covariance Parameters[a]

Parameter	Estimate	Std. Error	Wald Z	Sig.	95% Confidence Interval	
					Lower Bound	Upper Bound
Residual	2.546946E3	256.292935	9.938	.000	2091.054987	3102.230694
Intercept Variance [subject = School]	1.232590E5	3.765170E4	3.274	.001	6.773356E4	2.243023E5

a. Dependent Variable: Exam.

their scores on the college entrance exam tend to go down, but each school has a different level from which they started (or a different intercept). Furthermore, this variable is considered relevant to the model given that is both statistically significant ($p < .001$) and able to explain approximately 69.12% of the level 1 variance in the outcome:

$$\sigma^2_{explained} = \frac{\sigma^2_{null} - \sigma^2_{conditional}}{\sigma^2_{null}} = \frac{8250 - 2546.94}{8250} = 69.12\% \qquad (6.9)$$

In testing this model, we also consider three statistics. The first is the chi-square (χ^2) model fit statistic. In comparing Models M_0 and M_1, we see that the difference in the chi-square is 205 (i.e., 2691 – 2486). If we consider that the difference between the two models is the simple addition of one parameter (the fixed effect for "Hrs"), we can compute whether or not the addition of the parameter improves the overall model fit by a statistically significant amount. In testing one parameter (or degree of freedom) on a chi-square value of 205, we see that this value is statistically significant ($p < .001$). We can therefore conclude that the addition of the "Hrs" variable improved model fit, or lowered the deviance, by a statistically significant amount, and the addition of this parameter is needed.

The other two model fit indices are the AIC and the BIC. Smaller values of AIC and BIC indicate better fit, whereas higher values indicate less adequate fit. The AIC penalizes the fit of a model for the number of parameters being estimated, while the BIC applies a greater penalty for models with more parameters (West, Ryu, Kwok, & Cham, 2011). In this example, both AIC and BIC decreased, suggesting that the addition of the variable Hrs produced a better fit than the previous model and is therefore warranted in the interpretation of the LMM.

CONCLUSION

The reality for researchers in the educational and social sciences is that data are often nested within higher-level structures. Ordinary least squares analyses do not take into consideration correlated error within these structures. As such, the purpose of this chapter was to provide a brief introduction to the potential problems associated with violations to the assumption of observation independence and how linear mixed modeling can be implemented to model correlated errors in the data.

Three models were presented to illustrate this point, along with the differences in interpretation of each: a least squares model, an LMM null model, and a model with a one-way ANCOVA with random effects and one level 1 predictor. The results from this heuristic dataset demonstrate how different statistical approaches can produce varied results. Specifically, the intercepts for each of the j or level 2 units changed as a result of the linear mixed model approach. In addition, the direction of the slopes for each of the j or level 2 units was negative rather than positive, as first interpreted in the OLS regression model. This illustrates why linear mixed modeling should be considered when the data are nested. Below, we provide a sample write-up for the null model and a one-way ANCOVA with random effect with one level 1 predictor.

SAMPLE WRITE-UP

Our aim in the heuristic dataset was to examine the effect of part-time employment on students' scores on standardized college entrance exams within a sample, given its relevance in the literature (Astin, 1993; Dundes & Marx, 2006; Pascarella & Terenzini, 2005; Riggert et al., 2006). A linear mixed model was specified in SPSS to test the relationship between the number of part-time hours worked (level 1 predictor variable) and exam scores (level 1 criterion variable).

First, a null or unconditional model was specified to determine the amount of variance that existed between and within institutions. The results of this null model (M_0) suggested that students generally scored below the national average ($\beta_{00} = 1050$, 95%CI [965.85, 1134.15]) with a standard deviation of 188.15. This exam score was statistically different from zero ($t = 25.876$, $p < .001$). The examination of the level 1 and level 2 variance components with no predictors revealed a high ICC ($\rho = .811$). This suggests that 81% of the variance in exam scores lies within institutions at the student level, and 19% of the variance lies at the student level (i.e., between students within schools).

Table 6.2 Results of Multilevel Models

	M_0: Null		M_1: + Hours	
	estimate	*S.E.*	*estimate*	*S.E.*
Fixed Effects:				
Intercept	1050	40.578	1432.726	77.179
Hours			−25.438	1.230
Random Effects:				
σ_e^2	8250		2546.946	
τ_{00}	35400		123259.042	
Fit:				
χ^2	2691		2486	
AIC	2697		2494	
BIC	2708		2507	

Because variance existed at both individual and institutional levels of the data, the number of part-time hours worked as a student was then added at the individual level (M_1) to determine the amount of additional variance between students within schools explained by this variable. Unlike the OLS model, the unstandardized regression coefficient in the linear mixed model was negative (Figure 6.2) but still statistically significant (b = -25.44, $p < .001$). This suggested that students' exam scores were actually lower when students worked additional part-time hours, controlling for the school effect. Furthermore, the inclusion of the level 1 Hrs variable was able to explain approximately 69% of the residual error in the null model. Given that these coefficients are statistically significant, we conclude the effect of hours worked on exam score is negative in the LMM model and opposite of what is implied by the OLS model.

REFERENCES

Astin, A. W. (1993). *What matters in college?* San Francisco: Jossey-Bass.

Bliming, G. S., Pascarella, E. T., & Terenzini, P. T. (1996). Students' out-of-class experiences and their influence on learning and cognitive development: A literature review. *Journal of College Student Development, 37,* 149–162.

Coyle, T., Snyder, A., Pillow, D., & Kochunov, P. (2011). SAT predicts GPA better for high-ability students: Implications for Spearman's law of diminishing returns. *Personality and Individual Differences, 50*, 470–474.

DeSimone, J. S. (2008). *The impact of employment during school on college student academic performance* (NBER Working paper No/4006). Cambridge, MA: National Bureau of Economic Research.

Driscoll, D., Halcoussis, D., & Svorny, S. (2007). Gains in standardized test scores: Evidence of diminishing returns to achievement. *Economics of Educational Review, 27*, 211–220.

Dundes, L., & Marx, J. (2006). Balancing work and academics in college: Why do students working 10 to 19 hours per week excel? *Journal of College Student Retention, 8*, 107–120.

Ferron, J. M., Hogarty, K. Y., Dedrick, R. F., Hess, M. R., Niles, J. D., & Kromrey, J. D. (2008). Reporting results from multilevel analyses. In A. A. O'Connel & D. B. McCoach (Eds.), *Multilevel modeling of educational data.* Charlotte, NC: Information Age Publishing.

Harrison, D. M., & Raudenbush, S. W. (2006). Linear regression and hierarchical linear models. In J. L. Green, G. Camilli, P. B. Elmore, A. Skukauskaite, and E. Grace (Eds.), *Handbook of complementary methods in education research* (pp. 411–426). Mahwah, NJ: Lawrence Erlbaum.

King, J. E. (2002). *Crucial choices: How students' financial decisions affect their academic success.* Washington, DC: Center for Policy Analysis at the American Council on Education.

Kreft, I., & de Leeuw, J. (1998). *Introducing multilevel modeling.* Thousand Oaks, CA: Sage.

Lee, V. E. (2000). Using hierarchical linear modeling to study social contexts: The case of school effects. *Educational psychologist, 35*, 125–141.

Pascarella, E. T., & Terenzini, P. T. (2005). *How college affects students* (Vol. 2). San Francisco: Jossey-Bass.

Raudenbush, S. W., & Bryk, A. S. (2002). *Hierarchical linear models: Applications and data analysis methods* (2nd ed.). Thousand Oaks, CA: Sage.

Riggert, S. C., Boyle, M., Petrosko, J. M., Ash, D., & Rude-Parkins, C. (2006). Student employment and higher education: Empiricism and contradiction. *Review of Educational Research, 76*, 63–92.

Roberts, J. K. (2002). The importance of the intraclass correlation in multilevel and hierarchical linear modeling designs. *Multiple Linear Regression Viewpoints, 28*, 19–31.

Roberts, J. K. (2004). An introductory primer on multilevel and hierarchical linear modeling. *Learning Disabilities: A Contemporary Journal, 2*, 30–38.

Roberts, J. K., Monaco, J. P., Stovall, H., & Foster, V. (2011). Explained variance in multilevel models. In J. J. Hox & J. Kyle Roberts (Eds.), *The handbook of advanced multilevel analysis* (pp. 219–230). New York: Routledge.

Rothstein, J. M. (2004). College performance predictions and the SAT. *Journal of Econometrics, 121*, 297–317.

Snijders, T., & Bosker, R. (1999). Multilevel analysis: An introduction to basic and advanced multilevel modelling. London: Sage.

U.S. Department of Education, National Center for Education Statistics. (2010). *The condition of education 2010* (NCES 2010-028). Washington, DC: U.S. Government Printing Office.

West, S. G., Ryu, E., Kwok, O., & Cham, H. (2011). Multilevel modeling: Current and future applications in personality research. *Journal of Personality, 79*, 2–50.

Zhan, M., & Sherraden, M. (2011). Assets and liabilities, educational expectations, and children's college degree attainment. *Children and Youth Services Review, 33*, 845–854.

A Random Intercept Regression Model Using HLM

7

Cohort Analysis of a Mathematics Curriculum for Mathematically Promising Students

Carissa L. Shafto

Jill L. Adelson

The research focus of this study was on the effectiveness of a mathematics curriculum for mathematically promising elementary school students, Project M^3: Mentoring Mathematical Minds. All students were identified as mathematically promising prior to participation in the program using multiple criteria, including the Naglieri Nonverbal Ability Test (NNAT; Harcourt Brace Education Measurement, 1997) and the math scale of the Scales for Rating the Behavioral Characteristics of Superior Students (SRBCSS; Gavin, 2005). The development of the curriculum and the initial results from using the curriculum with intervention students compared to students who had "mathematics as usual" are reported in Gavin, Casa, Adelson, Carroll, and Sheffield (2009). Given the lack of mathematics curriculum that is challenging, in-depth, and research-based for mathematically promising elementary students, Gavin et al. sought to both develop and research such a curriculum. Because the curriculum is delivered within classrooms, with groups of students in each school being taught by different teachers, the research lends itself to multilevel modeling, which accounts for the nested nature of the data.

The Project M^3 curriculum combines exemplary teaching practices in both mathematics and gifted education literature (Gavin et al., 2007). Specifically, the curriculum uses the National Council of Teacher of Mathematics (NCTM) content standards (2000) and includes 12 curriculum units, 4 for each grade level from third through fifth that are both accelerated (i.e., address standards one to two grade levels above students' current grade) and enriched (e.g., go more in depth, address standards not typically addressed in the "mathematics as usual" curriculum). For each grade level, the Project M^3 curriculum has a unit addressing (a) number and operations, (b) algebraic reasoning, (c) geometry and measurement, and (d) data analysis and probability. At each grade level, students completed the Project M³ units as well as compacted lessons addressing any additional mathematics curriculum standards that were not addressed by the Project M³ curriculum, as the Project M³ units were not designed to be a comprehensive curriculum. In addition, the Project M³ units also focus on NCTM process skills, with an emphasis on verbal and written communication as well as problem solving. More details about the Project M³ curriculum and evidence of pre- and posttest results are discussed in Gavin et al. (2007).

The intervention (the Project M³ curriculum) was implemented over the course of 5 years with three groups: a Control Group, Intervention Group 1, and Intervention Group 2 (see Table 7.1). All students were identified as mathematically promising using the same methods, and all students were in the same schools but were cohorts going through third through fifth grade during different years of the project. The Control Group was identified as mathematically promising in third grade in the year prior to the intervention so that they were in the same schools but there was no contamination of the Project M³ curriculum. Students in the Control Group received "mathematics as usual." Although not all Control Group classes used the same mathematics curriculum, none of them used a curriculum specifically designed for mathematically promising students. For the most part, the "mathematics as usual" curricula were not reform-based and were not focused specifically on the NCTM standards.

Intervention Group 1 students were identified as mathematically promising using the same methods (e.g., NNAT and SRBCSS scores) and started third grade the following year in the same schools as the Control Group. Unlike the Control Group, they received the Project M³ curriculum. In the subsequent year, Intervention Group 2 students were identified as mathematically promising, once again using the same methods, and began the third grade in the same schools as the Control Group and Intervention Group 1, where they received the Project M³ curriculum. At the end of each school year, all students were given two tests on mathematics (see Table 7.1), which are discussed later in this chapter.

The intervention was implemented at the classroom level and was conducted across different schools. We were not interested in growth over time but instead were interested in cross-sectional analyses examining the efficacy of the Project

Table 7.1	Study Design				
Group	*Year 1*	*Year 2*	*Year 3*	*Year 4*	*Year 5*
Control	T3	T4	T5		
Intervention 1		T3	T4	T5	
Intervention 2			T3	T4	T5

Note. T*n* = Test in grade *n*. Each year that students were tested, they took two standardized mathematics assessments: the ITBS Concepts and Estimation Assessment and the Open-Response Assessment.

M^3 curriculum at each grade level (i.e., third grade, fourth grade, and fifth grade), because there were different units for each grade level. This allowed for an examination of the effectiveness of each grade-level Project M^3 curriculum rather than the complete 12-unit curriculum. Moreover, both units and grade levels were designed to stand on their own. Finally, the Open-Response Assessment (one of the mathematics outcome measures) was not vertically equated in a manner that allowed examination of change over time. Multilevel modeling is particularly appropriate for this kind of analysis, where the data illustrate the effect of an intervention at the cluster level (classroom) on outcomes assessed at the individual level (student). In particular, unlike in standard regression, a multilevel modeling approach allows the researcher to randomly vary the intercept so that each classroom can have a different average mathematics outcome score. This multilevel modeling approach was critical for evaluating the difference between classrooms on mathematics outcome scores as a way of determining the effectiveness of the Project M^3 curriculum. Moreover, the researchers were not controlling for any student-level variables (e.g., sex, ethnicity, socioeconomic status [SES]).

Within a given school, there were classrooms for each group: the Control Group receiving standard mathematics instruction and curriculum ("mathematics as usual") and Intervention Groups 1 and 2 receiving the Project M^3 curriculum. Within a given classroom, the students were either all receiving the Project M^3 curriculum or were all receiving "mathematics as usual." The research goal was to explore differences in mathematics achievement between mathematically promising students who were exposed to the Project M^3 curriculum (Intervention Groups 1 and 2) and a comparison group of mathematically promising students of similar backgrounds who were not exposed to the Project M^3 curriculum (Control Group).

SAMPLE

There were 10 elementary schools[1] in two states that participated. One classroom from each school participated in the research each year for 3 years, for a total of 30 classrooms of unique students per grade level. Based on the design, in which control and intervention groups were assigned based on year (Control Group in year 1, Intervention 1 in year 2, Intervention 2 in year 3), students in the Control Group and Intervention Groups 1 and 2 were grouped in classrooms with the same teachers. Thus, there was no random assignment.

Data were collected from students in Grades 3 through 5 who were in one of three groups (each offset by 1 school year; see Table 7.1). During the first year of the study, the teachers continued teaching the standard mathematics instruction to third graders (Control Group); during the second year of the study, the participating classroom in each school implemented the Project M^3 curriculum (Intervention Group 1) for third graders; and during the third year of the study, the participating classrooms implemented the Project M^3 curriculum with a new cohort of third graders (Intervention Group 2). At the first assessment (third grade), across the 10 Intervention Group 1 classrooms, there was a total of 184 students (51% female), with an average of 18.4 students (SD = 2.75) in each classroom. Across the 10 Intervention Group 2 classrooms, there was a total of 172 students (48% female), with an average of 17.2 students (SD = 3.26) in each (third grade) classroom. Across the 10 Control Group classrooms, there was a total of 211 students (45% female), with an average of 21.1 students (SD = 5.38) in each (third grade) classroom.

All children were identified as mathematically promising prior to participation in the program using multiple criteria, including the NNAT (Harcourt Brace Education Measurement, 1997) and the math scale of the SRBCSS (Gavin, 2005). Children in each classroom in each group were tested on mathematics ability in third, fourth, and fifth grade. At the end of each of the 3 school years, each student's mathematics achievement was assessed using a traditional assessment (the Iowa Tests of Basic Skills [ITBS] Mathematics Concepts and Estimation) and an Open-Response Assessment based on released items from National Assessment of Educational Progress (NAEP) and Trends in International Mathematics Science Study (TIMSS). Scores on these assessments were all continuous variables.

The ITBS has different possible scores for each grade level. The third-grade population mean score is 174.5, with a standard deviation of 17.7 and a possible range of 120 to 248. The fourth-grade population mean score is 190.4 (SD = 20.2, range = 123 to 270), and the fifth-grade population mean score is 205.3 (SD = 23.7, range = 127 to 289). Because the Open-Ended Assessment consisted of released test items and was not an existing assessment, there are no population norms. The possible scores on the Open-Ended Assessment ranged from 0 to 16. The descriptive statistics for all three groups on the two assessments at each grade level are provided in Table 7.2.

Table 7.2 Descriptive Statistics on Mathematics Assessments for Intervention and Control Groups

Grade and variable	Intervention Group 1			Intervention Group 2			Control Group		
	M	SD	N	M	SD	N	M	SD	N
Third									
ITBS	200.63	23.88	185	203.52	16.45	172	194.42	20.35	211
Open-Response	8.74	2.36	184	8.40	2.30	172	6.33	2.38	208
Fourth									
ITBS	226.24	20.70	178	224.66	19.69	156	214.06	20.95	180
Open-Response	10.11	3.51	177	9.91	3.23	159	6.49	3.22	180
Fifth									
ITBS	241.62	22.18	163	246.42	21.50	142	233.18	22.96	147
Open-Response	7.64	2.66	162	8.25	2.33	143	5.73	2.50	147

Note. ITBS is the Concepts and Estimation subtest of the Iowa Tests of Basic Skills.

Source: From Gavin, M. K., Casa, T. M., Adelson, J. L., Carroll, S. R., & Sheffield, L. J. (2009). The impact of advanced curriculum on the achievement of mathematically promising elementary students. *Gifted Child Quarterly, 53,* 188–202.

There were no level 1 predictors. The level 2 predictors were Group, which was entered as two dummy codes with the Control Group being the reference group (i.e., zero), and School, which was entered as nine dummy codes. This dataset had the limitation of the classes being nested within a small number of clusters (10 schools); thus, we were not able to model a third level but instead accounted for school differences at level 2.

SOFTWARE AND PROCEDURE

To investigate differences in mathematics achievement as measured using a traditional assessment (the ITBS Concepts and Estimation test) and an Open-Response Assessment across intervention and control groups, we conducted a series of two-level multilevel models using the HLM2 module of hierarchical linear modeling software (HLM), version 7.0 (Raudenbush, Bryk, & Congdon, 2011). Data files containing both level 1 and level 2 data were created using SPSS software (SPSS Inc., 2008). A single data file was created with both level 1 and level 2 data included, although this is not necessary when using the HLM 7.0 software. The dependent variables of interest were scores on the Concepts and Estimation section of the ITBS and scores on the Open-Response Assessment for each grade level.

Although data were collected at the student level, we were interested in testing classroom-level effects to determine the efficacy of the Project M^3 curriculum. Level 1 contained mathematics outcome scores for students; level 2 contained classroom information, that is, information for a particular intervention or control group, and School. Exposure to the Project M^3 curriculum was the independent variable and included three conditions—the Project M^3 Intervention Group 1, the Project M^3 Intervention Group 2, and the Control Group. Because we had three groups, we used two dummy codes—M3_IntI (Intervention Group 1 was coded 1; the other groups were coded 0) and M3_Int2 (Intervention Group 2 was coded 1; the other groups were coded 0), and we entered these two variables at level 2. For the other level 2 variable, School, we created nine dummy codes for the 10 cohorts of students. When using dummy codes in multilevel modeling, one of the members of that category (in this example, School) has to be labeled as zero in order to have a reference point for the differentials from the other members of that category. In this study, we were not interested in comparisons across schools but were including School to account for school differences. Therefore, we asked the professional development staff which school they would consider "average" and used that as the reference school (coded as zero). Given the small level 2 sample size, we used restricted maximum likelihood estimation (REML; Raudenbush & Bryk, 2002).

ANALYZING THE DATA[2]

We began analyzing each of the six outcomes (two assessments at three grade levels each, i.e., T3, T4, and T5 in Table 7.1) by estimating an unconditional model with no predictors at either level so that we could estimate the intraclass correlation (ICC), a measure of the proportion of variance at the school level in relation to the total variance. The formula for the unconditional model for each dependent variable is

$$\text{OUTCOME}_{ij} = \gamma_{00} + u_{0j} + r_{ij},$$

where γ_{00} is the intercept (average outcome score in third, fourth, or fifth grade), u_{0j} is the incremental effect of school j to the observed outcome (level 2 error), and r_{ij} is the incremental effect of child i in school j (level 1 error).

The results of each unconditional model for the ITBS Concepts and Estimation scores are in Table 7.3. For all three grade levels of the test, the ICC was about .30 (Grade 3 = .26, Grade 4 = .30, Grade 5 = .28). This was calculated as

$$\frac{\tau_{00}}{\sigma^2 + \tau_{00}},$$

where τ_{00} is the between-class (level 2) intercept variance and σ^2 is the within-class (level 1) variance. For example, the Grade 3 ITBS Concepts and Estimation test ICC was calculated as $\frac{113.52}{329.67 + 113.52} = .26$ (using values from Table 7.3). An ICC value of .26 indicates that about 26% of the variance in ITBS Concepts and Estimation scores in third grade lay between classes. This value is consistent with other studies analyzing mathematics achievement with students clustered in schools (Hedges & Hedberg, 2007). An ICC of this magnitude, as well as a statistically significant τ_{00}, indicates the need for multilevel modeling. In fact, an ICC as small as .05 with as few as 10 classrooms can lead to type I error due to underestimated standard errors (see McCoach & Adelson, 2010).

Table 7.4 displays the results of each Open-Response Assessment unconditional model. The ICCs for the Open-Response Assessment at each grade level were somewhat more variable than for the ITBS Concepts and Estimation. For third grade, the Open-Response Assessment ICC was .31, for fourth grade it was .48, and for fifth grade it was .39. This indicates that between 31% and 48% of the variance in Open-Response Assessment scores at each grade level lay between classes.

We were interested in the effects of the Project M^3 curriculum and did not include any level 1 covariates. In addition, the relatively large ICC values suggested significant clustering at level 2. Therefore, we next estimated the full level 2 models, which included School cohort (nine dummy codes) and Project M^3 Group (two dummy codes) at level 2. Because the level 2 variables were dummy codes, they were all entered into the model uncentered. As indicated in Chapter 2 of this textbook, binary variables (including dummy codes) typically are not centered. The formula for the full model for each dependent variable, including School cohort and Project M^3 Group, is

$$\text{OUTCOME}_{ij} = \gamma_{00} + \gamma_{01}{}^*\text{M3\_Int1} + \gamma_{02}{}^*\text{M3\_Int2} + \gamma_{03}{}^*\text{SCHOOL2} +$$
$$\gamma_{04}{}^*\text{SCHOOL3} + \gamma_{05}{}^*\text{SCHOOL4} + \gamma_{06}{}^*\text{SCHOOL5} + \gamma_{07}{}^*\text{SCHOOL6} +$$
$$\gamma_{08}{}^*\text{SCHOOL7} + \gamma_{09}{}^*\text{SCHOOL8} + \gamma_{10}{}^*\text{SCHOOL9} + \gamma_{11}{}^*\text{SCHOOL10} + u_{0j} + r_{ij},$$

Table 7.3 Summary of REML Parameter Estimates for Two-Level Model of ITBS Concepts and Estimation, Grades 3, 4, and 5

Parameter	Third grade				Fourth grade				Fifth grade			
	Unconditional model		Full model		Unconditional model		Full model		Unconditional model		Full model	
	Parameter estimate	SE	Parameter estimate	SE	Parameter estimate	SE	Parameter estimate	SE	Parameter estimate	SE	Parameter estimate	SE
Fixed effect												
Intercept (γ_{00})	199.24***	2.10	178.27***	2.94	221.44***	2.28	200.54***	3.59	239.66***	2.45	220.99***	3.65
M3_Int1 (γ_{01})			6.26***	2.05			12.35***	2.42			9.43***	2.40
M3_Int2 (γ_{02})			9.70***	2.09			11.21***	2.47			13.99***	2.47
School2 (γ_{03})			18.19**	3.88			14.35***	4.52			17.74***	4.52
School3 (γ_{04})			26.89***	3.88			30.23***	4.51			27.89***	4.50
School4 (γ_{05})			1.49	4.13			5.21	4.88			-6.76	5.07
School5 (γ_{06})			10.24*	3.76			5.25*	4.55			6.22	4.67
School6 (γ_{07})			12.94*	3.67			9.07**	4.38			6.54*	4.35
School7 (γ_{08})			22.51***	3.70			18.92***	4.44			17.59***	4.32
School8 (γ_{09})			29.59***	4.03			28.10***	4.83			26.72***	4.84
School9 (γ_{010})			26.36***	3.69			18.27***	4.38			13.53*	4.42
School10 (γ_{011})			8.39	3.82			0.77	4.57			-4.08	4.76
Variance estimate												
Level-1 variance (σ^2)	329.67		329.56		321.11		321.47		385.91		383.83	
Intercept variance (τ_{00})	113.52***		4.12		135.67***		10.70		153.22***		3.35	
Deviance (number of REML parameters)	4959.05 (2)		4854.79 (2)		4481.58 (2)		4378.91 (2)		4025.60 (2)		3915.66 (2)	

Note. REML = restricted likelihood estimation. M3_Int1 and M3_Int2 (Project M³ Intervention Groups 1 and 2) are indicators of treatment group and are dummy coded 0 for Control and 1 for participation in the respective Intervention Group. Nine dummy codes were created to represent the 10 school cohorts.

* $p < .05$. ** $p < .01$. *** $p < .001$.

Source: From Gavin, M. K., Casa, T. M., Adelson, J. L., Carroll, S. R., & Sheffield, L. J. (2009). The impact of advanced curriculum on the achievement of mathematically promising elementary students. *Gifted Child Quarterly, 53*, 188–202.

Table 7.4 Summary of REML Parameter Estimates for Two-Level Model of Open-Response Assessment, Grades 3, 4, and 5

| | Third grade | | | | Fourth grade | | | | Fifth grade | | | |
| | Unconditional model | | Full model | | Unconditional model | | Full model | | Unconditional model | | Full model | |
Parameter	Parameter estimate	SE	Parameter estimate	SE	Parameter estimate	SE	Parameter estimate	SE	Parameter estimate	SE	Parameter estimate	SE
Fixed effect												
Intercept (γ_{00})	7.77***	0.28	5.66***	0.34	8.76***	0.49	5.16***	0.68	7.06***	0.34	4.76***	0.51
M3_Int1 (γ_{01})			2.44***	0.24			3.65***	0.46			2.08***	0.35
M3_Int2 (γ_{02})			2.15***	0.24			3.49***	0.47			2.61***	0.35
School2 (γ_{03})			0.91***	0.45			3.25**	0.86			2.08*	0.64
School3 (γ_{04})			2.26***	0.45			3.11***	0.86			2.00**	0.64
School4 (γ_{05})			−0.73**	0.48			−1.24	0.90			−1.71*	0.70
School5 (γ_{06})			0.32**	0.43			−0.44	0.86			0.51	0.66
School6 (γ_{07})			0.08	0.42			0.10	0.84			0.05	0.63
School7 (γ_{08})			1.01	0.43			2.24***	0.85			1.02	0.63
School8 (γ_{09})			1.18***	0.47			3.75***	0.90			1.41	0.67
School9 (γ_{010})			1.78***	0.43			2.76***	0.84			2.50**	0.63
School10 (γ_{011})			−0.89***	0.45			−1.44**	0.87			−0.72	0.67
Variance estimate												
Level-1 variance (σ^2)	4.69		4.66		7.48		7.49		4.82		4.81	
Intercept variance (τ_{00})	2.09***		0.04		6.82***		0.64***		3.04***		0.28*	
Deviance (number of REML parameters)	2536.82 (2)		2468.69 (2)		2570.41 (2)		2492.88 (2)		2060.27 (2)		1997.40 (2)	

Note. REML = restricted likelihood estimation. M3_Int1 and M3_Int2 (Project M³ Intervention Groups 1 and 2) are indicators of treatment group and are dummy coded 0 for Control and 1 for participation in the respective Intervention Group. Nine dummy codes were created to represent the 10 school cohorts.

* $p < .05.$ ** $p < .01.$ *** $p < .001.$

Source: From Gavin, M. K., Casa, T. M., Adelson, J. L., Carroll, S. R., & Sheffield, L. J. (2009). The impact of advanced curriculum on the achievement of mathematically promising elementary students. *Gifted Child Quarterly, 53,* 188–202.

where γ_{00} is the intercept (the predicted outcome score for a student in that grade at School 1; all School dummy codes = 0) in the Control Group (M3_IntI = 0 and M3_Int2 = 0)], γ_{01} is the differential for a student who participated in Project M^3 Intervention Group 1, and γ_{02} is the differential for a student who participated in Project M^3 Intervention Group 2. In addition, the coefficient for the nine School cohorts (γ_{03} to γ_{11}) represented the differential between average scores for students at the other nine schools and School 1, the variance of u_{0j} is the residual between-class (level 2) variance in the outcome after accounting for School and the Project M^3 group, and the variance of r_{ij} is the residual within-class (level 1) variance.

To calculate the proportion of variance explained by Project M^3 Group, above and beyond what School explains, we also ran level 2 models with just School cohorts as predictors to determine the amount of variance remaining to be explained after accounting for School. The formula to calculate the proportion of between-class variance explained is

$$\frac{\tau_{00 \text{ baseline model}} - \tau_{00 \text{ full model}}}{\tau_{00 \text{ baseline model}}},$$

where $\tau_{00 \text{ baseline model}}$ is τ_{00} (the between-class variance) from the level 2 model with only School cohort as a predictor, and $\tau_{00 \text{ full model}}$ is τ_{00} from the level 2 model that includes both School and Project M^3 Group as predictors. To work through an example, the proportion of variance explained by Project M^3 Group in scores on the ITBS Concepts and Estimation in third grade was $\frac{26.66 - 4.12}{26.66} = 0.845$ (using values from Figure 7.1). This means that after accounting for School, 85% of the remaining between-class variance in ITBS Concepts and Estimation score in third grade was explained by the Project M^3 Group (i.e., whether they were in the Control Group or one of the two Intervention Groups). Figure 7.1 illustrates the HLM 7.0 output for the variance components in both of these level 2 models (for the ITBS Concepts and Estimation scores in third grade). Table 7.5 lists the t_{00} (between-class variance) from the level 2 model with only the School cohort, the t_{00} from the level 2 model with both the School cohort and Project M^3 Group, and the proportion of between-class variance explained by the Project M^3 Group for each of the six outcomes (two assessments at three grade levels each).

OUTPUT AND ANALYSIS

Figures 7.2 and 7.3 are screen shots of the output from the HLM 7.0 software. Figure 7.2 displays the regular fixed effects table with conventional standard errors. Figure 7.3 displays the fixed effects table with robust standard errors, as well as a table of the variance components and the deviance statistic. These figures illustrate the HLM 7.0 analysis output for ITBS Concepts and Estimation scores when the children were third graders. For space, we omitted the output for

Figure 7.1	Output from HLM 7.0 software displaying the model equations and variance components for the baseline model on the left (Only SCHOOL as Predictors) and the full model on the right (SCHOOL and Group as predictors). The outcome variable is ITBS Concepts and Estimation scores in third grade

---

Summary of the model specified

Level-1 Model

$ITBS\_3_{ij} = \beta_{0j} + r_{ij}$

Level-2 Model

$\beta_{0j} = \gamma_{00} + \gamma_{01}*(SCHOOL2) + \gamma_{02}*(SCHOOL3) + \gamma_{03}*(SCHOOL4) + \gamma_{04}*(SCHOOL5) + \gamma_{05}*(SCHOOL6) + \gamma_{06}*(SCHOOL7) + \gamma_{07}*(SCHOOL8) + \gamma_{08}*(SCHOOL9) + \gamma_{09}*(SCHOOL10) + u_{0j}$

Mixed Model

$ITBS\_3_{ij} = \gamma_{00} + \gamma_{01}*SCHOOL2_j + \gamma_{02}*SCHOOL3_j + \gamma_{03}*SCHOOL4_j + \gamma_{04}*SCHOOL5_j + \gamma_{05}*SCHOOL6_j + \gamma_{06}*SCHOOL7_j + \gamma_{07}*SCHOOL8_j + \gamma_{08}*SCHOOL9_j + \gamma_{09}*SCHOOL10_j + u_{0j} + r_{ij}$

Run-time deletion has reduced the number of level-1 records to 568

Final Result-Iteration 4

Iterations stopped due to small change in likelihood function

$\sigma^2 = 329.50740$

τ

INTRCPT1, β_0 26.65720

Baseline Model τ_{00}

Summary of the model specified

Level-1 Model

$ITBS\_3_{ij} = \beta_{0j} + r_{ij}$

Level-2 Model

$\beta_{0j} = \gamma_{00} + \gamma_{01}*(M3\_INT1) + \gamma_{02}*(M3\_INT2)_j + \gamma_{03}*(SCHOOL2)_j + \gamma_{04}*(SCHOOL3)_j + \gamma_{05}*(SCHOOL4) + \gamma_{06}*(SCHOOL5)_j + \gamma_{07}*(SCHOOL6)_j + \gamma_{08}*(SCHOOL7)_j + \gamma_{09}*(SCHOOL8)_j + \gamma_{010}*(SCHOOL9)_j + \gamma_{011}*(SCHOOL10)_j + u_{0j}$

Mixed Model

$ITBS\_3_{ij} = \gamma_{00} + \gamma_{01}*M3\_INT1_j + \gamma_{02}*M3\_INT2_j + \gamma_{03}*SCHOOL2_j + \gamma_{04}*SCHOOL3_j + \gamma_{05}*SCHOOL4_j + \gamma_{06}*SCHOOL5_j + \gamma_{07}*SCHOOL6_j + \gamma_{08}*SCHOOL7_j + \gamma_{09}*SCHOOL8_j + \gamma_{010}*SCHOOL9_j + \gamma_{011}*SCHOOL10_j + u_{0j} + r_{ij}$

Run-time deletion has reduced the number of level-1 records to 568

Final Result-Iteration 2

Iterations stopped due to small change in likelihood function

$\sigma^2 = 329.55999$

τ

INTRCPT1, β_0 4.12039

Full Model τ_{00}

Table 7.5	Proportion of Between-Class (Level 2) Variance Explained by Project M3 Group for Both Outcomes at Grades 3, 4, and 5					
	ITBS Concepts and Estimation			*Open-Response Assessment*		
	Grade 3	*Grade 4*	*Grade 5*	*Grade 3*	*Grade 4*	*Grade 5*
Baseline Model (only School as Level 2 predictor) τ_{00}	26.66	55.50	46.71	1.77	4.77	2.16
Full Model (School and M^3 Group as Level 2 predictors) τ_{00}	4.12	10.70	3.35	0.04	0.64	0.28
Proportion of Variance Explained by M^3 Group	0.85	0.81	0.93	0.98	0.87	0.87

the other five outcomes as the output would look similar but with different numbers. We will now discuss the values one by one with a description of what each signifies.

The first statistic of interest in Figure 7.2 is γ_{00}, the intercept (the mathematics outcome score). The value of 178.27 is the predicted score on the ITBS Concepts and Estimation test for a third grader in School 1 in the Control Group. The *p*-value indicates that this score is significantly greater than zero. This is what we should expect because the range of possible scores on the ITBS Concepts and Estimation test in third grade is 120 to 248, all of which is well above zero. The next two values—γ_{01} and γ_{02}—represent the differentials for students who participated in one of the intervention groups. The value of 6.26 (γ_{01}) means that a third grader who participated in Intervention Group 1 is predicted to have an ITBS Concepts and Estimation score that is 6.26 points higher than a third grader in the same school who was in the Control Group ($\gamma_{00} + \gamma_{01}$; 178.27 + 6.26 = 184.53). The fact that this differential is statistically significant ($p < .001$) means that it is statistically significantly greater than zero, so this is a significantly higher score. The value of 9.70 (γ_{02}) means that a third grader who was in Intervention Group 2 is predicted to have an ITBS Concepts and Estimation score of 9.70 points higher than a third grader in the same school who was in the Control Group ($\gamma_{00} + \gamma_{02}$; 178.27 + 9.70 = 187.97). Going down that column in Figure 7.2, the next coefficient value (γ_{03}) is 18.19. This is the differential for School 2, which means that a third grader in the Control Group in School 2 is predicted to have an ITBS Concepts and Estimation score that is 18.19 points greater than a third grader in the Control Group in School 1. The remaining coefficients (γ_{04}–γ_{11}) are the differentials in ITBS Concepts and Estimation score in third grade for the other eight schools and would be described in a similar fashion to γ_{03}.

The table at the bottom of Figure 7.3 lists the variance components. The first value (τ_{00}; listed as the variance component for u_0) is the residual between-class

| Figure 7.2 | Output from HLM 7.0 software displaying the fixed effects estimates with conventional standard errors for the full level 2 model for ITBS Concepts and Estimation scores in third grade |

Final Results – Iteration 2

Iterations stopped due to small change in likelihood function
$\sigma^2 = 329.55999$

τ
INTRCPT1, β_0 4.12039

Random level-1 coefficient	Reliability estimate
INTRCPT1, β_0	0.190

The value of the log-likelihood function at iteration 2 = −2.427393E + 003

Final estimation of fixed effects:

Fixed Effect	Coefficient	Standard error	t-ratio	Approx. d.f.	p-value
For INTRCPT1, β_0					
INTRCPT2, γ_{00}	178.266126	2.944182	60.549	18	<0.001
M3_INT1, γ_{01}	6.261348	2.054471	3.048	18	0.007
M3_INT2, γ_{02}	9.704319	2.085448	4.653	18	<0.001
SCHOOL2, γ_{03}	18.190260	3.876635	4.692	18	<0.001
SCHOOL3, γ_{04}	26.886598	3.875006	6.938	18	<0.001
SCHOOL4, γ_{05}	1.490728	4.125639	0.361	18	0.722
SCHOOL5, γ_{06}	10.236598	3.761732	2.721	18	0.014
SCHOOL6, γ_{07}	12.934848	3.670148	3.524	18	0.002
SCHOOL7, γ_{08}	22.505176	3.700120	6.082	18	<0.001
SCHOOL8, γ_{09}	29.585163	4.034989	7.332	18	<0.001
SCHOOL9, γ_{010}	26.364145	3.688216	7.148	18	<0.001
SCHOOL10, γ_{011}	8.391004	3.815518	2.199	18	0.041

Figure 7.3 Output from HLM 7.0 software displaying the fixed effects with robust standard errors, the variance components, and the deviance statistic for ITBS Concepts and Estimation scores in third grade

Final estimation of fixed effects (with robust standard errors)

Fixed Effect	Coefficient	Standard error	t-ratio	Approx. d.f.	p-values
For INTRCPT1, β_0					
INTRCPT2, γ_{00}	178.266126	4.724220	37.735	18	<0.001
M3_INT1, γ_{01}	6.261348	1.459435	4.290	18	<0.001
M3_INT2, γ_{02}	9.704319	1.705998	5.688	18	<0.001
SCHOOL2, γ_{03}	18.190260	4.945633	3.678	18	0.002
SCHOOL3, γ_{04}	26.886598	4.755234	5.654	18	<0.001
SCHOOL4, γ_{05}	1.490728	5.035882	0.296	18	0.771
SCHOOL5, γ_{06}	10.236598	4.476301	2.287	18	0.035
SCHOOL6, γ_{07}	12.934848	4.463886	2.898	18	0.010
SCHOOL7, γ_{08}	22.505176	4.880096	4.612	18	<0.001
SCHOOL8, γ_{09}	29.585163	4.540490	6.516	18	<0.001
SCHOOL9, γ_{010}	26.364145	4.960211	5.315	18	<0.001
SCHOOL10, γ_{011}	8.391004	4.569938	1.836	18	0.083

The robust standard errors are appropriate for datasets having a moderate to large number of level 2 units. These data do not meet this criterion.

Final estimation of variance components

Random Effect	Standard Deviation	Variance Component	d.f.	χ^2	p-value
INTRCPT1, u_0	2.02987	4.12039	18	22.18770	0.223
level-1, r	18.15379	329.55999			

Statistics for current covariance components model

Deviance = 4854.786139

Number of estimated parameters = 2

(level 2) variance in the ITBS Concepts and Estimation score in third grade, after accounting for School and Project M³ Group (Control, Intervention 1, or Intervention 2). This value is 4.12, and the p-value ($p = .22$) indicates that it is not statistically significant. This means that after School and Project M³ Group are accounted for, there is not a statistically significant amount of remaining between-class (level 2) variance in third-grade ITBS Concepts and Estimation score to be explained. Directly underneath τ_{00} in Figure 7.3 is σ^2 (listed as the variance component for r), which is 329.56 (σ^2 is also listed at the top of the HLM 7.0 output, which can be seen in Figure 7.2). This is the within-class (level 1) residual variance in the ITBS Concepts and Estimation score in third grade. This value barely changed at all from the unconditional mode, which is not surprising. As no student-level (level 1) predictors were added to the model, we did not explain the within-class variability.

CONCLUDING RESULTS

Table 7.3 displays the results of the three full models for the ITBS Concepts and Estimation, and Table 7.4 displays the results of the three full models for the Open-Response Assessment. This information can be used to determine the predicted score for different students, after taking into account the nested structure of the data. For instance, the predicted ITBS Concepts and Estimation score for a student in Grade 3 ($\gamma_{00} = 178.27$) at School 3 ($\gamma_{04} = 26.89$) who was in Intervention Group 2 ($\gamma_{02} = 9.70$) was 214.86 ($\gamma_{00} + \gamma_{04} + \gamma_{02}$; 178.27 + 26.89 + 9.70), whereas the predicted score for a third grader in the same school but in the Control Group was 205.16 ($\gamma_{00} + \gamma_{04}$; 178.27 + 26.89). The predicted score for a student in the Control Group is different from that of the student in Intervention Group 2 because for that student, there is no differential for the effect of the Project M³ curriculum (γ_{01} or γ_{02}).

Of greatest interest to us were the effects of the Project M³ curriculum (M3_IntI and M3_Int2). For all three grade levels, both Intervention Group 1 and Intervention Group 2 had statistically significantly ($p < .001$) higher scores on the ITBS Concepts and Estimation compared to the Control Group. As shown in Table 7.6, the Cohen's d effect sizes on this test ranged from 0.30 to 0.60, which are small to medium effect sizes (Cohen, 1992). These effect sizes were calculated using the equation suggested by Raudenbush, Spybrook, Liu, and Congdon (2005, p. 16):

$$\frac{treatment\ gamma}{\sqrt{\tau_{00} + \sigma^2}},$$

where *treatment gamma* is equal to γ_{01} or γ_{02} (the fixed effect for a dummy code representing treatment) and where τ_{00} (the between-class variance component) and σ^2 (the within-class variance component) are taken from the unconditional or null model (before any variability has been explained). There is no general formula for effect sizes in multilevel modeling, but this formula does apply to this two-level random intercepts regression model in which we are examining the differences between two groups (i.e., Intervention Group 1 versus Control and Intervention Group 2 versus Control). As an example, for a student in the third grade in Intervention Group 1, the effect size for the score on the ITBS Concepts and Estimation was calculated as $\dfrac{6.26}{\sqrt{113.53+329.67}}$, which equals 0.30 (see Table 7.3 for the coefficients).

Table 7.6   Cohen's *d* Effect Sizes for All Outcome Measures

Intervention Group	ITBS Concepts and Estimation			Open-Response Assessment		
	Grade 3	*Grade 4*	*Grade 5*	*Grade 3*	*Grade 4*	*Grade 5*
1	0.30	0.58	0.41	0.94	0.97	0.74
2	0.46	0.52	0.60	0.83	0.92	0.93

Source: From Gavin, M. K., Casa, T. M., Adelson, J. L., Carroll, S. R., & Sheffield, L. J. (2009). The impact of advanced curriculum on the achievement of mathematically promising elementary students. *Gifted Child Quarterly, 53*, 188–202.

As shown in Tables 7.3 and 7.4, the results from the ITBS Concepts and Estimation test, a standardized, multiple-choice assessment, were corroborated by those obtained on the Open-Response Assessment. Like on the ITBS Concepts and Estimation test, both Intervention Group 1 and Intervention Group 2 scored statistically significantly higher ($p < .001$) than the Control Group on the Open-Response Assessment at all three grade levels. The Cohen's *d* effect sizes on this assessment, which also are displayed in Table 7.6, ranged from 0.74 to 0.97, which are medium to large effect sizes (Cohen, 1992). These results indicate that both of the Project M[3] intervention groups, on average, outperformed students in the Control Group on both the ITBS Concepts and Estimation and the Open-Response Assessment in Grades 3, 4, and 5.

SUMMARY

The goal of this study was to see if there was a difference in mathematics achievement between mathematically promising students who were exposed to the Project M[3] curriculum (Intervention Groups 1 and 2) and mathematically promising students of similar backgrounds who were not exposed to the Project M[3] curriculum (Control Group). The main finding was that students exposed to the Project M[3] curriculum consistently had statistically significantly higher scores in all three grades (Grades 3, 4, and 5) compared to students in the Control Group (who had "mathematics as usual") on tests of mathematical abilities, with medium to large effect sizes.

ACKNOWLEDGMENTS

The data reported here were funded in part by the Jacob K. Javits Students Education Act, grant no. S206A020006, and the writing of this chapter was funded in part by a grant from the NIH to CLS (F31 DC010281). The opinions, conclusions, and recommendations expressed in this article are those of the authors and do not necessarily reflect the position or policies of the U.S. Department of Education or the NIH.

NOTES

1. Technically, there were 11 schools, but 1 of the elementary schools only went up to fourth grade, and then those students fed into a middle school. Because that particular elementary and then middle school represent the same students and because the analyses are conducted by grade level, we treated them as one school. Therefore, all analyses have 10 schools.

2. Data analyses for this chapter vary somewhat from those reported in Gavin et al. (2009). For pedagogical purposes, we made slightly different decisions when creating the .mdm. file, running the analyses, and interpreting the results. However, the general findings remain the same.

REFERENCES

Cohen, J. (1992). A power primer. *Psychological Bulletin, 112,* 155–159.

Gavin, M. K. (2005, Fall/Winter). Are we missing anyone? Identifying mathematically promising students. *Gifted Education Communicator,* 24–29.

Gavin, M. K., Casa, T. M., Adelson, J. L., Carroll, S. R., & Sheffield, L. J. (2009). The impact of advanced curriculum on the achievement of mathematically promising elementary students. *Gifted Child Quarterly, 53,* 188–202.

Gavin, M. K., Casa, T. M., Adelson, J. L., Carroll, S. R., Sheffield, L. J., & Spinelli, A. M. (2007). Project M^3: Mentoring Mathematical Minds—A research-based curriculum for talented elementary students. *Journal of Advanced Academics, 18,* 566–585.

Harcourt Brace Education Measurement. (1997). *Naglieri Nonverbal Ability Test (NNAT).* San Antonio, TX: Harcourt Brace.

Hedges, L. V., & Hedberg, E. C. (2007). Intraclass correlation values for planning group randomized trials in education. *Educational Evaluation and Policy Analsyis, 29,* 60–87.

McCoach, D. B., & Adelson, J. L. (2010). Dealing with dependence (Part I): Understanding the effects of clustered data. *Gifted Child Quarterly, 54,* 152–155.

National Council of Teachers of Mathematics. (2000). *Principles and standards for school mathematics.* Reston, VA: Author.

Raudenbush, S. W., & Bryk, A. S. (2002). *Hierarchical linear models* (2nd ed.). Thousand Oaks, CA: Sage.

Raudenbush, S. W., Bryk, A. S., & Congdon, R. (2011). *HLM 7: Hierarchical linear and nonlinear modeling* [Computer software]. Lincolnwood, IL: Scientific Software International, Inc.

Raudenbush, S. W., Spybrook, J., Liu, X., & Congdon, R. (2005). *Optimal Design for Longitudinal and Multilevel Research, Version 1.55* [computer software]. Retrieved December 21, 2011, from http://sitemaker.umich.edu/group-based/optimal_design_software

SPSS Inc. (2008). *SPSS Statistics, Version 17* [Computer software]. Chicago: Author.

Random Coefficients Modeling With HLM 8

Assessment Practices and the Achievement Gap in Schools

Gregory J. Palardy

The random coefficients (RC) model is a type of hierarchical linear model that has a random intercept and at least one random slope in the level 1 model (Snijders & Bosker, 2011). Fixed coefficients (i.e., fixed effects) may also be included in the level 1 and level 2 models. There are a multitude of applications of the RC model in the social sciences. It might be helpful to begin with a few examples.

In research on developmental processes, repeated measures collected over time can be conceived of as nested within individuals. An RC growth model can be used to estimate the association between the repeated measurements and a variable measuring the passage of time. In this model the random intercept coefficients estimate the expected value on the outcome for each individual when the TIME variable equals zero, while the random slope coefficients on TIME estimate the change in the outcome for each individual per unit change in TIME. In other words, the model estimates a growth trajectory for each individual that is characterized by an intercept and a slope coefficient. Variation in the neighborhood crime rates could be modeled using measures of resident and neighborhood characteristics.

Another example is in the field of criminology, where scholars sometimes examine the effects neighborhoods have on the attitudes and behaviors of residents. In this case, residents are conceived of as nested in neighborhoods. The association between an outcome measuring the crime rate and a predictor measuring individual attitudes about crime may vary across neighborhoods. An RC model would be suitable for modeling this association. The random intercepts and slopes estimate the crime rate and the association between crime and individuals' attitudes in each neighborhood. Variation in the neighborhood intercepts and slopes could be modeled using measures of neighborhood characteristics.

A third example is the effect of family socioeconomic status (SES) on the educational outcomes of children, which might depend on the characteristics and practices of the schools the children attend (Raudenbush & Bryk, 2002). In this case, children are nested in schools. To study this relationship, an RC model could be fit to an achievement outcome with random intercepts and slopes that estimate the achievement level and achievement–SES association at each school. Variation in the intercepts and slopes could be modeled using school measures.

In all of the above examples, there is a unique intercept and slope estimate for each level 2 unit; therefore, a regression line is estimated for each level 2 unit. Figure 8.1 shows a graphic depiction of the results of an RC model for the third example above, the effect of SES on READING ACHIEVEMENT. The graph was constructed using HLM 7 software (Raudenbush, Bryk, Cheong, Congdon, & du Toit, 2011) and data from 1,261 elementary school children nested in 87 schools. Note that a regression line is estimated for each school. The lines differ in terms of their intercepts and slopes and the range of SES of the children attending. The location of the intercept of each line is the value for READING ACHIEVEMENT (vertical axis) that corresponds to an SES (horizontal) of zero. Because SES in this example is a standard normal variable with a mean of zero, the intercept can also be interpreted as the expected value on READING ACHIEVEMENT for children with average SES. The graph clearly shows that the intercepts vary substantially in this sample of schools; the slopes also vary, but far less so.

Figure 8.1 The Achievement–SES association in 87 elementary schools

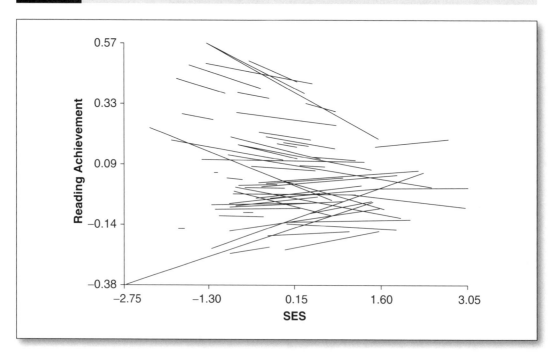

An RC model is suitable for addressing two general research questions:

1. To what degree do the intercepts and slopes vary and covary across level 2 units?

2. What individual and group factors account for variation in the intercepts and slopes?

Elaborating on the third example above, an RC growth model can address whether mean initial achievement and mean achievement growth vary across schools, and if so, which student and school factors are associated with that between-school variation. Of course, the research questions for any given empirical investigation would be precisely tailored and, ideally, theoretically informed. Note that some scholars restrict an RC model to include only level 1 predictors (e.g., Raudenbush & Bryk, 2002), in which case the second research question would be restricted to individual factors. When defined that way, another model, the so-called intercepts-and-slopes-as-outcomes model, is an extension of the RC model that includes level 2 predictors. However, the present chapter considers the intercepts-and-slopes-as-outcomes model to be a special case of the more general RC model and not a separate model.

STATISTICAL FORMULATIONS

In developing a deeper understanding of the RC model, it will be necessary to discuss details of the model and its specification. In order to express that precisely, the formulations for the RC model are provided below in Equation Set 1. Note that the multilevel equation system shown here is consistent with the widely used system of Raudenbush and Bryk (2002), which has a single equation at level 1 and an equation at level 2 model for each coefficient in the level 1 model.

Equation Set 1: The General Multilevel Equations for the Random Coefficient Model

Level 1

$$Y_{ij} = \beta_{0j} + \sum_{p=1}^{P} \beta_{pj}(X_{pij} - \overline{X}_{p.j}) + \sum_{q=P+1}^{Q} \beta_q X_{qij} + r_{ij} \qquad r_{ij} \sim N(0,\sigma^2)$$

Level 2

$$\beta_{0j} = \gamma_{00} + \sum_{r=1}^{R} \gamma_{0l} W_{lj} + u_{0j}$$

$$\beta_{pj} = \gamma_{p0} + \sum_{r=1}^{R} \gamma_{1l} W_{lj} + u_{pj}$$

$$\beta_q = \gamma_{q0}$$

$$\mathbf{u}_j \sim N(\mathbf{0}, \mathbf{T}) \quad \mathbf{u}_j = \begin{bmatrix} u_{0j} \\ \cdot \\ \cdot \\ \cdot \\ u_{pj} \end{bmatrix}, \mathbf{0} = \begin{bmatrix} 0 \\ \cdot \\ \cdot \\ \cdot \\ 0 \end{bmatrix}, \mathbf{T} = \begin{bmatrix} \tau_{00} & & & \\ \cdot & \cdot & & \\ \cdot & & \cdot & \\ \cdot & & & \cdot \\ \tau_{0p} & \cdot & \cdot & \cdot & \tau_{pp} \end{bmatrix}$$

Beginning with level 1, Y is the outcome and the subscripts ij represent the nested structure of the data in that level 1 units, "i" (presumably individuals), are nested in level 2 units, "j." Note that subscripts also indicate which terms are variables. For example, terms with an "i" subscript are variables with values for each level 1 unit, while terms with no "i" but a "j" subscript are variables with values for each level 2 units. Terms with i or j subscripts are not variables and only one estimate is produced for each. On the right side of the equation are the predictors or independent variables (represented by Xs) and associated coefficients (represented by β s). β_{0j} represents the intercept coefficients. The j subscript indicates there is an estimate for each level 2 unit, and therefore it is a random coefficient. Note that random coefficients can be considered latent variables because they are not measured directly, but rather estimated or inferred from other variables by the model.

Next is the capital Greek character sigma (Σ), which is the summation notation in statistics, meaning what follows is repeated additively. There are P slope coefficients (β_{pj}) and associated predictors (X_{pij}) that are enumerated from 1 to p. These slopes are random coefficients, as signified by the j subscripts, and hence, there is an estimate for each level 2 unit. Note that the predictors are centered on the mean of their level 2 unit ($X_{pij} - \overline{X}_{p \cdot j}$). That is, for each X, the mean of the group is subtracted from the individual's score. This group-mean centering technique for level 1 variables has two important consequences. First, it provides more accurate estimates of the slope within each level 2 unit and therefore a more accurate estimate of the mean of the slopes and the variability between the slopes of the level 2 units (Raudenbush & Bryk, 2002, p. 136). This is highly desirable because the primary objectives when specifying a slope as random are to obtain accurate estimates of the mean and variation of the slopes. Second, the intercepts are not statistically adjusted for the group-mean centered predictor. That is, the variance in the intercepts is not altered by the inclusion of the group-mean centered predictors in the level 1 model; therefore, such predictors cannot be considered "control covariates" in the vein of an ANCOVA model. For this reason, the group-mean centered predictors account for variation in the outcome within the level 1 units (i.e., reduces σ^2), but do not alter the variance in the intercepts at level 2 (i.e., τ_{00} does not change).

The next set of terms consists of Q minus P fixed slope coefficients and associated covariates that are numbered from $P + 1$ to Q. The coefficients are fixed (and therefore have no j subscript) in that there is one estimate that applies to all level 2 units. Note that the predictors associated with these fixed effects are typically specified as uncentered (as shown) or grand-mean centered, in which case the sample mean of the variable is subtracted from each level 1 unit's score. Either way, in contrast with group-mean centering, the inclusion of these variables will adjust the intercepts for differences on the covariate across level 2 units. As a result, these covariates not only account for variation in the level 1 residuals, but may also alter the variance in the level 2 residuals, typically reducing it, but occasionally increasing it. For these reasons, uncentered and grand-mean centered covariates can be considered "control covariates." The last term is the level 1 residual, which captures variance in the outcome within the level 1 units that is not accounted for by the covariates in the model. In other words, the residual is a variable that measures the difference between the observed and model-predicted value for each individual. To the right of the level 1 equation is a description of the assumed distribution of the level 1 residuals, which is approximately normal, with a mean of zero, and some variation (σ^2).

Each coefficient in the level 1 model has an equation at level 2 that may or may not include predictors. Predictors and associated coefficients in level-2 equations are represented by Ws and gammas (γ), respectively. Note that the Ws in the slope equations interact with the level-1 X variable associated with the respective random slope to create what is referred to as a cross-level interaction effect (i.e., $X*W$). Also, each random coefficient in the level-1 equation will have a residual term in its level-2 equation (i.e., u_{pj}) that captures the unexplained variation in the coefficient. Including the residual for the random intercept, there will be $P + 1$ residual terms in the level-2 model. The assumed distribution of these residuals can be expressed succinctly in matrix form as shown below the equations. There is a vector of residual terms ($\mathbf{u}$), one for each random coefficient, each of which is assumed to be normally distributed, has a mean of zero, and some variance that is represented by the diagonal terms in the tau matrix ($\mathbf{T}$). The off-diagonal terms in the tau matrix are covariances between the random effects.

AN APPLICATION OF THE RC MODEL: ASSESSMENT PRACTICES AND THE ACHIEVEMENT GAP IN SCHOOLS

The remainder of this chapter will focus on applying the RC model using HLM 7 software and data from a large-scale survey to study the minority–White achievement gap in schools. This achievement gap may originate from a number of factors including inequity of educational opportunity. Documented research on this gap in American schools has accumulated since at least the civil rights movement when Congress commissioned the Coleman Report (Coleman et al., 1966) to address this and other issues related to inequity. In subsequent decades, the minority–White achievement gap has reduced; however, it has remain substantial (Gamoran & Long, 2006).

The present application focuses on how assessment practices adopted in schools during the early grades can contribute to differential learning rates between minority (Black and Hispanic) children and White children. The data structure is hierarchical in that students are nested in elementary schools. The most basic question in considering this research problem is whether the magnitude of the gap varies across schools—a question that is highly suitable for an RC model, as we shall see. Once that has been established, the next question is how schools might contribute to that variation. This application addresses the following three research questions:

1. Does the first-grade reading achievement gains gap vary across schools? This question addresses whether school effects potentially contribute to the gap. To answer this question the variance of the random slopes for the MINORITY predictor is tested for significance.

2. To what degree does variation in the reading achievement gap across schools depend on the background characteristics of the students? This question addresses the extent to which the gap is due to differences in the background characteristics of students attending the schools.

3. Do the assessment practices employed by schools contribute to the achievement gains gap? If so, which practices are the most effective or ineffective? Note that this question focuses on the association between school factors and the achievement gains gap, which is level 2 of the RC model.

SAMPLE

This application uses data from the Early Childhood Longitudinal Study Kindergarten Cohort (ECLS-K), which is a large-scale survey of 1998 kindergarteners who were followed as they progressed through middle school (National Center for Education Statistics [NCES], 2002). Survey items and test scores were collected on the children, their teachers, and school principals, making this a good data source for studying school effects, particularly in the early grades. This study uses only the first-grade sample. Students without teacher or school IDs and students who repeated kindergarten were omitted, as were a small percentage of students who met the above criteria but had missing test scores. The final sample included 3,496 students nested in 254 schools. Sampling weights provided with the data were applied to produce a nationally representative sample of 1998 kindergarteners.

The outcome variable is READING ACHIEVEMENT GAINS during first grade. Because the reading test was administered at the beginning and end of first grade, the gain measurement does not include summer; this is a critical design advantage when modeling the effect schools have on the achievement gap because research shows that much of the gap accumulates over summer, a period that cannot be attributed to school effects (Alexander, Entwisle, & Olsen, 2001; Palardy, 2010). Besides READING ACHIEVEMENT GAINS and the primary independent variable, MINORITY, an indicator of whether the child is African American or Hispanic, this application uses student measures of SES, ethnicity (ASIAN, OTHER), AGE, PRIOR READING ACHIEVEMENT, and a measure

of the amount of time between the pre- and posttests for reading achievement
(TIME CHANGE). The last variable is needed to control for duration between the
fall and spring testing dates, which arbitrarily varies across the sample of schools
and is correlated with the achievement gains. Failing to control for that variable
will wrongly benefit schools where the duration was longer.

At level 2, the school-level model, eight measures are used to model the association between the achievement gains gap and school factors. Three variables are
used as controls for contextual aspects of the school; these variables can impact
student learning and may be associated with assessment practices, but are largely
beyond the control of school personnel. They include MEAN SES (average student SES), NEIGHBORHOOD BLIGHT (the prevalence of crime, gangs, traffic,
drugs, and unkempt or vacant structures), and SCHOOL MONITORING (teachers patrol hallways, hall passes required, restricted restroom use, all visitors must
sign in, locked exits during the day). The latter is a proxy measure for school
security necessitated by neighborhood factors. The other five school variables
measure assessment practices including standards-based, commercial, teacher-
made, performance, and behavioral assessment practices. With the exception of
MEAN SES, which is the mean of an equally weighted composite of five student
measures (mother's and father's education level and occupational status, and
family income), all school variables are principal components constructed from
two to seven measures. For ease of interpretation, all continuous variables are
standardized with the exception of two student variables, AGE and TIME
CHANGE, because their scale (months) is inherently meaningful. Table 8.1 provides further information on the variables described above.

Table 8.1   Variable List and Descriptive Statistics

Variable Name	Mean	SD	Min	Max	Description
Student Variables (Level 1, N = 3,496)					
Achievement Test Scores					
Reading Gains	0	1	−3.18	4.19	First-grade achievement reading gains
Fall Reading	0	1	−2.16	3.89	Fall first-grade reading achievement
Time Change	6.84	0.65	4.83	9.01	Time in months between fall and spring test administrations
Demographic Characteristics					
Minority	0.30	0.46	0	1	African American or Hispanic
Asian	0.02	0.14	0	1	Asian ethnicity

(Continued)

Table 8.1   (Continued)

Variable Name	Mean	SD	Min	Max	Description
Other	0.05	0.22	0	1	Not African American, Asian, Hispanic, or White
Age	86.97	4.21	74.23	96.00	Months since birth
SES	0	1	−2.81	3.75	Socioeconomic status
Gender	0.49	–	0	1	Coded 0 = male, 1 = female
School Variables (Level 2, N = 254)					
School Context					
Mean SES	0	1	−1.81	3.00	Mean school SES
Neighborhood Blight	0	1	−2.38	7.72	Degree of crime, gangs, traffic, drugs, unkempt, vacant (PC)
School Monitoring	0	1	−1.79	1.48	Access and use of facilities is carefully monitored (PC)
Assessment Factors					
Standards-based Assessment	0	1	−3.78	2.90	Relative to standard or the class (PC)
Commercial Assessment	0	1	−2.37	3.04	Commercially tests or textbooks (PC)
Teacher-Made Assessment	0	1	−4.62	2.41	Teacher-made tests and worksheets (PC)
Performance Assessment	0	1	−4.90	2.56	Individual or group projects or work samples (PC)
Behavioral Assessment	0	1	−2.92	1.86	Effort, participation, attendance, cooperation, etc. (PC)

Note. All student variables are weighted using the appropriate sampling weights; PC = principal component.

SOFTWARE AND PROCEDURE

HLM 7 was used to fit the models in the application. HLM is one of the original multilevel software packages and is capable of estimating a broad range of MLMs. HLM has several specialized modules for fitting models such as cross-classified, spatial, and multivariate multilevel models. Because HLM software is described in Chapter 3, minimal additional information is provided here. The reader is also referred to a review of the latest version of HLM 7

(Palardy, 2011) and the user's manual, which is freely available in pdf format (Raudenbush et al., 2011).

As described above, three sequential models are fit to the data, including the Baseline, Student, and School models. The graphing capabilities, while not extensive, are very convenient for testing modeling assumptions and developing figures to accentuate results (unfortunately, there is insufficient space in this chapter to demonstrate how to test model assumptions). After running a model with HLM 7, various aspects of the results can be graphed using the pull-down menu. Figure 8.1 (above) is an example of a graph of the level 1 equation for a sample of schools. It is helpful for visually examining the variability of the intercepts and slopes of an RC model.

ANALYZING THE DATA

A sequential or hierarchical model-building process is often employed in studies that use multilevel models, because such processes can disentangle effects and help address research questions. Three models were estimated to address the research questions in the current study including the Baseline, Student, and School models. The rationale for each model and its specification are provided below.

Baseline model. A typical starting point in model building is the null or unconditional model, which is the one-way ANOVA with random effect and has no covariates. This model can provide baseline estimates of the variability in the outcome at level 1 and level 2 which can be used to test whether there is significant variance in the means (intercepts) in the sample of schools. The baseline model can also be used to compute the intraclass correlation coefficient (ICC), which is the proportion of the total variance in the outcome that is between level 2 unit means. However, the unconditional model should not be the default starting point for every MLM study. Instead, the starting point should depend on the study's focus and research questions. In studies like the present one, where the focus is on the variability of a random slope (i.e., the minority achievement gap across a sample of schools), the null model is of limited utility because there is no substantive interest in the variability of the outcome means across schools, and it provides no insight about the variances component that is the focus of the study (i.e., variation in the random slopes). Note that even if the variance in mean achievement gains between schools is not statistically significant, the MINORITY slope coefficient may vary significantly across schools. For these reasons, the appropriate starting point for many studies employing RC modeling is a model that includes the random slope(s) that are the focus of the study, and thus, the present study begins with a baseline RC model with the dummy-coded MINORITY variable specified as random. Also included in the baseline model are dummy-coded variables for ASIAN and OTHER ethnic categories, which are fixed. ASIAN and OTHER are included so that the reference category is White children. TIME CHANGE is also included in the baseline model.

In this application the key purpose of the baseline model is to test whether the MINORITY effect varies across the sample of schools. The model also provides a set of parameters that can be compared with subsequent models to determine how estimates change as variables are added.

Student model. Consistent with the advice of Raudenbush and Bryk (2002), before adding level 2 predictors, the level 1 model should be finalized. To that end, the next model is the student model, which includes additional student covariates over and above those in the baseline model. These additional covariates may be of substantive or theoretical interest in the study, or they may be statistical controls (i.e., control covariates). In the current application, SES, AGE, GENDER, and PRIOR ACHIEVEMENT are all added as control covariates. None are of substantive interest in the present study, but the literature suggests that all are correlated with reading achievement gains in the first grade (Palardy & Rumberger, 2008). Because the means of these covariates may differ across the sample of schools, but are generally not considered to be school effects, it is critical that they be included when modeling school effects. Failing to include such variables raises concerns about the internal validity of the study, specifically, whether any observed school effects were due to differences in the characteristics of students who enrolled in respective schools rather than contextual school factors or the effectiveness of the practices school personnel use (Ballou, Sanders, & Wright, 2004). The student model is useful in that it will provide information that can be used to calculate the proportion of the variance accounted for by the addition of the student control covariates. A likelihood ratio test (i.e., chi-square difference test) can be used to test whether those variables collectively account for significant variation in the outcome.

When adding these covariates to the level 1 model, one will have to decide whether to specify them as fixed or random. This decision may be based in part on practical issues such as characteristics of the data source, as well as the focus of the study as articulated by the research questions. For example, if the data source has a very large number of observations per level 2 unit, it might be practical to begin the analysis with all level 1 covariates specified as random and then fix those with non-significant random effects. Yet, typically the number of observations per level 2 unit will be rather small, in which case a more restrictive model-building approach will be necessary. Recall that when level 1 covariates are specified as random, an estimate is generated for each level 2 unit, whereas if these covariates are specified as fixed, only one estimate is produced that applies to all level 2 units. Because of this, accurate estimates of random effects require far more observations per level 2 unit than do accurate estimates of fixed effects. Furthermore, including random coefficients with non-significant random effects can result in estimation problems. If the number of observations per level 2 unit is fairly large (e.g., $\bar{N}_j > 30$), a viable strategy is to specify and test level 1 covariates as random, one by one. If the random effect is not significant, the covariate can be fixed to prevent estimation problems and to promote model parsimony.

The objectives of the given study may also play a role in this decision. If a research question pertains to one or more specific random coefficients, it is essential that they be specified as random. If the number of observations per level 2 unit in the data source is small and the research questions pertain to only one random coefficient, all other level 1 covariates may be fixed for practical reasons. In this application, the data source includes approximately 14 students per school, which limits the number of level 1 covariates that can be specified as random. For this reason, all level 1 covariates other than the MINORITY variable are fixed.

School model. The last model estimated for this application is the school model, which includes the eight school-level measures described above. There are two types of school-level variables that have been strategically selected. The first type consists of school-level contextual variables, which in the present analysis can be considered school-level control variables. This includes MEAN SES, NEIGHBORHOOD BLIGHT, and SCHOOL MONITORING. While they are not of substantive interest in the present application, they are associated with student learning and school assessment practices and therefore may confound estimates of the achievement gap in schools. Hence, failing to control for such factors in the model may bias estimates of the effects of the assessment practices on reading gains. The second set of school variables contains five assessment practices, which were outlined above.

OUTPUT AND ANALYSIS

In this section, excerpts from the HLM 7 outputs for the three sequential models are provided along with annotations. In the *Conclusion* section, these results are interpreted.

The analysis begins with the baseline model, which is described in Equation Set 2. Note that two of the five level 1 coefficients are specified as random, including the intercept and the MINORITY slope.

Equation Set 2: The Baseline Model

LEVEL 1

READING GAINS$_{ij}$ = β_{0j} + β_{1j}*(OTHER$_{ij}$) + β_{2j}*(ASIAN$_{ij}$) + β_{3j}*(MINOR$_{ij}$) + β_{4j}*(TIME CHANGE$_{ij}$) + r$_{ij}$

LEVEL 2

$\beta_{0j} = \gamma_{00} + u_{0j}$
$\beta_{1j} = \gamma_{10}$
$\beta_{2j} = \gamma_{20}$
$\beta_{3j} = \gamma_{30} + u_{3j}$
$\beta_{4j} = \gamma_{40}$

Table 8.2-A shows the tau matrix of the variance/covariance terms for the level 2 random effects with the correlation (−0.37) in the upper right cell.

Table 8.2-B provides the average reliability of the intercept and slope estimates of the sample of 254 schools. The reliability measures the ratio of the parameter variance and the total variance for each school. This is primarily a function of (a) sample size (in this case, the number of students in the given school's sample), (b) error variance (σ^2), and (c) parameter variance (i.e., τ_{00} for the intercept and $\tau_{11}\sigma_x^2$ for the slope, where σ_x^2 is the variance in the MINORITY variable). Small within-school samples, large error variance, and small parameter variance all undermine the reliability of the random coefficient estimates. Raudenbush and Bryk (2002, p. 125) interpret these reliabilities as the amount of the observed variation in the respective random coefficient that is potentially explainable. They suggest that values less than 0.05 indicate there is potentially insufficient explainable variability in the coefficient for modeling and hence, it should be fixed. Note that average reliabilities below 0.05 will typically coincide with non-significant variance estimates on the random coefficient unless the sample size is very small.

Table 8.2-C shows the fixed effects, while Table 8.2-D shows the random effects. Note that robust standard errors are shown with the fixed effects. The HLM output provides model-based standard errors (not shown in Table 8.2-C) as well as robust standard errors. The robust standard errors have the advantage of being consistent even when some violations of the model assumptions are present. The two sets of standard errors can be used as a diagnostic tool: If they differ substantially, there are likely violations of the model assumptions that merit further investigation.

Table 8.2-A Baseline Model Tau Matrix of Level 2 Variances and Covariance of Random Effects

INTRCPT1,β_0	0.11583 (0.01616)	−0.37000
MINOR,β_3	−0.04031 (0.02330)	0.10251 (0.05353)

Upper right cell is the correlation coefficient; Standard errors are in parentheses.

Table 8.2-B Baseline Model Reliability Estimates

Random level 1 coefficient	Reliability estimate
INTRCPT1,β_0	0.639
MINOR,β_3	0.187

Table 8.2-C Baseline Model Fixed Effects (with robust standard errors)

Fixed Effect	Coefficient	Standard error	t-ratio	Approx. d.f.	p-value
For INTRCPT1, β_0					
INTRCPT2, γ_{00}	0.001553	0.028647	0.054	253	0.957
For OTHER slope, β_1					
INTRCPT2, γ_{10}	−0.033334	0.076337	−0.437	2985	0.662
For ASIAN slope, β_2					
INTRCPT2, γ_{20}	−0.245924	0.099706	−2.466	2985	0.014
For MINOR slope, β_3					
INTRCPT2, γ_{30}	−0.099911	0.061787	−1.617	253	0.107
For TIME_CHANGE slope, β_4					
INTRCPT2, γ_{40}	0.186111	0.037709	4.935	2985	<0.001

Table 8.2-D Baseline Model Variance Components

Random Effect	Standard Deviation	Variance Component	d.f.	χ^2	p-value
INTRCPT1, u_0	0.34033	0.11583	178	524.95598	< 0.001
MINOR slope, u_3	0.32017	0.10251	178	223.20278	0.012
level 1, r	0.92501	0.85564			

Deviance = 9671.60; number of estimated parameters = 9.

Equation Set 3 shows the student model. Compared with the baseline model, four additional control covariates were added, including SES, AGE, GENDER, and PRIOR ACHIEVEMENT.

Equation Set 3: The Student Model

LEVEL 1

$$READING\ GAIN_{ij} = \beta_{0j} + \beta_{1j}*(OTHER_{ij}) + \beta_{2j}*(ASIAN_{ij}) + \beta_{3j}*(GENDER_{ij}) + \beta_{4j}*(MINOR_{ij}) + \beta_{5j}*(TIME\ CHANGE_{ij}) + \beta_{6j}*(AGE_{ij}) + \beta_{7j}*(PRIOR\ ACHIEVE_{ij}) + \beta_{8j}*(SES_{ij}) + r_{ij}$$

LEVEL 2

$$\beta_{0j} = \gamma_{00} + u_{0j}$$
$$\beta_{1j} = \gamma_{10}$$
$$\beta_{2j} = \gamma_{20}$$
$$\beta_{3j} = \gamma_{30}$$
$$\beta_{4j} = \gamma_{40} + u_{4j}$$
$$\beta_{5j} = \gamma_{50}$$
$$\beta_{6j} = \gamma_{60}$$
$$\beta_{7j} = \gamma_{70}$$
$$\beta_{8j} = \gamma_{80}$$

Table 8.3-A   Student Model Fixed Effects (with robust standard errors)

Fixed Effect	Coefficient	Standard error	t-ratio	Approx. d.f.	p-value
For INTRCPT1, β_0					
INTRCPT2, γ_{00}	−0.030147	0.034139	−0.883	253	0.378
For OTHER slope, β_1					
INTRCPT2, γ_{10}	−0.060683	0.077297	−0.785	2981	0.432
For ASIAN slope, β_2					
INTRCPT2, γ_{20}	−0.174497	0.090103	−1.937	2981	0.053
For GENDER slope, β_3					
INTRCPT2, γ_{30}	0.049098	0.036486	1.346	2981	0.179
For MINOR slope, β_4					
INTRCPT2, γ_{40}	−0.131663	0.060153	−2.189	253	0.030
For TIME CHANGE slope, β_5					
INTRCPT2, γ_{50}	0.178314	0.037127	4.803	2981	<0.001
For AGE slope, β_6					
INTRCPT2, γ_{60}	−0.015700	0.004913	−3.195	2981	0.001
For PRIOR ACHIEVE slope, β_7					
INTRCPT2, γ_{70}	−0.243870	0.022310	−10.931	2981	<0.001
For SES slope, β_8					
INTRCPT2, γ_{80}	0.093536	0.022287	4.197	2981	<0.001

Table 8.3-B	Student Model Variance Components				
Random Effect	*Standard Deviation*	*Variance Component*	*d.f.*	χ^2	*p-value*
INTRCPT1, u_0	0.33907	0.11497	178	557.82651	<0.001
MINOR slope, u_4	0.31661	0.10024	178	223.30499	0.012
level 1, r	0.89568	0.80224			

Deviance = 9457.87; Number of estimated parameters = 13.

Equation Set 4 shows the school model. Only the level 2 equations are provided because the level 1 equation has not changed from the student model. The level 2 equations show that eight school variables were added to the INTERCEPT and MINORITY slope equations. Note that the same set of variables is included in each equation. This specification may strike some as unexpected, given that the research questions did not directly necessitate the inclusion of the school factors in the INTERCEPT equation. Recall that the random effects for the INTERCEPT and MINORITY slope are specified to covary. The covariance will depend in part on the covariates that are included in the model. Omitting important variables is a concern. To protect against that, it is prudent to include the same set of variables in both equations, at least as a starting point in model building. The model may then be reduced if desired by omitting the non-significant predictors. When a large number of predictors are being considered, reducing the model becomes a more attractive option due to the virtues of model parsimony and concerns with collinearity.

Equation Set 4: The School Model

LEVEL 2

$\beta_{0j} = \gamma_{00} + \gamma_{01}*(\text{MEAN SES}_j) + \gamma_{02}*(\text{MONITOR}_j) + \gamma_{03}*(\text{BEHAVORIAL}_j) + \gamma_{04}*(\text{AUTHENTIC}_j) + \gamma_{05}*(\text{STANDARDS}_j) + \gamma_{06}*(\text{COMMERCIAL}_j) + \gamma_{07}*(\text{TEACHER DEV}_j) + \gamma_{08}*(\text{NEIGHBORHOOD}_j) + u_{0j}$

$\beta_{1j} = \gamma_{10}$

$\beta_{2j} = \gamma_{20}$

$\beta_{3j} = \gamma_{30}$

$\beta_{4j} = \gamma_{40} + \gamma_{41}*(\text{MEAN SES}_j) + \gamma_{42}*(\text{MONITOR}_j) + \gamma_{43}*(\text{BEHAVORIAL}_j) + \gamma_{44}*(\text{AUTHENTIC}_j) + \gamma_{45}*(\text{STANDARDS}_j) + \gamma_{46}*(\text{COMMERCIAL}_j) + \gamma_{47}*(\text{TEACHER DEV}_j) + \gamma_{48}*(\text{NEIGHBORHOOD}_j) + u_{4j}$

$\beta_{5j} = \gamma_{50}$

$\beta_{6j} = \gamma_{60}$

$\beta_{7j} = \gamma_{70}$

$\beta_{8j} = \gamma_{80}$

Table 8.4-A   School Model Fixed Effects (with robust standard errors)

Fixed Effect	Coefficient	Standard error	t-ratio	Approx. d.f.	p-value
For INTRCPT1, β_0					
INTRCPT2, γ_{00}	−0.025798	0.032732	−0.788	245	0.431
MEAN SES, γ_{01}	0.125276	0.029851	4.197	245	<0.001
MONITOR, γ_{02}	−0.041727	0.027980	−1.491	245	0.137
BEHAVORIAL, γ_{03}	−0.029994	0.027345	−1.097	245	0.274
AUTHENTIC, γ_{04}	−0.017249	0.029441	−0.586	245	0.558
STANDARDS-BASED, γ_{05}	−0.023991	0.029862	−0.803	245	0.423
COMMERCIAL, γ_{06}	0.073182	0.029358	2.493	245	0.013
TEACHER DEV, γ_{07}	0.030569	0.035875	0.852	245	0.395
NEIGHBORHOOD, γ_{08}	−0.002157	0.020466	−0.105	245	0.916
For MINOR slope, β_4					
INTRCPT2, γ_{40}	−0.195881	0.054616	−3.586	245	<0.001
MEAN SES, γ_{41}	−0.023828	0.053599	−0.445	245	0.657
MONITOR, γ_{42}	0.082894	0.049706	1.668	245	0.097
BEHAVORIAL, γ_{43}	−0.220122	0.050366	−4.370	245	<0.001
AUTHETHIC, γ_{44}	0.217435	0.058171	3.738	245	<0.001
STANDARDS-BASED, γ_{45}	−0.017563	0.063572	−0.276	245	0.783
COMMERCIAL, γ_{46}	−0.037192	0.059583	−0.624	245	0.533
TEACHER DEV, γ_{47}	−0.026701	0.064551	−0.414	245	0.679
NEIGHBHOOD, γ_{48}	−0.027389	0.040534	−0.676	245	0.500

Table 8.4-B   Student Model Variance Components

Random Effect	Standard Deviation	Variance Component	d.f.	χ^2	p-value
INTRCPT1, u_0	0.31466	0.09901	170	509.70543	<0.001
MINOR slope, u_4	0.15254	0.02327	170	194.17873	0.099
level 1, r	0.89578	0.80243			

Deviance = 9404.5511; number of estimated parameters = 29.

CONCLUSION

Baseline Model

The tau matrix (Table 8.2-B) shows that the correlation between mean READING ACHIEVEMENT GAINS and the MINORITY-READING ACHIEVEMENT GAINS gap in the sample of 254 schools is −0.37. This means that schools with relatively high mean achievement gains tend to have relatively small minority–White achievement gains gaps. This suggests that schools that are effective in raising reading achievement in general are particularly effective for raising reading achievement for Black and Hispanic children. The standard errors of the tau can be used to develop a t-test for the significance of this covariance (t = −0.040/0.023 = −1.73, 0.10 > p > 0.05), which indicates it is not statistically significant at $\alpha = 0.05$, but it is at $\alpha = 0.10$.

Table 8.2-C shows the fixed effects. The mean of the school intercepts (γ_{00}), which is the expected reading gain during first grade for White children, is not significantly different from zero ($\gamma_{00} = 0.001553, t = 0.054, p = 0.957$). This is not surprising because the outcome variable has a standard normal distribution with a mean of zero. Also note that the mean minority–White reading gains gap is not statistically significant ($\gamma_{30} = -0.099911, t = -1.617, p = 0.107$). This finding may come as a surprise, given the amount of attention achievement gaps have received in the literature. Yet recall that the outcome used in this study is different from most of the achievement gap literature. The outcome is reading achievement gains within a single school year and does not include summer in the gains estimates. In fact, these results are not inconsistent with previous research that found most of the achievement gap accumulates over summer (Alexander et al., 2001).

Table 8.2-D displays the variance component estimates. There is significant variance in both the intercepts for mean reading achievement gains ($Var(u_0) = \tau_{00} = 0.11583, \chi^2_{178} = 524.96, p < 0.01$) and the slope for the minority–White achievement gains gap ($Var(u_3) = \tau_{33} = 0.10251, \chi^2_{178} = 223.20, p < 0.05$). Note that the significant variance (random effect) estimate for the MINORITY slope addresses Research Question 1: The minority–White achievement gains gap varies in our sample of schools. This is true even though the results above show the fixed effect for MINORITY is not statistically significant, indicating that on average, reading achievement gains for minority and White children are not different. To clarify, the random effects shows that the MINORITY–White achievement gains gap varies across the schools, whereas the fixed effect shows it is approximately zero, on average. These parameters and the deviance statistic for the baseline model (provided below Table 8.2-D) will be compared to subsequent models to gauge how they change as variables are added.

A common practice in multilevel modeling is to compute the intraclass correlation coefficient (ICC) for the baseline model, which is typically the unconditional model. Computing the ICC is very straightforward for the unconditional model; however, it becomes increasingly complex as random coefficients are added. Note that an ICC can be calculated for each level 2 random effect, which describes the proportion of the total variance that is accounted for by the respective random effect, although the computation becomes increasingly complex as random coefficients are added. The ICC for the INTERCEPT

is $ICC_0 = \dfrac{\tau_{00}}{\tau_{00} + \sigma_e^2 + \tau_{11}\sigma_x^2 + \mu_x\tau_{01}} = \dfrac{0.11583}{0.11583 + 0.85564 + 0.10251*0.2101 - 0.04031*0.3001} = 0.1181$ or 11.81%, where

σ_e^2 is the level 1 random effect (Table 8.2-D), σ_x^2 and μ_x are the variance and mean of the MINORITY variable (Table 8.1), and τ_{01} is the covariance between the level 2 random effects (Table 8.2-A). Similarly, the ICC for the MINORITY slope is as follows:

$ICC_3 = \dfrac{\tau_{11}\sigma_x^2}{\tau_{00} + \sigma_e^2 + \tau_{11}\sigma_x^2 + \mu_x\tau_{01}} = \dfrac{0.10251*0.2101}{0.11583 + 0.85564 + 0.10251*0.2101 - 0.04031*0.3001} = 0.0220$ or 2.2%. From these

computations, we see that the proportion of the total variance in reading achievement gains accounted for by the random effect of the minority–White achievement gains gap is small. Note, however, it is a statistically significant amount, as indicated by the chi-square test results in Table 8.2-D.

Student Model

Table 8.3-A (see page 196) shows that the majority of the student variables are significantly associated with reading gains at $\alpha = 0.05$. After adding the four student control covariates to the model, the minority–White achievement gains gap increases in magnitude by 32 percent and becomes statistically significant ($\gamma_{40} = -0.13$, p < 0.05). This increase may seem counterintuitive because SES and prior achievement are both negatively associated with minority status. A post-hoc analysis provides an explanation. The increase in the magnitude of the effect is almost completely due to minority children making greater gains in reading achievement during first grade than expected given their prior achievement. This results in a greater downward adjustment for minority children when prior achievement is added. By comparison, SES did not moderate the minority–White gap. This new estimate of the minority gap is closer to the true minority gap because the confounding effect of prior achievement has been removed. The mean reading achievement gain during first grade for Black and Hispanic children is approximately 0.13 standard deviations less than the mean gain for White children, after controlling for age, prior reading achievement, SES, and gender. The model deviance statistic can be compared with that of the baseline model to construct a likelihood ratio test (LRT, also known as the chi-square difference test) to determine if adding the set of student control variables accounted for a significant amount of variation. Comparing Table 8.2-D with Table 8.3-B, (see page 197), we see that compared with the baseline model, the student model deviance statistic was reduced by 213.73 on 4 degrees of freedom, a highly significant improvement in model fit ($LRT: \Delta\chi_4^2$ = 213.73, $p < 0.01$). We also see that variance in the 3 random effects were reduced, albeit, only to a small to moderate degree. The level 1 variance (σ^2) was reduced from 0.85564 to 0.80224 or 6.2%. The variation in the level 1 intercepts (τ_{00}) was reduced from 0.11583 to 0.11497 or 0.7%, whereas the variance in the MINORITY slopes (τ_{33}) was reduced from 0.10251 to 0.10024 or 2.2%. The addition of the four covariates in the level 1 model accounted for these reductions in the variability of the random effects.

Note that these results address Research Question 2. The level 1 control covariates account for only 2.2% of the variation in the achievement gains gap across the sample of schools. A highly significant amount of variation remains. The reading achievement gains gap does not seem to be closely linked with student background characteristics. The next model will examine whether it is associated with school context and assessment practices.

School Model

Recall that the school factors are all standardized principal components with means of zero and standard deviations of 1, resulting in the magnitude of their coefficients being directly comparable. Also recall that each of the factors in the level 2 MINORITY equation is a cross-level interaction effect. That is, each depends on the value of the level 1 variable, MINORITY. When MINORITY is zero, the term drops from the equation. When it is 1, the coefficient applies to describe the expected change in the achievement gap per unit (standard deviation) change in the predictor.

The fixed effect results displayed in Table 8.4-A show that two assessment practices stand out in terms of magnitude of effect and statistical significance. Each standard deviation increase in the use of *behavioral* assessments is associated with an increase in the achievement gains gap of 0.22 standard deviations ($\gamma_{43} = -0.22$, $p < 0.01$). Conversely, the use of *authentic* assessments, while equal in magnitude, is associated with a significant reduction in the achievement gains gap ($\gamma_{44} = 0.22$, $p < 0.01$). The other three types of assessment practices examined were not associated with the reading achievement gains gap. These results show that assessment practices potentially play a role in the formation of the achievement gap at the early grades.

The results indicate the minority achievement gains gap could differ immensely in two schools based on differences in assessment practices. For example, using the school model results, we can predict the achievement gains gap in two schools, one that relies heavily on authentic assessment (AUTHENTIC = 2) and avoids behavioral assessment (BEHAVIORAL = −2), compared with another school where behavioral assessment is strongly preferred (BEHAVIORAL = 2) and authentic assessment practices are largely ignored (AUTHENTIC = 2). In the latter school, the achievement gains gap will be approximately 1.76 (i.e., 0.22*8) standard deviations greater.

Compared with the student model, the deviance statistic (Table 8.4-B) was reduced by a significant amount (LRT = 53.32, df =16, $p < 0.01$), indicating the addition of the eight school factors accounted for significant variation in reading achievement gains. Note that on Table 8.4-B compared with Table 8.3-B, the level 1 variance is not altered when level 2 predictors are added to the model. Therefore, σ^2 did not change, which is expected given that the school variables are constants for students within schools. However, the variation in the mean achievement gains in the sample of schools (τ_{00}) was reduced from 0.11487 to 0.09901 (13.9%), whereas the variance in the achievement gains gap (τ_{44}) was reduced from 0.10024 to 0.02327 (76.8%), a highly substantial amount. After adding the school contextual controls and assessment methods, the variance in the achievement gains gap is no longer statistically significant.

These finding may tempt one to conclude that the minority–White achievement gap is caused at least in part by the assessment methods schools employ. While that might be correct, caution is recommended before making such causal claims with non-experimental data, as the statistical associations estimated by the model are correlational. The associations could be due to selectivity bias or spurious correlations. That the outcome measures achievement gains during the school year, that student and school controls are included, and that the model explains essentially all of the variance of the minority–White gap all improve the validity of such a causal claim. However, still stronger statistical controls, as well as quasi-experimental methods (e.g., propensity score matching), and econometric methods (e.g., instrumental variables and "fixed effects") can be employed to further strengthen the validity of causal inferences. These methods can be employed within the multilevel modeling framework.

Note that in a more comprehensive analysis, the school model could be estimated in two or more steps. For example, first the contextual controls may be added and the model estimated; then, the assessment factors may be added, along with the contextual controls, and the model estimated a second time. This two-step process would produce results that can be used to differentiate the effects of the contextual controls from the assessment factors to determine the net effect of the assessment factors.

In summary, the random coefficients model is a flexible and potentially complex multilevel model with a vast array of applications in the social sciences. This chapter was designed to introduce the model and some of that complexity, and provide guidance on model specification and results interpretation. Happy modeling.

REFERENCES

Alexander, K. L., Entwisle, D. R., & Olsen, H. R. (2001). Schools, achievement, and inequality: A seasonal perspective. *Educational Evaluation and Policy Analysis, 23,* 171–191.

Ballou, D., Sanders, W., & Wright, P. (2004). Controlling for student background in value added assessment of teachers. *Journal of Educational and Behavioral Statistics, 29,* 37–65.

Coleman, J. S., Campbell, E. A., Hobson, C., Mc Partland, J., Mood, A., Weinfeld, F., et al. (1966). *Equality of educational opportunity.* Washington, DC: U.S. Government Printing Office.

Gamoran, A., & Long, D. A. (2006). *Equality of educational opportunity: A 40-year retrospective.* Wisconsin Center for Education Research (Working Paper No. 2006-9). Madison: University of Wisconsin. Retrieved October 18, 2009, from http://www.wcer.wisc.edu/publications/workingpapers/Working_Paper_No_2006_09.pdf

National Center for Educational Statistics. (2002). *User's guide to the longitudinal kindergarten-first grade public-use data file.* Washington, DC: U.S. Department of Education.

Palardy, G. J. (2010). The multilevel crossed random effects growth model with applications for estimating teacher and school effects: Issues and extensions. *Educational and Psychological Measurement, 70,* 401–419.

Palardy, G. J. (2011). Review of HLM 7. *Social Science Computer Review, 29,* 515–520.

Palardy, G. J., & Rumberger, R. W. (2008). Teacher effectiveness in first grade: The importance of background qualifications, attitudes, and instructional practices for student learning. *Educational Evaluation and Policy Analysis, 30,* 111–140.

Raudenbush, S. W., & Bryk, A. S. (2002). *Hierarchical linear models: Applications and data analysis methods* (2nd ed.). Newbury Park, CA: Sage.

Raudenbush, S. W., Bryk, A. S., Cheong, Y. F., Congdon, R. T., & du Toit, M. (2011). *HLM 7: Hierarchical linear and nonlinear modeling.* Chicago: Scientific Software International.

Snijders, T. A. B., & Bosker, R. J. (2011). *Multilevel analysis: An introduction to basic and advanced multilevel modeling* (2nd ed.). London: Sage.

Emotional Reactivity to Daily Stressors Using a Random Coefficients Model With SAS PROC MIXED

9

A Repeated Measures Analysis

Shevaun D. Neupert

When the primary research question focuses on micro-level variables that are nested within a larger grouping, a random coefficients regression model is appropriate (Raudenbush & Bryk, 2002). In this example using SAS PROC MIXED, repeated occasions (Level 1) are nested within individuals (Level 2). Therefore, time-varying measures are associated with Level 1, and time-invariant, person-level measures are associated with Level 2. The specific within-person (Level 1) research question that will be addressed is whether days with more stressors are associated with increases in psychological distress, which is also known as emotional reactivity.

I use publicly available daily diary data (www.icpsr.umich.edu) to examine the within-person (Level 1) relationship between daily stressors and psychological distress. Daily stressors are the routine challenges of day-to-day living, and although they may be relatively minor, they are tangible events that can have immediate negative impacts on psychological well-being (Almeida, 2005; Almeida, Wethington, & Kessler, 2002; Bolger, DeLongis, Kessler, & Schilling, 1989). The present chapter examines emotional reactivity to daily stressors, which is defined as an increase in distress in response to stressors (Neupert, Almeida, & Charles, 2007). Importantly, reactivity is a within-person process, so the variables of interest were measured and modeled at Level 1. Specifically, the number of daily stressors and the level of psychological distress were measured repeatedly for 8 consecutive days. Age was also included as a person-level covariate at Level 2 because it is important to control for age-related differences in the average level of psychological distress, as older adults typically report less distress than younger adults (Neupert et al., 2007). Although the example here uses daily diary data where days are nested within people, the structure of the model and the analytic process is the same for repeated measures data with shorter or longer intervals as well as for data where people are nested within larger groups.

SAMPLE AND PROCEDURE

Data for the analyses are from the National Study of Daily Experiences (NSDE). Respondents were 1,031 adults (562 women, 469 men), all of whom had previously participated in the Midlife in the United States Survey (MIDUS), a nationally representative telephone-mail survey of 3,032 people, aged 25 to 74 years, carried out in 1995–1996 under the auspices of the MacArthur Foundation Research Network on Successful Midlife Development (for descriptions of the MIDUS project, see Brim, Ryff, & Kessler, 2004; Keyes & Ryff, 1998; Lachman & Weaver, 1998; Mroczek & Kolarz, 1998). Respondents in the NSDE were randomly selected from the MIDUS sample and received $20 for their participation in the project.

Over 8 consecutive evenings, respondents completed short telephone interviews about their daily experiences. Data collection was planned to span an entire year (March 1996 to March 1997), so 40 separate "flights" of interviews with each flight representing the 8-day sequence of interviews from approximately 38 respondents were used. The initiation of flights was staggered across the day of the week to control for the possible confounding between day of the study and day of week. Of the 1,242 MIDUS respondents contacted, 1,031 agreed to participate, yielding a response rate of 83%. Respondents completed an average of 7 of the 8 interviews, resulting in a total of 7,229 daily interviews. The NSDE subsample and the MIDUS sample had very similar distributions for gender, age, education, and race. The NSDE had slightly more females (54.5% vs. 51.5% of the MIDUS sample), was better educated (62.3% had 13 years or more of education vs. 60.8% of the MIDUS sample), and had fewer minority respondents than the MIDUS. Of the participants in the NSDE, 90.3% were Caucasian, 5.9% were African American, and 3.8% were all other races versus 87.8% Caucasian, 6.8% African American, and 4.4% other races in the MIDUS. Respondents for the present analysis were on average 47 years old.

MEASURES

Daily psychological distress was measured using 10 items designed specifically for the MIDUS. This scale was developed from the following well-known and valid instruments: the Affect Balance Scale (Bradburn, 1969), the University of Michigan's Composite International Diagnostic Interview (Kessler et al., 1994), the Manifest Anxiety Scale (Taylor, 1953), and the Center for Epidemiological Studies Depression Scale (Radloff, 1977). Respondents were asked questions such as how much of the time today did they feel worthless, hopeless, nervous, restless, or fidgety, that everything was an effort, and so sad that nothing could cheer them up. They rated their response on a 5-point scale from 0 *(none of the time)* to 4 *(all of the time)*. Scores across the 10 items were summed for each day. This scale has demonstrated good reliability and validity in previous studies (Kessler et al., 2002; Mroczek & Kolarz, 1998).

Daily stressors were assessed through the semi-structured Daily Inventory of Stressful Events (DISE; Almeida et al., 2002). The inventory consisted of a series of seven stem questions asking whether certain types of daily stressors (i.e., arguments, potential arguments, work stressors, home stressors, network stressors, discrimination stressors, and other stressors) had occurred in the past 24 hours. For each daily interview, affirmative responses to the stem questions received a value of 1, and a composite score was created by summing the number of affirmative responses. Therefore, the possible range of the stressor variable was 0 to 7, but the observed range was 0 to 6 ($M = 0.52$, $SD = 0.79$).

EQUATIONS

The equations below were used to examine emotional reactivity to daily stressors. In this example, individual variability is represented by a two-level hierarchical model where Level 1 reflects the daily diary information nested within the person-level information at Level 2.

$$\text{Level 1: DISTRESS}_{ti} = \beta_{0i} + \beta_{1ti}(\text{STRESSORS}) + r_{ti} \tag{1}$$

$$\text{Level 2:} \qquad \beta_{0i} = \gamma_{00} + \gamma_{01}(\text{AGE}) + u_{0i} \tag{2}$$

$$\beta_{1i} = \gamma_{10} + u_{1i} \tag{3}$$

Following the guidelines by Raudenbush and Bryk (2002), the lettered subscripts in the equations depict the nesting structure. Days/timepoints are represented by t (Level 1), and individuals are represented by i (Level 2).

In Equation 1, the intercept (β_{0i}) is defined as the expected level of psychological distress for person i on days when no stressors occurred (i.e., STRESSORS = 0) because the variable was uncentered. Although it would have been possible to person-mean or grand-mean center STRESSORS, I chose to leave this variable uncentered so that the interpretation of the intercept would be associated with a particular type of day (i.e., when no stressors were reported). In addition, this method allows for the focus to be on changes in absolute levels of stressors, rather than implying that a daily stressor score of 0 has a different meaning for people with different average levels of stress (which would be the case with person-mean centering) (Raudenbush & Bryk, 2002). The reactivity slope, β_{1ti}, is the expected change in psychological distress associated with days when stressors occur. For researchers with repeated measures data who are interested in modeling individual growth parameters for the dependent variable, the Level 1 predictor would then be an indication of time (e.g., number of trials, number of months since baseline). The error term (r_{ti}) represents a unique effect associated with person i (i.e., individual fluctuation around his or her own mean). The Level 1 intercept and slope become the outcome variables in the Level 2 equations. Equation 2 includes age as a covariate and therefore tests to see if age is related to the average level of psychological distress (γ_{01}). The intercept (γ_{00}) represents the average level of psychological distress for a 47-year-old because age was centered at the grand mean (CAGE [centered age] = 0). I chose to grand-mean center age to maintain an interpretable value of the intercept. Equation 3 provides the estimate (γ_{10}) representing reactivity for the sample: the average relationship between stressors and psychological distress. If age was included as a predictor in this equation, a cross-level interaction would have been specified (i.e., STRESSOR X CAGE), and the research question would have asked whether there were age differences (Level 2) in emotional reactivity (Level 1 relationship). Because the goal of the current example was to control for age and focus on the Level 1 relationship, age was not included in Equation 3. Interindividual fluctuations from the average level and slope are represented by u_{0i} and u_{1i}, respectively.

It is important to note that the models can also be represented in a single line. For the current example, the equation can be expressed as follows:

$$DISTRESS_{ti} = \gamma_{00} + \gamma_{10}(STRESSOR_{ti}) + \gamma_{01}(AGE_i) + r_{ti} + u_{0i} + u_{1i}$$

The interpretation of each of the components is the same as those reported above. The notable difference is that the beta terms from Level 1 are no longer included; only the gamma terms and the random effect terms are used.

SAS COMMANDS

I chose to present the current example using SAS PROC MIXED (SAS Institute Inc., 1997) because the ability to reduce, manage, and analyze in a single software package is a distinct advantage (Singer, 1998). By properly specifying the model within SAS, a user can fit an array of multilevel models, hierarchical models, and individual growth models that are popular in social science research (Hox & Kreft, 1994; Kreft, 1995; Singer, 1998).

As with other hierarchical linear models, the first step is often to conduct an unconditional (null) model with the dependent variable to partition the variance across both levels to determine, in this case, how much variance is associated with day-to-day fluctuations (i.e., Level 1 variance) and how much is associated with individual differences (i.e., Level 2 variance). In addition to partitioning the variance, this is an important first step for the current example because the residual variance estimates from the final model with predictors will be compared to the results from the unconditional model in order to calculate the percentage of variance explained at both levels. The SAS commands in Table 9.1 were used to partition the variance in daily psychological distress.

STRUCTURAL SPECIFICATION

The first line of the commands specifies that a procedure ("proc") for data with mixed levels will be conducted. The current dataset is called "merged." (The user can assign any name to the dataset, but "merged" was chosen in this case because

| Table 9.1 | SAS Commands for the Fully Unconditional Model |

```
proc mixed data=merged noclprint covtest;
title 'null model for daily psychological distress';
class caseid;
model distress=
  /solution ddfm=bw;
random intercept  /subject=caseid ;
run;
```

the NSDE and MIDUS datasets were merged together.) NOCLPRINT does not affect the analysis but prevents the printing of the CLASS-level information, which essentially condenses the amount of output generated. Singer (1998) suggests that the first time the program is run, the user may not want to include this option so that it is easy to ensure that all relevant groups are included in the analysis. The COVTEST command provides hypothesis tests (z- and corresponding p-values in the output) for the variance and covariance components. The second line creates a title for the output and is an optional command. The CLASS statement indicates that CASEID is a classification variable whose values do not contain meaningful quantitative information. In this example, CASEID is the Level 2 ID variable representing each person's ID. Note that the TYPE clause (which will be included in the final model) is omitted here, which means that the model defaults to a variance components (VC) model. VC null models are used to compute the intraclass correlation coefficient (ICC), which provides an estimate of the percentage of the total variance in the dependent variable that is associated with Level 2 effects.

MODEL SPECIFICATION

The MODEL statement specifies the fixed effects and provides an estimate of the grand mean (γ_{00}). Because this is a null or empty model, only the dependent variable and an equal sign appear in this statement. The estimate of the intercept (γ_{00}) is included by default. The /SOLUTION prompts SAS to print the estimates for the fixed effects, and DDFM=BW specifies that computations for denominator degrees of freedom for fixed effects be based on a "between-within" structure. In this example, the degrees of freedom for Level 1 observations will be based on the number of daily interviews, and the degrees of freedom for Level 2 observations will be based on the number of people. As noted in Chapter 2, the Kenward-Roger (KR) method is sometimes preferred over the BW method because KR works reasonably well with more complicated covariance structures when the sample sizes are moderate to small and the design is reasonably balanced. I have chosen to use the BW method for this example because I wanted to obtain exact denominator degrees of freedom (DDF) values. In addition, when the BW method is replaced with the KR method, the fixed and random effects results for this model remain the same.

The RANDOM statement is essential because this is where the random effects are specified. The Level 1 residual (i.e., r_{ti} corresponding to σ^2) is included by default. Including INTERCEPT in the RANDOM statement adds a second random effect, u_{0i} (corresponding to τ_{00}). Specifically, this indicates that the intercept should be treated not only as a fixed effect (represented by γ_{00}), but also as a random effect (Singer, 1998). The SUBJECT= option on the RANDOM statement specifies how the data are structured, indicating how the Level 1 units are nested within Level 2 units. In this example, the Level 1 units (days) are nested within individuals so the Level 2 ID variable (CASEID) is used: SUBJECT=CASEID.

UNCONDITIONAL MODEL OUTPUT

The output from the unconditional model is presented in Table 9.2. The Model Information section repeats the name of the dataset and dependent variable as well as the Level 2 ID variable ("Subject Effect"). The estimation method is REML by default, and the "between-within" degrees of freedom method was specified in the commands.

The Dimensions section summarizes the number of covariance parameters (two random effects in the current model: σ^2 and τ_{00}) and also repeats the number of Level 2 observations (Subjects=1031) and the maximum number of Level 1 observations within each Level 2 unit (8 days per person). The Number of Observations Read, Used, and Not Used are specified in the next section.

PROC MIXED is an efficient program, so the model converged quickly (Singer, 1998). However, increasingly complex models (e.g., those with several random effects) can increase the number of iterations as well as the computational time.

The next section provides the *covariance parameter estimates*. These are the estimates for the random effects in the model, which are used below to calculate the ICC. In this example, $\tau_{00} = 7.2201$ and $\sigma^2 = 6.2266$ and the hypothesis tests indicate that both variance components are significantly different from zero. (Note that Singer [1998] cautions that these tests may not be highly reliable.) The estimates were then used to obtain the ICC [$\rho = \tau_{00} / (\tau_{00} + \sigma^2) = 7.22/(7.22 + 6.23) = .54$].

The next section presents information that can be useful for comparing the goodness of fit of multiple models. A more detailed description of comparing models is described when the final model is presented.

The last section presents parameter estimates for the fixed effects. Because the unconditional model has only one fixed effect, the intercept (γ_{00}), the estimate of 1.8281 indicates that the average level of distress across all people was 1.83 units.

Table 9.2	SAS Output From the Fully Unconditional Model

```
The Mixed Procedure

                          Model Information

        Data Set                        WORK.MERGED
        Dependent Variable              distress
        Covariance Structure            Variance Components
        Subject Effect                  CASEID
        Estimation Method               REML
        Residual Variance Method        Profile
        Fixed Effects SE Method         Model-Based
        Degrees of Freedom Method       Between-Within


                             Dimensions

              Covariance Parameters           2
              Columns in X                    1
              Columns in Z Per Subject        1
              Subjects                     1031
              Max Obs Per Subject             8


                       Number of Observations

          Number of Observations Read        7229
          Number of Observations Used        7221
          Number of Observations Not Used       8


                        Iteration History

      Iteration    Evaluations      -2 Res Log Like       Criterion

              0              1      38814.11732590
              1              2      35958.91873320      0.00035413
              2              1      35954.51316766      0.00000956
              3              1      35954.40270116      0.00000001
```

(Continued)

Table 9.2   (Continued)

```
                    Convergence criteria met.

Covariance Parameter Estimates

                                    Standard          Z
    Cov Parm      Subject    Estimate      Error      Value      Pr > Z

    Intercept     CASEID       7.2201     0.3718      19.42      <.0001
    Residual                   6.2266     0.1125      55.35      <.0001


                        Fit Statistics

             -2 Res Log Likelihood          35954.4
             AIC (smaller is better)        35958.4
             AICC (smaller is better)       35958.4
             BIC (smaller is better)        35968.3


                    Solution for Fixed Effects

                        Standard
     Effect      Estimate     Error       DF     t Value     Pr > |t|

     Intercept    1.8281     0.08905     1030      20.53      <.0001
```

INTERPRETATION OF UNCONDITIONAL MODEL RESULTS

The following description is intended to be an example of how the results from the unconditional model could be written for publication. Results from the unconditional model revealed that there was significant within-person ($\sigma^2 = 6.23$, $z = 55.35$, $p < .0001$) as well as between-person variance ($\tau_{00} = 7.22$, $z = 19.42$, $p < .0001$). The ICC was .54, indicating that 54% of the variance in daily distress was between people and 46% was within people. In other words, individuals varied or fluctuated around their own averages almost as much as they differed from other people. These results indicate that there was sufficient variance at both levels to continue with subsequent models with predictors.

RANDOM COEFFICIENTS REGRESSION MODEL

The SAS commands in Table 9.3 were used to model Equations 1 through 3. Compared to the commands for the unconditional model, the structural specification of the model remains the same, but there are some differences in the

Table 9.3	SAS Commands for the Random Coefficients Regression Model

```
proc mixed data=merged noclprint covtest;
  class caseid;
  model distress= stress cage
   /solution ddfm=bw;
random intercept stress /subject=caseid type = un ;
run;
```

model specification. Specifically, STRESS (Level 1) and CAGE (Level 2 grand-mean centered age) are included as predictors in the MODEL statement. The/SUBJECT = command specifies the nesting structure and alerts SAS that STRESS is a Level 1 variable and CAGE is a Level 2 variable. The MODEL statement provides γ_{10} (STRESS) from Equation 3 and γ_{01} (CAGE) from Equation 2 as well as the default γ_{00} (intercept) from Equation 2. Adding a variable name to the RANDOM statement allows the slope between the specified variable and the dependent variable to vary across Level 2 units. Therefore, only Level 1 variables can be added to the RANDOM statement. In this example, STRESS was added to the RANDOM statement to allow the slope between stressors and distress to vary across people. Note that this corresponds to u_{1i} in Equation 3. If STRESS was not added to the RANDOM statement, the reactivity (β_1) slope would be constrained to be equal across all Level 2 units (people), and the model would represent a one-way ANCOVA with random effects. An option has been added that specifies the structure of the variance–covariance matrix for the intercepts and slopes. The structure used here, TYPE=UN, indicates an unstructured specification and was chosen to allow all three parameters (τ_{00}, τ_{01}, and τ_{11}) to be determined by the data.

RANDOM COEFFICIENTS REGRESSION OUTPUT

The output in Table 9.4 is structured in the same way as the output for the unconditional model. The Model Information remains the same, but the Number of Covariance Parameters under Dimensions has changed from two to four. This reflects the increase in the number of random effects from the unconditional model. Whereas the unconditional model had two random effects (σ^2 and τ_{00}), the current model has those two random effects as well as a random effect reflecting the covariance (τ_{10}) and one reflecting the variance around the slope (τ_{11}). These additional random effects are obtained because the unstructured type allows for covariance of random effects (unlike the VC type constraint used in the unconditional model) and because the Level 1 variable was included in the RANDOM statement. Notice that the Number of Observations Not Used is higher than in the unconditional model. This reflects the fact that two respondents had missing data for the CAGE variable. Missing data at Level 1 would not result in an observation being removed from the analysis, but missing data at Level 2 does result in removal.

The four rows for Covariance Parameter Estimates correspond to the four random effects. The first row (UN 1,1) corresponds to τ_{00}, reflecting the remaining Level 2 variance in the level of DISTRESS after accounting for CAGE. The second row (UN 2,1) corresponds to τ_{10}, reflecting the covariance between the intercept and slope. The third row (UN 2,2) corresponds to τ_{11}, reflecting the variance around the slope between STRESS and DISTRESS. The fourth row (Residual) corresponds to σ^2 and reflects the remaining Level 1 variance in DISTRESS after accounting for STRESS. Note that all four of the random effects are significant. This indicates that there is still significant variance left to explain at Level 1 (σ^2) and Level 2 (τ_{00}), and it also shows that there is a significant relationship between the intercept of DISTRESS and the relationship between STRESS and DISTRESS (significant covariance: τ_{10}). Lastly, the significant τ_{11} indicates that there is variance across people in the relationship between STRESS and DISTRESS; that is, not all people have the same emotional reactivity to daily stressors. In order to obtain an estimate of the percentage of variance explained by this model, separate calculations need to be conducted for Level 1 and Level 2. The proportion of variance explained at Level 1 can be calculated based on the following formula (Raudenbush & Bryk, 2002, p. 79): [σ^2 (unconditional model) − σ^2 (random coefficients model)]/σ^2 (unconditional model). For the current example, the result is .18 [(6.23−5.11)/6.23 = .18]. The proportion of variance explained at Level 2 can be calculated based on the following formula (Raudenbush & Bryk, 2002, p.74): [τ_{00} (unconditional model) − τ_{00} (random coefficients model)]/ τ_{00} (unconditional model). For the current example, the result is .54 [(7.22−3.29)/7.22 = .54].

The Fit Statistics follow and are helpful when comparing models that have the same fixed effects but different random effects (Singer, 1998). The two criteria that can be especially helpful are the AIC (Akaike's information criterion) and the −2 res log likelihood (deviance). For example, if one removed STRESS from the RANDOM line in the current example and wanted to compare that model to the current model, model comparison tests could be conducted. An excellent step-by-step guide for comparing models in this way is provided by Singer (1998) and is also described in Chapter 2.

The Solution for Fixed Effects provides the output for the three gamma coefficients. The Intercept corresponds to γ_{00} and indicates that the average level of distress for a 47-year-old on days with no stressors was 1.22. This value is significantly different from zero ($t = 18.34$, $p < .0001$). The next line corresponds to γ_{10} and indicates that there is a significant and positive relationship between stress and distress. On days when someone experiences an additional stressor, distress also increases by 1.0086 units. Notice that the number of degrees of freedom for this relationship is 6,176, reflecting the fact that STRESS is a Level 1 variable and is based on the number of days rather than the number of people in the sample. The last line corresponds to γ_{01} and indicates that there are significant age differences in the level of distress. Specifically, older adults report less distress than younger adults.

The Type 3 Tests of Fixed Effects presents the F statistics for the γ_{10} and γ_{01} results. In this case, the value of the F statistic is t^2, so these results are redundant with the Solution for Fixed Effects above.

Table 9.4	SAS Output From the Random Coefficients Regression Model

```
The Mixed Procedure

                          Model Information

          Data Set                    WORK.MERGED
          Dependent Variable          distress
          Covariance Structure        Unstructured
          Subject Effect              CASEID
          Estimation Method           REML
          Residual Variance Method    Profile
          Fixed Effects SE Method     Model-Based
          Degrees of Freedom Method   Between-Within


                             Dimensions

             Covariance Parameters          4
             Columns in X                   3
             Columns in Z Per Subject       2
             Subjects                    1029
             Max Obs Per Subject            8


                       Number of Observations

           Number of Observations Read        7229
           Number of Observations Used        7206
           Number of Observations Not Used      23


                         Iteration History

    Iteration    Evaluations    -2 Res Log Like       Criterion

            0              1     38103.70457346
            1              3     34705.09095009      0.00024440
            2              1     34702.27170731      0.00000380
            3              1     34702.23047768      0.00000000
```

(Continued)

Table 9.4   (Continued)

```
                         Convergence criteria met.

                      Covariance Parameter Estimates

                                     Standard         Z
   Cov Parm    Subject    Estimate     Error       Value       Pr Z

   UN(1,1)     CASEID      3.2904      0.2247       14.64      <.0001
   UN(2,1)     CASEID      1.6656      0.1402       11.88      <.0001
   UN(2,2)     CASEID      1.8895      0.1827       10.34      <.0001
   Residual                5.1146      0.09883      51.75      <.0001


                            Fit Statistics

              -2 Res Log Likelihood           34702.2
              AIC (smaller is better)         34710.2
              AICC (smaller is better)        34710.2
              BIC (smaller is better)         34730.0


                  Null Model Likelihood Ratio Test

             DF      Chi-Square       Pr > ChiSq

              3        3401.47          <.0001


                     Solution for Fixed Effects

                          Standard
   Effect       Estimate    Error       DF      t Value     Pr > |t|

   Intercept     1.2198     0.06650     1027      18.34      <.0001
   STRESS        1.0086     0.06580     6176      15.33      <.0001
   cage         -0.01145    0.004975    1027      -2.30      0.0215


                   Type 3 Tests of Fixed Effects

                      Num      Den
            Effect     DF       DF     F Value     Pr > F

            STRESS      1      6176     234.97     <.0001
            cage        1      1027       5.30     0.0215
```

INTERPRETATION OF RANDOM COEFFICIENTS REGRESSION RESULTS

The following description is intended to be an example of how the results from the random coefficients regression model could be written for publication. Results from this model indicate that days with increased stressors are associated with increased distress ($\gamma_{10} = 1.01$, $t = 15.33$, $p < .0001$). Stated another way, there is significant emotional reactivity to daily stressors. In addition, older adults reported less distress than younger adults ($\gamma_{01} = -0.01$, $t = -2.30$, $p = .02$). Using the equations for the proportion of variance explained (Raudenbush & Bryk, 2002), this model accounted for 18% of the within-person and 54% of the between-person variance in daily distress.

CONCLUSION

The random coefficients regression model is a flexible and useful tool when the primary research question of interest involves a Level 1 relationship. This chapter focused on the Level 1 relationship of within-person emotional reactivity to daily stressors. It also showed how covariates can be added at Level 2, how the output from SAS PROC MIXED can be interpreted, and how the results can be written for publication. Extensions of this model are simple; covariates can also be added at Level 1 and additional covariates can be added at Level 2. These extensions are made by adding the relevant variable names to the MODEL statement.

REFERENCES

Almeida, D. M. (2005). Resilience and vulnerability to daily stressors assessed via diary methods. *Current Directions in Psychological Science, 14*, 64–68.

Almeida, D. M., Wethington, E., & Kessler, R. C. (2002). The daily inventory of stressful events: An investigator-based approach for measuring daily stressors. *Assessment, 9*, 41–55.

Bolger, N., DeLongis, A., Kessler, R. C., & Schilling, E. A. (1989). Effects of daily stress on negative mood. *Journal of Personality and Social Psychology, 57*, 808–818.

Bradburn, N. (1969). *The structure of psychological well-being.* Chicago: Aldine.

Brim, O. G., Ryff, C. D., & Kessler, R. C. (2004). *How healthy are we? A national study of well-being at midlife.* Chicago: University of Chicago Press.

Hox, J. J., & Kreft, I. G. G. (Eds.). (1994) Multilevel analysis methods [Special issue]. *Sociological Methods and Research, 22*(3).

Kessler, R. C., Andrews, G., Colpe, L. J., Hiripi, E., Mroczek, D. K., Normand, S. L. T., et al. (2002). Short screening scales to monitor population prevalence and trends in non-specific psychological distress. *Psychological Medicine, 32*, 959–976.

Kessler, R. C., McGonagle, K. A., Zhao, S., Nelson, C. B., Hughes, M., Eshleman, S., et al. (1994). Lifetime and 12-month prevalence of DSM-III-R psychiatric disorders in the United States: Results from the national comorbidity survey. *Archives of General Psychiatry, 51,* 8–19.

Keyes, C. L. M, & Ryff, C. D. (1998). Generativity in adult lives: Social structural contours and quality of life consequences. In D. P. McAdams & E. de St. Aubin (Eds.), *Generativity and adult development: How and why we care for the next generation* (pp. 227–263). Washington, DC: American Psychological Association.

Kreft, I. G. G. (Ed.). (1995). Hierarchical linear models: Problems and prospects [Special issue]. *Journal of Education and Behavioral Statistics, 20*(2).

Lachman, M. E., & Weaver, S. L. (1998). Sociodemographic variations in the sense of control by domain: Findings from the MacArthur studies on midlife. *Psychology and Aging, 13*, 553–562.

Mroczek, D. K., & Kolarz, C. M. (1998). The effect of age on positive and negative affect: A developmental perspective on happiness. *Journal of Personality and Social Psychology, 75*, 1333–1349.

Neupert, S. D., Almeida, D. M., & Charles, S. T. (2007). Age differences in reactivity to daily stressors: The role of personal control. *Journal of Gerontology: Psychological Sciences, 62B*, P216–P225.

Radloff, L. S. (1977). The CES-D scale: A self-report depression scale for research in the general population. *Applied Psychological Measurement, 1*, 385–401.

Raudenbush, S. W., & Bryk, A. S. (2002). *Hierarchical linear models*. Thousand Oaks, CA: Sage.

SAS Institute Inc. (1997). *SAS/STAT software: Changes and enhancements through Release 6.12*. Cary, NC: Author.

Singer, J. D. (1998). Using SAS PROC MIXED to fit multilevel models, hierarchical models, and individual growth models. *Journal of Educational and Behavioral Statistics, 24*, 323–355.

Taylor, J. A. (1953). A personality scale of manifest anxiety. *Journal of Abnormal and Social Psychology, 48*, 285–290.

Hierarchical Linear Modeling of Growth Curve Trajectories Using HLM

10

David F. Greenberg

Julie A. Phillips

THE CHALLENGES POSED BY LONGITUDINAL DATA

Social and behavioral scientists often study change over time in some attribute or characteristic of an entity. In this chapter, the entity (or case) of interest is a county, but in other applications the case could be a person, an organization, or a country. The attribute or characteristic may be measured by a binary variable (such as whether or not a person commits at least one crime during a given time period), a count (such as the number of crimes someone commits in a given stretch of time), or a continuous variable (such as a crime rate).

Latent growth trajectory models—also known as growth curve models—are one of several ways social scientists conceptualize and analyze this type of change. With these models, researchers can not only describe the pattern of change over time experienced by these entities but can also determine how different entity characteristics affect those patterns of change. The growth trajectory model is a particularly fruitful tool for studying change when data are available for a number of different entities, and when the change occurs fairly smoothly. However, when data are available for just one entity, time series methods will be more appropriate.

This chapter shows how to formulate and estimate latent growth trajectory models. The chapter begins by explaining how an approach originally devised to study cross-sectional data can be adapted to study change. It demonstrates how to set up such models for both a continuous dependent variable and a count outcome using the HLM program. Tests for the adequacy with which a model fits the data are also presented. To illustrate the procedures, we analyze a dataset with information on annual robbery counts and rates in a sample of 400 U.S. counties between the years 1985 and 1999. The chapter concludes by identifying the strengths and weaknesses of the hierarchical linear modeling approach and indicates when alternative methods might be preferable.

The hierarchical linear modeling (or multilevel) approach to the estimation of growth trajectory models is designed to deal with two problems that arise when analyzing repeated measures for the same entities: the lack of independence of the observations and unmeasured heterogeneity. As discussed in earlier chapters, inferential statistics in ordinary least squares (OLS) regression are based on the assumption that the observations are independent. That is, the value of a variable for a particular observation in the dataset is completely unrelated to the value of that same variable for another observation, conditional on (that is, controlling for) the values of the independent variables. When this assumption holds, the value of a residual for one case in a regression analysis should carry no information as to the value of a residual for another case. If this assumption is false, significance tests do not have their conventional distributions, and their associated probability levels are inaccurate.

Unmeasured heterogeneity often arises when researchers do not sufficiently control for variables that influence the dependent variable, either due to data constraints or lack of knowledge about their importance. This sort of unmeasured heterogeneity can produce biased parameter estimates. Unmeasured heterogeneity can also occur when the coefficients for a set of predictors on an outcome of interest vary across cases. The assumption underlying conventional OLS regression is that the same intercept and regression coefficients are valid for all cases in the dataset. Although OLS procedures allow for interaction terms, thereby permitting a regression coefficient to vary across cases according to the level of other variables in the dataset, they do not allow for variability on the basis of unmeasured contributions. Failure to take this sort of interaction into account can lead to heteroscedasticity as well as nonindependence of residuals. These problems will reduce the precision of OLS estimates, bias significance tests, and fail to provide full information about individual variability in trajectories.

As Garson points out in Chapter 1, hierarchical linear modeling is a set of statistical techniques for addressing these issues. The original applications of HLM were not to longitudinal (over-time) data; they were developed for analyzing cross-sectional data where observations are "nested" in larger settings—for example, residents living in different neighborhoods. Observations nested in this way are unlikely to be independent. Two subjects drawn randomly from the same neighborhood are more likely to be similar to one another than two subjects drawn randomly from the entire population of residents in a city, even when controlling for individual traits that are known to be important to the explanation of the outcome, such as age and socioeconomic status (SES). This resemblance may be due to such factors as social interaction of residents in the neighborhood, or shared attributes not represented in the dataset, such as lifestyle preferences or access to community resources. The HLM approach allows this dependence and unmeasured heterogeneity to be taken into account.

THE HIERARCHICAL MODELING
APPROACH TO LONGITUDINAL DATA

Longitudinal data have the same nested structure—repeated measures for a set of cases over time—and thus similar issues arise when analyzing longitudinal data. Observations at consecutive time points for the same case are more likely to be similar to one another than observations at the same two time points for two different cases. This resemblance stems from the stability of many personal traits and characteristics of the social world. Students who have exceptional math skills in one year are likely to have exceptional math skills in subsequent years. Likewise, neighborhoods with unusually high or low crime rates at one point in time tend to have exceptionally high or low rates in later years. In statistical terms, the observations are not independent of one another. This dependence must be taken into account to avoid misleading results.

In principle, the dependence of a dependent variable on time could take many forms. In many applications, the time dependence can be well represented by a polynomial with low order. For example, a continuous dependent variable y measured on individuals (i) might be expressed as a linear function of *time*, with the level 1 equation

$$y_{it} = \pi_0 + \pi_1 time_{it} + e_{it} \tag{1}$$

In this equation, π_0 represents the expected value of y_{it} at *time* = 0 (usually chosen to be the first wave of observations); the subscript $t = 1, 2, 3 \ldots$ indexes the time metric (waves of observation); and e_{it} is a random shock assumed to be normally distributed with a mean of zero, and uncorrelated with *time* and with shocks at other times and for other cases.

If the relationship between time and the outcome is nonlinear, adding a quadratic term to the right-hand side in Eq. (1) may sufficiently account for the curvilinearity, as in Eq. (2):

$$y_{it} = \pi_0 + \pi_1 time_{it} + \pi_2 time_{it}^2 + e_{it} \tag{2}$$

This equation describes a curve that is symmetric about its maximum or minimum, which occurs at *time* = $-\pi_1/2\pi_2$. Real-life curves are not always symmetric. To accommodate departure from symmetry when present, cubic and higher-power terms in *time* can be added. It should be kept in mind that the number of additional power terms is constrained by the number of waves. If there are T waves of data, no more than $T - 1$ powers of *time* can appear in the equation. Thus, if one has three waves of data, one could include at most a linear and quadratic term.[1] The introduction of cubic or higher powers of *time* can lead to severe multicollinearity and, as a result, estimation problems. The addition of these higher-order terms can also lead to over-fitting and to prediction curves that poorly describe observed temporal patterns. Consequently, they should be used with caution.

Alternatively, generalized linear models can accommodate nonlinearity between the dependent variable and the independent variables with a transformation of the dependent variable so that the outcome can be expressed as a linear additive function of the predictors. For example, a pattern of exponential growth can be linearized by a logarithmic transformation.[2] Transformation of the dependent variable can be a convenient way of handling binary, categorical, ordered, and count outcomes. However, the implicit assumption with all these approaches is that the coefficients π_0, π_1, and π_2 are the same for all cases.

Multilevel modeling relaxes this assumption by allowing the intercept and slopes to vary randomly or systematically across entities. This variability can be captured in a "level 2" equation expressing the coefficients in the level 1 equation (Eqs. 1 or 2 above) as a linear additive function of the time-stable characteristics of the level 2 predictors. If, for example, there are Q characteristics of the various entities (z_{1it}, z_{2it}, ..., z_{Qit}), we can express their influence on the level 1 intercepts and slopes through the following equations:

$$\pi_{0i} = \beta_{00} + \beta_{01}z_1 + ... + \beta_{0Q}z_{Qi} + r_{0i} \qquad (3)$$

$$\pi_{1i} = \beta_{10} + \beta_{11}z_1 + ... + \beta_{1Q}z_{Qi} + r_{1i} \qquad (4)$$

$$\pi_{2i} = \beta_{20} + \beta_{21}z_{1i} + ... + \beta_{2Q}z_{Qi} + r_{2i} \qquad (5)$$

The r error terms are taken to be normally distributed with a mean of 0 and are assumed to be uncorrelated with the z variables; they may, however, be correlated with one other. The absence of a subscript for time indicates that the r residuals are assumed to be time-invariant—that is, they represent stable features of the entities that are not captured by the z variables.

Interpretation of the coefficients is facilitated by inserting these level 2 expressions into the level 1 equation (Eq. 1). To prevent the equations from becoming too complicated, we suppose that there is just one level 2 predictor. We then obtain

$$y_{it} = (\beta_{00}+\beta_{01}z_{1i} + r_{0i}) + (\beta_{10} +\beta_{11}z_{1i}+r_{1i})time_{it} + e_{it}. \qquad (6)$$

To grasp the meaning of the different terms, consider first what this equation says at $time = 0$, the first wave of observations. The equation states that y depends linearly on an independent variable z_1, along with a random shock r_{0i} that varies across cases and that allows each case to have its own distinct intercept, and another random shock e_{i0} that varies randomly across cases. With data for only the first wave, we would have no way to distinguish the two types of random shocks. With additional waves of data, it is possible to estimate the separate contributions of the two types of shocks. The term $\beta_{10}time$ expresses the tendency of the outcome variable to rise and fall linearly with $time$ when $z = 0$, while the term $\beta_{11}z_{1i}time$ represents an interaction between $time$ and the variable z. It allows the effect of z_1 to change linearly with $time$, or equivalently, it allows the growth of y

over *time* to depend on the value of z_1. The total effect of time thus receives contributions from three different terms: β_{10} (which is common to all cases), $\beta_{11}z_{1i}$ (which varies across cases according to the value of the variable z), and r_{1i} (which varies randomly across cases). Because *time* is a level 1 variable and z is a level 2 variable, the product of the two variables is sometimes referred to as a "cross-level" effect. In this way, the model allows for both systematic (fixed) and random contributions to the intercept and slope. The level 1 equation can be extended to incorporate a quadratic term (as in Eq. 2), which would allow the intercept and both the linear and quadratic slopes for *time* to vary systematically according to case characteristics, as well as randomly across cases.

To better understand these different contributions, we can rearrange the terms in Eq. 6 and distinguish the fixed and random contributions. Doing this, we have

$$y_{it} = (\beta_{00} + \beta_{01}z_{1i} + \beta_{10}time_{it} + \beta_{11}z_{1i}time_{it}) + (r_{0i} + r_{1i}time_{it} + e_{it}) \qquad (7)$$

The first term in parentheses on the right-hand side represents the fixed part of the model, while the second term is the random part. Prior to the introduction of hierarchical linear modeling, researchers would have dealt with case-specific trends by using just the first term, with independent and identically distributed error terms tacked on. This approach, however, would have ignored two of the three random contributions of the second term.

Up to this point, we have been assuming that the entity characteristics in the level 2 equations (3–5) do not change over time. This assumption is needed for logical consistency. The coefficients on the right-hand side of Eqs. 2 and 3 are assumed to be unchanging features of the individual cases. The coefficients representing the influence of the case characteristics on these coefficients are also assumed to be time-invariant. Consistency thus requires that the z variables themselves be constant over time. However, in many research settings, there will be change over time in some of the entity characteristics that we would expect to influence the coefficients of the level 1 equation. For example, a level 1 equation might represent a county's robbery rate in a given year as a function of that county's unemployment rate. The effect of unemployment could itself depend on the region in which a county is located (a time-stable characteristic) and the proportion of young people living in the county in that year. In setting up the model, time-invariant level 2 variables that characterize the case should be handled as level 2 variables while time-varying case characteristics (measured for each case at each time) should be treated as level 1 variables (Hox, 2002; Singer, & Willett, 2003).

The approach just outlined can be extended to handle nominal, ordinal, and count data through the use of a link variable that transforms the original outcome variable to one that can plausibly be represented as a linear function of the predictors. For example, for a count outcome, the relevant distribution of outcomes is the Poisson. In this case, if the long-term rate at which events happen to an individual is λ (lambda), and there are N individuals to whom events are happening randomly over a time span, the expected number of counts is $N\lambda$. The link function that is assumed to depend linearly on the predictors is then $\ln(\lambda)$. The coefficients of the predictor variables in the link function can be assumed to be fixed (the same for all entities) or random (variable across entities). Error terms for the level 2 model, however, are assumed to be multivariate normal, as in the linear case.

It is the lambda in this model that is being referenced with the phrase "latent" growth trajectory. It is not measured directly, but only indirectly through the events that occur in a finite time span. If that time span were to be extended without limit, the number of events observed per unit time would be lambda. In a finite time span, the observed rate, as defined by the ratio of counts to the length of the time span, would not necessarily equal lambda, but would approach it as the length of the observation time is extended.

As noted in other chapters, researchers working with cross-sectional hierarchical data often center the independent variables in the level 1 equation to facilitate interpretation of the coefficients and to reduce problems of multicollinearity (Enders & Tofighi, 2007; Hofman & Gavin, 1998; Raudenbush & Bryk, 2002; Paccagnella, 2006). In latent growth curve analysis, however, when the independent variable *time* is not centered, the intercept represents the predicted value of the dependent variable at the first time point (when *time* = 0), and the coefficients of the predictors have a natural interpretation. They specify the expected change in the dependent variable when *time* (or *age*) is increased by one unit (e.g., 1 year) while the others are held constant. Nonetheless, at times it may be computationally advantageous to center the predictors to reduce multicollinearity between time and time raised to higher powers. Moreover, researchers may want to center other variables in the level 1 equation, such as time-varying case characteristics, to ease interpretation and reduce multicollinearity.[3]

APPLICATION: GROWTH TRAJECTORIES OF
U.S. COUNTY ROBBERY RATES

We illustrate these procedures by showing their application to the study of robbery rates (defined as the number of robberies per 100,000 population) in a sample of 400 of the largest U.S. counties for the years 1985 through 1999. The data are hierarchical—county-years are nested within counties—and thus a multilevel approach is appropriate. We are interested in determining the factors that influenced the rise and fall of the robbery rates during this time period.

For this purpose, we consider the unemployment rate (*unemprt*); the percent of the population that is Black (*perblack*); the percent that is male (*permale*); the percent that is between 15 and 34 years old (*per1534*); and dummy variables (*regionS, regionW, regionMW*) coded 1 if the county is in the South, 1 if in the West, 1 if in the Midwest, and 0 otherwise. The reference category is the Northeast. Detailed descriptions of the dataset and information about the sources of the variables can be found in Phillips (2006) and Phillips and Greenberg (2008). We carry out the estimations in version 6 of the HLM program. A detailed description of this program and basic information about how to use it can be found in Raudenbush, Bryk, Cheong, Congdon, and du Toit (2004) and in Chapter 3 of this book.

Exploratory Analyses

We begin by examining the distribution of the outcome variable to help us decide what type of analysis to conduct. If the outcome is continuous but empirically clustered into relatively discrete groups with little overlap, a finite-mixture modeling approach might be preferable to a hierarchical linear model. If, on the other hand, the distribution appears to be smooth and continuous without evidence of pronounced clustering, we would want to adopt a model that assumes continuity. This phase of the analysis cannot be done in HLM; we did it from the raw data in SPSS version 19. The histogram shown in Figure 10.1 displays the distribution of robbery rates (across all counties and years).

Figure 10.1   Histogram of County Robbery Rates

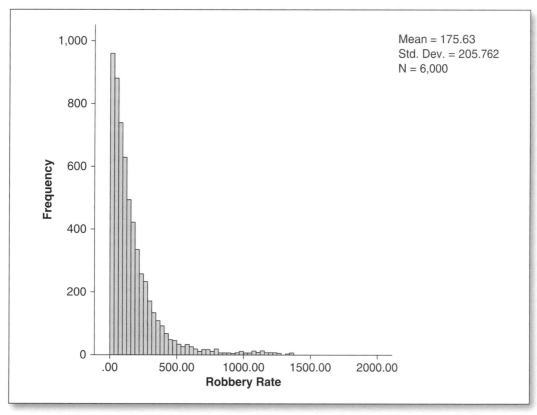

The distribution is clearly continuous, but quite skewed. Most counties had relatively few robberies, while a small number had many. Many researchers would respond to such a distribution by taking the natural logarithm of the crime rate, justifying this transformation on the grounds that it reduces skewness. When this is done, the coefficients can be interpreted as semi-elasticities. If the coefficient of a level 1 predictor for a logged dependent variable is π, then a unit change in the predictor implies a proportional change of π in the outcome variable in its original metric. In our case, logging the robbery rate is a problematic procedure because some counties had no robberies in some years, and the logarithm of 0 is not defined. Dropping these observations would bias the analysis. Some researchers avoid losing these cases by adding 1 to the variable before logging it. This procedure is now considered dubious because the choice of 1 as the constant to be added to each observation is arbitrary, and yet the results may be influenced by this choice (Gould, 2011; Nichols, 2010). Moreover, it is an unnecessary choice. In OLS regression, it is actually not a requirement that the dependent variable be normally distributed (Greene, 2003; Johnston & DiNardo, 1997).

In a longitudinal analysis, it is also helpful at an early stage in the analysis to get a sense of trends in the data so as to identify an appropriate provisional time dependence for the level 1 equation. To do this graphically, we totaled up all the robberies in a given year for the 400 counties and divided that total by the total population of all the counties in that year to obtain an overall robbery rate for the 400 counties in that year.[4] We then used Stata's graphics facilities to create the "two-way" plot shown in Figure 10.2. The figure shows that robbery rates rose for a number of years, and then fell. Apart from a small dip in 1987, the rise and fall seem to have been approximately symmetric, peaking in 1992. Consequently, we assume provisionally that the robbery rates between 1985 and 1999 depend quadratically on time. We will want to model this dependence in such a way as to allow the *time* coefficients to vary across counties, so that the trajectories of the different counties can have different initial levels of robbery, as well as different rates of increase and decrease, and different times of peaking.

We illustrate two different procedures for analyzing this type of data. One is to adopt the untransformed robbery rate as the dependent variable in a hierarchical linear model; the other is to treat the number of robberies in a county as a count variable in a hierarchical generalized linear model.[5] The latter approach is appealing because, in principle, a linear model for the rate allows predicted rates to be negative, which is not possible.[6] Count models are constructed in such a way that this cannot happen. However, we begin our exposition with the linear model, as much published research uses this model. Moreover, in other applications, the linear model may be more appropriate. After outlining the procedures for estimating linear models, we take up the Poisson model for counts.

Estimation of the Linear Hierarchical Model

Having determined the shape of the level 1 equation on the basis of Figure 10.2, we now proceed to estimate a linear model for the county robbery rates using

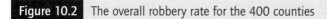

Figure 10.2 | The overall robbery rate for the 400 counties

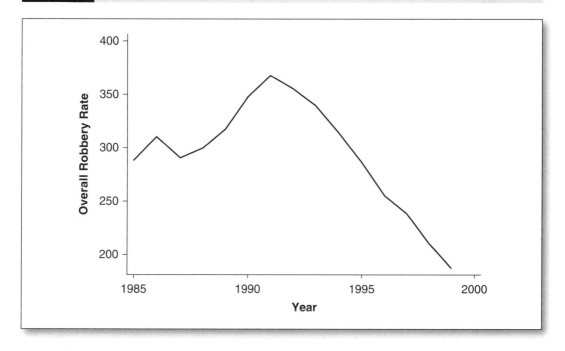

version 6.02 of the HLM program.[7] Before doing this, however, we must carry out certain preliminary procedures (transformations of variables, creation of interaction terms) in a general statistical package.

To ease the computational problems associated with the squaring of large numbers, and to facilitate the interpretation of our estimations, we rescaled time in SPSS so that the year 1985 is coded 0 before importing the data into HLM. Had we failed to do this, the intercept would tell us the estimated robbery rate in the year 0, two millennia earlier than the period covered by our dataset, rather than in 1985, the year our dataset actually begins.

As already discussed, time-varying county characteristics that contribute to the explanation of robbery rates are placed in the level 1 equation. Because we will want to allow these variables to influence the coefficients for *year* and *year*^{2} as well as the intercepts, we create products (that is, interaction terms) of these variables with *year* and *year*^{2} in SPSS before we open HLM.

When the HLM program is first opened, it will ask whether we want to estimate a two-level or three-level model. As our model involves only two levels, we choose HLM2 and indicate that we will input data from a stat package file rather than an ASCII file. From the screen that pops up, we choose "Make new MDM matrix." Rather than carry out computations directly on the raw data, the HLM program first computes a multivariate data matrix (mdm) and uses it in subsequent procedures, speeding up computation. From the screen that appears, we tell

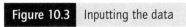

Figure 10.3   Inputting the data

HLM which statistical package created the dataset we are inputting. In our case, it is SPSS. Users are also asked to name and save an mdmt matrix that contains information about the data, including any specifications as to missing data. We have none. For the estimation of a growth trajectory model, we check the menu item certifying that observations are nested within individuals.[8] We use the "browse" button to choose the level 1 dataset and the level 2 dataset. They can be the same, but need not be. For each dataset, the researcher chooses all the variables that will figure in the analysis. A figure of the screen showing the location of these different boxes is shown in Figure 10.3.

In choosing the variables for each level, it is necessary to link the two files. We do this by choosing *fips* as the variable identifying each unique county in each equation.[9] In the level 1 equation, we choose *robrate, year,* and *year²* (year squared) as our variables. We also include the time-varying variables (such as unemployment rate and percentage Black) whose effects on the intercept and slopes (coefficients of *year* and *year²*) we want to assess in the level 1 equation. This includes the cross-level interaction terms involving the time variables and the county characteristics whose construction we discussed previously. We put the time-invariant county characteristics (in our case, the dummy variables for region) in the level 2 equation. The screen showing the complete model, involving both levels, is shown in Figure 10.4.

Figure 10.4   Specifying the level 1 and level 2 models in HLM

Once the variables are chosen, the researcher asks HLM to construct the MDM file by pressing the button in the lower left-hand corner of the window. Once this is done, the researcher can look at summary statistics for the dataset to make sure that all cases and variables have been successfully read in. The output, displayed in Table 10.1, shows that we have complete information for all 400 counties for the 15 years covered by our panel, for a total of 6,000 observations.[10] This information is stored in a file with the extension sts. With the possible exception of *permale*, there is sufficient variation about the mean to enable us to detect the influence of each variable on the robbery rate if it has a nontrivial effect.

| **Table 10.1** | Descriptive Statistics as Produced by HLM |

LEVEL 1 DESCRIPTIVE STATISTICS

Variable Name	N	Mean	SD	Minimum	Maximum
YEAR	6000	7.00	4.32	0.00	14.00
YEAR2	6000	67.67	62.72	0.00	196.00
YEAR3	6000	735.00	855.99	0.00	2744.00
YEAR4	6000	8512.47	11595.97	0.00	38416.00
UNEMPRT	6000	6.99	2.74	2.26	19.02
PERBLACK	6000	10.69	11.68	0.06	67.91
PERMALE	6000	48.66	1.28	45.21	60.02
PER1534	6000	35.07	3.87	21.81	54.64
ROBRATE	6000	175.63	205.76	0.00	1714.14
ROBBERIES	6000	1297.03	3949.79	0.00	68959.00

LEVEL 2 DESCRIPTIVE STATISTICS

Variable Name	N	Mean	SD	Minimum	Maximum
REGIONS	400	0.30	0.46	0.00	1.00
REGIONW	400	0.16	0.37	0.00	1.00
REGIONMW	400	0.27	0.44	0.00	1.00

Note. To conserve space, we omit from this table the descriptive statistics for those level 1 variables defined as products of *year* and *year²* with the *unemprt, perblack, permale,* and *per1534.*

To proceed, we must tell HLM something about the character of the outcome variable and its distribution. We do this by clicking on "Basic Settings." Our variable, the robbery rate, is a continuous variable, and we assume that its distribution, conditional on the independent variables, is normal. Consequently, we accept HLM's default. We are given the option of fixing the error variance of the level 1 equation at a particular value or estimating it. We have no basis for fixing the error variance, so we write the word "computed" in the blank space. By clicking on the error terms that appear on the screen for the level 2 equations, they can either be fixed at zero or freely estimated. In the latter case, the HLM program will also estimate the covariances between the level 2 residuals. We are also given an opportunity to save the residuals from the level 1 and level 2 equations. We will demonstrate the uses to which they can be put below. If the user wants to keep all files associated with this project in a special folder, the full file path should be provided so that the files can be accessed easily at a later time.

The other menu item of relevance to us is "Other Settings," in particular, the "Estimation Settings" choice. As we will not conduct formal comparisons of different specifications for the level 2 equations through likelihood ratio tests (requiring full maximum likelihood estimation), we accept the default setting, "Restricted Maximum Likelihood." (Note that in version 7, the default is Full Information Maximum Likelihood. For detailed instructions as to how one chooses these settings, see Raudenbush et al., 2004.)

After choosing all settings, the user should save the model so that it can be run again without having to recreate it. To do this, press the "Save and Run" button, give the file a name, and specify where on the computer it is to be saved. After the estimation is completed, the output can be accessed by clicking on "File/View Output."

We begin by estimating a baseline model with only *year* and *year²* as level 1 predictors and no level 2 predicators. However, we allow all three of the level 2 equations to have random error terms. The HLM output for this model is displayed in Table 10.2. It contains four panels of information.

The fixed and random effects estimates given in the output file are displayed in Panels D and C, respectively. HLM uses Latin letters for estimates of the

Table 10.2 Parameter Estimates for Linear Model (level 1 variables only)

Panel A. Tau Matrix (as correlations)

INTRCPT1, P0	1.000	0.600	−0.781
YEAR, P1	0.600	−0.781	−0.952
YEAR2, P2	−0.781	−0.952	1.000

Panel B. Reliability Estimates for Random Level 1 Estimates

Random Level 1 Coefficient	Reliability Estimate
INTRCPT1, PO	.976
YEAR, P1	.901
YEAR2, P6	.918

Panel C. Final Estimation of Variance Components

Random Effect	Standard Deviation	Variance Component	df	Chi-square	P-value
INTRCPT1, R0	176.09	31007.42	399	16730.31	0.000
YEAR SLOPE, R1	27.51	756.76	399	4024.91	0.000
YEAR2 SLOPE, R2	2.11	4.44	399	4885.05	0.000
LEVEL-1, E	40.38	1630.19			

Panel D. Final Estimation of Fixed Effects (with robust standard errors)

Fixed Effect	Coefficient	Standard Error	T-ratio	Approx. d.f.	P-value
For INTRCPT1, PO					
INTRCPT2, B00	148.18	8.90	16.65	399	0.000
For YEAR SLOPE, P1					
INTRCPT2, B10	15.99	1.45	11.05	399	0.000
For YEAR2 SLOPE, P2					
INTRCPT2, B20	−1.25	0.11	−11.37	399	0.000

Deviance = 655145.708
Number of estimated parameters = 7

model parameters that it represents with Greek letters. Thus, estimates of π are denoted P, and estimates of β are denoted B. Looking first at Panel D, we can retrieve the estimated prediction equation

$ROBRATE = 148.18 + 15.99YEAR - 1.25YEAR^2$

All coefficients have an associated probability less than .001. Consistent with the earlier exploratory analysis, robbery rates are estimated to rise with $YEAR$, peaking at $YEAR = 15.99/[2(1.25)] = 6.40$. In calendar years, this corresponds to about 5 months into 1991. This figure is obtained by recalling that 1985 is year 0. We consequently compute $1985 + 6.40 = 1991.4$.

Panel C of Table 10.2 displays the estimated variance components or random effects of the model; they are highly significant, indicating that substantial random variation in the level and change over time in robbery rates exists among the counties in our sample. In other words, there is significant variation in the model intercept and slopes for time across counties. Thus, it may be worthwhile to examine possible county characteristics that could account for this variability in the level 1 parameters.

Panel A shows the correlations among the level 1 error terms. HLM denotes the matrix of these correlations or covariances with the Greek letter *tau* in the output. The positive correlation of 0.600 between the intercept and slope indicates that robberies tended to rise faster in states that had an overall higher level of robberies. The correlation of $-.781$ between the intercepts and quadratic slopes shows that robberies tended to drop faster in counties with higher levels of robberies. Finally, the correlation of $-.952$ between the estimates for the linear and quadratic slopes is quite high. The three reliabilities, displayed in Panel B of the table, are all high. Here, *reliability* has the same meaning as in classical measurement theory: It indicates how much of the variability in a parameter is due to variability in the true score, relative to the total variability, which also includes random error contributions.

Before going any further, we wanted to make sure that higher powers of *year* are not needed, so we estimated a model with linear and quadratic terms in *year*, treating all coefficients as fixed, without random variation across counties. Then we added cubic and quartic terms to the model, keeping their coefficients fixed as well.[11] To see whether the additional term made a significant contribution, we carried out a likelihood ratio test. This is done by comparing the difference of the deviance statistics for the two models, or twice the difference of the log-likelihoods, with the chi-square distribution, using as the degrees of freedom the number of parameters constrained to nest one model within the other. In our case, the model with a cubic term has one more free parameter than the model with only linear and quadratic terms; the model with cubic and quartic terms has two more. These tests showed that the additional terms did not significantly improve the fit. Furthermore, the more complex models suffered from extreme multicollinearity. Consequently, we settled for the model with just linear and quadratic slopes. Multicollinearity is high even with this restricted model, but it is manageable.

Modeling the Variability of the Level 1 Coefficients

Having ascertained that the intercept and two slopes for time vary randomly across counties, we want to determine which county characteristics influence these level 1 coefficients. We do this by specifying the county factors that influence the level 1 coefficients. As all but the dummy variables for region of the county are time-varying, we incorporate them into the level 1 equation and re-estimate the model. In principle, we could allow each of these time-varying county characteristics to have an impact on the robbery rate that varies randomly across counties. Doing so, however, would complicate the model and make it harder to estimate. For this exposition, we fix the random contributions to the effects of the time-varying covariates at 0 (which is the common practice). The correlation of residuals for the level 1 estimates, shown in Panel A of Table 10.3,

Table 10.3	Parameter Estimates for Linear Model (Levels 1 and 2)

Panel A. Tau Matrix (as correlations)

INTRCPT1, P0	1.00	0.232	−.585
YEAR, P1	.232	1.000	−.900
YEAR2, P2	−.585	−.899	1.000

Panel B. Reliability Estimates for Random Level 1 Estimates

Random Level 1 Coefficient	Reliability Estimate
INTRCPT1, PO	.964
YEAR, P1	.817
YEAR2, P6	.848

Panel C. Final Estimation of Variance Components

Random Effect	Standard Deviation	Variance Component	df	Chi-square	P-value
INTRCPT1, R0	139.69	19397.573	396	10880.333	0.000
YEAR SLOPE, R1	18.912	357.672	396	2150.046	0.000
YEAR2 SLOPE, R2	1.454	2.115	396	2586.102	0.000
LEVEL-1, E	39.595	1567.775			

Panel D. Final Estimation of Fixed Effects (with robust standard errors)

Fixed Effect	Coefficient	Standard Error	T-ratio	Approx. df	P-value
For INTRCTP1, PO					
INTRCPT2, B00	484.654	210.770	2.299	396	.022
UNEMPRT, B01	5.872	1.256	4.675	5976	.000

(Continued)

Table 10.3   (Continued)

Fixed Effect	Coefficient	Standard Error	T-ratio	Approx. df	P-value
PERBLACK, B02	9.946	1.258	7.904	5976	.000
PERMALE, B03	−10.427	4.889	−2.133	5976	.033
PER1534, B04	1.957	1.801	1.086	5976	.278
REGIONS, B05	−100.451	31.006	−3.240	396	.002
REGIONW, B06	33.490	21.657	1.546	396	.123
REGIONMW, B07	−52.171	20.599	−2.533	396	.012
For YEAR slope, P1					
INTRCPT2, B10	32.583	38.533	.846	396	.399
UNEMPRT, B11	.295	.284	1.038	5976	.300
PERBLACK, B12	1.682	.290	5.795	5976	.000
PERMALE, B13	−.377	.865	−.435	5976	.663
PER1534, B14	−.578	.252	−2.291	5976	.022
REGIONS, B15	−7.140	4.815	−1.483	306	.399
REGIONW, B16	6.998	3.180	2.201	396	.028
REGIONMW, B17	2.264	2.885	.785	396	.433
For YEAR2 slope, P2					
INTERCPT2, B20	−1.140	2.952	−.386	396	.699
UNEMPRT, B21	−.071	.021	−3.460	5976	.001
PERBLACK, B22	−.133	.020	−6.549	5976	.000
PERMALE, B23	.007	.064	.113	5976	.911
PER1534, B24	.036	.015	2.356	5976	.663
REGIONS, B25	.905	.373	2.427	396	.016
REGIONW, B26	−.289	.230	−1.256	396	.210
REGIONMW, B27	.022	.206	.109	396	.914

Deviance: 64506.358
Number of estimated parameters = 7

sustain our earlier conclusion that counties with high levels of robberies tended to incur higher increases than counties that did not, but not to the extent indicated in Table 10.2. This means that some of the higher correlations found in the level 1–only estimation shown in Table 10.2 were due to the level 2 contributions that are now controlled. The correlation of −.585 between the intercept and quadratic slope is still substantial, and the correlation of −.899 shows that counties experiencing especially high increases in robbery in the late 1980s tended to see especially rapid drops in the 1990s for reasons unrelated to the county characteristics we have included in the model.

Panel C of Table 10.3 shows the final estimates of the variance components. By taking the ratio of the variance component in this table to that of the corresponding variance component in Panel C of Table 10.2, we obtain ratios of 0.63 for the intercept, 0.47 for the linear slope, and 0.48 for the quadratic slope. This is the proportion of the total variation in the estimated coefficient that remains unexplained by our level 2 variables. The variance in the level 1 coefficients explained by the level 2 variables is consequently 0.37, 0.53, and 0.52, respectively. The variables we have chosen to characterize the counties evidently explain a fair amount of the heterogeneity in robbery rate trajectories, but a substantial proportion of the variance in these coefficients remains unexplained.

The first grouping of coefficients in Panel D tells us the extent to which counties with particular characteristics had levels of robbery that were higher or lower than average. The larger the percent Black in a county and the higher its unemployment rate, the higher was its robbery rate in 1985, while a disproportionate number of males, counterintuitively, tended to reduce it. Controlling for these variables, robbery rates were significantly lower in the South and in the Midwest than in the Northeast.

The coefficients for the second grouping of variables show the sources of variability in the factors that influenced the linear slope. Remarkably, the intercept is consistent with 0. Thus, in counties in the Northeast (our reference region), where there were very few Blacks, males, and young people, and where unemployment was extremely low, robbery rates did not tend to rise systematically in the late 1980s. The linear slope was higher where there were more Blacks and in the West; it was reduced by a disproportionate number of young people.

The third grouping of variables shows the sources of variability in the factors that influenced the quadratic slope. Here, too, the intercept is consistent with 0. In the same reference counties identified in the previous paragraph, there was no systematic tendency for robbery rates to fall. However, robbery rates dropped faster in counties containing a disproportionate number of Blacks and high levels of unemployment. Rates dropped slower in the South than elsewhere. These estimates imply that the gross patterns of change in robbery rates for the years 1985–1999 cannot be understood exclusively as a national phenomenon. They rose faster, and then declined faster, in cities with particular demographic makeups.

Residual Analysis

As in other regression-type analyses, examination of the level 1 and level 2 residuals can provide information about the appropriateness of the model. This examination must be conducted in a statistical package other than the HLM program. The inferential statistics computed in HLM assume that the level 1 residuals are normally distributed. To test the validity of this assumption using SPSS, we open the level 1 residual file created in HLM in SPSS, and choose "Analyze" from the choices on the toolbar, then choose "Descriptive Statistics." We select "Q-Q plot," and put the variable *l1resid* in the variable box. It is the residual for the level 1 equation, with a value for each of the 6,000 observations in the dataset. We leave the *test distribution* at its default, "normal." This gives us the Q-Q plot shown in Figure 10.5. If the residuals are normally distributed, the points will lie

Figure 10.5 Q-Q plot of level 1 residuals for the linear model

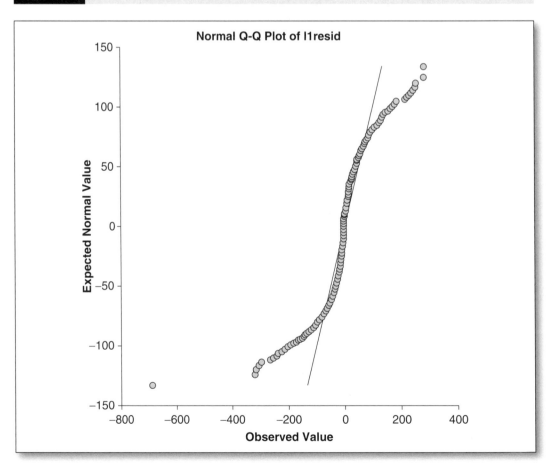

on a straight line. Here we see some deviations at either end of the distribution, pointing to some departures from normality. This is not surprising: Robbery rates cannot be truly normally distributed because they can never be negative.

The nature of the departure can be seen by going to "Graphs/Legacy Dialogs/ Histogram" in SPSS. Choose the variable *l1resid*. Clicking the option that asks for a display of the normal curve to be superimposed on the histogram gives us the graph shown in Figure 10.7. We see at once that the histogram has the general shape of a symmetric, unimodal curve, but it is more peaked than a normal distribution would be. The impact of this departure from normality should be minimized by using robust standard errors in the estimation[12] (as we did).

Chapter 3 reviews several ways of comparing the relative goodness of fit for multilevel models. It can also be of interest to have an absolute measure of a model's goodness of fit, assessing how closely the observed and predicted values of the outcome variable coincide. For continuous variables, the Pearson correlation coefficient for the observed and predicted dependent variable is a familiar

Figure 10.6   Histogram of level 1 residuals for the linear model

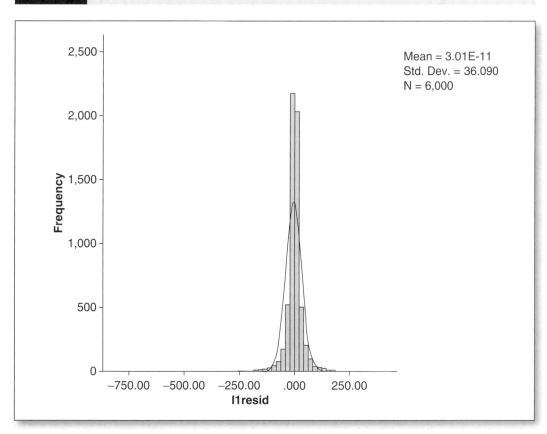

Mean = 3.01E-11
Std. Dev. = 36.090
N = 6,000

Figure 10.7 Scatterplot of level 1 residuals plotted against predicted robbery rates

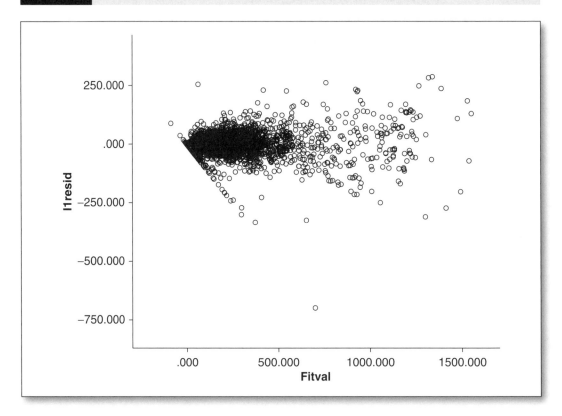

way of assessing the linear absolute goodness of fit. To estimate it, go to "Analyze/Correlate/Bivariate" in SPSS, and ask for the Pearson correlation between the robbery rate and the *fitvalue*. We find a correlation of 0.985, which is spectacular. Correlations this large are uncommon in the social sciences, making one wonder why the fit here is so good. The reason is that the fit includes the random error for the level 1 equation in the computation of the fit.

It may also be of interest to examine the distribution of the dependent variable predicted by the model. To do this, go to "Analyze/Descriptive Statistics/ Descriptives." The SPSS output shows that the smallest value of *fitvalue* is −102.99 (compared to a mean of 175.63 and a maximum of 201.29). The prediction of a negative rate for 31 county-years—which is impossible—is an undesirable feature of our model.

Another informative graph plots the level 1 residual against the predicted value of the robbery rate, *fitvalue*. Ideally, the residuals should be randomly distributed above and below zero, with no evident curvilinearity, and have a dispersion that is approximately constant across the range of values of *fitvalue*.

The first two conditions appear to hold, at least approximately (see Figure 10.8), but there is evidence of heteroscedasticity. The spread of the residuals is wider in the extreme right-hand part of the graph, where there are fewer cases, than in the left-hand part of the graph.

To detect curvilinearity in the level 2 equation, the researcher can create a scatterplot of the estimated intercept and slopes for the level 1 equation against each of the level 2 variables. If the level 2 equation is specified using just the first power of each level 2 variable, curvilinearity in the scatterplot is an indication that the model should be modified by introducing another term capturing that curvilinearity into the model. We do not illustrate this procedure here because all of our level 2 variables are dummies; as they are coded 0 or 1 only, raising these variables to higher powers would only give us back the original variables. Including them would tell us nothing new. In other applications, where continuous variables appear in the level 2 equation, this procedure could identify functional misspecifications of the level 2 equation.

Estimating a Model for Counts

We next treat the outcome as a count variable and return to Basic Settings after selecting our outcome variable, *robberies*. We choose the Poisson distribution. To

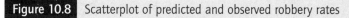

Figure 10.8   Scatterplot of predicted and observed robbery rates

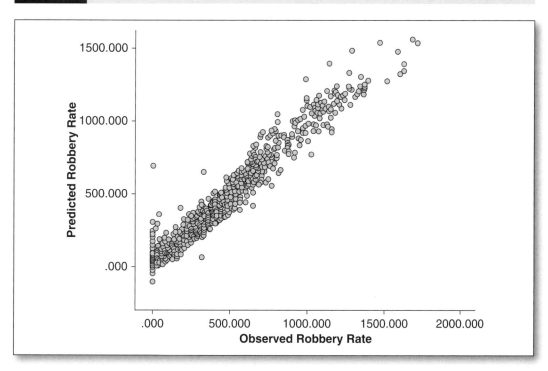

take into account our expectation that states with larger populations will have more robberies for that reason alone, we check Variable Exposure and choose *poptot* (total population) to control for differential exposure among the counties.

In a true Poisson distribution, the mean and the variance of the distribution should be equal. Yet it often happens that this equality does not hold empirically. To test this assumption, researchers allow for overdispersion, i.e., a conditional variance that is larger than the conditional mean. Overdispersion can arise in various ways, for example, from an omitted random variable. HLM users can allow for overdispersion in the Basic Settings menu. The output yields an estimate for sigma; if this quantity is greater than 1, overdispersion is present. The rest of our model is identical to that estimated with the robbery rate as the dependent variable. Because we will need it for post-estimation analysis, we also include *poptot* in the level 2 residual file. We show the REML estimates, which are actually restricted penalized quasi-likelihood estimates, in Table 10.4.

Table 10.4 Poisson Regression for Robbery Counts (with overdispersion)

Panel A. Tau Matrix (as correlations)

INTRCPT1, P0	1	−.180	−.105
YEAR,P1	−.180	1	−.753
YEAR2, P2	−.105	−.753	1

Panel B. Reliability Estimates for Random Level 1 Estimates

Random Level 1 Coefficient	Reliability Estimate
INTRCPT1, PO	.881
YEAR, P1	.501
YEAR2, P2	.548

Panel C. Final Estimation of Variance Components

Random Effect	Standard Deviation	Variance Component	df	Chi-square	P-value
INTRCPT1, R0	.760	.578	396	48499.587	.000
YEAR SLOPE, R1	.064	.004	396	2319.467	.000
YEAR2 SLOPE, R2	.005	.000	396	2614.114	.000
Level 1 E	4.778	22.82734			

Panel D. Final Estimation of Fixed Effects (with robust standard errors)

Fixed Effect	Coefficient	Standard Error	T-ratio	Approx. df	P-value
For I NTRCTP1, PO					
INTRCPT2, B00	−5.672	1.209	−4.691	396	.000
UNEMPRT, B01	.054	.005	10.868	5976	.000
PERBLACK, B02	.057	.004	14.755	5976	.000
PERMALE, B03	−.046	.027	−1.694	5976	.000
PER1534, B04	−.001	.009	−.165	4976	.869
REGIONS, B05	−.064	.114	−.561	396	.575
REGIONW, B06	.566	.130	4.365	396	.000
REGIONMW, B07	−.138	.111	−1.251	396	.212
For YEAR slope, P1 (×100)					
INTRCPT2, B10	25.276	20.789	1.216	396	.225
UNEMPRT, B11	−.293	.001	−2.183	5976	.029
PERBLACK, B12	.196	.405	4.825	5976	.000
PERMALE, B13	−.098	.448	−.219	5976	.827
PER1534, B14	−.521	.111	−4.782	5976	.000
REGIONS, B15	4.159	20.789	1.268	396	.001
REGIONW, B16	2.679	1.563	1.714	396	.087
REGIONMW, B17	4.971	1.351	3.681	396	.000
For YEAR2 slope, P2 (×1000)					
INTERCPT2, B20	−12.812	15.553	−.824	396	.411
UNEMPRT, B21	−.224	.098	−2.285	5976	.029
PERBLACK, B22	−.185	.028	−6.639	5976	.000
PERMALE, B23	−.053	.323	−.165	5976	.869
PER1534, B24	.451	.071	6.326	5976	.000
REGIONS, B25	−1.885	.945	−1.995	396	.046
REGIONW, B26	−1.207	1.171	−1.031	396	.304
REGIONMW, B27	−4.946	1.011	−4.894	396	.000

The reliability for the intercept in this model remains high; the reliabilities for the two time slopes are not as high as they were in the linear model (see Panel B of Table 10.4). A comparison of the different sets of estimates must take into account an important difference in the models: The Poisson regression in Table 10.4 takes the log of the latent robbery rate as the outcome variable, while the model presented in Table 10.3 presents the estimates for the unlogged rate. For this reason, we do not necessarily expect the two sets of estimates to agree perfectly. Nevertheless, if we compare the two sets of models, there is quite strong agreement. Most of the estimates have the same sign in both models. Most that are significant in one model are significant in the other; most that are not significant in one are not significant in the other. There are some slight differences in the impact of the regional dummy variables: Compared to the reference region (Northeast), Table 10.3 shows southern and midwestern counties to have lower robbery rates (estimates for the intercepts), whereas in Table 10.4, western counties have elevated rates. In the estimates for the coefficients of the quadratic term in *year*, Table 10.3 shows the regional dummy for South to be significantly positive, whereas in Table 10.4, it is significantly negative. In addition, the dummy for Midwest in Table 10.3 is positive but not significant; in Table 10.4, it is significantly negative. In our discussion of the linear model, we noted that the model made unrealistic negative predictions for some of the robbery rates; that it did this for only 31 of the 6,000 observations in the dataset—just 0.5%—might suggest that the violations of the Poisson assumptions are too few to make a big difference. Our finding of few differences between the models tends to confirm this reasoning, but it also shows that the model differences are not totally inconsequential either.

How well does the Poisson model perform in predicting observed robbery counts? We can compute the predicted robbery counts from the output in the level 1 residual file. Recall that the expected number of robberies in a county is equal to the population total of that county times the estimate of λ, and that $\lambda = \exp(a + b_1 x_1 + ...)$. We obtain the estimate of lambda from our output by exponentiating *fitval*. When we do this, and multiply the estimate by N, we can compute the correlation between estimated and predicted robbery counts. It is 0.997. The fit displays a small degree of heteroscedasticity, with the spread of residuals being slightly larger in counties with many robberies than in counties with relatively few. This graph is shown in Figure 10.9. When compared with Figure 10.8, it is clear that the values predicted by the Poisson regression correspond more closely to the observed values than was the case for the linear model for robbery rates.

The Q-Q plot for the level 1 residuals from the Poisson regression (not shown here) is not perfect, but it looks a little better at the lower-left part of the graph than it did when we were analyzing robbery rates. Unlike the linear model discussed earlier, now there are no negative predicted robbery rates. Given that the count model is statistically more justifiable than the model for rates (because it does not make assumptions that cannot possibly be valid and it fits the data marginally better than the linear model), we prefer the Poisson regression results to those of the

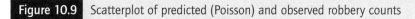

Figure 10.9 Scatterplot of predicted (Poisson) and observed robbery counts

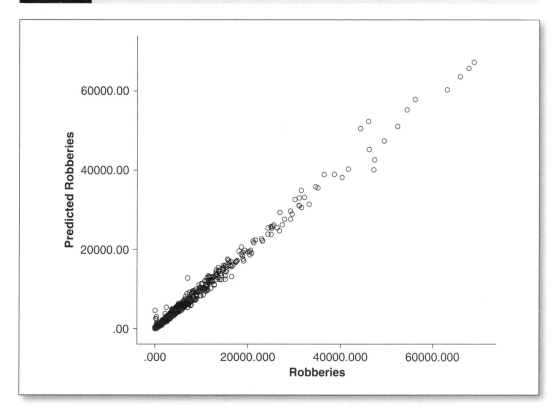

linear model. These results furnish new and provocative insights into the nature of trends in robbery during the years 1985 through 1999. Paying attention only to the coefficients for *year* and *year²* that achieved statistical significance, we find that in the northeastern part of the country (our reference region), counties with very few blacks had no significant increase in robberies, nor did they experience significant declines in the latter part of the time period. The major changes in robbery rates in the late 1980s were to a significant degree a racial phenomenon.

ASSESSMENT OF THE METHODS

We have seen that panel data permit us to address questions about the factors that influence causal variables in a manner that would be impossible with cross-sectional data. Had we collected data on robberies and their correlates in a single year, we could have examined the factors that influence the number of robberies or the robbery rate in U.S. counties in that year only. A time series analysis for the national robbery rate would have revealed the aggregate national trend, but not local variation in robbery rate trends. Separate time series analyses for each county would have yielded 400 sets of coefficients, each of them based on just 15 years—a guaranteed way to obtain unreliable estimates for each county.

By contrast, panel data pool cross-sectional and longitudinal information in the outcome of interest, to enable investigation of possible random variation across counties in both the levels of robberies and changes in those levels of robberies over time. Furthermore, hierarchical linear modeling enables researchers to identify factors that explain the variation in levels and rates of change over time.

The flexibility of the HLM program permits us to analyze the data by alternately treating robbery as a continuous variable, or as a count by estimating a Poisson regression. In our example, most of the findings were similar for the two models. However, for a few of the estimates the conclusions were substantively different from one another, indicating that the model choice can be consequential.

In the econometric approach to the analysis of panel data, it is common to deal with the issue of unmeasured heterogeneity in the intercepts in a slightly different manner from that used in multilevel modeling. In the econometric approach, one stacks the cross-sections and then adds random contributions to the intercept as we did here, but does not initially assume them to be uncorrelated with the level 1 predictors. The assumption that these correlations vanish is a strong one. If the random contributions contain unmeasured variables that are correlated with the level 1 predictors, potential bias in the estimates of the level 1 coefficients can result (Baltagi 1995; Cameron & Trivedi, 2005; Greene, 2003; Johnston & DiNardo, 1997). In our case, any omitted influence on robberies that correlates with *year* or *year²* would lead to such a bias. For example, prison populations were growing between 1985 and 1999 and could have reduced robberies through deterrence and incapacitation.

To determine whether this type of correlation is a potential problem, econometricians conduct Hausman tests to see whether there are systematic differences in the estimates obtained from a "fixed effects" model that takes these possible correlations into account, and a "random effects" model in which they are assumed to be absent. If the Hausman test is significant, the researcher opts for the fixed effects model and purges one source of unmeasured heterogeneity—stable, time-invariant effects that influence the outcome—by subtracting the mean of each variable from that variable and working with the "de-meaned" data[13] (Cameron & Trivedi, 2005; Greene, 2003). The group-mean centering option in the HLM program easily allows the researcher to de-mean the level 1 and level 2 predictors in a way that yields the same estimators as the fixed effects model for panel data (Phillips & Greenberg, 2008; Raudenbush, 2009). We did not do this in the present analysis.

The wider limitations of the multilevel model should also be noted. We were able to represent the overall temporal change in robbery rates only because they were relatively smooth. If the robbery rates had varied in a highly erratic manner, a polynomial of a higher order would have been necessary to fit the fluctuations. We would then have had to contend with severe multicollinearity and large standard errors, resulting in grossly imprecise estimates in which little confidence could be placed. In principle, dummies for each time period could be introduced, but this would be messy, as the output would contain a set of level 2 coefficients for each of the dummy variables. In this circumstance, the research might better be carried out in the fashion of econometricians, by pooling of time series and cross-sections (Baltagi, 1995; Cameron & Trivedi, 2005; Greene, 2003; Phillips & Greenberg, 2008). The HLM approach, however, is convenient for estimating the variance components, which tell us how much unexplained level 1 variance there is, and how the level 1 estimates are correlated with one another. It helps the researcher to identify interactions between time and the level 2 covariates and is more easily extended to models with higher levels of nesting (Curran, Obeidat, & Losardo, 2010).

A further limitation of the hierarchical linear modeling approach is that the software packages for doing this type of estimation are not equipped for handling measurement models for latent variables (Curran et al., 2010), or instrumental variable estimation. The latter limitation means that they are not well-suited for handling problems involving reciprocal causation. They also ignore the possibility of nonstationarity in the dataset (which can lead to spurious regressions and biased significance tests) and co-integration of variables. Where these issues are salient, statistical packages equipped for structural equation modeling or advanced econometrics procedures may be preferable to HLM.[14]

ACKNOWLEDGMENTS

We are grateful to G. David Garson, Steven Raudenbush, David Rindskopf, and Shevaun Neupert for helpful comments and suggestions.

NOTES

1. This means that at least three waves of data are needed if anything is to be learned about the curvature of the trajectory.

2. There are two senses in which an expression can be said to be linear. The common-sense meaning is that none of the powers of the predictors is different from 1. From the point of view of statistical estimation, however, it is linearity in the coefficients, not linearity in the variables, that is important.

3. A more extensive discussion of coding schemes for time in growth models can be found in Singer and Willett (2003) and Biesanz, Deeb-Sossa, Papadakis, Bollen, and Curran (2004).

4. Researchers may also find it useful to get a sense of how much variability there is in the shape of trajectories across cases. This can be done in Stata by first using the xtset command to identify the case and time variables and then using the xtline command with the overlay option. If there are many cases in the dataset, the resulting graph will be too dense to be informative, so the researcher may want to select a small number of cases—10, say—at random, and graph the trajectories for just these cases.

5. In principle, we could estimate the linear model using robbery counts instead of rates. We do not do so because we would encounter extreme multicollinearity. By working with rates when we estimate the linear model, we remove the common factor of county population size from the level 2 predictors (Firebaugh, 1988; Firebaugh & Gibbs, 1985, 1986). When we later estimate a statistical model designed for count data, multicollinearity will not be a problem.

6. In many applications, this will not be a serious problem. If the rate is sufficiently high, there will be few negative predicted values, if any. In this circumstance, the misfit will not have a large impact on the estimates.

7. To the best of our knowledge, the newly released version 7 does not differ from version 6.02 in the procedures we are presenting here.

8. HLM specifies "individuals" as the level 2 unit. The user should check this box even when the level 2 unit is something else. In this case, it is the county, not an individual.

9. The U.S. government assigns a unique *fips* code to each distinct city, county, and state in the United States.

10. To save space, we omit the descriptive statistics for the predictors that are defined as interaction terms involving other variables.

11. When we estimated a model in which all coefficients were random (a preferable procedure), HLM was unable to carry out the estimation.

12. The output contains the robust standard errors for all runs; the user does not need to request them.

13. The de-meaning procedure, we should point out, only protects the estimation from bias originating in time-invariant unmeasured predictors. It does not eliminate bias from the omission of time-varying covariates. If the procedure is adopted, it will not be possible to obtain estimates of the effects of time-invariant level 2 predictors.

14. Introductions to latent growth curve modeling in a structural equation modeling framework can be found in Bollen and Curran (2006); Duncan, Duncan, and Strycker (2006); and Preacher, Wichman, MacCallum, and Briggs (2008).

REFERENCES

Baltagi, B. (1995). *Econometric analysis of panel data*. New York: Wiley.

Biesanz, J. C., Deeb-Sossa, N., Papadakis, A. A., Bollen, K. A., & Curran, P. J. (2004). The role of coding time in estimating and interpreting growth curve models. *Psychological Methods, 9*(1), 30–52.

Bollen, K. A., & Curran, P. J. (2006). *Latent curve models: A structural equation perspective*. Hoboken, NJ: Wiley.

Cameron, A. C., & Trivedi, P. K. (2005). *Microeconomics: Methods and applications*. New York: Cambridge University Press.

Curran, P. J., Obeidat, K., & Losardo, D. (2010). Twelve frequently asked questions about growth curve modeling. *Journal of Cognition and Development, 11*(2), 121–136.

Duncan, T. E., Duncan, S. C., & Strycker, L. A. (2006). *An introduction to latent growth curve modeling: Concepts, issues, and applications* (2nd ed.). Mahwah, NJ: Lawrence Erlbaum.

Enders, C. K., & Tofighi, D. (2007). Centering predictor variables in cross-sectional multilevel models: A new look at an old issue. *Psychological Methods, 12*(2), 121–138.

Firebaugh, G. (1988). The ratio variables hoax in political science. *American Journal of Political Science, 32*(2), 523–535.

Firebaugh, G., & Gibbs, J. P. (1985). User's guide to ratio variables. *American Sociological Review, 30*(5), 713–722.

Firebaugh, G., & Gibbs, J. P. (1986). Using ratio variables to control for population size. *Sociological Methods & Research, 15*(1–2), 101–117.

Gould, W. (2011). *Use Poisson rather than regress; tell a friend.* Retrieved August 29, 2011, from http://blog.stata.com/2011/08/22

Greene, W. H. (2003). *Econometric analysis* (5th ed.). Upper Saddle River, NJ: Prentice Hall.

Hofmann, D. A., & Gavin, M. B. (1998). Centering decisions in hierarchical linear models: Implications for research in organizations. *Journal of Management, 24*(5), 623–641.

Hox, J. (2002). *Multilevel analysis: Techniques and applications.* Mahwah, NJ: Lawrence Erlbaum.

Johnston, J., & DiNardo, J. (1997). *Econometric methods* (4th ed.). New York: McGraw-Hill.

Nichols, A. (2010). *Regression for nonnegative skewed dependent variables.* Retrieved December 27, 2011, from http://repec.org/bost10/nichols_boston2010.pdf

Paccagnella, O. (2006). Centering or not centering in multilevel models? The role of the group mean and the assessment of group effects. *Evaluation Review, 30*, 66–85.

Phillips, J. A. (2006). The relationship between age structure and homicide rates in the United States, 1970–1999. *Journal of Research in Crime & Delinquency, 43*(3), 230–260.

Phillips, J. A., & Greenberg, D. F. (2008). A comparison of methods for analyzing criminological panel data. *Journal of Quantitative Criminology, 24*(1), 51–72.

Preacher, K. J., Wichman, A. L., MacCallum, R., & Briggs, N. E. (2008). *Latent growth curve modeling.* Thousand Oaks, CA: Sage.

Raudenbush, S. W. (2009). Adaptive centering with random effects: An alternative to the fixed effects model for studying time-varying treatments in school settings. *Education Finance and Policy, 4*(4), 468–491.

Raudenbush, S. W., & Bryk, A. S. (2002). *Hierarchical linear modeling: Applications and data analysis.* Thousand Oaks, CA: Sage.

Raudenbusch, S., Bryk, A., Cheong, Y. F., Congdon, R., & du Toit, M. (2004). *HLM6: Hierarchical linear and nonlinear modeling.* Lincolnwood, IL: Scientific Software.

Singer, J. D., & Willett, J. B. (2003). *Applied longitudinal data analysis: Modeling change and event occurrence.* New York: Oxford University Press.

A Piecewise Growth Model Using HLM 7 to Examine Change in Teaching Practices Following a Science Teacher Professional Development Intervention

11

Jaime L. Maerten-Rivera

Many studies are conducted where the variable of interest is measured from the same subject repeatedly over time in order to study growth or change. HLM provides a method for estimating random effects change models by treating the data as nested, such that the repeated measures are nested within individuals (Raudenbush & Bryk, 2002; Singer & Willett, 2003). The level 1 model considers the within-person change over time (intraindividual), while the level 2 model considers the between-person variation in change (interindividual).

A major advantage of using HLM to model change is that it is easily fit to unbalanced data (i.e., data with varying numbers of data collection points), provided there are enough participants with enough waves of data. The approach can readily incorporate all participants who have participated in at least one wave of data collection. The model uses full information maximum likelihood estimation to compute parameter estimates based on the data collected for each person. These estimates are unbiased, provided that attrition is random (Schafer & Graham, 2002; Singer & Willett, 2003). It has even been shown that in many realistic applications, departures from missing at random are not large enough to effectively invalidate the results of the estimates obtained using a missing data procedure, assuming data are missing at random (Collins, Schafer, & Kam, 2001).

Another advantage is that in the HLM framework, change is not limited to a single linear or constant change trajectory. Nonlinear change can be modeled by adding additional time measurement variables. Similarly, piecewise (Raudenbush & Bryk, 2002) or discontinuous (Singer & Willett, 2003) change can be specified such that change is treated in separate though related pieces by modeling two or more linear slopes.

When analyzing change models using HLM, there is a common error covariance structure that is tested. Singer and Willett (2003) review this error covariance structure and refer to it as the "standard" multilevel model for change. It is the default provided by many HLM software programs. In this model, there is a within-person error structure and a composite error structure. As a result of the time variable being included in the model, the within-person structure can be both heteroscedastic (with a minimum that will increase parabolically and symmetrically over time on either side of its minimum) and correlated over time. The composite residuals are expected to be normally distributed with zero means. In other words, the blocks of the error covariance matrix are identical across people as a result of a homogeneity assumption that the composite residuals may be heteroscedastic and dependent within people, but the error structure is repeated identically across people.

However, alternative error covariance structures, such as unstructured, first-order autoregressive, and compound symmetric structures can easily be tested (see Chapter 2 of text for explanation of each). Refining hypotheses about the error covariance structure rarely changes the fixed effects parameter estimates obtained. However, it can affect the precision of estimates of the fixed effects, and therefore impacts hypothesis testing and confidence intervals (Singer & Willett, 2003). As the error covariance structure of a model is better represented, the standard errors may decline, increasing the likelihood of rejecting the null hypothesis.

The data used to demonstrate the above were collected as part of a larger research project funded by the National Science Foundation (NSF). The chapter addresses measurement and missing data issues in longitudinal studies and illustrates how these issues are handled in HLM. In this particular example, a piecewise change model was examined where two linear slope factors were modeled. The first growth factor examined the initial change in teaching practices after first participating in the intervention, whereas the second examined the change that occurred from the first year through the third year of the intervention. Finally, this example addresses alternative error covariance structures in longitudinal models. Recent advancements in HLM software (Raudenbush, Bryk, & Congdon, 2005) allow a number of covariance structures to be examined with relative ease, and this chapter demonstrates how this can be done.

SAMPLE

Longitudinal data obtained from a science teacher professional development project were used. The research project aimed at improving science and English literacy achievement of English language learning (ELL) students. Over a 5-year period, the research implemented an educational intervention consisting of curriculum units and teacher workshops. The research involved teachers from Grades 3 through 5 and their students at six elementary schools in a large urban school district. During the first year (2004–2005), third-grade teachers and their students began the intervention. In the second year (2005–2006), the intervention was started with the fourth-grade teachers. In the third year (2006–2007), the intervention was started with the fifth-grade teachers. Each grade participated in 3 years of the intervention. All of the schools enrolled relatively high proportions of ELL students and students from low socioeconomic status (SES) backgrounds and had traditionally performed poorly according to the state's accountability policies.

A main goal of the intervention was to increase the use of reform-oriented teaching practices (ROP) in science, and this was the outcome variable examined in the study. The ROP scale consisted of 10 items asking the teacher the frequency in which he or she used reform-oriented practices for understanding and inquiry while teaching science. An example stem item asks the teacher how often he or she "Used science process skills (e.g., hypothesize, organize, infer, analyze, evaluate, describe patterns, make models or simulations)" with the response options of "Never or almost never," "Some lessons," "Most lessons," and "Every lesson." For a list of all items and results pertaining to the baseline scores, see Maerten-Rivera, Penfield, Myers, Lee, and Buxton (2009); for further piecewise analysis of measures pertaining to the study, see Lee and Maerten-Rivera (in press).

The score for the ROP scale was computed using the average of the responses to the items that comprised the scale. Teacher-level predictors (i.e., race or ethnicity, highest degree, number of years teaching, number of science classes taken in college, and grade taught) were examined for their impact on both initial status in ROP and change over time in ROP. There were 191 teachers included in this study, with varying data points collected. The missing data were primarily the result of teacher attrition over the 5 years in which the professional development took place. The number of teachers per school ranged from 17 to 43 with a mean of 31 teachers per school.

At the end of each school year, all third-, fourth-, and fifth-grade teachers were asked to complete a questionnaire. For the purpose of this research, when a teacher completed the questionnaire prior to beginning the intervention, the time was coded as Baseline or Time 0. When a teacher completed the questionnaire at the end of his or her respective first year of participating in the intervention, time was coded as Time 1. Similarly, at the end of his or her respective second year of participating in the intervention, time was coded as Time 2, and at the end of his or her respective third year of participating in the intervention, time was coded as Time 3. A teacher could start participation at any time during the 5-year intervention. If a third-grade teacher started teaching at a participating school during Year 3 of the intervention, when the teacher completed the questionnaire at the end of the year, the time would be coded as Time 1 since it was his or her first year of participating in the intervention.

Table 11.1 shows the number of teachers who completed the questionnaire at each time. The maximum number of time points that a teacher could have is 4 (Group 1), in which case the teacher completed a baseline questionnaire, then participated in 3 years of the intervention, and completed the questionnaire at the end of each year. Groups 8 through 11 represent cases where a teacher was unavailable at a scheduled time to complete the questionnaire. The other groups (Groups 2 through 7) represent missing data due to teacher attrition (i.e., either leaving a school prior to participating in all 3 years of the intervention or entering a school after the baseline data had been collected).

	N	Baseline	Time 1	Time 2	Time 3
Group 1	18	X	X	X	X
Group 2	19	X	X	X	
Group 3	17	X	X		
Group 4	31	X			
Group 5	15		X	X	X
Group 6	28		X	X	
Group 7	58		X		
Group 8	1			X	
Group 9	1		X		X
Group 10	2	X		X	
Group 11	1	X		X	X
Totals	191	88	156	84	35

Table 11.1 Patterns of Data Collected (N = 191)

SOFTWARE AND PROCEDURE

The data storage and preparation was conducted using SPSS 19, and this data file was then used in HLM 7 (Raudenbush et al., 2005) to analyze the multilevel models. The first series of models was analyzed using the hierarchical linear models (HLM) module of the HLM software. The .mdm files in the HLM software were created in a typical fashion as illustrated in Chapter 3, but it is important to note that in making the file, the "Structure of data" selection was changed from the default of "cross-sectional" (persons within groups) to "longitudinal" (occasions within persons), since this was a longitudinal analysis. (This changes the notation of the output.) Once the .mdm file was created, models were specified by assigning the appropriate variables as outcomes and predictors using the point-and-click method. All models were examined using full maximum likelihood estimation, which can easily be specified in HLM (Other Settings → Estimation Settings → Full Maximum Likelihood). Full maximum likelihood estimation was chosen because it allows model comparisons for the entire model (both fixed effects and variance components), whereas when using restricted maximum likelihood, only the variance components can be tested.

In this research, a model-building approach was generally employed, as suggested by Raudenbush and Bryk (2002). Broadly, a growth model was built, and then person-level predictors were added to the model to evaluate their effect on initial status and the growth parameters. All predictors were entered uncentered because they were typically dummy coded and therefore easy to interpret as they were. In the process, competing models were compared using the deviance statistic, also called the likelihood ratio or model chi-square statistic. HLM includes the deviance statistic and degrees of freedom (df) as output for each model. The HLM software was used to test the current model against a previous model by computing the chi-square statistic once the competing model information was entered (Other Settings → Hypothesis Testing).

In addition, the proportion of variance accounted for (PVAF)[1] or pseudo-R^2 (Raudenbush & Bryk, 2002; Singer & Willett, 2003) is often used as an estimate of effect size. This estimate compares a model with the predictor(s) of interest (fitted model) to a model without the predictor(s) (baseline model). Thus, in this example the PVAF in ROP by predictors was computed throughout. The R^2 can be interpreted as values of less than .09 having a small effect, between .09 and .25 having a medium effect, and greater than .25 having a large effect (Cohen, 1977), and therefore, the PVAF was interpreted in the same way.

Finally, the hierarchical multivariate linear models (HMLM) module of HLM was used in order to compare alternative error covariance structures for the final model. HMLM allows an unrestricted or unstructured error covariance (where each element of the error covariance structure takes on the value that the data demand) to be defined and allows comparisons to other error covariance structures. Note that the unrestricted model cannot be examined within the standard HLM. The model is examined by first specifying HMLM as the analysis being conducted when HLM first prompts the user for the type of model. When selecting variables for the level 1 file, there will be an additional column labeled "Indicator." In the column, the dummy variables that were created for whether the measurement occasion (in this case, *T0*, *T1*, *T2*, *T3*) is collected should be checked. Once the .mdm file is created, these measures will by default appear in the level 1 measurement equation. The user can then select the other variables to be used in the level 1 and level 2 portions of the model. The different covariance structure models can be selected by clicking on "Basic Settings." A screen such as that displayed in Figure 11.1 will appear from which the error covariance

Figure 11.1   HMLM basic settings screen

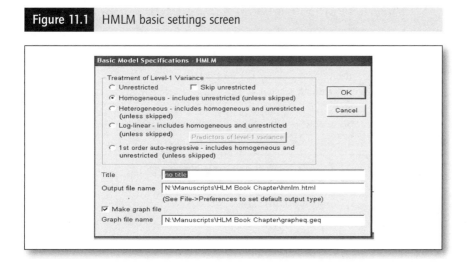

structures to be examined can be selected. Note that by clicking on "1st order auto-regressive," by default the model will be compared to the unrestricted and homogeneous level 1 structures. The compound symmetric covariance structure can be examined by clicking on the homogeneous structure but specifying that all random effects be fixed to 0. (In HLM, clicking on the variance component allows you to unhighlight it, and thus it is not estimated in that model.)

ANALYZING THE DATA

Preparing the Data

The first step in the analyses was to prepare the SPSS files so that HLM could read them and convert them for use. The level 1 file was created first, followed by a level 2 file.

The data for each year of the project were entered into separate SPSS files and contained a variable denoting the time point (0, 1, 2, 3) of measurement for that individual's data. The files for each year were merged together in SPSS (Data → Merge Files → Add Cases). Next, the two variables were created to measure the piecewise growth model. In the piecewise growth model, two linear slope factors were modeled. The first growth factor examined the initial change in ROP after first participating in the intervention, while the second examined the change that followed after completing the first year of the intervention. This was done by coding the first time variable, *PWTIME1,* with the values of *0, 1, 1, 1* representing baseline, T1, T2, and T3, respectively. The second time variable, *PWTIME2,* had the values of *0, 0, 1, 2* representing baseline, T1, T2, and T3, respectively. This was done using the SPSS syntax below.

RECODE TIMEPOINT (0=0) (1=1) (2=1) (3=1) INTO PWTIME1.
EXECUTE.
RECODE TIMEPOINT (0=0) (1=0) (2=1) (3=1) INTO PWTIME2.
EXECUTE.

Note that the intercept of the model represents the average score at baseline, as the baseline measurement is always coded as 0.

The final variables in the level 1 file were used in testing the alternative error covariance structures using the HMLM function of HLM. These variables are dummy variables with a value of *1* if the respondent has data for that time point and a *0* if the data are missing. These are labeled *T0, T1, T2,* and *T3* in the level 1 file.

Figure 11.2 is a screenshot of the data for selected participants. The *TIMEPOINT* variable represents the actual time point (Baseline, T1, T2, T3) of the data collected, while the *PWTIME1* and *PWTIME2* are the variables to be used in order to fit a piecewise growth model. Teacher 202 has data for baseline

Figure 11.2	Level 1 data file

	ID	TIMEPOINT	PWTIME1	PWTIME2	ROPMEAN	T0	T1	T2	T3
1	202	0	0	0	3.10	1.00	.00	.00	.00
2	202	1	1	0	3.20	.00	1.00	.00	.00
3	206	0	0	0	2.80	1.00	.00	.00	.00
4	206	1	1	0	3.70	.00	1.00	.00	.00
5	206	2	1	1	3.80	.00	.00	1.00	.00
6	206	3	1	2	3.90	.00	.00	.00	1.00
7	207	0	0	0	2.50	1.00	.00	.00	.00
8	207	1	1	0	3.00	.00	1.00	.00	.00
9	207	2	1	1	2.90	.00	.00	1.00	.00
10	207	3	1	2	3.00	.00	.00	.00	1.00
11	209	0	0	0	1.90	1.00	.00	.00	.00
12	209	1	1	0	3.20	.00	1.00	.00	.00
13	210	0	0	0	3.00	1.00	.00	.00	.00

and T1, and thus has two rows of data. The missing data are also reflected by the value of *0* for both *T2* and *T3* in all rows associated with the teacher.

Next, the level 2 data file was created. This file contained one row of data for each respondent and contained person-level variables. All variables were dummy coded as follows: grade (GR4: 1 = Grade 4 teacher, 0 = other grade; GR5 1 = Grade 5 teacher, 0 = other grade), highest degree (DEG: 1 = master's, 0 = bachelor's), gender (GEN: 1 = female, 0 = male), ethnicity (BLK: 1 = Black, 0 = other; HSP: 1 = Hispanic, 0 = other). In this file, school dummy variables were created to denote at which of the six schools the teacher taught. This was used as a level 2 variable to reduce variance since the sample size did not allow a three-level model to be fit. Figure 11.3 is a screenshot of the data for the selected participants.

HLM Data Analyses

As the first step in this analysis, graphs of the *ROP* variable over time were examined to explore the type of change displayed. The graph trajectories were examined for displaying no change, linear change, quadratic change, or piecewise change. This information, in addition to a priori expectations, led us to focus on the piecewise change model. The first growth factor examined the initial change in ROP after first participating in the intervention, while the second examined the change that followed after completing the first year of the intervention (secondary change).

Figure 11.3	Level 2 data file

	ID	GR4	GR5	DEGREE	GEN	BLK	HSP	SCH1	SCH2	SCH3	SCH4	SCH5
1	202	0	0	0	1	1	0	1	0	0	0	0
2	206	1	0	1	1	0	0	1	0	0	0	0
3	207	1	0	1	1	0	1	1	0	0	0	0
4	209	0	1	0	0	0	1	1	0	0	0	0
5	210	0	1	1	1	1	0	1	0	0	0	0

EXAMINATION OF TIME

First, an unconditional multilevel model in which no predictors were included, except individual, was imposed. This provided the intraclass correlation coefficient (ICC),[2] which was an estimate of the variance in ROP attributed to individual differences. Next, an unconditional change model was examined in which only the time variables were entered as uncentered predictors. Since the unconditional variance of the secondary change random effect was not statistically significant ($p > .05$), a model with this random effect fixed to 0 across individuals was examined. This finding suggests that there was not significant variation between individuals in the level of secondary change, or that most teachers changed at the same rate.

LEVEL 2 PREDICTORS

The limited sample size did not allow for a three-level model to be analyzed, though the data may have an additional level of nesting since the teachers were clustered within six different schools. In order to test the degree to which the assumption of independent observations was violated, in the first step of the analyses, school was dummy coded into five variables and examined as a person-level predictor. Separate models were examined with the school predictors entered as a predictor of each random coefficient (in this case, the intercept and initial change slope since the secondary change slope was fixed). A model comparison was conducted using the likelihood ratio test based on differences in deviance (as described above) and demonstrated that these variables as predictors of the intercept did improve the model, though they did not as predictors of the primary change slope. Note that these variables were not retained because they are of direct interest, but because they are control variables.

In the next step, background predictors were examined, such as number of years teaching, as predictors of the intercept, but were not retained because they did not contribute to the model and had at most small effects. The school variables were then added to the model as predictors of the initial change slope. These variables did not significantly improve the model and therefore were not retained. Finally, the background variables were added as predictors of the initial change slope. These variables were not retained because they did not significantly improve the model and had at most small effects. Note that variables were not examined as predictors of the secondary change slope because the variance was fixed to zero, since it was not statistically significant in previous models.

FINAL MODEL

The uncombined (by level) equation below summarizes the final HLM model. Note that in the level 2 model, PWTIME1 is modeled as a random effect, while PWTIME2 is not. This was because, as stated previously, the random effect for PWTIME2 was not significant.

Level 1 model:

$$ROP_{ti} = \pi_{0i} + \pi_{1i} PWTIME1_{ti} + \pi_{2i} PWTIME2_{ti} + e_{ti}$$

Level 2 model:

$$\pi_{0i} = \beta_{00} + \beta_{01} SCH1_{1i} + \beta_{01} SCH2_{1i} + \beta_{01} SCH3_{1i} + \beta_{01} SCH4_{1i} + \beta_{01} SCH5_{1i} +$$
$$\beta_{01} GR4_{1i} + \beta_{01} GR5_{1i} + r_{0i}$$
$$\pi_{1i} = \beta_{10} + r_{1i}$$
$$\pi_{2i} = \beta_{20}$$

ALTERNATIVE ERROR COVARIANCE STRUCTURES

Exploratory comparisons of the error covariance structure were conducted beginning with the unrestricted error covariance structure, since it is the least restrictive and will always have the lowest deviance statistic (Singer & Willett, 2003). The models were examined using the following error covariance structures in this order: (1) unrestricted, (2) random slopes, homogeneous level 1 variance (common error covariance structure used in HLM longitudinal models), (3) first-order autoregressive, and (4) compound symmetry.

Since the models were nested, model comparisons were conducted as discussed above using a likelihood ratio chi-square statistic, and results are provided in the HLM output. In addition, the Akaike information criterion (AIC; Akaike, 1974) and Bayesian information criterion (BIC; Schwartz, 1978) were used to compare models. These can be calculated based on the deviance statistic and degrees of freedom for the model provided in the HLM output. Each of these fit statistics compares models based on the log likelihood statistic, but the AIC penalizes based upon the number of model parameters, whereas the BIC penalizes based on the number of parameters and sample size (i.e., in larger samples, the researcher needs a larger improvement before the complex model is preferred over a simpler model). The model with the smaller information criterion fits "better."

OUTPUT AND ANALYSIS

Examination of Time

First, the unconditional multilevel was examined. Results from the model are provided in Table 11.2. Using the information provided for the variance components from the model, the ICC was computed as 0.22 (0.069/[0.069 + 0.246]), suggesting that 22% of the variance in ROP was due to interindividual teacher differences (level 2), while 78% of the variance in ROP was due to intraindividual differences (level 1).

In the next step, an unconditional piecewise change model was examined. The results from this model are displayed in Table 11.3. The variance of the random effect for the secondary change slope (τ_{22}; 0.00252, $p = 0.085$) was not significant,

Table 11.2 HLM Output: Fixed Effects and Variance Components for Fully Unconditional Model

Final estimation of fixed effects

Fixed Effect	Coefficient	Standard error	t-ratio	Approx. df	p-value
For INTRCPT1, π_0					
INTRCPT2, β_{00}	3.010717	0.033240	90.575	190	<0.001

Final estimation of variance components

Random Effect	Standard Deviation	Variance Component	df	χ^2	p-value
INTRCPT1, r_0	0.26249	0.06890	190	291.82738	<0.001
level-1, e	0.49635	0.24637			

Statistics for the current model

Deviance = 598.129492

Number of estimated parameters = 3

Table 11.3 HLM Output: Fixed Effects and Variance Components for Piecewise Model

τ

INTRCPT1, π_0	0.20835	−0.13384	0.00472
PLTIME, π_1	−0.13384	0.21834	−0.01993
PLTIME2, π_2	0.00472	−0.01993	0.00252

Standard errors of τ

INTRCPT1, π_0	0.04670	0.04882	0.02105
PLTIME, π_1	0.04882	0.07364	0.02502
PLTIME2, π_2	0.02105	0.02502	0.01345

τ (as correlations)

INTRCPT1,π_0	1.000	−0.628	0.206
PLTIME,π_1	−0.628	1.000	−0.849
PLTIME2,π_2	0.206	−0.849	1.000

Final estimation of fixed effects

Fixed Effect	Coefficient	Standard error	t-ratio	Approx. df	p-value
For INTRCPT1, π_0					
INTRCPT2, β_{00}	2.527722	0.056420	44.802	190	<0.001
For PLTIME slope, π_1					
INTRCPT2, β_{10}	0.629634	0.063711	9.883	190	<0.001
For PLTIME2 slope, π_2					
INTRCPT2, β_{20}	0.039918	0.028043	1.423	190	0.156

Final estimation of variance components

Random Effect	Standard Deviation	Variance Component	df	χ^2	p-value
INTRCPT1, r_0	0.45645	0.20835	37	131.07051	<0.001
PLTIME slope, r_1	0.46727	0.21834	37	87.87626	<0.001
PLTIME2 slope, r_2	0.05021	0.00252	37	49.28607	0.085
level-1, e	0.29123	0.08482			

Note. The chi-square statistics reported above are based on only 38 of 191 units that had sufficient data for computation. Fixed effects and variance components are based on all the data.

Statistics for the current model

Deviance = 448.208184

Number of estimated parameters = 10

so a model comparison was conducted to determine if a model with the secondary change slope constant across individuals fit the data significantly worse. The decrease in model deviance from the unconditional piecewise change model with the variance of secondary change fixed (i.e., baseline model) to the unconditional piecewise change model with the variance of secondary change random (i.e., fitted model) was not statistically significant, χ^2_{LR} (3)= 1.62, $p > .500$ (see Table 11.4 for model comparison). Therefore, the unconditional piecewise change model with the variance of secondary change fixed (i.e., baseline model) was retained. The results from this model are presented in Table 11.4. The PVAF by the time predictors was computed (see formula in endnote 1) to be 0.64 ([0.25 − 0.09]/0.25), where 0.25 is the baseline within-groups variance labeled "level-1, e" in Table 11.2, and 0.09 is the corresponding fitted model statistic in Table 11.4. This suggests that the time predictor variables accounted for 64% of the within-teacher variance in ROP scores.

Table 11.4	HLM Output: Fixed Effects and Variance Components for Piecewise Model With Secondary Slope Fixed

τ

INTRCPT1,π_0	0.20714	−0.12730
PLTIME,π_1	−0.12730	0.18993

Standard errors of τ

INTRCPT1,π_0	0.04586	0.04470
PLTIME,π_1	0.04470	0.06097

τ (as correlations)

INTRCPT1,π_0	1.000	−0.642
PLTIME,π_1	−0.642	1.000

Final estimation of fixed effects

Fixed Effect	Coefficient	Standard error	t-ratio	Approx. df	p-value
For INTRCPT1, π_0					
INTRCPT2, β_{00}	2.526546	0.056551	44.677	190	<0.001
For PLTIME slope, π_1					
INTRCPT2, β_{10}	0.630636	0.062770	10.047	190	<0.001
For PLTIME2 slope, π_2					
INTRCPT2, β_{20}	0.040391	0.029000	1.393	362	0.165#

The p-vals above marked with a "#" should be regarded as a rough approximation.

Final estimation of variance components

Random Effect	Standard Deviation	Variance Component	df	$\chi 2$	p-value
INTRCPT1, r_0	0.45512	0.20714	56	193.77026	<0.001
PLTIME slope, r_1	0.43581	0.18993	56	134.38727	<0.001
level-1, e	0.29652	0.08792			

Note. The chi-square statistics reported above are based on only 57 of 191 units that had sufficient data for computation. Fixed effects and variance components are based on all the data.

Statistics for the current model

Deviance = 449.826868

Number of estimated parameters = 7

Model comparison test

χ^2 statistic = 1.61868

Degrees of freedom = 3

p-value = >.500

At this point, the level 1 model is discussed. Parameters of interest in Table 11.4 are the fixed effect coefficients, variance components and covariances of r (i.e., τ_{00}, τ_{11}, and τ_{01}) at the between-individual level, and variance of e (i.e., σ^2) at the within-individual level. The coefficient for the intercept (β_{00}) was 2.53, which was statistically significant, indicating that the average true ROP across teachers at baseline was 2.53 points. The coefficient for initial change (β_{10}) was 0.63, which was statistically significant, indicating that the average true change in ROP across teachers from baseline to 1 year after the intervention was 0.63 points. The coefficient for secondary change (β_{20}) was 0.04, which was not statistically significant, indicating that the average true change in ROP across teachers from 1 year after the intervention to 3 years after the intervention was not different from zero. Figure 11.4 graphically depicts the change in ROP based on the model results. This figure was constructed in SPSS using the model results.

Also, in Table 11.4, the estimate of the level 1 variance component (σ^2; see output of Table 11.4 for level-1, e) was 0.09, which was statistically significant, suggesting that there was a significant amount of within-teacher variance in ROP from baseline to Time 3, even after controlling for both initial change and secondary change. The estimate of the variance component for the intercept (see top portion of Table 11.4 for INTRCPT1, π_0) was 0.21, which was statistically significant, suggesting that there was a significant amount of between-teacher variation around the average true ROP scores at baseline. The estimate of the variance component for the initial change slope (see top portion of Table 11.4 for PLTIME, π_1) was 0.19, which was statistically significant, suggesting that there was a significant amount of between-teacher variation around the average initial true change in ROP. The

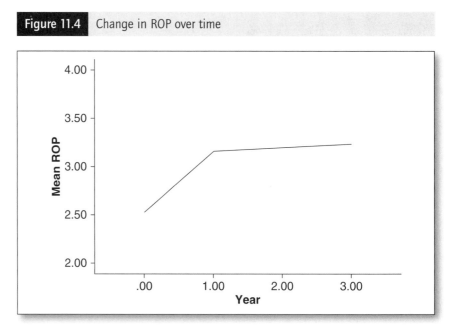

Figure 11.4 Change in ROP over time

estimate of the covariance component (see top portion of Table 11.4 for INTRCPT1, π_0) was -0.13 (the correlation was -0.64; see "τ as correlations"), which was statistically significant (note test of significance is not included in HLM output, but can be computed from information provided), suggesting that there was a significant amount of between-teacher covariation between the within-teacher estimates of true ROP at baseline and the within-teacher estimates of initial true change in ROP across teachers. On average, teachers with lower ROP at baseline experienced a larger initial increase in ROP after 1 year of the intervention.

SCHOOL AS A LEVEL 2 PREDICTOR

In the next model, the school dummy predictors were included as predictors of the intercept (τ_{00}). The results of this model are presented in Table 11.5. The deviance from the unconditional piecewise change model (i.e., baseline model) to the model with the school as a level 2 predictor of the intercept (i.e., fitted model) was statistically significant, χ^2_{LR} (5) $= 19.78$, $p = .002$ (see Table 11.5). Therefore, the model with the school as a level 2 predictor of the intercept was retained. The PVAF in the intercept by the group of school predictors was 0.05, suggesting that the school predictors accounted for 5% of the variation in the average true ROP across teachers at baseline. Overall, there were small differences in initial (or baseline) ROP based on the school in which the teacher taught.

At this point, it should be noted that the teacher background variables were examined as predictors of the initial or baseline ROP, but were not retained

Table 11.5	HLM Output: Fixed Effects and Variance Components for Piecewise Model With Schools in Level 2 Intercept

τ

INTRCPT1,π0	0.19654	−0.13150
PLTIME,π1	−0.13150	0.18787

Standard errors of τ

INTRCPT1,π0	0.04431	0.04415
PLTIME,π1	0.04415	0.06002

τ (as correlations)

INTRCPT1,π0	1.000	−0.684
PLTIME,π1	−0.684	1.000

Final estimation of fixed effects

Fixed Effect	Coefficient	Standard error	t-ratio	Approx. df	p-value
For INTRCPT1, π_0					
INTRCPT2, β_{00}	2.536603	0.056100	45.215	185	<0.001
SCH1, β_{01}	0.225070	0.131409	1.713	185	0.088
SCH2, β_{02}	0.399943	0.120010	3.333	185	0.001
SCH3, β_{03}	0.191865	0.118556	1.618	185	0.107
SCH4, β_{04}	0.035651	0.121507	0.293	185	0.769
SCH5, β_{05}	0.054911	0.120688	0.455	185	0.649
For PLTIME1 slope, π_1					
INTRCPT2, β_{10}	0.614737	0.062750	9.797	190	<0.001
For PLTIME2 slope, π_2					
INTRCPT2, β_{20}	0.041326	0.028892	1.430	355	0.153#

The p-values above marked with a "#" should be regarded as a rough approximation.

(Continued)

Table 11.5 (Continued)

Final estimation of variance components

Random Effect	Standard Deviation	Variance Component	df	χ^2	p-*value*
INTRCPT1, r_0	0.44333	0.19654	51	192.57559	<0.001
PLTIME slope, r_1	0.43344	0.18787	56	136.16872	<0.001
level-1, e	0.29614	0.08770			

Note: The chi-square statistics reported above are based on only 57 of 191 units that had sufficient data for computation. Fixed effects and variance components are based on all the data.

Statistics for the current model

Deviance = 430.051177

Number of estimated parameters = 12

Model comparison test

χ^2 statistic = 19.77569

Degrees of freedom = 5

p-value = .002

because they did not contribute to the model and had at most small effects. The school variables were then added to the model as predictors of the initial change slope. This tests whether there were differences in the rate of change, based on the school in which the teacher taught. These variables did not significantly improve the model and therefore were not retained. Finally, the background variables were added as predictors of the initial change slope. Again, this tests if certain characteristics of teachers caused them to change at a different rate (e.g., teachers new to profession have higher rate of change than those teaching for longer period of time). These variables were not retained because they did not significantly improve the model and had at most small effects. Note that variables were not examined as predictors of the secondary change slope because the variance was fixed to zero, since it was not statistically significant in previous models.

ALTERNATIVE ERROR COVARIANCE STRUCTURES

The HMLM output results from the models examining the alternative error covariance structures are presented in Table 11.6 and 11.7. Table 11.6 displays the variance and covariance components for the different models.[3] The covariance

Table 11.6   HLM Output: Variance and Covariance Components of Different Error Covariance Models

A. Variance and Covariance Components for Unrestricted Model

Δ

T0	0.28112	0.06294	0.04799	0.09851
T1	0.06294	0.22234	0.12019	0.12824
T2	0.04799	0.12019	0.18305	0.08773
T3	0.09851	0.12824	0.08773	0.20579

Δ (as correlations)

T0	1.000	0.252	0.212	0.410
T1	0.252	1.000	0.596	0.600
T2	0.212	0.596	1.000	0.452
T3	0.410	0.600	0.452	1.000

Variance and Covariance Components for Homogeneous Level 1 Model

Δ

T0	0.28430	0.06508	0.06508	0.06508
T1	0.06508	0.20911	0.12141	0.12141
T2	0.06508	0.12141	0.20911	0.12141
T3	0.06508	0.12141	0.12141	0.20911

Δ (as correlations)

T0	1.000	0.267	0.267	0.267
T1	0.267	1.000	0.581	0.581
T2	0.267	0.581	1.000	0.581
T3	0.267	0.581	0.581	1.000

(Continued)

Table 11.6 (Continued)

Variance and Covariance Components for First-Order Autoregressive Model
Δ

T0	0.28426	0.06348	0.06701	0.06687
T1	0.06348	0.20909	0.12062	0.12416
T2	0.06701	0.12062	0.20909	0.12062
T3	0.06687	0.12416	0.12062	0.20909

Δ (as correlations)

T0	1.000	0.260	0.275	0.274
T1	0.260	1.000	0.577	0.594
T2	0.275	0.577	1.000	0.577
T3	0.274	0.594	0.577	1.000

Variance and Covariance Components for Compound Symmetric Model
Δ

T0	0.22820	0.10060	0.10060	0.10060
T1	0.10060	0.22820	0.10060	0.10060
T2	0.10060	0.10060	0.22820	0.10060
T3	0.10060	0.10060	0.10060	0.22820

Δ (as correlations)

T0	1.000	0.441	0.441	0.441
T1	0.441	1.000	0.441	0.441
T2	0.441	0.441	1.000	0.441
T3	0.441	0.441	0.441	1.000

Table 11.7	HLM Output: Model Fit and Model Comparisons of Different Error Covariance Models

Summary of Model Fit Unrestricted, Homogeneous Level 1, and First-Order Autoregressive Models

Model	Number of Parameters	Deviance
1. Unrestricted	18	428.71205
2. Homogeneous σ^2	12	431.88905
3. First-order autoregressive	13	431.84971

Model Comparison	χ^2	d.f.	p-value
Model 1 vs. Model 2	3.17700	6	>0.500
Model 1 vs. Model 3	3.13766	5	>0.500
Model 2 vs. Model 3	0.03934	1	>0.500

Summary of Model Fit Unrestricted and Compound Symmetric Models

Model	Number of Parameters	Deviance
1. Unrestricted	18	428.71205
2. Homogeneous σ^2	10	448.63603

Model Comparison	χ^2	d.f.	p-value
Model 1 vs. Model 2	19.92399	8	0.011

matrix for the unrestricted model represents the values determined by the data without restrictions (note that there are more parameters freely estimated here than in the output for other models). The variance of the baseline measurement (0.28) was higher than that of the other three measurements, which were very similar (0.22, 0.18, 0.21). This suggests that over time, the teachers' use of ROP became more similar.

In addition, the correlation matrix shows that generally the correlations between the baseline measurement and the other measurements were lower than the correlations between the latter measurement occasions, with the interesting exception of the baseline measure with the T3 measure. This general pattern was captured fairly well by Model 2 (homogeneous level 1). Recall that the secondary change slope was fixed, while the initial change slope was random. Since the time predictor pertaining to the initial change slope had the values of 0, 1, 1, 1, the covariance and correlation matrices of the homogeneous level 1 model reflect this pattern, as the error covariance components are weighted by this time variable. In the homogeneous level 1 model, the variance for the baseline time point differs from the variance estimate pertaining to times 1, 2, and 3. Similarly, the covariance and correlation estimates are aligned such that those including the baseline measure differ from those of the other time points.

The top portion of Table 11.7 shows the deviance and chi-square comparison statistics for the unrestricted, random slope homogeneous level 1 and first-order autoregressive models, and the bottom portion shows this information for the unrestricted and compound symmetry models. Table 11.8 displays much of this information along with additional model comparisons and the AIC and BIC estimates for the models in a more understandable format. The unrestricted model (Model 1) had the lowest deviance. However, this model estimated the most

Table 11.8 Comparison of Alternative Models

(a) Models Summary	Deviance	# of parameters estimated	AIC	BIC	χ^2
(1) Unrestricted	428.71	18	464.71	523.25	$\chi^2(16) = 21.05$, $p = .177$
(2) Random slope, homogeneous level-1	431.89	12	455.89	494.92	$\chi^2(22) = 24.23$, $p = .335$
(3) First-order autoregressive	447.95	11	469.96	505.73	$\chi^2(23) = 40.30$, $p = .014$
(4) Compound symmetry	448.64	10	468.64	501.16	$\chi^2(24) = 40.98$, $p = .017$

(b) Model Comparisons	Difference in Deviance	df	p
Model 1 versus Model 2	3.18	6	>.500
Model 1 versus Model 3	19.24	7	.008
Model 1 versus Model 4	19.93	8	.011
Model 2 versus Model 3	16.06	1	<.001
Model 2 versus Model 4	16.75	2	<.001
Model 3 versus Model 4	0.69	1	<.500

parameters. Results from the model comparisons displayed in Table 11.8 show that the random slopes, homogeneous level 1 model (Model 2) did not fit the data significantly worse than the unrestricted model (Model 1) (χ^2_{LR} (6) = 3.18, $p >$ .500). The first-order auto regressive model (Model 3) was slightly more parsimonious than the homogeneous level 1 model (Model 2) and did fit the data significantly worse than both Model 2 (χ^2_{LR} (1) = 16.06, $p <$ .001) and Model 1 (χ^2_{LR} (7) = 19.24, $p =$ .008). The compound symmetry model (Model 4) did fit the data significantly worse than Model 1 (χ^2_{LR} (8) = 19.93, $p =$ .011) and Model 2 (χ^2_{LR} (2) = 16.75, $p <$ .001), but did not fit the data significantly worse than Model 3 (χ^2_{LR} (1) = 0.69, $p >$ .500). Though it is not presented, it is worth noting that the fixed effect parameter estimates did not change notably based on the change in the error covariance structure.

The AIC and BIC both favor Model 2. Based on these results, it would seem reasonable to accept Model 2, which is the structure commonly used in multilevel models and the default structure used in HLM.

CONCLUSION

Discussion of Results

The current study used data collected as part of a teacher professional development intervention in science, which took place over 5 years and consequently had missing data. The model was able to converge using HLM despite the moderate sample size and lack of complete data for all respondents at all time points. In support of one widely noted advantage of HLM to handle missing data, this research demonstrates that this modern approach was able to conduct longitudinal analysis of missing data with relative ease, whereas it would have been difficult using more traditional analysis approaches (e.g., ANOVA, regression).

This research provided an applied example of the use of a piecewise change model in an education setting and demonstrated how to code the variables related to time. Three patterns of results about teacher change in ROP are noteworthy. First, analyses of the ROP variable showed that the change trajectory did not follow a single linear trend or a model quadratic in time. Rather, two separate linear trajectories were modeled. The results from the models demonstrated that the teachers' use of ROP increased after participating in the first year of the intervention and that this level was sustained, though it did not increase significantly in subsequent years. This finding is similar to that of another study on teacher professional development in science where large gains occurred during the first year but no change was seen in the second and third years (Supovitz, Mayer, & Kahle, 2000), and the pattern was described as short-term growth and long-term stability.

Second, the standardized covariance estimate between the estimates of initial ROP and change in ROP suggests a relationship in which teachers with lower

ROP at baseline experience a larger initial increase in ROP. Yet none of the background predictor variables entered into the model were significant predictors of teacher change.

Finally, there appeared to be more variation in the use of ROP at baseline, and this variation decreased in subsequent years. This information tells us that the intervention was successful in that after participating in the intervention, the teachers tended to use reform-oriented practices more frequently. The success of the intervention did not depend on any of the predictors that we assessed, and, as a group, the teachers became more similar in their use of ROP over time.

Recent advancements in software allow certain predefined error covariance structures to be examined using the HLM framework. This chapter shows how this can be done using available software and demonstrates the use of a number of statistics to compare models. The deviance statistic can be obtained and models can be compared by examining the χ^2 difference statistic, AIC, and BIC computed from information from the deviance. In this example, these fit indices suggest that the model with the traditional HLM covariance structure fit the data. However, this may not always be the case; therefore, the researcher should examine this as part of the analyses. As the error covariance structure of a model is better represented, the standard errors may decline, increasing the likelihood of rejecting the null hypothesis.

Limitations of the Study

This study suffered from a few limitations. First, the sample size (specifically, the number of schools) was small, which limited the complexity of the model. The main limitation that this created was that the effect of school as another level of dependency was not able to be examined. Since this could not be done, school was entered as a predictor at the teacher level in order to control for its effect.

Another limitation was in the number of time points in which data were collected. Data were collected at four different occasions. If collected at more occasions, we could have examined additional change that might have occurred after teachers had been involved in the intervention for a longer period of time or even studied the effects of sustainability once the intervention had ended. In addition, if more occasions had been included, additional error covariance structures could have been examined, such as a random slopes and heterogeneous level 1 variance model. Although the number of time points was relatively modest, the time over which the data were collected was spread out such that we could reasonably expect change in the outcome.

Even with these limitations, the results are useful, as the study does offer an applied example from an educational setting. A moderate sample size was used, and the research suffered from missing data. This type of situation is often encountered when conducting research in educational settings.

NOTES

1. Congruent with Raudenbush and Bryk (2002), proportion of variance explained estimates for the level 1 model were determined from the following formula:

$$\frac{\sigma^2 \text{ (baseline model)} - \sigma^2 \text{ (fitted model)}}{\sigma^2 \text{ (baseline model)}}$$

and proportion of variance explained estimates for the level 2 model were determined from the following formula:

$$\frac{\tau_{qq} \text{ (baseline model)} - \tau_{qq} \text{ (fitted model)}}{\tau_{qq} \text{ (baseline model)}}$$

Here, σ^2 is the residual within-groups level 1 variance estimate of the intercept, and τ_{qq} is the between-groups variance at level 2.

2. Congruent with Raudenbush and Bryk (2002), the interclass correlation coefficient was determined from the following formula:

$$\frac{\tau_{00}}{\tau_{00} + \sigma^2}$$

where τ_{00} = the estimated level 2 variance for the model and σ^2 = the estimated level 1 variance for the model.

3. In Table 11.6, column headers are not shown but correspond to the row labels. Variances appear on the diagonal and covariances on the off-diagonal.

REFERENCES

Akaike, H. (1974). Information theory as an extension of the maximum likelihood principle. In B. N. Petrov & F. Csaki (Ed.), *Second international symposium of information theory* (pp. 267–228). Budapest, Hungary: Akademiai Kiado.

Cohen, J. (1977). *Statistical power analysis for the behavioral sciences.* New York: Academic Press.

Collins, L. M., Schafer, J. L., & Kam, C. (2001). A comparison of inclusive and restrictive strategies in modern missing data procedures. *Psychological Methods, 6*(4), 330–351.

Lee, O., & Maerten-Rivera, J. (in press). Teacher change in elementary science instruction with English language learners: Results of a multi-year professional development intervention across multiple grades. *Teachers College Record.*

Maerten-Rivera, J., Penfield, R., Myers, N., Lee, O., & Buxton, C. (2009). School and teacher predictors of science instruction practices with English language learners in urban elementary schools. *Journal of Women and Minorities in Science and Engineering, 15*(2), 93–118.

Raudenbush, S., & Bryk, A. (2002). *Hierarchical linear models: Applications and data analysis methods.* Thousand Oaks, CA: Sage.

Raudenbush, S., Bryk, A., & Congdon, R. (2005). *Hierarchical linear and nonlinear modeling (HLM).* Lincolnwood, IL: Scientific Software International.

Schafer, J. L., & Graham, J. W. (2002). Missing data: Our view of the state of the art. *Psychological Methods, 7*(2), 147–177.

Schwartz, G. (1978). Estimating the dimensions of a model. *Annals of Statistics, 6,* 461–464.

Singer, J., & Willett, J. (2003). *Applied longitudinal data analysis: Modeling change and event occurrence.* New York: Oxford.

Supovitz, J. A., Mayer, D. P., & Kahle, J. B. (2000). Promoting inquiry-based instructional practice: The longitudinal impact of professional development in the context of systemic reform. *Educational Policy, 14*(3), 331–356.

Studying Reaction to Repeated Life Events With Discontinuous Change Models Using HLM

12

Maike Luhmann

Michael Eid

Over the last years, multilevel modeling has become a standard method for analyzing longitudinal data. Multilevel models are appropriate because longitudinal data have, by definition, a hierarchical structure: Time points (level 1) are nested within individuals (level 2). A major reason for the growing popularity of multilevel models is their flexibility. For instance, it is possible to include all participants in the analyses, regardless of whether they missed one or more time points or even dropped out of the study altogether. Furthermore, multilevel models allow the modeling of very different change patterns, for instance, linear change, nonlinear change, or discontinuous change.

The most common multilevel model to analyze change is the linear growth curve model (Singer & Willett, 2003). In linear growth curve models, changes in the outcome variable are linearly related to changes in time. Time can be scaled in any meaningful unit and may range from seconds or hours to months or years. In many research contexts, however, it is implausible to assume that the outcome will increase or decrease continuously and at the exact same rate over long time periods. For instance, a variable might increase over the first half of the selected time frame, but stagnate over the second half. Or, a variable might stagnate over long time periods and then suddenly drop. These patterns are examples of discontinuous change (also known as piecewise change). Generally speaking, discontinuous change refers to change patterns where the level of the outcome variable, the shape of change (e.g., linear vs. nonlinear), and/or the rate of change *differ between different time periods*. Discontinuous change can be modeled by modifying and extending the simple linear growth model.

In the present chapter, we will illustrate the application of a discontinuous change model by examining the following research question: How does life satisfaction change in response to repeated unemployment? From previous research, it is well established that people become significantly less satisfied with their lives when they lose their jobs (Lucas, Clark, Georgellis, & Diener, 2004). However, much less is known about how their life satisfaction changes when they become unemployed a second or third time in life. We have analyzed this question in detail (Luhmann & Eid, 2009) and considered three different possible patterns (see Figure 12.1): First, life satisfaction at Unemployment 2 might be similar to life satisfaction at Unemployment 1 (*no differences*). Second, life satisfaction at Unemployment 2 might be higher than at Unemployment 1, for instance, because people got used to this situation and know from their previous experience that they will be able to find a new job (*adaptation pattern*). Finally, life satisfaction at Unemployment 2 might be lower than at Unemployment 1, for instance, because people become increasingly hopeless (*sensitization pattern*). To investigate which of these patterns applies, it is necessary to compare the level of life satisfaction at one time period (Unemployment 1) to that at another time period (Unemployment 2) and to test whether the difference between these levels is statistically significant.

Figure 12.1 Three different change patterns in the context of repeated unemployment

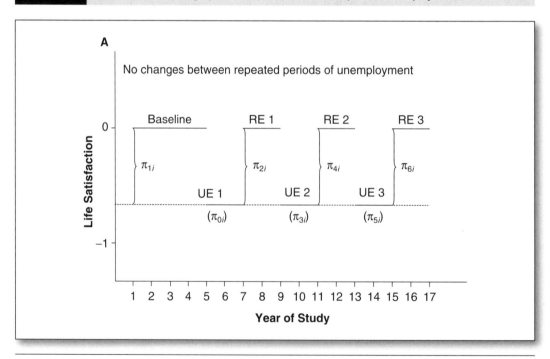

Notes: Baseline encompasses all years prior to the first unemployment. UE1, UE2, and UE3 refer to the years when the participants were unemployed for the first, second, or third time, respectively. RE1, RE2, and RE3 refer to the years when the participants were reemployed for the first, second, or third time, respectively. The π parameters reflect the coefficients in the analytic model (see text).

Source: Adapted from Luhmann & Eid (2009).

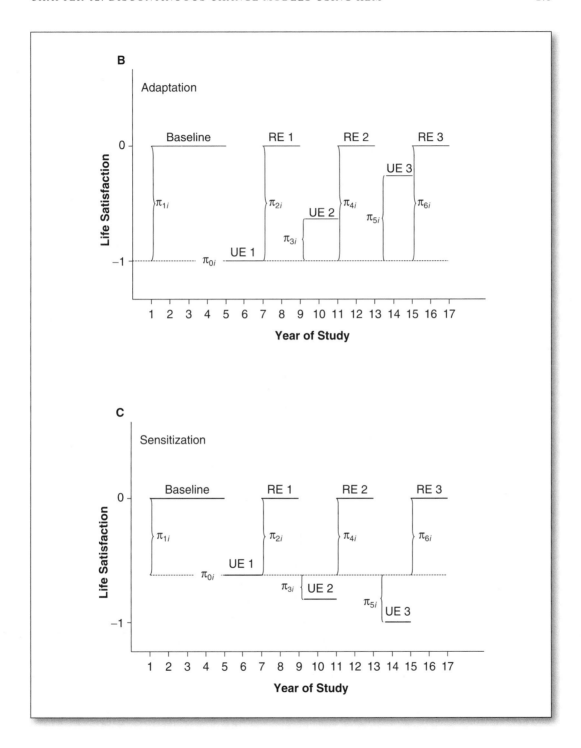

In this chapter, we will present a discontinuous change model that allows the examination of these kinds of change patterns. For this purpose, we will reanalyze the data by Luhmann and Eid (2009) and explain step-by-step how discontinuous change models are interpreted and how they can be applied using the software HLM (Raudenbush, Bryk, & Congdon, 2005). For the sake of brevity, we will focus on a rather simple discontinuous change model where each time period is represented in a single time variable and no level 2 variables are included. The chapter is organized as follows: First, we describe the sample that provided the longitudinal data. Second, we briefly discuss the general procedure and the software packages used in each step (SPSS for data preparation and HLM for the analyses). Third, we provide a detailed description of the data structure and the analytic model. Concerning the analytic model, we specifically focus on the interpretation of the model parameters. Fourth, we present selected tables of the HLM output and examine the most important findings. Finally, we conclude by giving an outlook on how our rather simple model can be extended, for instance, by modeling more complex change patterns or by adding level 2 variables to explain individual differences in change.

SAMPLE

The longitudinal data came from the German Socio-Economic Panel Study (SOEP), a large and nationally representative panel study where data on various economic, sociodemographic, and psychological variables are collected on an annual basis. The study started in 1984 with a sample of 12,245 individuals. Over the years, the sample was extended with several refreshment samples; for instance, in 1990, an additional 4,453 East Germans joined the survey (for detailed information on the aims and scope of the SOEP, see Wagner, Frick, & Schupp, 2007). For the purpose of our analyses, we used data from 24 annual waves (years 1984 to 2007) and selected those participants (a) who were never unemployed before joining the study; (b) who became unemployed at least once during their participation in the study; and (c) who provided data on their personality, which was only assessed in 2005. The size of this subsample was $N = 3,350$ (49% women; age at first unemployment: $M = 35.71$, $SD = 13.70$), including 787 persons (23.5%) who became unemployed at least twice (for an extensive description of this sample, see Luhmann & Eid, 2009). Unemployment status was contingent on whether a person was officially registered as being unemployed and seeking work. Thus, unemployment is not equivalent to not working (e.g., being a homemaker). Life satisfaction was assessed annually with a single item ("How satisfied are you with your life, all things considered?") on an 11-point scale ranging from 0 (*completely dissatisfied*) to 10 (*completely satisfied*). In order to control for variation in overall life satisfaction due to historical events (e.g., fall of the Berlin Wall), we centered the scores on the means for the total sample within each wave. Standard deviations ranged from 1.74 (wave 18) to 2.14 (wave 1).

SOFTWARE AND PROCEDURE

We used SPSS 18 to prepare the data and HLM 7 (Raudenbush et al., 2005) to analyze the multilevel models. In HLM, it is not possible to manipulate existing variables (except for group-mean or grand-mean centering) or to compute new variables. For this reason, the data preparation needs to be completed before the dataset is imported into HLM.

The data preparation consisted of two major steps: First, the data had to be transformed from wide format into long format. Most datasets are structured in a wide format, which means that all data belonging to one person are represented in a single row. Data of the same construct that were assessed at different time points are stored in different variables, for instance, *LS1984* (life satisfaction in the year 1984), *LS1985* (life satisfaction in the year 1985), and so forth. HLM, however, requires the longitudinal data to be structured in long format. In this format, each row represents the data of one person at one time point. Hence, the data of a single person are now stored in multiple rows, one for each time point at which this person participated. Longitudinal data of the same construct are now stored in a single variable (e.g., *LS*). Below, we will describe how the data can be transformed from wide to long format using SPSS.

Second, new time variables had to be computed. In linear growth curve models, it is sufficient to code time in a single variable. In the case of discontinuous change, however, time needs to be coded in multiple variables. This allows us to treat time much more flexibly, but it also requires thinking carefully about which coding is appropriate for the specific research objective (see below).

ANALYZING THE DATA

To analyze longitudinal data in HLM, the data must be structured in long format. As this might be unfamiliar to some readers, we will first describe some useful SPSS commands for the data preparation before moving on to the actual multilevel analyses that were performed in HLM.

Figure 12.2 SPSS screenshot of longitudinal data of six participants in wide format

id	sex	ls1984	ls1985	ls1986	ls1987	ls1988	ls1989
203	1	.	2.77	.71	1.87	1.98	1.94
602	2	-3.39	-2.23	-1.29	-1.13	-2.02	-3.06
1601	1	-2.39	.	.	-2.13	.	-2.06
1704	2	.	.77	2.71	1.87	2.98	1.94
5201	1	.61	-.23	-2.29	-5.13	-3.02	-2.06
5202	2	-.39	.77	-.29	-2.13	-2.02	2.94

Preparing the Data

Figure 12.2 presents the data on the first variables of six persons in wide format. Each row represents one person, and the longitudinal data on life satisfaction are stored in separate variables for each year. In SPSS, these data can be transformed into the long format by using the VARSTOCASES command. This command has different subcommands: The subcommand /MAKE lists all variables in the wide format that shall be transformed into a single variable in the long format. For each variable in the long format, a separate /MAKE subcommand is needed. The /KEEP subcommand lists all time-constant variables that should be kept in the long format but not be transformed. Finally, the subcommand /INDEX specifies the name of the variable that codes the wave of each row. For the example data in Figure 12.2, the complete SPSS command is

```
VARSTOCASES
  /MAKE ls FROM ls1984 TO ls2007
  /MAKE ue FROM ue1984 TO ue2007
  /KEEP id sex
  /INDEX = wave.
```

The index variable (here: *WAVE*) simply enumerates all time points. This variable can be transformed into more appropriate values. For instance, we used the COMPUTE command to calculate the year: COMPUTE year = wave + 1983.

Figure 12.3   SPSS screenshot of longitudinal data of Participant 5201 in the long format

id	sex	year	ls	ls_auto	ue	base	ue1	re1	ue2	re2	ue3	re3
5201	1	1984	-.23	.	0	1	0	0	0	0	0	0
5201	1	1985	-2.29	-.23	0	1	0	0	0	0	0	0
5201	1	1986	-5.13	-2.29	1	0	1	0	0	0	0	0
5201	1	1987	-3.02	-5.13	1	0	1	0	0	0	0	0
5201	1	1988	-2.06	-3.02	0	0	0	1	0	0	0	0
5201	1	1989	.73	-2.06	0	0	0	1	0	0	0	0
5201	1	1990	-2.10	.73	1	0	0	0	1	0	0	0
5201	1	1991	-5.03	-2.10	1	0	0	0	1	0	0	0
5201	1	1992	-.98	-5.03	1	0	0	0	1	0	0	0
5201	1	1993	-1.89	-.98	0	0	0	0	0	1	0	0
5201	1	1994	-2.86	-1.89	0	0	0	0	0	1	0	0
5201	1	1995	-.89	-2.86	0	0	0	0	0	1	0	0
5201	1	1996	-2.75	-.89	0	0	0	0	0	1	0	0
5201	1	1997	-6.93	-2.75	1	0	0	0	0	0	1	0
5201	1	1998	-6.96	-6.93	1	0	0	0	0	0	1	0
5201	1	1999	-6.07	-6.96	1	0	0	0	0	0	1	0
5201	1	2000	-6.09	-6.07	1	0	0	0	0	0	1	0
5201	1	2001	2.09	-6.09	0	0	0	0	0	0	0	1
5201	1	2002	-3.86	2.09	0	0	0	0	0	0	0	1
5201	1	2003	-3.65	-3.86	0	0	0	0	0	0	0	1
5201	1	2004	-3.82	-3.65	0	0	0	0	0	0	0	1

Figure 12.3 is an SPSS screenshot of the long-format data of participant 5201. For better presentation, we reduced this dataset to the most central level 1 variables. As can be seen in the variable *YEAR*, this person participated between 1984 and 2004 and provided data on life satisfaction (variable *LS*) in each of these years. Since life satisfaction values were centered on the mean of the total sample within each wave, positive scores reflect life satisfaction above average, and negative scores reflect life satisfaction below average. The variable *LS_AUTO* is the life satisfaction score in the previous wave. For instance, life satisfaction in 1984 was −.23, which is also the score of *LS_AUTO* in 1985. This variable was used to control for the autoregressive stability of life satisfaction (see below). In SPSS, this autoregressive variable can be computed in the wide format as well as in the long format. In the wide format, a new variable for each time point must be defined, for instance, COMPUTE ls1985_auto = ls1984. In the long format, the values of the original life satisfaction variable are copied and shifted down one row, for instance, with COMPUTE ls_auto = lag(ls), or with

SHIFT VALUES VARIABLE=ls

   RESULT=ls_auto LAG=1.

In any case, the first time point for each person must be deleted because no autoregressive value is available for this time point, and HLM does not allow for missing values on level 1 variables. (It does allow, however, for missing time points, which means that a whole row of data in the long format is missing.) Consequently, the first wave of data of each person is not considered in the analyses.

All of the remaining variables in this screenshot are dummy variables, which means that they either take on values of 0 (does not apply) or 1 (does apply). The variable *UE* represents unemployment status in each wave. Person 5201 was unemployed three times: from 1986 to 1987, from 1990 to 1992, and from 1997 to 2000. The variable *BASE* is coded with 1's in all years before the very first unemployment, and with 0's in all subsequent years. The variables *UE1*, *UE2*, and *UE3* are coded with 1's if the respective year falls into the first, second, or third unemployment period, respectively. Note that each time period can comprise multiple years, and that the duration of each period varies between persons. Finally, the variables *RE1*, *RE2*, and *RE3* are coded with 1's if the respective year falls into the first, second, or final reemployment period, respectively. The reason for this type of coding will become clearer when we discuss the analytic model in the next section. Importantly, we did not examine any later unemployment periods, so it is possible that some individuals became unemployed again during the period *RE3*. This has to be kept in mind in the interpretation of this specific time period.

Analytic Model

The most important decision in discontinuous change models concerns the definition of the time variables. Contrary to classic growth curve models, a single time variable is not sufficient to model discontinuous change. Instead, time is split into different periods, and each period is represented by (at least) one level 1 variable. In our case, we analyzed seven periods that were defined by employment status: baseline (before the very first unemployment), Unemployment 1, Reemployment 1, Unemployment 2, Reemployment 2, Unemployment 3, and Reemployment 3 (which may include subsequent unemployment periods). Each of these periods was represented in a separate dummy variable (see Figure 12.3). Similarly to dummy coding in normal regression models, one time period is chosen as the reference time period. The time variable representing the reference time period is not included in the model, but rather, it is represented in the intercept of the model. Since the reference time period can comprise multiple years, the intercept reflects the average level of the outcome variable across all years of the reference time period. The coefficients of the remaining dummy-coded time variables reflect the mean-level deviation of the outcome during the respective time period, relative to the intercept. A statistically significant coefficient signals that the outcome during this time period differs significantly from the reference time period.

There is no general rule as to which time period should be reflected in the intercept. It is therefore crucial to choose a reference time period that is meaningful and facilitates the interpretation of all model parameters (Biesanz, Deeb-Sossa, Papadakis, Bollen, & Curran, 2004). Often, it makes sense to use the very first time period as a reference. For instance, Lucas, Clark, Georgellis, and Diener (2003) used the SOEP data to study changes in life satisfaction in the context of marital transitions, a question very similar to ours. They were particularly interested in whether people adapt completely to getting married or becoming widowed. To examine this question, they split time into three time periods: baseline, reaction, and adaptation. The baseline period included all years preceding the reaction phase and served as the reference time period against which the coefficients of the other time periods were tested. The reaction period was coded with 1's on the year before a specific event, the year of the event itself, and the year following the event, and with 0's on all other years. The adaptation period was coded with 1's on all years following the reaction period and with 0's on all other years. To test whether people adapt completely to getting married, the authors simply examined the regression coefficient for the adaptation period: A nonsignificant coefficient meant that the level of life satisfaction during the adaptation period did not differ from the level of life satisfaction at baseline, indicating complete adaptation.

Our model is a direct extension of the model by Lucas and colleagues (2003). However, we were not interested in whether any of the later time periods differed from the baseline, but rather, we wanted to examine whether the level of life satisfaction during the second and third unemployment differed significantly from the level of life satisfaction during the first unemployment. For this reason, our reference time period was not the baseline, but Unemployment 1. This time period was not included in the model as a dummy variable, but instead, it was reflected in the intercept of the model. As a second extension, we included life satisfaction in the previous year as an additional predictor. In longitudinal data, one can often find an autoregressive structure among the residuals, meaning that the residuals of two adjacent time points are correlated (e.g., Rovine & Walls, 2006). By predicting life satisfaction in Wave t by life satisfaction in wave $t - 1$, we were able to control for these autoregressive trends. The level 1 model can be formalized as

$$LS_{ti} = \pi_{0i} + \pi_{1i} \cdot (BASE_{ti}) + \pi_{2i} \cdot (RE1_{ti}) + \pi_{3i} \cdot (UE2_{ti}) + \pi_{4i} \cdot (RE2_{ti}) + \pi_{5i} \cdot (UE3_{ti}) + \pi_{6i} \cdot (RE3_{ti}) + \pi_{7i} \cdot (LS_{(t-1)i}) + e_{ti}$$

where LS_{ti} denotes the observed life satisfaction of an individual i at occasion t, $BASE_{ti}$ is the dummy-coded variable indicating the years before the first unemployment (baseline), $UE2_{ti}$ and $UE3_{ti}$ are the dummy-coded variables indicating Unemployment 2 and Unemployment 3, $RE1_{ti}$ to $RE3_{ti}$ are the dummy-coded variables indicating Reemployment 1 to Reemployment 3, $LS_{(t-1)i}$ indicates the grand-mean centered autoregressive parameter, and e_{ti} indicates the level 1 random effect.

To clarify the interpretation of the coefficients in the simple level 1 model, we illustrate the coding of the time periods and the change patterns in Figure 12.1. The coefficient π_{0i} represents the life satisfaction score of individual i during the first unemployment period (UE1). This period serves as the reference time period. Since life satisfaction was centered on the means of the total sample within each wave, a non-zero coefficient π_{0i} indicates that life satisfaction in the subsample during this time period is significantly different from life satisfaction in the total sample. The coefficients π_{3i} and π_{5i} represent the contrasts between life satisfaction at the later unemployment periods (UE2, UE3) and life satisfaction at Unemployment 1, respectively. For instance, if $\pi_{3i} = -1$, this means that the average level of life satisfaction during Unemployment 2 for individual i is 1 scale point lower than it had been during the reference time period Unemployment 1. In Figure 12.1A, the coefficients π_{3i} and π_{5i} do not differ significantly from zero, which means that on average, life satisfaction during the later unemployment periods does not differ significantly from life satisfaction during the first unemployment period. In Figure 12.1B, the coefficients π_{3i} and π_{5i} are positive, which means that life satisfaction during later unemployment periods is higher than during the first unemployment period (adaptation pattern). In Figure 12.1C, finally, the coefficients π_{3i} and π_{5i} are negative, which means that life satisfaction during later unemployment periods is lower than during the first unemployment period (sensitization pattern). The coefficients π_{1i}, π_{2i}, π_{4i}, and π_{6i} represent the contrasts between life satisfaction during the (re)employment periods (baseline, RE1, RE2, RE3) and Unemployment 1, respectively.

As noted before, all regression coefficients reflect mean-level differences with respect to the reference time period Unemployment 1. To test whether life satisfaction at Unemployment 2 differs significantly from Unemployment 3, we contrasted the coefficients π_{3i} and π_{5i} using the general linear hypothesis function in HLM (Hypothesis Setting → Multivariate hypothesis tests). We will provide more details on this contrast when we present that part of the output below.

Finally, we were also interested in gauging individual differences in the reaction to repeated unemployment. The index i of the level 1 parameters indicates that these parameters vary between individuals. To model these individual differences, a separate level 2 equation is defined for each level 1 parameter. For instance, the level 2 equation for the intercept π_{0i} is

$$\pi_{0i} = \beta_{00} + r_{0i},$$

where β_{00} denotes the fixed effect representing the average intercept across all individuals, and r_{0i} denotes the random effect representing the deviation of the intercept π_{0i} of individual i. The variance of r_{0i} quantifies the amount of individual differences in the intercept. In the study presented here, random effects were specified for each level 1 parameter. An HLM screenshot of this model is presented in Figure 12.4.

Figure 12.4 Screenshot of the HLM input file

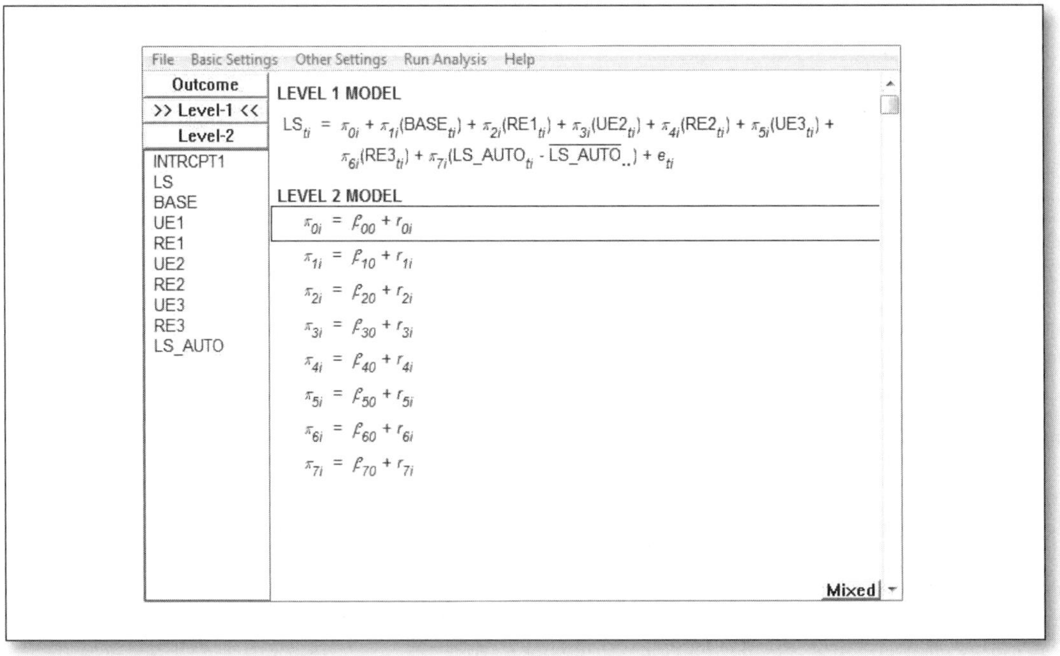

Notes: The autoregressive variable LS_AUTO was centered on the grand mean in HLM. The other time variables were left uncentered, as zero was a meaningful value for these variables.

OUTPUT AND ANALYSIS

In this section, we will examine the HLM output files for our model. We will focus on those parts of the output that are particularly relevant for our research question. The first tables in the results section present data on the variances, covariances, and correlations of the random effects. Here, we only discuss the correlation matrix for the random components (Table 12.1).

The rows are labeled, but the columns are not. But just as in any regular correlation matrix, the order of the variables for the columns is the same as for the rows. Hence, the first column reflects how the random effects of the predictor variables are related to the intercept. We can see, for instance, that the correlation between the intercept π_0 (life satisfaction at Unemployment 1) and the parameter π_3 (change in life satisfaction from Unemployment 1 to Unemployment 2) is negative, $r = -.434$, indicating that higher levels of life satisfaction at Unemployment 1 are associated with a greater drop in life satisfaction at Unemployment 2. We also see strong positive correlations among the later time periods, indicating that people who were more satisfied during one time period were also more satisfied during another time period.

Next, we take a look at the fixed effects (Table 12.2). For each level 1 parameter, we get the estimated level 2 coefficient and the corresponding standard error, t-value, degrees of freedom (df), and p-value. The overall intercept β_{00} reflects the average level of life satisfaction during Unemployment 1. Its value, -0.51, can be interpreted directly because we centered all life satisfaction scores on the mean of the total sample within each wave. Thus, this estimate tells us that the average level of life satisfaction during Unemployment 1 was significantly lower than the average level of life satisfaction in the total sample. The other coefficients have to be interpreted with respect to the intercept. The coefficients β_{30} (Unemployment 2)

| Table 12.1 | HLM Output 1: τ (as correlations) |

INTRCPT1,π_0	1.000	−0.692	−0.573	−0.434	−0.550	−0.289	−0.495	−0.017
BASE,π_1	−0.692	1.000	0.665	0.447	0.526	0.314	0.488	−0.096
RE1,π_2	−0.573	0.665	1.000	0.610	0.674	0.309	0.689	−0.146
UE2,π_3	−0.434	0.447	0.610	1.000	0.648	0.403	0.660	0.023
RE2,π_4	−0.550	0.526	0.674	0.648	1.000	0.756	0.907	−0.102
UE3,π_5	−0.289	0.314	0.309	0.403	0.756	1.000	0.798	−0.082
RE3,π_6	−0.495	0.488	0.689	0.660	0.907	0.798	1.000	−0.072
LS_AUTO,π_7	−0.017	0.096	−0.146	0.023	−0.102	−0.082	−0.072	1.000

Table 12.2	HLM Output 2: Final Estimation of Fixed Effects

Fixed effect	Coefficient	Standard error	t-ratio	Approx. df	p-value
For INTRCPT1, π_0					
INTRCPT2, β_{00}	−0.512819	0.025098	−20.433	3349	<0.001
For BASE slope, π_1					
INTRCPT2, β_{10}	0.462953	0.023976	19.309	3349	<0.001
For RE1 slope, π_2					
INTRCPT2, β_{20}	0.343668	0.024274	14.158	3349	<0.001
For UE2 slope, π_3					
INTRCPT2, β_{30}	−0.164193	0.045584	−3.602	3349	<0.001
For RE2 slope, π_4					
INTRCPT2, β_{40}	0.193639	0.043554	4.446	3349	<0.001
For UE3 slope, π_5					
INTRCPT2, β_{50}	−0.435706	0.089872	−4.848	3349	<0.001
For RE3 slope, π_6					
INTRCPT2, β_{60}	0.002755	0.076931	0.036	3349	0.971
For LS_AUTO slope, π_7					
INTRCPT2, β_{70}	0.227824	0.005584	40.803	3349	<0.001

and β_{50} (Unemployment 3) are negative and significantly different from zero. This means that the average level of life satisfaction during these periods is significantly lower than during the first unemployment. Specifically, the predicted level of life satisfaction during Unemployment 2 is −0.51 − 0.16 = −0.67 scale points below average, and the predicted level of life satisfaction during Unemployment 3 is −0.51 − 0.44 = −0.95 scale points below average. Thus, people sensitize to becoming unemployed; later unemployment experiences feel worse than the first one.

We also note that life satisfaction is, on average, higher when people are not unemployed: The coefficients for the baseline, Reemployment 1, and Reemployment 2 are all positive and significantly different from zero. For instance, the predicted level of life satisfaction before the first unemployment is −0.51 + 0.46 = −0.05. The only exception is Reemployment 3 where life satisfaction does not differ significantly from life satisfaction during Unemployment 1. However, it has to be kept in mind that this time period might also include subsequent unemployment periods.

We found that later unemployment periods feel worse than the first one. But how do these periods differ among each other? Above, we already noted that the predicted level of life satisfaction during Unemployment 3 is lower than during

Table 12.3	HLM Output 3: Results of General Linear Hypothesis Testing—Test 1

	Coefficients	*Contrast*
For INTRCPT1, π_0		
INTRCPT2, β_{00}	−0.512819	0.0000
For BASE slope, π_1		
INTRCPT2, β_{10}	0.462953	0.0000
For RE1 slope, π_2		
INTRCPT2, β_{20}	0.343668	0.0000
For UE2 slope, π_3		
INTRCPT2, β_{30}	−0.164193	1.0000
For RE2 slope, π_4		
INTRCPT2, β_{40}	0.193639	0.0000
For UE3 slope, π_5		
INTRCPT2, β_{50}	−0.435706	−1.0000
For RE3 slope, π_6		
INTRCPT2, β_{60}	0.002755	0.0000
For LS_AUTO slope, π_7		
INTRCPT2, β_{70}	0.227824	0.0000
Estimate		0.2715
Standard error of estimate		0.0941

χ^2 statistic = 8.332361

Degrees of freedom = 1

p-value = 0.004212

Unemployment 2. To test whether this difference is statistically significant, we contrasted these two coefficients using the general linear hypothesis function in HLM (Hypothesis Setting → Multivariate hypothesis tests; see Figure 12.5). Table 12.3 presents the estimated regression coefficients and the contrast coefficients as we specified them before running the model. We only specified contrast coefficients for those parameters that we actually wanted to compare; the contrast coefficients for the remaining parameters were set to zero. The contrast coefficient for parameter β_{30} was 1, and the contrast coefficient for β_{50} was −1. It is crucial that all contrast coefficients add up to zero because we test the hypothesis that $1 \cdot \beta_{30} + (-1) \cdot \beta_{50} = 0$. If this test is not significant, it indicates that β_{30} and β_{50} do not differ significantly from each other. In our case, however, the test was significant: $\chi^2(1) = 8.33$, $p = .004$ (see bottom of the table). Hence, we reject the null hypothesis that β_{30} equals β_{50} and conclude that life satisfaction at Unemployment 3 does indeed differ significantly from life satisfaction at Unemployment 2. Contrasts are very powerful and flexible tools to test a wide array of hypotheses. Apart from simple contrasts such as the one in our example, more complex contrasts can also be tested.

Finally, we take a closer look at the table for the random effects (Table 12.4). In this table, we see the standard deviation and variance as well as a statistical test of each random effect. To test whether the variance differs significantly from zero, a chi-square test is used. Remember that the random effects capture individual deviations from the average fixed effects presented above. A significant variance thus indicates significant individual differences that might be worth exploring by adding level 2 variables. In our example, this was true for all of the random effects.

Figure 12.5   Screenshot of the general linear hypothesis window in HLM (Hypothesis Setting → Multivariate hypothesis tests)

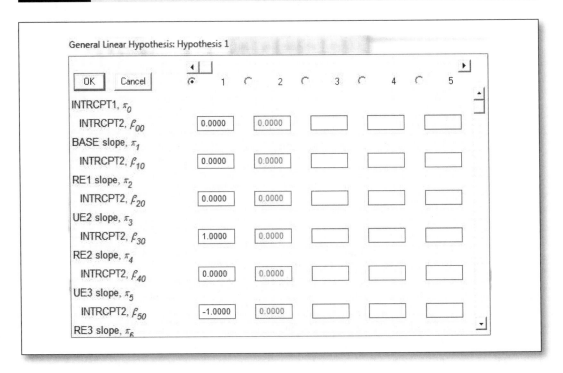

| Table 12.4 | HLM Output 4: Final Estimation of Variance Components |

Random effect	Standard deviation	Variance component	df	χ^2	p-value
INTRCPT1, r_0	1.05905	1.12159	134	366.46160	<0.001
BASE slope, r_1	0.67107	0.45033	134	214.72134	<0.001
RE1 slope, r_2	0.68973	0.47573	134	212.46240	<0.001
UE2 slope, r_3	0.73005	0.53297	134	205.51848	<0.001
RE2 slope, r_4	0.85046	0.72329	134	211.21209	<0.001
UE3 slope, r_5	0.73653	0.54248	134	219.98593	<0.001
RE3 slope, r_6	0.83746	0.70134	134	218.59108	<0.001
LS_AUTO slope, r_7	0.16191	0.02622	134	309.18158	<0.001
level-1, e	1.29803	1.68489			

Note. The chi-square statistics reported above are based on only 135 of 3,350 units that had sufficient data for computation. Fixed effects and variance components are based on all the data.

CONCLUSION

Multilevel models are powerful statistical tools to examine several research questions simultaneously. In reporting the results, it is therefore critical to guide the reader through the myriad analyses and to highlight the most important findings. In our case, the most important findings were as follows: (a) Repeated unemployment is associated with a downward trend in life satisfaction. In our analyses, we found a mean sensitization effect for repeated unemployment, which means that, on average, life satisfaction decreases more and more with each unemployment period, controlling for autoregressive stability. (b) There are significant individual differences in life satisfaction during repeated unemployment, as indicated by the statistically significant variance components.

To conclude this chapter, we would like to provide an outlook on extensions of discontinuous change models. First, the simple model we presented in this chapter can be extended to include level 2 variables to explain some of the individual differences. Main effects as well as cross-level interactions can be examined. For instance, we found that men were, on average, less satisfied at Unemployment 1 than women (main effect of gender), and that men reacted more negatively to becoming unemployed a second time than women (cross-level interaction between gender and Unemployment 2; for more results, see Luhmann & Eid, 2009).

Second, the number and definition of the different time periods depends entirely on the specific data situation. For repeated unemployment, it made sense to distinguish between periods of unemployment and (re)employment. In the same paper, we also examined reactions to repeated marriages and repeated divorces (Luhmann & Eid, 2009). If we had defined the time periods in the same fashion as for the unemployment example (e.g., Baseline, Marriage 1, Divorce 1, Marriage 2), we could only have examined whether life satisfaction during the first marriage was, on average, different from life satisfaction during the second marriage. We were, however, particularly interested in whether the *reaction* to the first marriage differed from the reaction to the second marriage. For this reason, the time periods when people were married were divided into two specific periods, respectively: the first year of the marriage and all subsequent years of this marriage. To examine our specific research question, we chose the first year of Marriage 1 as a reference time period that was contrasted with the first year of Marriage 2. In short, researchers should think hard about how they define their time periods and which time period to choose as a reference. This decision should always be based on conceptual reasoning.

Third, the simple discontinuous change model we introduced here can be extended to model linear or nonlinear change *within* each time period. In this case, additional time variables must be added to the model. These models can become complex very quickly, but they also allow the researcher to model change in very flexible ways. An excellent introduction to these kinds of models is provided by Singer and Willett (2003).

Finally, the range of statistical tests is not restricted to testing regression coefficients and variance components. For instance, it is possible to specify contrasts and test general linear hypotheses, as we demonstrated for a simple example. Alternatively, researchers might find it useful to constrain specific fixed effects. HLM offers this option (Other settings → Estimation Setting → Constraint of fixed effects). Typically, one will constrain two or more fixed effects to be equal, and then compare this model to a second model where these fixed effects are allowed to differ. The model with the constrained effects is more parsimonious, but it will necessarily have a worse fit than the unconstrained model. By comparing these models with a deviance test that is also available in HLM, it is possible to determine whether the model fit differs significantly and which model should be chosen. Specifically, a significant deviance test indicates that the more complex model (without constraints) fits significantly better and should therefore be preferred, whereas a non-significant deviance test indicates that the two models do not differ significantly in fit, and therefore the more parsimonious model (with constraints) should be preferred. Again, we recommend the illuminative book by Singer and Willett (2003) for more details.

Change can occur suddenly, it can be faster in some periods than in others, it can even be reversed, but it is rarely perfectly linear. Multilevel models allow researchers to model complex change patterns. The primary goal of this chapter was to provide an introduction to one of these more complex change models. The secondary, but more important goal, however, was to inspire researchers to think of change in more flexible ways.

REFERENCES

Biesanz, J. C., Deeb-Sossa, N., Papadakis, A. A., Bollen, K. A., & Curran, P. J. (2004). The role of coding time in estimating and interpreting growth curve models. *Psychological Methods, 9*(1), 30–52.

Lucas, R. E., Clark, A. E., Georgellis, Y., & Diener, E. (2003). Reexamining adaptation and the set point model of happiness: Reactions to changes in marital status. *Journal of Personality and Social Psychology, 84*(3), 527–539.

Lucas, R. E., Clark, A. E., Georgellis, Y., & Diener, E. (2004). Unemployment alters the set point for life satisfaction. *Psychological Science, 15*(1), 8–13.

Luhmann, M., & Eid, M. (2009). Does it really feel the same? Changes in life satisfaction following repeated life events. *Journal of Personality and Social Psychology, 97*(2), 363–381.

Raudenbush, S., Bryk, A., & Congdon, R. (2005). *Hierarchical linear and nonlinear modeling (HLM)*. Lincolnwood, IL: Scientific Software International.

Rovine, M. J., & Walls, T. A. (2006). Multilevel autoregressive modeling of interindividual differences in the stability of a process. In T. A. Walls & J. L. Schafer (Eds.), *Models for intensive longitudinal data* (pp. 124–147). New York: Oxford University Press.

Singer, J. D., & Willett, J. B. (2003). *Applied longitudinal data analysis: Modeling change and event occurrence.* New York: Oxford University Press.

Wagner, G. G., Frick, J. R., & Schupp, J. (2007). The German Socio-Economic Panel Study (SOEP). Scope, evolution and enhancements. *Schmollers Jahrbuch, 127*, 139–169.

A Cross-Classified Multilevel Model for First-Year College Natural Science Performance Using SAS

13

Brian F. Patterson

A dvanced Placement (AP) is a program of college-level courses and examinations offered by the College Board that began in 1955. Content and skills taught in each AP course are continuously and rigorously aligned with the content and skills taught in corresponding introductory college-level courses. The exam grade scale has five discrete levels (1 through 5), and based on students' exam score and the credit- or placement-granting policy of the college or university (henceforth, simply "college") that students attend, exemption from or credit for the relevant introductory course or courses may be granted. The program has gone through many changes in terms of the number of courses and exams offered, but as of the 2010–2011 academic year, there were 34 courses and exams in a variety of subject areas.

The Advanced Placement program is administered at the high school level, but the outcome for this study (i.e., mean natural science course grade) was observed at the college level, hence the use of a cross-classified multilevel model. In other words, since students from a given high school went on to attend a variety of colleges and universities and since a particular university drew from many different high schools, we can say that the students are cross-classified with respect to the high school from which they graduated and the college that they attended. At the outset, we put forth hypotheses that (a) high schools may differ in their ability to prepare students for college-level coursework in natural science; and (b) colleges may differ on natural science course grading standards and/or on science course difficulty. Alternative hypotheses include that the underlying mean student ability in natural sciences differs across high schools and colleges, due perhaps to sample selection.

The model to be estimated, which will be described later, is consistent with the supposition that substantial and significant random variation in intercepts may exist at the high school and college levels, lending weight to the decision to estimate a cross-classified random intercepts model. Such a model has a number of desirable properties with respect to the analytic problem at hand. The most important of these is that the model does not assume that individual students' residuals are independent between either high school or college, but rather that they are independent within those crossed groups and that the groups' mean natural science GPAs vary. In other words, within a given high school or college, there may be some residual dependence that is not accounted for by a non-multilevel regression method. Failing to account for the cross-classified nature of the data and the expected dependence structure within colleges and high schools by using a method such as ordinary least squares (OLS) would violate the assumption of residual independence required by that model and hence lead to potentially faulty inferences. In particular, the standard error for the fixed parameter estimates would be biased downward and may lead us to commit a type I error, by rejecting the null hypothesis of the true parameter being zero, when in fact it is zero.

Another desirable feature of the cross-classified random intercepts model is the generalizability of the results. The sample described below is based on a relatively small proportion of all 4-year colleges and universities in the United States and only includes high schools from which those colleges' students graduated. If we were to estimate high school and college effects as fixed, then we would only be able to draw inferences about those specific groups. Ideally, for the model assumptions to be perfectly met, ours would have to be a true random sample of all 4-year colleges in the United States, so we must consider the possibility that the mechanism through which colleges selected to participate in the study may have reduced the representativeness of our sample as it refers to the population. However, the notion inherent in random effects modeling is that the sampled high schools and colleges are drawn from well-defined populations and therefore that the results are the best linear unbiased estimates of the population values. In other words, we are not limited to making conclusions about the validity of natural science AP exam participation and performance for the sampled high schools and colleges, but rather can draw conclusions about the larger populations of all high schools and all 4-year colleges and universities in the United States.

SAMPLE

The SAT[1] is a standardized assessment that colleges in the United States use, in addition to other measures and information, for the purposes of determining undergraduate admittance. In March 2005, the College Board made major changes to the SAT; in particular, it added a new writing section as well as made minor changes in content to the verbal and mathematics sections. Since the changes were substantial, the College Board contacted colleges and universities to request first-year college performance data from the fall 2006 entering undergraduate cohort. In the end, 110 colleges and universities provided the necessary data, yielding a sample of 151,316 students with complete data on self-reported high school grade point average (HSGPA), first-year college GPA, and scores from each of the three sections of the SAT (mathematics, critical reading, and writing).

The colleges and universities participating in the SAT validity study were roughly representative of the population, defined as the 726 four-year colleges and universities that (a) received at least 200 SAT score reports from the 2005 cohort of college-bound high school seniors; (b) enrolled at least 250 first-time, first-year students in 2006; and (c) responded to the College Board's Annual Survey of Colleges (College Board, 2006). It should be noted, however, that these institutions chose to participate in the study and received a nominal stipend to defray the costs of preparing and providing their student data file. Therefore, they may not represent a truly random sample from the population; see Kobrin, Patterson, Shaw, Mattern, and Barbuti (2008) for more information on the sample and population.

The current study of Advanced Placement natural science exams required that we look at performance in the individual natural science college courses. Thus, we selected the subset of first-year students who had taken at least one natural science course, which we identified by reviewing course names and where necessary their official descriptions from individual college catalogs and websites. We estimated the mean natural science GPA, weighting courses by the credits that they bore. The result was that from the possible sample of 151,316 students with full data on the predictors of interest, we obtained a sample of 91,596 individual first-year students from 7,267 high schools who were attending 110 colleges.

Predictors

The purpose of the original research was to examine the effects of natural science Advanced Placement (i.e., biology, chemistry, physics: B, physics: C mechanics, physics: C electricity and magnetism, environmental science) exam participation and performance on college grades in natural science, relative to non-AP examinees.[2] AP exam participation was operationalized as the number of AP exams taken in natural science. AP exam performance was operationalized as the mean AP exam grade in natural science, which was rounded to the nearest score scale value and treated as a categorical predictor, where the reference group was non-AP examinees. The frequency of students within the sample who earned each mean AP natural science grade was as follows: 5, 5.1%; 4, 7.1%; 3, 7.5%; 2, 5.7%; 1, 4.1%; non-AP natural science students made up the remaining 70.4% of the sample.

In order to control for general ability and other demographic and socioeconomic differences, we considered a number of additional predictors. The SAT scores and high school GPA were included in the final model, grand-mean centered to ease interpretation and to make the fixed intercept effect more meaningful. In addition, because we anticipated significant differences in natural science course performance by gender, racial or ethnic identity group, and highest parental education level, we also included those categorical predictors in the series of models that we estimated.

SOFTWARE AND PROCEDURE

The SAS system's SAS/STAT®[3] software (version 9.1.3, service pack 2, executed on Windows XP; SAS Institute Inc., 2004a, 2004b) contains a number of procedures capable of estimating cross-classified random intercepts models of the sort that we built. The procedure that we used was the MIXED procedure, SAS's linear mixed model procedure, whose syntax is structured similarly to the OLS regression or REG procedure, with the addition of a RANDOM statement. The data for SAS's MIXED procedures should be configured such that each observation represents the smallest unit of analysis—in our case, that is the student level. Unique identifiers for the two levels (i.e., high school and college) should be included, identifying the high school from which each student graduated and the college where they subsequently enrolled. If we were interested in attempting to account for the random variation in intercepts at either the college or high school levels, then the data also ought to contain the higher-level predictors on each student's record.

| Figure 13.1 | Screenshot of a SAS dataset simulated to follow the pattern of estimated effects from the final model |

Note: Note the following features: (a) the cross-classified nature of the data in terms of high school and college IDs; (b) the racial/ethnic group and parental education variables were assigned values to ensure that the desired reference group would sort as the last unique value; (c) the mean natural science AP exam grade was rounded to the nearest scale score, and non-AP examinees were assigned a value of "N," as they were the desired reference group for the multilevel analyses; (d) HSGPA and SAT sections were grand-mean centered, and the SAT sections were rescaled.

See Figure 13.1 for an example[4] of how the SAS dataset was structured for cross-classified analysis—in particular, note how the high school and college ID variables do not follow a strict hierarchy.

SAS's MIXED procedure does not contain the ability to center predictors automatically, so some preparatory manipulation is required. Table 13.1 shows how we used the STDIZE procedure that is included in SAS to grand-mean center the four quantitative predictors.

We also divided each SAT section score by 100, so that the disparate scales of HSGPA (which had a range of 0.00 to 4.33) and SAT sections (which had ranges of 200 to 800) would be closer and so that their parameter estimates would not be overly small in absolute terms. The results of the grand-mean centering and rescaling of the HSGPA and SAT section variables may be seen in the respective columns of Figure 13.1.

Some variables in this dataset were stored as categorical, but the CLASS statement in SAS procedures automatically creates the requested effect coding (e.g., dummy coding) within the procedure itself. Unlike some other SAS procedures where we can specify the desired reference level (i.e., the level whose effect would not be explicitly estimated and would hence serve as the basis for comparison or "reference") on the CLASS statement (e.g., the LOGISTIC procedure), the MIXED procedure by default uses the last sorted (i.e., highest) value as its reference level. To ensure the desired reference level was specified for each variable, one could recode the variables such that, for example, the racial or ethnic identity value associated with White students was the greatest numeric value. We had our predictors saved as character strings, so we took the approach of adding a number before each value, such that the desired reference level would sort as the last level—for example, we transformed the highest parental education level of "Bachelor's Degree" to "9: Bachelor's Degree" and coded the other levels with integers smaller than 9. Figure 13.1 shows how these numeric prefixes were assigned in order to ensure that the intended levels were treated as the reference level.

When analyzing large datasets with many random subjects, we recommend using the LOGNOTE option in the MIXED procedure. Later SAS code demonstrates how LOGNOTE may be used to request that SAS provide more detailed feedback at each iteration and at the conclusion of estimation. For the null model estimated under maximum likelihood, the log file contained the information shown in Table 13.2.

Table 13.1   SAS PROC STDIZE Code for Grand-Mean Centering of Predictors Treated as Continuous

```
PROC STDIZE DATA= AP_Data METHOD= MEAN OUT= AP_Data_Ctr;
  VAR HS_GPA SAT_CR SAT_M SAT_W;
RUN;
```

| Table 13.2 | Example of Detailed Output From the LOGNOTE Option Within PROC MIXED |

```
NOTE: Levelizing effects.
NOTE: Processing subject and group effects.
NOTE: Setting up data.
NOTE: Loading data.
NOTE: Computing likelihood in iteration 0.
NOTE: Computing G derivatives in iteration 1.
NOTE: Computing likelihood in iteration 1.
...
NOTE: Computing likelihood in iteration 4.
NOTE: Computing G derivatives in iteration 4.
NOTE: Convergence criteria met.
NOTE: Computing likelihood in iteration 5.
NOTE: Computing Cholesky root of cross-products matrix.
NOTE: Computing H matrix.
NOTE: Computing Type 3 sums of squares.
NOTE: The data set WORK.AP_DATA_0b_IC has 1 observations and 7 vari-
      ables.
NOTE: The data set WORK.AP_DATA_0b_FIT has 4 observations and 2 variables.
NOTE: The data set WORK.AP_DATA_0b_COV has 3 observations and 9 variables.
NOTE: The data set WORK.AP_DATA_0b_FIX has 1 observations and 9 variables.
NOTE: PROCEDURE MIXED used (Total process time):
      real time 2:13:18.07
      user cpu time 2:12:50.26
      system cpu time 5.59 seconds
      Memory 428764k
```

If the model did not converge, then the details from the LOGNOTE option would help us diagnose the source of the problem and in turn develop a solution that would enable us to estimate the desired model. For further detail on the particular notes written to the log file, please refer to the "Mixed Models Theory" subsection of the "Details" section of the MIXED procedure documentation (SAS Institute Inc., 2004c).

Finally, we recommend that readers become familiar with the SAS system's Output Delivery System (ODS), which serves as the backbone for all output that SAS generates. In the examples to follow, we output results to HTML files so that they may be easily read by colleagues, and because the structured tables that are generated when outputting to HTML are far easier to work with than the text in the default listing output. An example of the code that we used to set up the HTML output appears in Table 13.3.

Table 13.3	SAS ODS HTML Statements

```
ODS _ALL_ CLOSE;
ODS NOPROCTITLE;
ODS HTML STYLE= MINIMAL FILE= "AP_Mixed.html"
    PATH= "C:\" (URL=NONE);
/* INSERT SAS CODE FOR RELEVANT PROCEDURES */
ODS _ALL_ CLOSE;
ODS LISTING;
```

More detail on the options and commands in the above section of code may be found in SAS's web-based references for the Output Delivery System, and information on the ODS table names, to which we will refer later, may be found in the ODS Table Names subsection of the Details section for each statistical procedure (SAS Institute Inc., 2004c).

ANALYZING THE DATA

Evaluating Residual Variability Due to the Cross-Classified Levels

As with any multilevel analysis, the first consideration is whether there is empirical evidence for the need for a multilevel approach. A unique consideration in the context of cross-classified data is whether we ought to include random effects for the interaction between the cross-classified levels. We must consider this issue both from a theoretical standpoint (i.e., is it reasonable to expect that a non-additive random intercept interaction effect may exist between high schools and colleges?); from a statistical standpoint (i.e., do we have enough statistical power to estimate such an effect); and, of course, from a practical standpoint (i.e., can we estimate such a model with existing computational resources?). A response of "no" to any of these questions may lead us to not include a random interaction effect, but in an ideal world, we would put this question to the test empirically. For example, is it theoretically reasonable to expect that natural science teaching styles in a given high school and a specific college could be so complementary that the random cross-level interaction of high school and college would be positive for that high school and college combination? Or are there relationships between colleges and the high schools that surround them that are well enough established to expect that high schools would teach natural sciences in a way that is especially conducive to success at those particular local colleges? Whether such suppositions are theoretically reasonable and whether, given those suppositions, their effects are large enough for the data to support their estimation are two separate matters. For an excellent example of how the covariance structure of cross-classified models may be carefully built, we refer readers to George Leckie's treatment of the theory (in the "Analyzing the Data" section) and the consideration of results (in the "Output and Analysis" section) in Chapter 14 of this volume.

In particular, we would estimate the model—using the SAS code that appears in Table 13.4—to determine if the random intercept interaction effect were significant, both statistically and practically.

If we found that the variance parameter associated with interaction between high school and college were neither statistically nor practically significant, we would drop it from the model and reestimate the above model, removing the third RANDOM statement. Note that a third variable identifying the unique combination of high school and college with which each student was associated was necessary to specify the random interaction effect, and that such a variable would have to have been created in a prior DATA step. We also note that the "0a:" that precedes the MODEL statement serves as a convenient label that appears in the ODS output and any ODS graphics that the user requests. Such labels are useful in keeping results organized.

Choice of estimation method is particularly important when estimating mixed effects models such as those considered in this chapter. Under maximum likelihood, all model parameters are estimated simultaneously—in other words, SAS simultaneously estimates both the fixed model parameters and the variances and covariances of the random effects and the residual variance. We estimated the empty model (a.k.a., null or unconditional model) under REML because that method yields unbiased estimates for the random covariance terms (Raudenbush & Bryk, 2002). Finding that there was substantial and significant random intercept variation at both the high school and college levels, we then estimated all subsequent models in full maximum likelihood, because we were interested in making inferences about the fixed effects. We simply changed the option on the PROC MIXED line to METHOD=ML and reestimated the null model.

Table 13.4   SAS PROC MIXED Code for Estimating the Null (a.k.a., Unconditional, Empty) Model

```
PROC MIXED DATA= AP_Data_Ctr METHOD= REML
  IC COVTEST NOCLPRINT LOGNOTE;
0a: MODEL Natural_Sci_GPA = INTERCEPT / SOLUTION;
RANDOM INTERCEPT / SUBJECT= High_School_ID TYPE= VC;
RANDOM INTERCEPT / SUBJECT= College_ID TYPE= VC;
RANDOM INTERCEPT / SUBJECT= High_School_by_College_ID TYPE= VC;
ODS OUTPUT FitStatistics = AP_Data_0a_Fit InfoCrit = AP_Data_0a_IC
  CovParms = AP_Data_0a_Cov SolutionF = AP_Data_0a_Fix;
RUN;
```

Specifying a Covariance Structure

Since we were interested in controlling for the dependence structure of students' residuals within high schools and colleges, we only modeled the intercept as random. As such, we had separate, single random variance parameters associated with the high school and college levels. If we were to include slopes that randomly varied with the high school or college levels, then the covariance matrices of random effects for the high school and college levels would be more complex and require additional consideration, which is beyond the scope of this chapter.

Building the Student-Level Model

We then turned to building the student-level model. We began by specifying only the intercept as random and all other effects as fixed, with the option to revisit the specification of student-level effects as random if there were empirical support for doing so, in the form of practically and statistically significant random slope variation. There were three blocks of variables that we expected to be important in the prediction of natural science college course performance: (a) demographic and socioeconomic status indicators, (b) measures of general academic ability, and (c) AP exam participation and performance measures. Since we were interested in determining the effects of AP exam participation and performance above and beyond the other predictors, we began by entering the demographic and general ability variables, in what we denoted in the original paper as Model 1; the corresponding SAS code is given in Table 13.5.

We estimated Models 2 and 3, adding to Model 1 the AP exam participation and performance variables, respectively. Model 4 is the fully specified model, which contains all predictors of interest. The SAS code associated with Model 4 is shown in Table 13.6.

Having no more student-level variables of interest, we stopped building the student-level model at this point.

Table 13.5   SAS PROC MIXED Code for Estimating Model 1

```
PROC MIXED DATA= AP_Data METHOD= ML IC COVTEST NOCLPRINT LOGNOTE;
  CLASS Gender Racial_Eth_ID High_Par_Educ;
    _1: MODEL Natural_Sci_GPA = Gender Racial_Eth_ID
    High_Par_Educ HS_GPA SAT_CR SAT_M SAT_W
    Num_Nat_Sci_APs Mean_Nat_Sci_AP_Gr / SOLUTION;
  RANDOM INTERCEPT / SUBJECT= High_School_ID;
  RANDOM INTERCEPT / SUBJECT= College_ID;
    ODS OUTPUT FitStatistics = AP_Data_4_Fit InfoCrit = AP_Data_4_IC
      CovParms = AP_Data_4_Cov SolutionF = AP_Data_4_Fix;
  RUN;
```

Table 13.6	SAS PROC MIXED Code for Estimating Model 4

```
PROC MIXED DATA= AP_Data METHOD= ML IC COVTEST NOCLPRINT LOGNOTE;
  CLASS Gender Racial_Eth_ID High_Par_Educ;
  _4: MODEL Natural_Sci_GPA = Gender Racial_Eth_ID High_Par_Educ
    HS_GPA  SAT_CR  SAT_M  SAT_W  Num_Nat_Sci_APs  Mean_Nat_Sci_AP_Gr  /
      SOLUTION;
  RANDOM INTERCEPT / SUBJECT= High_School_ID;
  RANDOM INTERCEPT / SUBJECT= College_ID;
  ODS OUTPUT FitStatistics = AP_Data_4_Fit InfoCrit = AP_Data_4_IC
    CovParms = AP_Data_4_Cov SolutionF = AP_Data_4_Fix;
RUN;
```

Building the College- and High School–Level Models

The focus of this study was neither to understand the particular contextual effects associated with high schools from which students graduate, nor to understand those linked to the colleges that they attend. With that said, it would be after building a complete student-level model that we would consider adding fixed effects at either the high school or college level. In our case, that could have included the control of the high school or college (e.g., public or private), mean test scores for the high school or college, or any other factors expected to affect the students' mean natural science course performance in high school.

We could have considered specifying random slopes for any of the student-level predictors in the model above, but as we wanted to keep the analyses as computationally manageable as possible and to avoid possible estimation issues that arise when many random effects are included for effects that have relatively little variation across the cross-classified units, we chose not to re-specify existing fixed effects as random.

Evaluating Model Fit

At the outset, we decided to use the Akaike information criterion (AIC; Akaike, 1974) for model comparison. Having estimated all models but the null model under maximum likelihood, we could just as appropriately have used likelihood ratio test results to guide our model-building efforts. Instead, using the rule of thumb that if the AIC were reduced by twice the difference in the number of parameters to be estimated, we would prefer a larger model (i.e., one requiring that more parameters be estimated) over a smaller one. For example, in order to select the larger model, we would want to see the AIC reduced by at least four, if the larger model had two more parameters than the smaller model.

OUTPUT AND ANALYSIS

Evaluating Residual Variability
Due to the Cross-Classified Levels

The first things to check are reported in the default SAS output and are (a) whether the expected number of observations were read in and used, and (b) whether the model converged according to the default (or user-supplied) convergence criterion. An example of the output for the null model under maximum likelihood is given in Figure 13.2.

Figure 13.2	SAS ODS tables NObs, IterHistory, and ConvergenceStatus indicate the number of observations read and used, track the iteration history of the estimation method, and report whether the default (or user-supplied) convergence criterion was met, respectively. This corresponds to the null, empty, or unconditional model estimated under maximum likelihood.

Number of Observations	
Number of Observations Read	91596
Number of Observations Used	91596
Number of Observations Not Used	0

Iteration History			
Iteration	Evaluations	−2 Log Like	Criterion
0	1	250458.55243741	
1	2	243151.11950591	0.00007815
2	1	243147.75144068	0.00000751
3	1	243147.44811323	0.00000013
4	1	243147.44309994	0.00000000

Convergence criteria met.

All of the observations ($n = 91{,}596$) were read in by SAS's MIXED procedure and used in the estimation of the model. The model converged after four iterations, with the default convergence criterion, which varies by operating system.

During the original research, Patterson, Packman, and Kobrin (2011) were constrained by the computational resources available to them and so simply could not estimate the null model with a random interaction between high school and college level. Indeed with 7,267 high schools and 110 colleges, the sheer number of combinations of high school and college was astronomical. We did not expect any substantial non-additivity in the random intercept effects that could have been attributed to the interaction between high school and college, so this limitation did not seriously hamper our ability to complete a rigorous study. As such, we considered output from the null model where random intercept main effects were estimated for high school and college.

This table demonstrates that 8.48% {=100% * [0.07810 / (0.07810 + 0.04198 + 0.8013)]} of the variance in mean natural science GPA was attributed to the college (see "College ID" in Figure 13.3) that students attended, while 4.56% of the variance was due to the high school from which students graduated (see "High School ID" in Figure 13.3). That left 87% of the variance in mean natural science GPA unexplained, so it is natural to expect that additional predictors are warranted for inclusion.

Specifying a Covariance Structure

Since we simply have random intercepts for the high school and college levels, the default covariance structure for SAS's MIXED procedure called "variance components" was used. An alternative covariance structure—which would have been equivalent to variance components since only intercepts randomly varied— is the unstructured covariance matrix. Whereas the variance components structure restricts all off-diagonal elements of the covariance matrix to zero, the unstructured type makes no restrictions on the random effects' covariance matrix

Figure 13.3	SAS ODS CovParm table for the null model estimated with random intercepts for high school and college, with the COVTEST option from the MIXED procedure. The "Estimate" column contains the random intercept variance accounted for by college (Subject = Institution_Number) and high school (Subject = CPM_AI_Code) attended.

Covariance Parameter Estimates								
Cov Parm	Subject	Estimate	Standard Error	Z Value	Pr Z	Alpha	Lower	Upper
Intercept	**College ID**	0.07810	0.01099	7.11	<.0001	0.01	0.05581	0.1157
Intercept	**High School ID**	0.04198	0.002069	20.29	<.0001	0.01	0.03710	0.04784
Residual		0.8013	0.003875	206.77	<.0001	0.01	0.7914	0.8114

elements. If there were random slopes included, then more attention should be given to the specification of the random covariance parameters, but for this random intercepts model, no such additional consideration was needed.

Building the Student-Level Model

From the SAS code for Model 1 above, we obtained ODS output from SAS, and Figure 13.3 demonstrates how that raw output got formatted and ultimately published as Table 13 in Patterson et al. (2011).

Figure 13.4 SAS ODS output for Model 1 compared with formatted Table 13 from p. 21 of Patterson, Packman, and Kobrin (2011). These three ODS tables combined to characterize Model 1, summarized in the first column of the formatted table.

Table 13
Natural Science Cross-Classified Multilevel Model Results

Variable	Value / Group	Model 1 Est. (p)	Model 2 Est. (p)	Model 3 Est. (p)	Model 4 Est. (p)
Fixed-Effects					
Intercept		2.753 (0.000)	2.731 (0.000)	2.725 (0.000)	2.725 (0.000)
Gender	Female	0.079 (0.000)	0.082 (0.000)	0.084 (0.000)	0.085 (0.000)
Racial or Ethnic Identity	American Indian	-0.123 (0.002)	-0.121 (0.002)	-0.122 (0.002)	-0.121 (0.002)
	Asian	-0.039 (0.000)	-0.057 (0.000)	-0.053 (0.000)	-0.056 (0.000)
	Black	-0.266 (0.000)	-0.270 (0.000)	-0.268 (0.000)	-0.268 (0.000)
	Hispanic	-0.175 (0.000)	-0.179 (0.000)	-0.174 (0.000)	-0.174 (0.000)
	Other	-0.084 (0.000)	-0.091 (0.000)	-0.089 (0.000)	-0.089 (0.000)
	Missing	-0.008 (0.885)	-0.003 (0.955)	-0.005 (0.931)	-0.006 (0.922)
Highest Parental Ed. Level	H.S. Diploma or Less	-0.102 (0.000)	-0.102 (0.000)	-0.102 (0.000)	-0.102 (0.000)
	Associate Degree	-0.072 (0.000)	-0.072 (0.000)	-0.071 (0.000)	-0.071 (0.000)
	Graduate Degree	0.025 (0.000)	0.022 (0.001)	0.020 (0.003)	0.020 (0.004)
	Missing	0.001 (0.918)	-0.002 (0.861)	-0.005 (0.673)	-0.005 (0.659)
High School GPA [a]		0.513 (0.000)	0.505 (0.000)	0.502 (0.000)	0.502 (0.000)
SAT Critical Reading [a, b]		0.072 (0.000)	0.069 (0.000)	0.060 (0.000)	0.060 (0.000)
SAT Mathematics [a, b]		0.157 (0.000)	0.146 (0.000)	0.139 (0.000)	0.138 (0.000)
SAT Writing [a, b]		0.080 (0.000)	0.079 (0.000)	0.076 (0.000)	0.076 (0.000)
Number of Nat. Sci. AP Exams			0.059 (0.000)		0.024 (0.002)
Mean AP Nat. Sci. Exam Grade	1			-0.102 (0.000)	-0.128 (0.000)
	2			0.002 (0.877)	-0.027 (0.075)
	3			0.074 (0.000)	0.043 (0.004)
	4			0.167 (0.000)	0.132 (0.000)
	5			0.301 (0.000)	0.263 (0.000)
Random Parameters					
Intercept	College	0.050 (0.000)	0.050 (0.000)	0.050 (0.000)	0.050 (0.000)
Intercept	High School	0.019 (0.000)	0.019 (0.000)	0.019 (0.000)	0.019 (0.000)
Residual		0.681 (0.000)	0.681 (0.000)	0.681 (0.000)	0.681 (0.000)
AIC (model parameters)		227,087 (19)	226,909 (20)	226,457 (24)	226,449 (25)

Note. The reference group was white males whose parents' highest education level was a bachelor's degree and who took zero subject area AP Exams. Models were estimated based on 91,596 students from 7,267 high schools attending 110 colleges.

[a] Variable was grand-mean centered. [b] Variable was divided by 100.

(Continued)

Figure 13.4 (Continued)

Solution for Fixed Effects

Effect	Gender [Cross-program Matched]	Ethnicity Limited [Cross-program Matched]	Highest Parental Education Band	Estimate	Standard Error	DF	t Value	Pr > |t|	Alpha	Lower	Upper
Intercept				2.7528	0.02275	92E3	121.01	<.0001	0.01	2.6942	2.8114
CPM_Gender	Female			0.07869	0.006053	92E3	13.00	<.0001	0.01	0.06309	0.09428
CPM_Gender	Male			0							
CPM_Ethnicity_Lim		1: American Indian or Alaska Native		-0.1234	0.03984	92E3	-3.10	0.0020	0.01	-0.2260	-0.02076
CPM_Ethnicity_Lim		2: Asian, Asian-American, or Pacific Islander		-0.03894	0.009932	92E3	-3.92	<.0001	0.01	-0.06452	-0.01335
CPM_Ethnicity_Lim		3: Black or African-American		-0.2657	0.01316	92E3	-20.19	<.0001	0.01	-0.2996	-0.2318
CPM_Ethnicity_Lim		4: Hispanic, Latino, or Latin American		-0.1752	0.01194	92E3	-14.67	<.0001	0.01	-0.2060	-0.1444
CPM_Ethnicity_Lim		5: Other		-0.08431	0.01654	92E3	-5.10	<.0001	0.01	-0.1269	-0.04172
CPM_Ethnicity_Lim		6: No Response		-0.00830	0.05743	92E3	-0.14	0.8851	0.01	-0.1562	0.1396
CPM_Ethnicity_Lim		9: White		0							
Highest_Par_Ed_Band			1: High School Diploma or Less	-0.1023	0.008060	92E3	-12.69	<.0001	0.01	-0.1230	-0.08152
Highest_Par_Ed_Band			2: Associate Degree	-0.07154	0.01227	92E3	-5.83	<.0001	0.01	-0.1032	-0.03993
Highest_Par_Ed_Band			3: Graduate Degree	0.02470	0.006881	92E3	3.59	0.0003	0.01	0.006976	0.04243
Highest_Par_Ed_Band			4: No Response	0.001216	0.01180	92E3	0.10	0.9179	0.01	-0.02919	0.03162
Highest_Par_Ed_Band			9: Bachelor Degree	0							
CPM_HS_GPA_DGM				0.5127	0.006986	92E3	73.38	<.0001	0.01	0.4947	0.5307
SAT_Crit_Read_Late_DGM				0.07175	0.005069	92E3	14.16	<.0001	0.01	0.05870	0.08481
SAT_Math_Late_DGM				0.1566	0.004577	92E3	34.20	<.0001	0.01	0.1448	0.1683
SAT_Writing_Late_DGM				0.08022	0.005310	92E3	15.11	<.0001	0.01	0.06655	0.09390

Covariance Parameter Estimates

Cov Parm	Subject	Estimate	Standard Error	Z Value	Pr Z	Alpha	Lower	Upper
Intercept	Institution_Number	0.05042	0.007270	6.94	<.0001	0.01	0.03576	0.07553
Intercept	CPM_AI_Code	0.01856	0.001240	14.97	<.0001	0.01	0.01572	0.02219
Residual		0.6814	0.003274	208.10	<.0001	0.01	0.6730	0.6899

Information Criteria

Neg2LogLike	Parms	AIC	AICC	HQIC	BIC	CAIC
227049	19	227087	227087	227049	227049	227068

Source: Advanced Placement® Exam-Taking and Performance: Relationships with First-Year Subject Area College Grades, Patterson, B. F., Packman, S., & Kobrin, J. L. © 2011 The College Board. Reproduced with permission. Advanced Placement® is a trademark registered and/or owned by the College Board, which was not involved in the production of, and does not endorse, this product.

Note the key elements included in the final, formatted table: (1) the estimates of the fixed effects, (2) the *p*-values associated with the fixed effect estimates, (3) the random (residual) variance parameter estimates for the high school and college levels, (4) the *p*-values associated with the random variance parameter estimates, and (5) the AIC and the number of model parameters. When it comes to evaluating the significance of the random intercept and residual variance components, we de-emphasize the individual *p*-values reported in this table—as they are based on approximations that may not be accurate with few higher-order units—and instead encourage the reader to perform likelihood ratio tests based on the full and restricted models being estimated under REML. Such an approach will minimize the possibility of incorrect inferences regarding the significance of the variance parameters. We requested that SAS output the ODS tables SolutionF,

CovParms, and InfoCrit to separate datasets for each model, and they were readily output to spreadsheets, where we formatted the final tables for comparison across models. We went on to estimate the additional three models, and the output from SAS was formatted in much the same way.

Evaluating Model Fit

In the original study, we presented each set of results for the four main models that we considered in building the student-level model for mean natural science GPA. In Figure 13.4, the AIC (and number of parameters) for Models 3 and 4 were 226,457 (24), and 226,449 (25), respectively. So, despite the addition of a single parameter, we selected Model 4 as "fitting best" because the AIC was reduced by approximately eight units. We use the term "best fitting" as convenient, though slightly inaccurate, shorthand for optimal, from an information theoretic point of view. At that point, we concluded that the model containing all demographic, socioeconomic status, and prior achievement indicators, as well as both the number of natural science AP exams and the mean score on those exams, fit the data best for predicting college mean natural science GPA.

Evaluating Residual Variability in the Final Model

After having built a complete student-level model with the available data, it is informative to review the residual variation that may be attributed to the high school, college, and student levels. Figure 13.5 shows the SAS ODS table called CovParms (see the ODS OUTPUT statement in Table 13.6) for the final model (Model 4).

There is still significant residual variation at the high school, college, and student levels ($p < .0001$ for each parameter), which indicates that if there were

| Figure 13.5 | SAS ODS CovParm table for the final model (Model 4) shows that significant residual variation remains at both the high school and college levels, even after building a complete student-level model for mean natural science GPA in college. |

Covariance Parameter Estimates								
Cov Parm	Subject	Estimate	Standard Error	Z Value	Pr Z	Alpha	Lower	Upper
Intercept	**College ID**	0.05237	0.007540	6.95	<.0001	0.01	0.03715	0.07840
Intercept	**High School ID**	0.01802	0.001222	14.74	<.0001	0.01	0.01523	0.02161
Residual		0.6768	0.003252	208.11	<.0001	0.01	0.6685	0.6852

additional variables to be added, the model may indeed support them. In particular, high school– or college-level variables could have been considered for addition into the model, which may have led to a large enough reduction in variation at one or both of those levels to warrant removing the random intercept effect associated with that level or levels.

As it stands, we can also compare the residual variance in the final model ($\hat{\sigma}^2 = 0.6814$) to that in the null or empty model ($\hat{\sigma}^2 = 0.8013$). After including the fixed effects discussed above, we reduced the residual variation in mean natural science GPA by 15.0% {=100% * [1 – 0.6814 / 0.8013)]}, which is substantial, considering all of the other unobserved or unmeasured variables that could explain additional variation in the outcome. We look at this reduction in residual variance as a practical measure of how good a job we did at specifying a model for mean natural science course grades in college, above and beyond mean differences due to different high school or college means.

CONCLUSION

Interpreting Fixed Parameter Estimates

Having selected Model 4 as the best fitting, we turned then to the interpretation of our fixed effects. Figure 13.6 shows the SAS output associated with Model 4's fixed effects.

Recall our discussion of the reference group that we identified. The SAS output demonstrates that we correctly specified the effects, since the cells containing the fixed effect estimate for males, White students, those whose highest level of parental education was a bachelor's degree, and those who took no natural science AP exams are fixed at zero. If non-zero estimates appeared in the rows associated with our desired reference levels, that would indicate a problem in how we formatted the predictors or how we identified their coding on the MIXED procedure's CLASS statement.

We begin by making a few notes about the intercept to the model. In particular, the intercept was estimated as 2.7247 and corresponds to the expected natural science GPA of a White male student whose parents completed at most a bachelor's degree; who took no AP exams in natural science; and who had high school GPA, SAT critical reading, mathematics, and writing scores equal to the grand mean of all students who took at least one natural science course in college. It is to this hypothetical student that the fixed effects discussed below make reference.

Next, looking at the demographic predictors, we can make a few interesting observations. Recall that the scale that most colleges in this sample used ranged from 0 to 4, with 4 typically being associated with a letter grade of "A," 3 with a grade of "B," and so forth. The scale of the dependent variable is important when considering the practical significance of our results. Females were expected to have earned slightly higher average natural science GPAs in college, relative to males, with an estimated effect of 0.0850. In fact, female students—relative to male students and controlling for the predictors in the model—tended to have earned

| Figure 13.6 | SAS ODS tables SolutionF for the final model (Model 4), which illustrates the relationships of the fixed effects with expected mean natural science college GPA |

Solution for Fixed Effects						
Effect	Level	Estimate	Standard Error	DF	t Value	Pr > ltl
Intercept		2.7247	0.0232	9.2E+04	117.4400	<.0001
Gender	Female	0.0850	0.0060	9.2E+04	14.0700	<.0001
Gender	Male	0.0000	.	.	.	.
Racial_Eth_ID	1: Amer. Indian	−0.1215	0.0397	9.2E+04	−3.0600	0.0022
Racial_Eth_ID	2: Asian	−0.0558	0.0100	9.2E+04	−5.5900	<.0001
Racial_Eth_ID	3: Black	−0.2682	0.0131	9.2E+04	−20.4500	<.0001
Racial_Eth_ID	4: Hispanic	−0.1742	0.0119	9.2E+04	−14.6300	<.0001
Racial_Eth_ID	5: Other	−0.0894	0.0165	9.2E+04	−5.4200	<.0001
Racial_Eth_ID	6: No Response	−0.0056	0.0572	9.2E+04	−0.1000	0.9217
Racial_Eth_ID	9: White	0.0000	.	.	.	.
High_Par_Educ	1: HS or Less	−0.1018	0.0080	9.2E+04	−12.6700	<.0001
High_Par_Educ	2: Assoc. Deg.	−0.0707	0.0122	9.2E+04	−5.7800	<.0001
High_Par_Educ	3: Grad. Deg.	0.0199	0.0069	9.2E+04	2.8900	0.0038
High_Par_Educ	4: No Response	−0.0052	0.0118	9.2E+04	−0.4400	0.6591
High_Par_Educ	9: Bach. Deg.	0.0000	.	.	.	.
HS_GPA		0.5020	0.0070	9.2E+04	71.8400	<.0001
SAT_CR		0.0598	0.0051	9.2E+04	11.7900	<.0001
SAT_M		0.1384	0.0046	9.2E+04	29.7900	<.0001
SAT_W		0.0758	0.0053	9.2E+04	14.3100	<.0001
Num_Nat_Sci_APs		0.0245	0.0079	9.2E+04	3.1100	0.0019
Mean_Nat_Sci_AP_Gr	1	−0.1284	0.0165	9.2E+04	−7.7800	<.0001
Mean_Nat_Sci_AP_Gr	2	−0.0274	0.0154	9.2E+04	−1.7800	0.0752
Mean_Nat_Sci_AP_Gr	3	0.0432	0.0149	9.2E+04	2.8900	0.0038
Mean_Nat_Sci_AP_Gr	4	0.1324	0.0162	9.2E+04	8.1600	<.0001
Mean_Nat_Sci_AP_Gr	5	0.2632	0.0186	9.2E+04	14.1300	<.0001
Mean_Nat_Sci_AP_Gr	N	0.0000	.	.	.	.

Note. This table was reformatted slightly from the original SAS output.

higher grades in college natural science courses, and this effect was significant ($p < 0.0001$), but quite small when we consider that for most colleges' grade scales, even the smallest difference for an individual course grade (i.e., the difference between a "B" and a "B+") was typically 0.3.

American Indian students were expected to significantly ($p = 0.0022$) underperform White students on mean natural science GPA by 0.1215. Asian students tended to have earned slightly, but significantly ($p < 0.0001$) lower mean college natural science GPAs, by a margin of 0.0558 GPA units. Black and Hispanic students were both expected to significantly ($p < 0.0001$ for both groups) underperform White students, by 0.2682 and 0.1742 mean natural science GPA units, respectively. Those students who reported their racial or ethnic identity as "Other" tended to have earned slightly but significantly ($p < 0.0001$) lower mean natural science GPAs in college, by 0.08942, relative to White students. Finally, students who did not indicate their racial or ethnic identity did not perform significantly ($\alpha = 0.01$) differently from White students. Given this non-significant result, it is inappropriate to discuss the estimate of the fixed effect or even to state the sign of the estimated effect associated with this group.

In consideration of the possible relationship of socioeconomic status with students' mean natural science GPA, we included the highest degree level of education completed between students' parents. In particular, we note that students who were children of parents who completed at most a high school degree were expected to have earned mean college natural science GPAs of 0.1018 lower ($p < 0.0001$) than students whose parents' completed at least a bachelor's degree between them. Students whose parents completed at most an associate's degree—relative to those whose parents completed at most a bachelor's degree—were expected to earn slightly but significantly ($p < 0.0001$) lower mean natural science GPAs in college, by 0.07066 on the GPA scale. Turning to students with at least one parent who completed a graduate or professional degree, they were expected to significantly ($p = 0.0038$) outperform students whose parents completed at most a bachelor's degree, but by only a very small margin: 0.01986 on the GPA scale. Finally, students who did not report their parents' educational attainment were not expected to perform significantly differently ($p = 0.6591$) from the reference group of students whose parents completed at most a bachelor's degree.

In terms of the measure of prior academic ability, each of the four predictors had significant ($p < 0.01$) positive relationships with expected mean natural science GPA in college. These predictors were grand-mean centered in order to ease the interpretation of results. With a unit increase on high school GPA, students were expected to earn mean natural science GPAs of 0.5020 higher, and this effect was significant ($p < 0.0001$). The SAT sections were rescaled to put their associated parameter estimates onto a reasonable scale for this prediction problem. The original SAT section scores each ranged from 200 to 800, and we rescaled them by dividing by 100 (i.e., the approximate population standard deviation for each SAT section score). This in turn affected the interpretation of the parameter estimates. For example, as SAT mathematics scores increased

100 points, students were expected to earn mean natural science GPAs of 0.1384 higher ($p < 0.0001$). If we had not rescaled the variables, the parameter estimate would simply have been shifted to 0.001384, and the output may have been truncated, leading to less decimal precision in the reporting of the results. The expected effects of an additional 100 points on SAT critical reading and writing were both smaller than the effect of the same increase on SAT mathematics—with estimates of 0.05983 and 0.07577, respectively—but both were significant, with p-values smaller than 0.0001.

Finally, we turn to the predictors that were the main focus of this study: the number of AP exams taken in natural science and the associated mean score on those exams. The effect of each additional Advanced Placement exam taken in natural science on expected mean natural science GPA was significant ($p = 0.0019$) but quite small at 0.02446 on the GPA scale. We note that the number of AP exams taken in natural science was entered linearly, but other researchers may have wished to estimate it in a more flexible manner, such as the nonlinear relationship implied by entering it as categorical. Such an approach would have enabled the marginal effect of an additional AP exam in natural science to vary when increasing from, say, zero to one exam, as opposed to increasing from one to two exams.

In order to ensure that our reference group was non-AP examinees in natural sciences, we assigned those examinees to a mean natural science AP exam score of "N" and used it as the reference level for that categorical variable. Students whose mean natural science AP exam score was a 1 were the only group of AP examinees who were expected to underperform non-AP examinees ($p < 0.0001$) and were expected to do so by 0.1284 points on the GPA scale. Students who scored on average a 2 on the AP exams that they took in natural science were not expected to perform differently in college natural science courses from those who took no AP exams at all ($p = 0.0752$). Those students whose average AP exam scores in natural science were 3, 4, or 5 all significantly ($p < 0.01$ for each of the three levels) outperformed non-AP examinees, having been expected to earn mean natural science GPAs of 0.04319, 0.1324, and 0.2632 higher than non-AP examinees, respectively.

The central finding of the study of Advanced Placement exam participation and performance for predicting first-year college natural science grades was that while the number of natural science AP exams taken had a small, positive, significant parameter estimate—indicating a positive association between that predictor and students' mean natural science course grades—the effects associated with each level of mean natural science AP exam grade tended to dominate. This result remained statistically significant, even after controlling for high school GPA, SAT scores, gender, racial or ethnic identity, and highest parental education level, and for random variation in mean natural science GPA attributable to the high school and college attended. It should be noted, however, that the expected difference in mean natural science GPA with each additional AP exam taken is quite small. So, while exposing prepared and motivated students to more rigorous natural science coursework in high school may be beneficial to their subsequent performance in first-year natural science courses, performance in exams related to those high school natural science courses is generally a more powerful predictor of subsequent success in that discipline.

NOTES

1. Advanced Placement, AP, and SAT are registered trademarks of the College Board, which was not involved in the production of, and does not endorse, this chapter. Furthermore, researchers are encouraged to freely express their professional judgment. Therefore, points of view or opinions stated herein do not necessarily represent official College Board position or policy.

2. The original study spanned nine college content areas (mathematics, computer science, engineering, natural science, social science, history, English, world language, and art and music), which corresponded to the broad categories of Advanced Placement courses and exams. For the sake of simplicity and brevity, only the natural science analyses are presented herein. For additional research on other subject areas, we encourage the reader to download the full paper (Patterson, Packman, & Kobrin, 2011) available on the College Board's Research and Development departmental website: www.collegeboard.org/research/.

3. SAS and all other SAS Institute Inc. product or service names are registered trademarks or trademarks of SAS Institute Inc. in the USA and other countries. ® indicates USA registration.

4. Note that the data in Figure 13.1 were simulated based on the estimated relationships among the predictors and outcome and do not represent valid observations of actual student outcomes.

REFERENCES

Akaike, H. (1974). A new look at the statistical model identification. *IEEE Transactions on Automatic Control, 19*(6), 716–723. doi:10.1109/TAC.1974.1100705.

College Board. (2006). *The College Board college handbook 2006* (43rd ed.). New York: Author.

Kobrin, J. L., Patterson, B. F., Shaw, E. J., Mattern, K. D., & Barbuti, S. M. (2008). *Validity of the SAT for predicting first-year college grade point average* (Research Rep. No. 2008-5). New York: College Board. Retrieved December 31, 2011, from http://professionals.collegeboard.com/data-reports-research/cb/validity-of-sat-predicting-fycgpa

Patterson, B. F., Packman, S., & Kobrin, J. L. (2011). *Advanced Placement exam-taking and performance: Relationships with first-year subject area college grades* (Research Rep. No. 2011-4). New York: College Board. Retrieved December 31, 2011, from http://professionals.collegeboard.com/data-reports-research/cb/RR2011-4/

Raudenbush, S. W. & Bryk, A. S. (2002). *Hierarchical linear models: Applications and data analysis methods* (2nd ed.). Thousand Oaks, CA: Sage.

SAS Institute Inc. (2004a). *Base SAS software.* Cary, NC: Author.

SAS Institute Inc. (2004b). *SAS/STAT software.* Cary, NC: Author.

SAS Institute Inc. (2004c). *SAS/STAT 9.1 user's guide.* Cary, NC: Author.

Cross-Classified Multilevel Models Using Stata

How Important Are Schools and Neighborhoods for Students' Educational Attainment?

George Leckie

14

S chools and neighborhoods are frequently cited as important influences on student educational attainment. Any attempt to quantify the relative impact of schools on attainment must therefore account for the role of neighborhoods. Similarly, studies of neighborhood effects on attainment must not ignore the influence of schools. When neighborhoods are nested within schools, the data form a three-level hierarchy. Students at level 1 in the data hierarchy would be nested within neighborhoods at level 2, which in turn would be nested within schools at level 3. However, pure hierarchies often do not arise in practice, and so we will often see that students from the same neighborhood attend several different schools. When pure hierarchies break down in this way, the data are described as nonhierarchical and cross-classified. Specifically, students are nested within the cells of a two-way cross-classification of schools by neighborhoods. Cross-classified multilevel models (crossed random effects models) can be fitted to these data to simultaneously account for clustering due to schools and clustering due to neighborhoods.

It is important to realistically model the different sources of response variable variation in multilevel models, as ignoring important sources of variation will lead us to misattribute variation to those sources that we do account for in our models. For example, if we ignore neighborhood effects when modeling student attainment, we will likely overestimate the importance of school and student effects. It is also important to realistically model the different sources of response variable variation in multilevel models to accurately model the nonindependence in the data. By ignoring important sources of clustering, we implicitly assume that units within those clusters are independent when they are actually correlated. This will lead us to estimate the effects of predictors measured at those missing levels with spurious precision. For example, by ignoring neighborhood effects, we would incorrectly assume that children from the same neighborhood are no more alike than children from different neighborhoods, and we would therefore underestimate the standard errors of neighborhood-level predictor variables. Cross-classified models allow us to account for multiple sources of variation or clustering even when our data are nonhierarchical.

In this chapter, we analyze a classic cross-classified educational dataset where students are nested within both schools and neighborhoods: the Scotland Neighborhood Study. The data were first studied by Garner and Raudenbush (1991), who set out to test the hypothesis that a neighborhoods level of social deprivation has a negative effect on a student's educational attainment even after controlling for the student's prior attainment and family background. The data were restudied by Raudenbush (1993) and were also used as one of the examples in the classic *Hierarchical Linear Models* textbook (Raudenbush & Bryk, 2002), as an exercise dataset in the excellent *Multilevel and Longitudinal Modeling Using Stata* book (Rabe-Hesketh & Skrondal, 2008), and as the illustrative application in the *Cross-Classified Multilevel Models* module of the free online multilevel modeling course provided by the Centre for Multilevel Modelling at the University of Bristol.[1] In our analyses of these data, we focus on quantifying the relative impact of schools and neighborhoods on educational attainment, but our analyses also replicate many of the results presented for these data by Raudenbush, and Raudenbush and Bryk.

SAMPLE

The study looked at 2,310 students who attended 17 secondary schools and resided in 524 neighborhoods. We note that 17 is rather a low number of units to have at a higher level in a multilevel analysis. Ideally, we would have a higher number of units to ensure a more reliable estimation of any school level random part parameters that we choose to include in our models. (The secondary schools in this study correspond to high schools in the United States, while the neighborhoods in this study are similar in size to U.S. census tracts.) A copy of these data is provided on the author's website and can be opened in any net-aware version of Stata by issuing the "Use" command in the Stata Command Window[2]:

```
. use http://www.bristol.ac.uk/cmm/media/leckie/scotland_
neighbourhood_study, clear
```

The web address for the Stata dataset scotland_neighborhood_study immediately follows the command. This in turn is followed by a comma, which denotes the start of the list of options associated with the command. Here we have specified the clear option to replace any data that might already be open in Stata.

To obtain a first impression of the structure of the cross-classified data, we use the table command to present the data as a two-way cross-tabulation of neighborhoods (neighid) by schools (schid). The high number of neighborhoods makes this table too long to report in its entirety here. Thus, for presentation purposes, and also in order to replicate Table 1 of Raudenbush (1993), we choose to restrict this cross-tabulation to the subset of neighborhoods in the sample with identifier values in the range 1 to 38, 251 to 263, or 793 to 803. Note that the choice of this particular subset is not in itself meaningful, and we could have just as easily examined a different subset of neighborhoods. We restrict the cross-tabulation to the specified subset by using the if and inrange qualifiers and the logical "or" operator denoted by the single vertical bar.

```
. table neighid schid if inrange(neighid,1,38) |
inrange(neighid,251,263) | inrange(neighid,793,803)
```

neighid	2	3	8	10	15	16	17	18	19	20
26										5
27										1
29								1		8
30										2
31								1		1
32								1		5
33								2		2
35										3
36										2
37										1
38								1		4
251							4		1	
252						1	3			1
253							3			
256										2
258					5					
259					6	1		2		
260					7					
261					4			3		
262					5		1	1		
263					14		1	1		
793			1	7						
794	1		1	12						
795	1			1						
796	9									
797	4		1							
798	9		1							
799	1			1						
800	2									
801	1	1								
803				4						

The rows of the cross-tabulation reference the neighborhoods, while the columns reference the schools. Note that the cross-tabulation has only 10 columns, as none of the selected neighborhoods sent students to the remaining seven schools. The cell counts give the number of students who belong to the relevant neighborhood and school combination. Straightaway, we see that most combinations of school and neighborhood do not exist, but where combinations do exist, they often contain multiple students. Looking more closely and across the columns of the cross-tabulation, we see that some neighborhoods sent students to multiple schools. For example, neighborhood 259 sent six students to school 15, one student to school 16, and two students to school 18. (Note that Raudenbush, 1993, labeled the 17 schools with different numeric identifiers from those used in our data; schools 15, 16, and 18 in our data correspond to schools 10, 11, and 16 in his data.) Similarly, looking down the rows of the cross-tabulation, we see that some schools taught students from multiple neighborhoods. The cross-tabulation clearly shows that the data are not a pure hierarchy. Rather, students are nested within the cells formed by the cross-classification of schools by neighborhoods.

To produce a table of descriptive statistics for the student variables used in the analyses, we use the `tabstat` command. The list of variables for which descriptive statistics are to be calculated immediately follows the command. We use the `stat()` option with the `mean` and `sd` arguments to request the mean and standard deviation for each of these variables. We use the `column(stat)` option to request that the variables be presented in the table rows and the statistics in the table columns, as opposed to the default where the variables and statistics are presented the other way around. Finally, the `format(%4.3f)` option is specified to present all statistics to three decimal places. The resulting table replicates Table 3 of Raudenbush (1993).

```
. tabstat attain p7vrq p7read male dadocc daded momed dadunemp,
stat(mean sd) columns(stat) format(%4.3f)

    variable |      mean          sd
-------------+--------------------------
      attain |     0.093       1.002
       p7vrq |     0.506      10.648
      p7read |    -0.044      13.888
        male |     0.480       0.500
      dadocc |    -0.464      11.782
       daded |     0.215       0.411
       momed |     0.248       0.432
    dadunemp |     0.109       0.312
-------------------------------------
```

The first variable, `attain`, which will be the response variable in our multilevel models, is a measure of total attainment. It is based on a series of national examinations taken at the end of compulsory secondary schooling in Scotland (age 16). Successful performance in these examinations is a crucial factor in decisions regarding employment and entrance to universities. Note that `attain` is approximately standardized (`attain` has a mean of approximately 0 and a standard deviation of 1) and therefore allows us to interpret the fixed covariate effects in our models in standard deviation units.

The variables `p7vrq` and `p7read` are verbal reasoning and reading prior attainment scores in tests administered at the end of primary schooling (age 12). The variable `male` is a simple gender dummy variable. The variable `dadocc` is a continuous score for father's occupation, a proxy for social class. The variables `daded`, `momed`, and `dadunemp` are binary indicator variables for whether students' fathers and mothers continued in school beyond the age of 15 and whether students' fathers were unemployed. The table shows that only 22% of the fathers and 25% of the mothers continued in school past the age of 15 and that 11% of the fathers were unemployed.

In Garner and Raudenbush (1991), the key predictor variable of interest was `deprive`, a neighborhood-level social deprivation score. We did not include this variable in the variable list for the `tabstat` command, as we must calculate the mean and standard deviation of this variable at the neighborhood level rather than at the student level. The mean and standard deviation of this variable are 0.0377 and 0.622, respectively. Neighborhoods with higher scores have higher concentrations of poverty, worse health, and poorer housing stock than neighborhoods with lower scores.

SOFTWARE AND PROCEDURE

Multilevel models for continuous response variables are fitted in Stata using the `xtmixed` command. (Multilevel models for binary and count response variables are fitted using the `xtmelogit` and `xtmepoisson` commands; the user-written `gllamm` command [Rabe-Hesketh & Skrondal, 2008] is available for other response types). While `xtmixed` is primarily designed for fitting multilevel models for pure hierarchies, cross-classified multilevel models can also be fitted within this framework, and we shall describe and demonstrate this in the following sections.

The default estimation procedure is to fit the model using the expectation maximization (EM) algorithm until convergence, or until 20 iterations have been reached, whichever happens sooner. At that point, maximization switches to a gradient-based method using Newton-Raphson iterations. By default, models are fitted by maximum restricted likelihood (REML); the `mle` option can be specified to instead fit the model by maximum likelihood (MLE). We use the command's default estimation options in our analyses.

There are a number of useful resources for researchers wishing to learn more about `xtmixed` and how it can be used to fit cross-classified models. The xtmixed help page fully documents the syntax and the wide range of options associated with the command: www.stata.com/help.cgi?xtmixed. The xtmixed entry in the Stata Longitudinal-Data/Panel-Data Reference Manual (StataCorp., 2011) gives a concise introduction to the multilevel theory underlying the command and provides a range of brief examples, including a cross-classified model. An excellent and more detailed introduction to multilevel modeling in Stata, which includes several examples of fitting cross-classified models, is provided by Rabe-Hesketh and Skrondal (2008). Further worked examples of fitting cross-classified multilevel models in Stata are provided in the free online multilevel modeling course provided by the Centre for Multilevel Modelling, based at the University of Bristol (www.cmm.bristol.ac.uk/learning-training/course.shtml).

ANALYZING THE DATA

To analyze the data, we shall fit five increasingly complex multilevel models. We describe each of these models below, together with the xtmixed command syntax for fitting them. The output for each model is presented and interpreted in the Output and Analysis section.

Model 1 is a two-level (students within schools) variance components model, which simply partitions the variation in attainment into between-school and within-school components. The model is an unconditional one; it includes no covariates. The school variance therefore summarizes the variability in school means and can be interpreted as a measure of school-level educational inequality or disparities. These will be driven by a mix of school differences in educational effectiveness (i.e., causal effects) and those in student attainment and other characteristics at intake (i.e., selection effects). The xtmixed command for fitting this model is as follows:

```
. xtmixed attain || schid:, variance
```

The response variable attain immediately follows the xtmixed command, and this would normally be followed by the list of fixed part explanatory variables, excluding the constant, as this is included by default. However, as our first model is an unconditional one, we do not specify any explanatory variables. The level 2 random part of the model is specified in the command syntax after two vertical bars. The level 2 identifier variable schid is specified first, followed by a colon and then by the list of explanatory variables that have random coefficients at that level, again excluding the constant, as this is included by default. However, as our first model contains no random coefficients, we do not specify any explanatory variables at this point, either. Finally, we specify the variance option to report the variances of the random intercept and any random coefficients included in the model, as opposed to the default of standard deviations.

Model 2 is a two-level (students within neighborhoods) variance components model, which simply partitions the variation in attainment into between-neighborhood and within-neighborhood components. The model is equivalent to Model 1 in Raudenbush (1993). Like our previous model, this is an unconditional model; it includes no covariates. The neighborhood variance therefore summarizes the variability in neighborhood means and can be interpreted as a measure of neighborhood-level educational inequality or disparities. These neighborhood differences will be driven by a mix of causal neighborhood effects on student attainment and nonrandom selection of students and their families into neighborhoods. The xtmixed command for fitting this model is similar to the earlier one except here, neighid is the level 2 identifier variable instead of schid:

```
. xtmixed attain || neighid:, variance
```

Whereas Model 1 accounted for school effects but ignored neighborhoods and Model 2 accounted for neighborhood effects but ignored schools, in Model 3 we will simultaneously account for both sources of attainment variation. Were neighborhoods strictly nested within schools, we would specify Model 3 as a three-level multilevel model. The xtmixed command for fitting such a model would be as follows:

```
. xtmixed attain || schid: || neighid:, variance
```

where the syntax for each higher level begins with two vertical bars. The order in which these are specified (from left to right) is significant: xtmixed assumes that neighid is nested within schid. However, our data are not a pure hierarchy; the data are cross-classified. We must therefore specify Model 3 as a cross-classified variance components model. This model is equivalent to Model 2 in Raudenbush (1993).

In our introduction to the xtmixed command, we stated that it is primarily designed for fitting multilevel models to hierarchical rather than nonhierarchical data. However, it turns out that it is possible to formulate cross-classified multilevel models as constrained hierarchical models, and doing so therefore enables us to fit Model 3 using xtmixed (see, e.g., Rabe-Hesketh & Skrondal, 2008). To specify the model as a constrained hierarchical model, we first specify a three-level model with an artificial level 3 identifier variable that has only one unit. Schools are then entered into the model as a series of 17 binary indicator variables, one for each school, where each indicator is given a random coefficient at level 3, rather than the usual fixed coefficient. Thus, the 17 schools are entered as 17 level 3 random effects rather than as 17 fixed effects. These 17 level 3 random coefficients give rise to a 17×17 level 3 variance–covariance matrix. The 17 variances in this matrix are constrained to be equal, while all covariances are constrained to be zero. This simplification results in a single random part parameter at level 3, the between-school variance. Neighborhoods are then treated as the level 2 units in the usual way.

Fortunately, `xtmixed` makes it easy to specify this constrained three-level model. First, we do not need to create the artificial level 3 identifier variable, as `xtmixed` accepts the cluster name `_all` for this purpose. Second, the syntax `R.schid` can be used to generate the 17 binary indicator variables as random effects and to automatically constrain their 17 variances to be equal and to constrain all their covariances to zero. The `xtmixed` command for fitting this model is therefore as follows:

```
. xtmixed attain || _all: R.schid || neighid:, variance
```

An important point to note in the above model is that we could equally have entered neighborhood as the series of random binary indicator variables at level 3 and treated schools as the level 2 units. While this second formulation would give exactly the same model results, it is computationally far less efficient than the first formulation, as it will lead to 524 binary indicator variables and a 524×524 level 3 variance–covariance matrix. It is therefore always recommended to specify the classification with fewer units as the one that is entered as the series of random binary indicator variables at level 3. See Rabe-Hesketh and Skrondal (2008, Chap. 11) for other techniques to fit complex cross-classified models computationally efficiently.

Like Models 1 and 2, Model 3 includes no covariates and so is again an unconditional model. Models 1 and 2 are in fact nested within Model 3, and thus likelihood ratio tests can be used to test whether Model 3 provides the best fit to the data.

As with multiple regression, the interpretation of each parameter in Model 3 is the effect that the parameter has having adjusted for the other parameters in the model. The estimate of the student variance, for example, should be interpreted as the variability between students having accounted for both school effects and neighborhood effects.

In Model 3, the school and neighborhood effects are assumed additive. However, the effects of school and neighborhood on attainment might interact. For instance, some schools may be more beneficial for students who live in particular neighborhoods. We can relax the additive random effects assumption by including a random interaction classification in the model to capture the interaction effects between schools and neighborhoods. The variance of these random interaction effects can be separated from the student variance because we observe multiple students for at least some combinations of school and neighborhood. If no combinations had more than one student, we would not be able to include these interaction effects. The student variance then captures the variability between students within the cells of the cross-classification. Prior to fitting this non-additive model, we must first create a new identifier variable, which we name `schidXneighid`, to index the unique combinations of school and neighborhood in the data. This can be done using the `egen` command, an extension to Stata's standard `generate` command, with the `group()` function. The `group()` function makes the new variable index the unique combinations of `schid` and `neighid` found in the data.

```
. egen schidXneighid = group(schid neighid)
```

We incorporate these random interaction effects into the model by specifying the interaction classification as a new lowest clustering level in the model. The new syntax `|| schidXneighid` is therefore added to the end of the command:

```
. xtmixed attain || _all: R.schid || neighid: ||
schidXneighid:, variance
```

Model 5 extends Model 3 by including the full set of covariates that we described earlier. This model is equivalent to Model 3 in Raudenbush (1993). Note that we could equally have introduced covariates into our Model 4, but the resulting model would no longer be comparable to that analyzed by Raudenbush. (While Raudenbush discusses the possibility of random interaction effects, he does not analyze them due to the computational difficulty in doing so at that time when he conducted his research.) In Model 5, we therefore do not include the `|| schidXneighid` syntax that appeared in Model 4. The seven student- and family-level covariates that we control for are all measured at the end of primary schooling. Adjusting for these covariates can therefore be seen as adjusting for the nonrandom assignment of students into schools, a likely major source of between-school differences in attainment. We also expect these variables along with the neighborhood social deprivation variable to explain a substantial proportion of the variation in attainment between neighborhoods. The `xtmixed` command for this model is as follows:

```
. xtmixed attain p7vrq p7read male dadocc daded momed
dadunemp deprive || _all: R.schid || neighid:, variance
```

The list of student- and neighborhood-level explanatory variables immediately follows the response variable. Note that no distinction is made between the student-level variables (p7vrq, p7read, male, dadocc, daded, momed, dadunemp) and the neighborhood-level variable (deprive) in how they are entered into the model. The random part of the `xtmixed` command remains identical to that in Model 3.

A wide range of modeling extensions can of course be made to each of the models presented in this section, including adding random coefficients at either higher level or even adding further classifications such as school districts. We discuss such extensions in the Conclusion of this chapter.

OUTPUT AND ANALYSIS

In this section, we present and interpret the model output associated with the five models described in the previous section.

Model 1 is the two-level variance components model for students nested within schools.

```
. xtmixed attain || schid:, variance

Performing EM optimization:

Performing gradient-based optimization:

Iteration 0:   log restricted-likelihood = -3222.7277
Iteration 1:   log restricted-likelihood = -3222.7277

Computing standard errors:

Mixed-effects REML regression            Number of obs      =      2310
Group variable: schid                    Number of groups   =        17

                                         Obs per group: min =        22
                                                        avg =     135.9
                                                        max =       286


                                         Wald chi2(0)       =         .
Log restricted-likelihood = -3222.7277   Prob > chi2        =         .

------------------------------------------------------------------------------
      attain |     Coef.   Std. Err.      z    P>|z|     [95% Conf. Interval]
-------------+----------------------------------------------------------------
       _cons |   .081839   .0782383     1.05   0.296    -.0715052    .2351833
------------------------------------------------------------------------------


------------------------------------------------------------------------------
  Random-effects Parameters |   Estimate   Std. Err.     [95% Conf. Interval]
----------------------------+-------------------------------------------------
schid: Identity             |
                var(_cons) |   .0954118   .0383529      .0433952    .2097788
----------------------------+-------------------------------------------------
               var(Residual) |   .9343739   .0276035      .8818085    .9900727
------------------------------------------------------------------------------
LR test vs. linear regression: chibar2(01) =    124.59 Prob >= chibar2 = 0.0000
```

The top left-hand section of the model output presents the estimation log. This consists of three parts, which appear sequentially as xtmixed performs each step of the estimation: (a) When "Performing EM optimization:" appears, xtmixed performs a set of expectation-maximization (EM) iterations to refine the starting values of the model parameters; (b) when "Performing gradient-based optimization:" appears, xtmixed performs gradient-based iterations until convergence. The log restricted-likelihood at each iteration is displayed, and from the output we see that the model converged in one iteration; (c) when "Computing standard errors:" appears, xtmixed computes standard errors for the model parameters. The output title, "Mixed-effects REML regression," informs us that our model was fitted using REML. Finally, we are informed that schid has been specified as the grouping level (i.e., the level 2 units).

The top right-hand section of the model output summarizes the multilevel structure of the estimation sample. The model is fitted to 2,310 level 1 observations (i.e., the students) nested within 17 level 2 groups (i.e., the schools) where there are between 22 and 286, with an average of 136, observations per group (i.e., students per school). The Wald test "Wald chi2(0) = .," which compares the current model to a restricted model with only a constant, has not been carried out, as the current model includes no explanatory variables and so is equivalent to the restricted model. Stata therefore reports a period (Stata syntax for a missing value) for the test statistic and associated p-value.

The first estimation table reports the fixed effects. We estimate that the intercept is 0.082 with standard error 0.078. The z-ratio, p-value, and 95% confidence intervals for this parameter estimate are also given. The intercept is not significantly different from zero ($p = 0.296$). This is expected, as the response variable is approximately standardized and therefore has a mean of approximately zero.

The second estimation table reports the estimated variance components. The first section of the table is labeled "schid: Identity," indicating that this section reports random part parameters at the school level. The row labeled "var(_cons)" reports the between-school variance, and this is estimated as 0.095. The second section of the table labeled "var(Residual)" displays the estimated within-school variance of 0.934. A useful way to interpret the relative magnitude of these two variance components is to compute the variance partition coefficient (VPC), which in this case gives the proportion of variation that lies between schools. Based on Model 1, this is 0.092 ($= 0.095/(0.095 + 0.934)$), and so 9% of the variation in attainment lies between schools. A second commonly computed statistic used to interpret the variance components is the intraclass correlation coefficient (ICC), which in this case gives the expected correlation in attainment between two students who attend the same school. For this model, the ICC coincides with the VPC, and thus the correlation in attainment between schoolmates is also 0.09.

Finally, a likelihood-ratio test comparing the current model with a single-level model with no school effects (i.e., linear regression) is provided and reports a p-value that is effectively zero ($p < 0.001$). This leads us to conclude that the variance in mean attainment at the school level is highly significant and that the multilevel approach is, as expected, favored over the single-level approach.

Having fitted the model, we can predict the empirical Bayes (i.e., posterior or shrunken) estimates of the school effects and their associated standard errors. We do this using the predict command with the reffects and reses options, respectively. We specify u0 and u0se as the corresponding new variable names:

```
. predict u0, reffects

. predict u0se, reses
```

We could now check whether these residuals are normally distributed by using the qnorm graph command to plot the predicted school effects as a quantile-quantile plot. However, we will instead examine the magnitudes of these effects to count how many schools differ significantly from the average school. We will do this by using the serrbar graph command to produce a "caterpillar plot" of the school effects. However, one thing that we must recognize before we proceed is that the school-level residuals and their standard errors have been calculated and stored for all 2,310 records in the data. Our graph and associated variables, on the other hand, should be based on a dataset with 17 records, one record per school. We therefore use the egen command with the tag function to generate a dummy variable pickone to pick one record per school.

```
. egen pickone = tag(schid)
```

Next, we generate a new variable u0rank using the egen command with the rank function to rank the predicted school effects for these 17 selected records. These ranks will be plotted on the x-axis of the caterpillar plot.

```
. egen u0rank = rank(u0) if pickone==1
```

Finally, we can issue the serrbar command

```
. serrbar u0 u0se u0rank if pickone==1, scale(1.96)
```

where we use the scale(1.96) option to create the 95% confidence intervals to allow each school to be compared to the average school (which has an effect of zero). The graph shows that only 8 out of the 17 schools differ significantly from the overall average. The difference between the highest and lowest scoring of these schools is approximately one standard deviation.

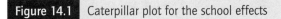

Figure 14.1   Caterpillar plot for the school effects

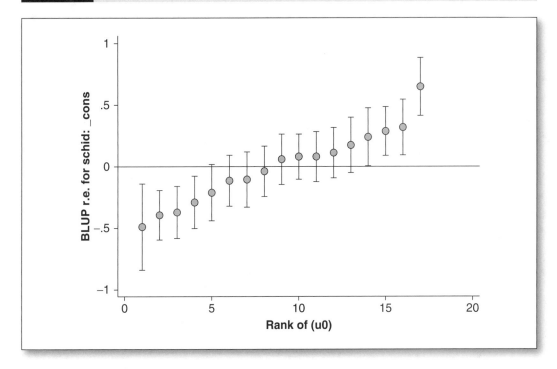

Model 2 is the two-level variance components model for students nested within neighborhoods and is equivalent to Model 1 in Raudenbush (1993). The model is effectively the same as our Model 1, except here neighborhoods are the clustering variable instead of schools.

```
. xtmixed attain || neighid:, variance

Performing EM optimization:

Performing gradient-based optimization:

Iteration 0:    log restricted-likelihood = -3210.6275
Iteration 1:    log restricted-likelihood = -3210.6254
Iteration 2:    log restricted-likelihood = -3210.6254

Computing standard errors:

Mixed-effects REML regression              Number of obs     =       2310
Group variable: neighid                    Number of groups  =        524
```

```
                                          Obs per group: min =             1
                                                         avg =           4.4
                                                         max =            16


                                          Wald chi2(0)          =           .
Log restricted-likelihood = -3210.6254    Prob > chi2           =           .

------------------------------------------------------------------------------
      attain |      Coef.   Std. Err.      z    P>|z|     [95% Conf. Interval]
-------------+----------------------------------------------------------------
       _cons |   .0820099   .0284661     2.88   0.004     .0262173    .1378025
------------------------------------------------------------------------------


------------------------------------------------------------------------------
  Random-effects Parameters  |   Estimate   Std. Err.     [95% Conf. Interval]
-----------------------------+------------------------------------------------
neighid: Identity            |
                 var(_cons)  |    .20236    .0258064      .1576062    .2598221
-----------------------------+------------------------------------------------
               var(Residual) |   .8043651   .0265749      .7539297    .8581744
------------------------------------------------------------------------------
LR test vs. linear regression: chibar2(01) =    148.80 Prob >= chibar2 = 0.0000
```

In Model 2, the between-neighborhood variance is 0.202 while the within-neighborhood variance is 0.804. Thus, 20% of the variation in attainment lies between neighborhoods, and the correlation in attainment between two children who live in the same neighborhood is 0.20. The between-neighborhood variance in Model 2 is considerably larger than the between-school variance in Model 1 and so greater disparities in attainment appear to lie between neighborhoods than between schools.

Model 3 is the cross-classified variance components model which simultaneously accounts for the nesting of students within schools and the separate nesting of students within neighborhoods.

```
. xtmixed attain || _all: R.schid || neighid:, variance

Performing EM optimization:

Performing gradient-based optimization:

Iteration 0:   log restricted-likelihood = -3180.0763
Iteration 1:   log restricted-likelihood = -3180.0484
Iteration 2:   log restricted-likelihood = -3180.0484
```

```
Computing standard errors:

Mixed-effects REML regression                    Number of obs      =        2310


-----------------------------------------------------------------
                |  No. of       Observations per Group
Group Variable  |  Groups    Minimum    Average    Maximum
----------------+------------------------------------------------
          _all  |      1      2310       2310.0       2310
        neighid |    524         1          4.4         16
-----------------------------------------------------------------


                                                 Wald chi2(0)       =         .
Log restricted-likelihood = -3180.0484           Prob > chi2        =         .


-----------------------------------------------------------------------------
      attain |     Coef.    Std. Err.     z    P>|z|    [95% Conf. Interval]
-------------+---------------------------------------------------------------
       _cons |   .0748585    .074656    1.00   0.316   -.0714646     .2211817
-----------------------------------------------------------------------------



-----------------------------------------------------------------------------
  Random-effects Parameters  |   Estimate   Std. Err.    [95% Conf. Interval]
-----------------------------+-----------------------------------------------
_all: Identity               |
               var(R.schid)  |    .08149    .0348397     .0352522     .1883744
-----------------------------+-----------------------------------------------
neighid: Identity            |
                 var(_cons)  |   .1410982   .0218534     .1041566      .191142
-----------------------------+-----------------------------------------------
                var(Residual)|   .7990432   .0263663     .7490018     .8524278
-----------------------------------------------------------------------------
LR test vs. linear regression:       chi2(2) =   209.95   Prob > chi2 = 0.0000
```

Note: LR test is conservative and provided only for reference.

In Model 3, the between-school variance is 0.081, the between-neighborhood variance is 0.141, and the student variance is 0.799. Thus, 8% of the variation lies between schools, while 14% lies between neighborhoods. Interpreted as ICCs, the correlation in attainment between two students who attend the same school but live in different neighborhoods is approximately 0.08, while the correlation in attainment between two students who live in the same neighborhood but attend different schools is 0.14. Finally, the correlation in attainment between two students who attend the same school and live in the same neighborhood is 0.22 ($0.217 = (0.081 + 0.141) / (0.081 + 0.141 + 0.799)$).

The Model 3 results contrast with those of Model 1, which suggest that 10% of the variation lies between schools, and Model 2, which suggest that 20% of the variation lies between neighborhoods. The Model 3 results demonstrate the importance of simultaneously accounting for both sources of influence on attainment. When we exclude one of the classifications, whether it be schools or neighborhoods, we overstate the importance of the classification that we do include. This leads us to draw potentially misleading conclusions.

By computing the deviance ($-2 \times$ the log likelihood) for each model, we can test whether Model 3 offers a significantly better fit than either Model 1 or Model 2. A comparison between the fit of Model 3 and Model 1 yields a reduction of deviance of $6445.46 - 6360.10 = 85.36$ associated with adding the neighborhood variance component to Model 1. Similarly, a comparison between the fit of Model 3 and Model 2 gives a reduction of deviance of $6421.25 - 6360.10 = 61.15$ associated with adding the school variance component to Model 2. Bearing in mind that the 5% point of a chi-squared distribution on 1 degree of freedom is 3.84, there is overwhelming evidence in favor of Model 3 over either Model 1 or Model 2. (Note that these deviance or likelihood ratio tests can be automatically calculated in Stata using the `lrtest` command.)

Model 4 extends Model 3 by including the random school-by-neighborhood interaction classification to allow the effects of schools and neighborhoods on attainment to potentially be non-additive.

```
. egen schidXneighid = group(schid neighid)

. xtmixed attain || _all: R.schid || neighid: || schidXneighid:, variance

Performing EM optimization:

Performing gradient-based optimization:

Iteration 0:    log restricted-likelihood = -3181.0944
Iteration 1:    log restricted-likelihood = -3178.0607
Iteration 2:    log restricted-likelihood = -3177.9791
Iteration 3:    log restricted-likelihood = -3177.9771
Iteration 4:    log restricted-likelihood = -3177.9771

Computing standard errors:

Mixed-effects REML regression                    Number of obs      =      2310
```

```
------------------------------------------------------------
             |  No. of     Observations per Group
Group Variable |  Groups  Minimum   Average   Maximum
---------------+--------------------------------------------
        _all  |      1      2310     2310.0      2310
      neighid |    524         1        4.4        16
   schidXneig~d |  784         1        2.9        14
------------------------------------------------------------
```

```
                                    Wald chi2(0)      =      .
Log restricted-likelihood = -3177.9771   Prob > chi2      =      .
```

```
------------------------------------------------------------------------
    attain |     Coef.   Std. Err.     z    P>|z|   [95% Conf. Interval]
-----------+------------------------------------------------------------
      _cons |  .0744393  .0748152   0.99   0.320   -.0721959   .2210744
------------------------------------------------------------------------
```

```
------------------------------------------------------------------------
 Random-effects Parameters |  Estimate  Std. Err.   [95% Conf. Interval]
---------------------------+--------------------------------------------
_all: Identity             |
          var(R.schid)     |  .0819288  .0352785    .0352297    .19053
---------------------------+--------------------------------------------
neighid: Identity          |
           var(_cons)      |  .0906067  .0335769    .0438252   .1873256
---------------------------+--------------------------------------------
schidXneig~d: Identity     |
           var(_cons)      |  .0684128  .0365626    .0240005   .1950086
---------------------------+--------------------------------------------
          var(Residual)    |  .7819341  .0271391    .7305114   .8369767
------------------------------------------------------------------------
LR test vs. linear regression:      chi2(3) =   214.10   Prob > chi2 = 0.0000
```

Note: LR test is conservative and provided only for reference.

In this model, the between-school variance is 0.082, the between-neighborhood variance is 0.091, the interaction variance is 0.068, and the student variance is 0.782. A comparison between the fit of Model 4 and Model 3 yields a reduction of deviance of 4.15 (4.15 = 6360.10 − 6355.95) for one additional parameter. This gives a p-value (output not shown) of 0.042, suggesting that the random interactions effects are large as well as significant. Model 4 is therefore preferred to Model 3.

Model 5 extends Model 3 by including the student and family background covariates and the neighborhood social deprivation covariate. This model is equivalent to Model 3 in Raudenbush (1993). As discussed above, we choose not to include the random interaction effects in this model, despite finding them to be significant in our Model 4. We do this so that our results remain comparable to those reported by Raudenbush.

```
. xtmixed attain p7vrq p7read male dadocc daded momed dadunemp deprive || _all:
R.schid || neighid:, variance

Performing EM optimization:

Performing gradient-based optimization:

Iteration 0:   log restricted-likelihood = -2421.0934
Iteration 1:   log restricted-likelihood = -2416.7366
Iteration 2:   log restricted-likelihood = -2416.7336
Iteration 3:   log restricted-likelihood = -2416.7336

Computing standard errors:

Mixed-effects REML regression                 Number of obs      =       2310

-----------------------------------------------------------
               |  No. of      Observations per Group
Group Variable |  Groups   Minimum   Average   Maximum
---------------+-------------------------------------------
          _all |       1      2310    2310.0      2310
       neighid |     524         1       4.4        16
-----------------------------------------------------------

                                              Wald chi2(8)       =    2504.87
Log restricted-likelihood = -2416.7336        Prob > chi2        =     0.0000

------------------------------------------------------------------------------
      attain |      Coef.   Std. Err.      z    P>|z|     [95% Conf. Interval]
-------------+----------------------------------------------------------------
       p7vrq |   .0275499   .0022678    12.15   0.000     .023105    .0319948
      p7read |   .0262531   .0017537    14.97   0.000     .022816    .0296903
        male |  -.0559831    .028443    -1.97   0.049    -.1117304   -.0002357
      dadocc |   .0080982   .0013631     5.94   0.000     .0054267    .0107698
       daded |   .1436937   .0408658     3.52   0.000     .0635982    .2237892
       momed |   .0593024   .0374486     1.58   0.113    -.0140956    .1327003
    dadunemp |  -.1210332   .0468652    -2.58   0.010    -.2128874    -.029179
```

```
   deprive |   -.1565115    .0257023    -6.09   0.000    -.2068871   -.1061359
     _cons |    .0858849    .0282789     3.04   0.002     .0304592    .1413105
```

Random-effects Parameters	Estimate	Std. Err.	[95% Conf. Interval]	
_all: Identity				
var(R.schid)	.0043361	.0028664	.0011869	.0158411
neighid: Identity				
var(_cons)	.0038204	.0067428	.0001202	.121464
var(Residual)	.4569292	.014911	.4286191	.4871091

```
LR test vs. linear regression:        chi2(2) =      7.55   Prob > chi2 = 0.0230
```

Note: LR test is conservative and provided only for reference.

In Model 5, the between-school variance is 0.0043, the between-neighborhood variance is 0.0038, and the student variance is 0.457. Comparing these estimates to those in Model 3 reveals that the covariates explain some 95% (−0.947 = (0.0043 − 0.081)/0.081) of school variance in attainment, 97% of neighborhood variance, and 43% of student variance. The covariates clearly have substantial explanatory power, particularly at the school and neighborhood levels.

When examining the fixed-part parameter estimates, it is helpful to recall that attain is approximately standardized and that this allows the effects of covariates to be interpreted in standard deviation units. We see that students who score higher in their age 12 verbal reasoning and reading prior attainment are predicted to have higher attainment at school-leaving age. Boys are predicted to score 0.056 of a standard deviation lower than girls, although this result is only borderline significant ($p = 0.049$). Students whose fathers are in higher social class occupations are predicted to score higher than students with fathers in lower social class occupations. Students whose fathers are educated beyond 15 years of age are predicted to score 0.143 of a standard deviation higher than students with less educated fathers. The corresponding effect for mothers, however, is smaller and not significant. Students whose fathers are unemployed are predicted to score 0.121 of a standard deviation lower than otherwise equivalent students. The final fixed-part parameter estimate is for neighborhood social deprivation. Garner and Raudenbush (1991) used these data to test the hypothesis that a neighborhood's level of social deprivation has a negative effect on a student's educational attainment, even after controlling for the student's prior attainment and family background. We see that this is indeed the case; the significant coefficient of -0.156 shows the importance of neighborhood deprivation in explaining mean neighborhood attainment, even after controlling for the other covariates. Furthermore, by recalling that the standard deviation of `deprive` is 0.622, we are able to calculate that a 1 standard deviation increase in neighborhood social deprivation is associated with a $0.10 (= -0.156 \times 0.622)$ standard deviation decrease in attainment. The magnitude of this effect is approximately twice the gender difference and similar in magnitude to the detrimental effect associated with paternal unemployment. Neighborhood social deprivation therefore has a substantial effect on student attainment as well as a significant effect.

CONCLUSION

An important class of multilevel models are those that involve nonhierarchical data where lower-level units are not strictly nested within single higher-level units. The data analyzed in this chapter involved students nested within both schools and neighborhoods, but where not all students from the same neighborhood attend the same school. Thus, rather than a three-level hierarchy of students within neighborhoods within schools, the data are cross-classified with students nested within the cells of a two-way cross-classification of schools by neighborhoods.

The analyses that we carried out in this chapter set out to quantify the relative importance of schools and neighborhoods as sources of variation in student educational attainment. Models 1 and 2 fitted separate two-level unconditional hierarchical models to estimate the magnitude of school and neighborhood differences in attainment, respectively. Model 3 then fitted a cross-classified multilevel model to simultaneously estimate the magnitude of each of these sources of variation while holding the other source constant. Model 3 revealed that a substantial part of the variation in Model 1 that we described as school variation is better described as neighborhood variation, and similarly a substantial part of the variation in Model 2 that we described as neighborhood variation is better described as school variation. These results highlight the importance of not omitting important sources of variation when carrying out multilevel analyses. Model 3 assumed that the school and neighborhood effects on attainment are additive. However, when we tested this assumption, by comparing Model 4 to Model 3, we found that there are in fact significant random interaction effects between schools and neighborhoods. This suggests that the effectiveness of schools differs for students from different neighborhoods. In other words, some schools are more beneficial for students who live in particular neighborhoods. Having quantified the school-level and neighborhood-level differences in unconditional attainment, our final model sought to explain these differences in terms of a variety of student and family background covariates and a measure of neighborhood social deprivation. The included covariates explain a substantial proportion of the variation at each level. The effect of neighborhood social deprivation on attainment, which was of particular research interest to Garner and Raudenbush (1991), was found to be strongly significant, even after adjusting for the student and family background covariates.

While our analyses focused on students who are cross-classified by schools and neighborhoods, there are many other examples of cross-classified data in educational research. For example, Rasbash, Leckie, Pillinger, and Jenkins (2010) analyze students who are cross-classified by primary schools and secondary schools, as not all students from the same primary school go on to attend the same secondary school. Leckie and Baird (2011) analyze the scores awarded by raters to students' essays. The scores are cross-classified by raters and students, as each rater scores every student and each student is scored by every rater.

Our analyses and the examples given above both involve two-way cross-classifications. However, cross-classified models can be extended to model data with additional classifications. For example, in the most complex models analyzed by Rasbash et al. (2010), students are modeled as nested within a four-way cross-classification of families, primary schools, secondary schools, and neighborhoods. Furthermore, secondary schools are in turn nested within local education authorities (i.e., school districts).

Cross-classified models can also be extended to model data where lower-level units belong to multiple higher-level units at one or more classifications. In the context of our application, when students change schools during secondary schooling, they can be seen as belonging to multiple schools. The contribution of all schools attended during secondary schooling should therefore be modeled, not just the contribution of the final school. Similarly, when students move neighborhoods during secondary schooling, the effects of every neighborhood resided in should be recognized, not just the final neighborhood. In previous work (Leckie, 2009), where we also studied the educational attainment of students who are cross-classified by schools and neighborhoods, we analyzed an extended version of the cross-classified models we have introduced in this chapter, which incorporates multiple membership structures to account for both schooling mobility and residential mobility.

An important issue in fitting cross-classified models with additional classifications and multiple membership structures is that these models are computationally challenging to estimate. This is especially true when using `xtmixed`, as this command is primarily designed for fitting multilevel models to hierarchical rather than nonhierarchical data. Bayesian model fitting using Markov chain Monte Carlo (MCMC) techniques can overcome such limitations. The MLwiN multilevel modeling software package can fit highly complex cross-classified and multiple membership models using MCMC. MLwiN can also be run from within Stata by using the `runmlwin` Stata command (Leckie & Charlton, 2011). Further information can be found at www.bristol.ac.uk/cmm/software/runmlwin/.

NOTES

1. www.bristol.ac.uk/cmm/learning/course.html
2. Online materials to accompany this book chapter can be found at www.bristol.ac.uk/cmm/team/leckie.html. These materials include the data and do-file to replicate all analyses presented in this chapter using Stata.

REFERENCES

Garner, C. L., & Raudenbush, S. W. (1991). Neighborhood effects on educational attainment: A multilevel analysis. *Sociology of Education, 64,* 251–262.

Leckie, G. (2009). The complexity of school and neighbourhood effects and movements of pupils on school differences in models of educational attainment. *Journal of the Royal Statistical Society: Series A, 172,* 537–554.

Leckie, G., & Baird, J.-A. (2011). Rater effects on essay scoring: A multilevel analysis of severity drift, central tendency and rater experience. *Journal of Educational Measurement., 48,* 399-418.

Leckie, G., & Charlton, C. (2011). *Runmlwin: Stata module for fitting multilevel models in the MLwiN software package.* Centre for Multilevel Modelling, University of Bristol.

Rabe-Hesketh, S., & Skrondal, A. (2008). *Multilevel and longitudinal modeling using Stata.* College Station, TX: Stata Corp.

Rasbash, J., Leckie, G., Pillinger, R., & Jenkins, J. (2010). Children's educational progress: Partitioning family, school and area effects. *Journal of the Royal Statistical Society: Series A, 173,* 657–682.

Raudenbush, S. W. (1993). A crossed random effects model for unbalanced data with applications in cross-sectional and longitudinal research. *Journal of Educational and Behavioral Statistics, 18,* 321.

Raudenbush, S. W., & Bryk, A. S. (2002). *Hierarchical linear models: Applications and data analysis methods.* Thousand Oaks, CA: Sage.

StataCorp. (2011). *Stata 12 longitudinal-data/panel-data reference manual.* College Station, TX: Stata Press.

Predicting Future Events From Longitudinal Data With Multivariate Hierarchical Models and Bayes' Theorem Using SAS

15

Larry J. Brant

Shan L. Sheng

The modeling of longitudinal data can be accomplished using models that are known as hierarchical, mixed-effects, multilevel, or random coefficient models, where a common feature is a hierarchy with the basic underlying structure of the measurements being nested within units of measure at a higher level. For example, in a longitudinal study, observed measurements pertaining to heart disease, taken at a series of time points, may be nested within subjects constituting the second level of the hierarchy. Longitudinal studies have shown that some individuals maintain a particular level of a variable over a long period of time, others demonstrate a gradual constant rate of change in the same variable, while yet others show a dramatic decline or increase in the variable over time. The pattern of change need not be the same for different variables for the same unit or individual. In the case of individual health care, an individual may show a greater-than-average increase in blood pressure over time, while maintaining a more gradual and less severe decline in pulmonary function.

Traditionally, classification methods have been based on measurements taken at a single time point or study baseline and have proceeded to make a classification or prediction of an event occurring within a certain follow-up period. These methods have been based on multinomial logistic regression or the proportional hazards regression.

For example, previously presented methods for dealing with the prediction of future events have used survival analysis methodology to develop risk-prediction models (e.g., coronary heart disease prediction scores or general cardiovascular risk profiles from the Framingham Heart Study) based on the Cox proportional hazards model. This approach utilizes data from only a single measurement time or at a study's baseline, and develops a risk equation that is a function of the modifiable predictor variables or risk factors along with other risk variables related to the unit or individual, such as age and sex in an epidemiological study. In addition, one important assumption of the Cox model is that all the risk factors in the model should satisfy the proportionality assumption. This is an assumption that may not be satisfied for continuous predictor variables such as age or another variable that represents a wide range of heterogeneity over its span (Brant et al., 2010).

The proportional hazards model also has the ability to handle risk factors or covariates that can change over time. Such an approach is much more complex than the Cox model with fixed or non–time-dependent covariates, in that it requires constructing a function of time that allows a covariate value to be present for every individual at each time in the follow-up period at which an event occurs. Also, a time-dependent proportional hazards model cannot usually be used to predict survival or the nonoccurrence of an event over time, since the estimated probability of an event occurring is not related to the hazard function in the usual manner. In the time-dependent covariate model, the model depends on the value of a changing quantity or covariate, and these values are usually unknown until they are observed in reality.

Using measurements taken at multiple time points, a method of classification using mixed models has been developed for the classification of individuals into one of several outcome categories such as different preclinical disease states, where categories are based on changes in longitudinally observed biological variables known to be related to the disease. The classification method considers each individual's data on repeated measurements using longitudinal data where there is no prior clinical evidence of the disease in question. This classification method was initially developed for classifying men in regard to prostate cancer using longitudinal prostate-specific antigen (PSA) measurements (Brant et al., 2003), and was further employed to screen for Alzheimer's disease (Brant, Sheng, Morrell, & Zonderman, 2005). In general, the classification method first models the longitudinal measurements for all individuals in the dataset and provides modeled trajectories for all the possible disease-related outcome categories. Using predicted probability density values representing the possible different trajectories, each individual's longitudinal screening data are considered one repeated measurement at a time over the subject's longitudinal follow-up period. Finally, posterior probabilities of the individual being in each of the different disease categories or states are calculated from Bayes' theorem, on the basis of data from other individuals with confirmed diagnoses of being in one of the disease states, and a classification is made on the basis of developed classification criteria.

The mixed-model classification method was initially based on longitudinal measurements from a single known disease marker. Recently, this method has been extended to a multivariate mixed-modeling approach where several disease-related variables can be modeled simultaneously. The classification method illustrated in this chapter is based on this multivariate model (Sheng & Brant, 2009, 2010). Figure 15.1 summarizes the design involved in this classification method for the case of three marker variables. The multivariate mixed model simultaneously models the longitudinal trajectories of all the variables considered in the classification process while accounting for the correlation between and within the measurements for all the variables. As in the case of the univariate classification method, the resulting predicted multivariate probability density values are used to calculate posterior probabilities of each individual being in the event or non-event class or group. These probabilities are calculated at each measurement time for each experimental unit in the dataset, and a decision is made based on a preassigned classification rule to classify the individual unit as a potential event or outcome category.

Figure 15.1 Hypothetical longitudinal data for an experimental unit

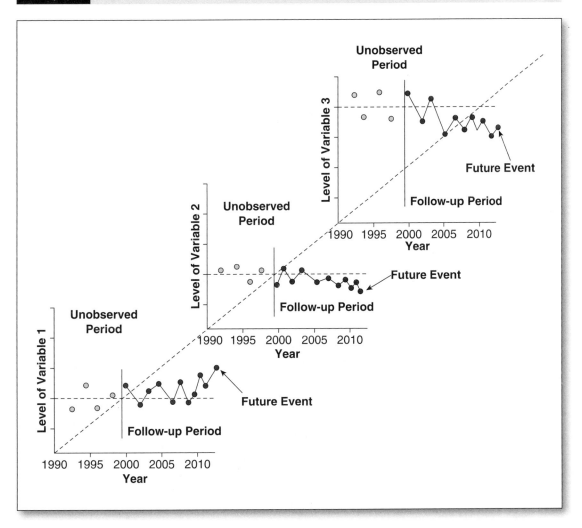

The methodology presented in this chapter can be used to make predictions of future events from data observed in longitudinal studies. For example, a researcher may wish to evaluate the need for governmental services, such as the number of schools, based on observed neighborhood longitudinal trends in births, housing, tax revenues, or other demographic factors while controlling for important neighborhood characteristics. The trends in longitudinally measured variables y can be modeled simultaneously in terms of the classifying variable and other x variables representing demographic or geographic characteristics of each of the governmental subunits used to develop the classification. To illustrate the multivariate hierarchical prediction method, the prediction of overt coronary heart disease (CHD) is given for individuals observed in a long-term longitudinal study based on modeled longitudinal trends in blood pressure, cholesterol, and glucose.

SAMPLE

The Baltimore Longitudinal Study of Aging (BLSA), begun in 1958 and conducted by the Intramural Research Program of the National Institute on Aging, is a cohort study of volunteer participants that is both prospective in the sense that individuals are examined longitudinally over time, and also open, since new participants are continually being enrolled in the study. In general, the participants are predominantly Caucasian; healthy; well-educated; middle- to upper-middle class; and reside in the Baltimore–Washington, D.C., metropolitan area. The BLSA recruits men and women ages 17 to 96 years to participate in repeated medical examinations and assessments of physical and psychological performance. Examinations occur approximately every 2 years during a 2- to 3-day visit to the research center in Baltimore. Participants are given a careful health screening at baseline to ensure that they are in excellent health with no known diseases (Brant et al., 2010).

Data collection follows a standard protocol approved by the Institutional Review Board of the MedStar Research Institute.

- Blood pressure is measured three times in both arms using a mercury sphygmomanometer appropriately sized to the arm of the participant, and the arithmetic mean of the measurements is used in the prediction.
- Mean arterial pressure (MAP in mm Hg) is determined as one third the sum of systolic and twice the diastolic blood pressure.
- Cholesterol and glucose measurements are both taken from fasting serum samples and are measured in mg/dl.
- Overt CHD is used as the study endpoint or final event and is defined as cardiac death or nonfatal myocardial infarction (MI). Cardiac death is defined by death due to acute MI, congestive heart failure, or a sudden death not due to another cause. Nonfatal MI includes clinical, characterized by chest pain accompanied by serial electrocardiogram (ECG) changes or enzyme elevation, or silent, characterized by Q-wave abnormalities on resting ECG (Minnesota codes 1:1 or 1:2) with confirmation by an independent BLSA cardiologist who reviews all ECG results.

The sample used for illustration of the multivariate prediction method consists of 892 males with 164 observed overt CHD events, during a maximum study period of 26 years.

SOFTWARE AND PROCEDURE

For the CHD prediction example, there are two classification groups, CHD and no CHD. The number of visits (visit) or repeated measurements for the 892 males studied ranged from 2 to 26 visits with a median of 5 visits. The software used in the classification is the SAS procedure MIXED that is adapted for the multivariate linear mixed-effects (MLME) regression for the three dependent variables: mean arterial pressure (map), total serum cholesterol (chol), and serum glucose (glu). Table 15.1 gives the annotated SAS computer code or program for the prediction of CHD based on PROC MIXED and Bayes' theorem. The program can also be found at www.grc.nia.nih.gov/branches/rrb/ Trivariate MLME SAS Program.doc. Basically, the program consists of three main parts: (a) fitting the multivariate

Table 15.1	Annotated SAS Computer Code for Multivariate Mixed-Model Prediction of CHD Using MAP, Cholesterol, and Glucose

*Step 1: Name the SAS working file "a," and input the eight variables used in the prediction from the previously created file "multivar," which includes ID (id), visit or observation number (visit), age at the first visit (fage), the follow-up time (time), CHD status (chd), as well as the predictor (dependent) variables mean arterial pressure (map), cholesterol (chol), and glucose (glu);
data a; infile multivar; input id visit fage time map chol glucose chd;

*Step 2: Sort the data by id and by visit within id;
proc sort data = a; by id visit; run;

*Step 3: Set up the three sets of variables for the multivariate analysis assigning y to map, chol and glu, adding the index variable (var) with values 1, 2, and 3 corresponding to map, chol, and glu, respectively, and using the prefixes of m, c, and g for the MAP, cholesterol, and glucose x (independent) variables, respectively;
data map; set a; var = 1; y = map; mint = 1; mfage = fage; mtime = mtime; mchd = chd;
keep id visit var y mint mfage mtime mchd; run;
data chol; set a; var = 2; y = chol; cint = 1; cfage = fage; ctime = time; cchd = chd;
keep id visit var y cint cfage ctime cchd; run;
data glu; set a; var = 3; y = glucose; gint = 1; gfage = fage; gtime = time; gchd = chd;
keep id visit var y gint gfage gtime gchd; run;

(Continued)

Table 15.1   (Continued)

*Step 4: Create the SAS working file "multlme" by stacking up the three datasets of "map", "chol," and "glu" defined in Step 3 with the "set" statement. For var = 1 (map) replace "." with "0" for all x variables with prefix of "c" or "g," for var = 2 (chol) replace "." with "0" for all x variables with prefix "m" or "g," and for var = 3 (glu) replace "." with "0" for all x variables with prefix "m" or "c";data multlme; set map chol glu; by id; if mint = . then mint = 0; if cint = . then cint = 0; if gint = . then gint = 0; if mfage = . then mfage = 0; if cfage = . then cfage = 0; if gfage = . then gfage = 0;   if mtime = . then mtime = 0; if ctime = . then ctime = 0; if gtime = . then gtime = 0; if mchd = . then mchd = 0; if cchd = . then cchd = 0; if gchd = . then gchd = 0;
if y = . then delete; run;

*Step 5: Use the MIXED procedure to run the hierarchical multivariate mixed model (MLME) for MAP, cholesterol, and glucose where the method of computation is chosen to be restricted maximum likelihood (REML), the data are "multlme" created in Step 4, the option noclprint is chosen so that the class or id numbers will not be listed on the PROC MIXED output, and the maximum iterations for convergence are limited to 200 (maxiter = 200);
proc mixed method = reml data = multlme noclprint maxiter = 200;
where var in (1, 2, 3); class id var visit;
model y = mint mfage mtime mtime*mtime mfage*mtime mfage*mtime*mtime mchd   mchd*mtime cint cfage ctime ctime*ctime cfage*ctime cchd cchd*cfage cchd*ctime cchd*ctime*ctime gint gfage gtime gtime*gtime gfage*gtime gfage*gtime*gtime gchd gchd*gtime / s noint;
random mint mtime mtime*mtime cint ctime ctime*ctime gint gtime gtime*gtime
/ subject = id type = un g; repeated var / subject = id*visit type = un;
ods output covparms = covb solutionF = betahat G = D;

*Step 6: Output and save the fixed-effects estimates of the betas, the variance-covariance matrix for the random effects D, and variance estimates needed in the calculations of the posterior probabilities for the classification or prediction of CHD;
 data betahat; set betahat; keep estimate; run; data covb; set covb; keep estimate; run;
data D; set D; keep col1 col2 col3 col4 col5 col6; run;

*Step 7: Set up the SAS data "p" based on "multlme" by adding a subject index variable (intid), e.g., intid = 1 for the first individual in the data file, and forming the variable "chd" for the set "p" derived from variables mchd, cchd, and gchd;
data id; set multlme; by id; if first.id; keep id; run;
data id; set id; intid=_n_; run; data p; merge id multlme; by id; chd = mchd + cchd + gchd; run; data p; set p; where var in (1, 2, 3); run;

*Step 8: Create SAS macro procedure "mvn" to calculate the marginal probabilities from the mixed model for each individual where x represents the input (observed) variables y, mu is the predicted (average) value of y, S is the estimated variance components using the mixed-model estimates from Step 5, and f is the computed (output) marginal probabilities;
%macro mvn(x, mu, S, f); p=nrow(&x); twopi=6.283185307;
&f=1./(twopi**(p/2)*sqrt(det(&S)))*exp(-0.5*(&x-&mu)`*inv(&S)*(&x-&mu));
%mend mvn;

*Step 9: Create the SAS macro procedure "postp" to calculate marginal probabilities of CHD occurring by looping over the subjects in the study from subject number 1 to subject number 892;
%macro *postp*; %do subi = 1 %to 892; %let first = 1;

*Step 9.1: Select the subset of the data "sub_i" for subject i;
data sub_i; set p; if intid = &subi; run;

*Step 9.2: Generate variable "numvis" giving the number of visits for subject i in data "sub_i";
data p1; set sub_i; if var = 1; run; data nvis; set p1; by id visit; retain numvis;
if first.id then numvis = 0; numvis = numvis+1; if last.id; keep id numvis; run;
data sub_i; merge sub_i nvis; by id; run;

*Step 9.3: Read the estimates derived from the mixed model and all data for subject i;
proc iml; use betahat; read all into betahat;
close betahat; use covb; read all into varcomp; close covb;
s11= VarComp[46] ; s12= VarComp[47] ; s22= VarComp[48] ;
s31= VarComp[49] ; s32= VarComp[50] ; s33= VarComp[51] ;
row1 = s11 || s12 || s31; row2 = s12 || s22 || s32;
row3 = s31 || s32 || s33; SIGMA = row1 // row2 // row3; use D; read all into covb;
close D; use sub_i; read all var {id visit y mfage mtime cfage ctime gfage gtime chd numvis};
close sub_i;

*Step 9.4: Loop over repeated observations within subject I, and form the matrices for later multivariate calculations;
nvisi = numvis[1]; postmat=shape(0, nvisi, 2); do j=1 to nvisi; int=J(j,1,1);
zero=J(j,1,0); yj=y[1:j] // y[1+nvisi:nvisi+j] // y[1+2*nvisi:2*nvisi+j] ;
mint= int // zero // zero ;
mfagej=mfage[1:j] // mfage[1+nvisi:nvisi+j] //mfage[1+2*nvisi:2*nvisi+j] ;
mf2=mfagej#mfagej;
mtimej=mtime[1:j] // mtime[1+nvisi:nvisi+j] // mtime[1+2*nvisi:2*nvisi+j] ;
mt2=mtimej#mtimej; mft=mfagej#mtimej; mf2t=mf2#mtimej; mft2=mfagej#mt2;
cint= zero // int // zero;
cfagej=cfage[1:j] // cfage[1+nvisi:nvisi+j] // cfage[1+2*nvisi:2*nvisi+j] ;
cf2=cfagej#cfagej;
ctimej=ctime[1:j] // ctime[1+nvisi:nvisi+j] // ctime[1+2*nvisi:2*nvisi+j] ;
ct2=ctimej#ctimej; cft=cfagej#ctimej; cf2t=cf2#ctimej; cft2=cfagej#ct2;
gint= zero // zero // int;
gfagej=gfage[1:j] // gfage[1+nvisi:nvisi+j] // gfage[1+2*nvisi:2*nvisi+j] ;
gf2=gfagej#gfagej;
gtimej=gtime[1:j] // gtime[1+nvisi:nvisi+j] // gtime[1+2*nvisi:2*nvisi+j] ;
gt2=gtimej#gtimej; gft=gfagej#gtimej; gf2t=gf2#gtimej; gft2=gfagej#gt2;
zero=J(3*j,1,0);
Xicon = mint || mfagej || mtimej || mt2 || mft || mft2 || zero || zero ||
        cint || cfagej || ctimej || ct2 || cft || zero || zero || zero || zero ||
        gint || gfagej || gtimej || gt2 || gft || gft2 || zero || zero;

(Continued)

Table 15.1 (Continued)

Xichd = mint || mfagej || mtimej || mt2 || mft || mft2 || mint || mtimej ||
    cint || cfagej || ctimej || ct2 || cft || cint || cfagej || ctimej || ct2||
    gint || gfagej || gtimej || gt2 || gft || gft2 || gint || gtimej;
Zi = mint || mtimej || mt2 || cint || ctimej || ct2 || gint || gtimej || gt2;

*Step 9.5: Compute marginal means and covariance matrices for subject i at visit j with regard to the non-CHD and CHD classification groups, respectively;
mucon = Xicon*betahat; muchd = Xichd*betahat;
SI = SIGMA @ diag(int); V = Zi * covb * Zi` + SI;

*Step 9.6: Compute the marginal probabilities for subject i at visit j being in the non-CHD (fcon) and CHD (fchd) groups using the SAS macro "mvn" created in Step 8;
%mvn(yj, mucon, V, fcon); %mvn(yj, muchd, V, fchd);
postmat[j,1]=fcon; postmat[j,2]=fchd; end;

*Step 9.7: Finish looping within subject i;
create post_prob from postmat; append from postmat ; close post_prob; quit;

*Step 9.8: Finish looping over all subjects;
%if &subi = &first %then %do; data pp; set post_prob; run;
%end; %else %do; data pp; set pp post_prob; run; %end; %end;

*Step 9.9: Save marginal probabilities in the file "pp" for later use;
%mend postp; proc printto log = logfile new; run; %postp; proc printto; run;

*Step 10: Read the data for the marginal probabilities previously derived for all subjects;
data mtemp.pp_blsa_MCG_post; set pp; run;

*Step 11: Format the table necessary to display the various classification-related quantities such as sensitivity, specificity, TPP (true proportion positive), etc.;
data s0; input TPP TPN FPP FPN TrueP TrueN PredP PredN Sensitivity Specificity One_Spec Accuracy Distance PPV NPV; datalines; 0 0 0 0 0 0 0 0 0 0 0 0 0 0 0 ; run;

*Step 12: Set up the SAS macro procedure "ss" to compute the posterior probabilities using Bayes' theorem with prior probability 0.5, and probability cut points for the classification ranging from 0.24 to 0.75 with 0.05 increments;
%macro ss(data, prior, start, end, by, eval); %let prior = &prior;
%do c = &start %to &end %by &by; %let cutoff = %sysevalf(&c/&eval);

*Step 12.1: Combine the data of marginal probabilities from the mixed model by CHD status, and calculate the posterior probabilities "postchd" as a function of the prior probabilities and the marginal probabilities for all patients using Bayes' theorem;

```
data pp; set mtemp.&data; run; data ids; set b; keep id chd; run; data pp; merge ids pp;
fcon=COL1; fchd=COL2; priorchd = %sysevalf(&prior); priorcon=1-priorchd;
postchd = priorchd*fchd/(priorcon*fcon+priorchd*fchd);
drop col1 col2; run;
```

*Step 12.2: Create the SAS data "predict" necessary for the computations of sensitivity, 1 – specificity, accuracy, distance, etc., at each cut point for all subjects;

```
data id1; set ids; by id; if first.id; run; data pred; set pp; by id; if postchd>&cutoff;
pchd = 1; run; data predict; set pred; by id; if first.id; run;
data predict; merge id1 predict; by id; if pchd = . then pchd = 0; run; data d1;
set predict; proc means noprint; class CHD PCHD; var id; output out = d2;  run;
data c (keep = pchd chd N); set d2; if _STAT_ = "N"; if pchd ne . and chd ne .;
rename _FREQ_ = N; run; data TPP (keep = TPP); set c; if pchd = 1 and chd = 1;
rename N = TPP; run; data TPN (keep = TPN); set c; if pchd = 0 and chd = 0;
rename N = TPN; run; data FPP (keep = FPP); set c; if pchd = 1 and chd = 0;
rename N = FPP; run; data FPN (keep = FPN); set c; if pchd = 0 and chd = 1;
rename N = FPN; run; data table; merge TPP TPN FPP FPN;
```

*Step 12.3: Compute sensitivity, specificity, accuracy, distance, and other quantities summarizing the classification results of all subjects;

```
TrueP = TPP + FPN; TrueN = TPN + FPP; PredP = TPP + FPP; PredN = FPN + TPN;
Sensitivity = TPP/TrueP; Specificity = TPN/TrueN; One_Spec = 1 - Specificity;
X = 1-Specificity; Accuracy = (TPP+TPN)/(TrueP+TrueN);
Distance = sqrt((1-Sensitivity)*(1-Sensitivity)+(1-Specificity)*(1-Specificity));
PPV = TPP/PredP; NPV = TPN/PredN;
CPT = symget('cutoff'); run;  proc freq data = predict noprint; tables pchd*chd;
title2 Actual vs. Predicted CHD: Prior = &Prior , Cutoff = &cutoff ; run;
data prediction; set s0 table; if TPP = 0 and TPN = 0 then delete; run;
data s0; set prediction; run; %end; %mend ss;
%ss(pp_blsa_MCG_post, 0.5, 24, 74, 5, 100);
```

*Step 13: Display CHD prediction results of sensitivity, specificity, accuracy, distance, etc., for all subjects based on the posterior probabilities at each of the cut points ranging from 0.24 to 0.74 by increments of 0.05;

```
data mtemp.pred; set prediction; rename trueP = TOP; rename trueN = TON;
Sensitivity = round(Sensitivity, 0.01);  One_Spec = round(One_Spec, 0.01);
Distance = round(Distance, 0.0001); Accuracy = round(Accuracy, 0.01);
options nodate; options pageno = 1;
title 'Results of Predictions based on posterior prob. for pp_blsa_MCG';
title2 'TPP - Correctly predicted positive, TPN - Correctly predicted negative';
title3 'TOP - True observed positive, TON - True observed negative';
title4 'CPT - Cutoff point'; proc print;
var TPP TPN TOP TON Sensitivity One_Spec Accuracy Distance CPT; run;
```

mixed model using all the data for every individual, (b) computing the marginal probabilities based on the mixed-model results at every observation time (visit) for each individual in the dataset, and (c) computing the posterior probabilities at every visit for each individual using Bayes' theorem and using these probabilities to classify all the individuals into the CHD and non-CHD classification groups.

Before the program can be executed, a dataset needs to be created, similar to the data illustrated in Table 15.2, where the data are given for a non-CHD case (unit id = 015) and a CHD case (unit id = 031). In Steps 1 through 4 of the program, the data are entered corresponding to the three dependent variables, mean arterial pressure (map), cholesterol (chol), and glucose (glu), to be used in the multivariate analysis (Step 1), and sorted by id and visit (Step 2). Then, the dependent and independent variables are created (Step 3) and organized to be put into a multivariate array format "multlme" for the regression analysis (Step 4). In Step 5, the MIXED procedure in SAS is run for the multivariate linear mixed model (MLME) where the covariates or independent variables for

| Table 15.2 | Individual Observed Data for Individual or Unit ID Numbers 015 and 031* |

Unit ID	Visit	FAge	Time	MAP	Chol	Glucose	CHD
015	1	51.0	0	88.0	195	94	0
015	2	51.0	2.72	86.7	186	98	0
015	3	51.0	8.98	83.3	189	106	0
015	4	51.0	12.83	80.7	185	103	0
015	5	51.0	14.91	94.0	199	101	0
015	6	51.0	18.98	98.7	176	102	0
015	7	51.0	21.04	96.7	166	100	0
⋮	⋮	⋮	⋮	⋮	⋮	⋮	⋮
031	1	61.6	0	98.0	143	108	1
031	2	61.6	3.22	83.3	193	107	1
031	3	61.6	6.65	96.7	204	108	1
031	4	61.6	8.65	100.0	204	107	1
031	5	61.6	12.75	110.0	209	119	1
031	6	61.6	16.75	101.3	181	115	1
031	7	61.6	18.75	94.7	149	122	1

*First age (FAge) and Time are measured in years, MAP in mm Hg, Cholesterol (Chol) and Glucose in mg/dl, and CHD = 0 (non-CHD case) or 1 (CHD case).

the three dependent variables have the prefixes "m" for map, "c" for cholesterol, and "g" for glucose. In examples representing longitudinal measurements
of persons, first age (fage), time, and the diagnostic group (CHD) are present
along with necessary interaction terms involving these variables (e.g.,
cchd*cfage and cchd*ctime in the model statement of Step 5). Note that the
choice of the fixed effects given in the model statement, along with the choice
of the random effects given in the random statement, need not be the same for
each of the three dependent variables. Also, note that a random term for intercept
(int) is usually chosen, since its variance represents the between-subject or -
persons variability.

Step 6 of the program saves all the MLME estimates in files to be used in later
computations, while Step 7 organizes the working file "multlme" by a subject
index variable (intid) in preparation of the classification of subjects by CHD
status. Step 8 creates the SAS macro "mvn" to calculate the marginal probabilities for each subject based on the normal distribution assumptions for the linear
mixed model. The calculation of all the marginal probabilities for each of the 892
subjects at all visits is accomplished using the SAS macro "postp" created in Step 9
and its nine subsequent Substeps 9.1 through 9.9. After setting up the subject
id (Step 9.1) and visits (Step 9.2), Step 9.3 reads the MLME estimates and the
data for subject i, while Step 9.4 loops over the repeated measurements j for
subject i and creates the necessary matrices for the marginal means and covariances with regard to the non-CHD and CHD classification groups (Step 9.5). Step
9.6 gives the marginal classification probabilities (fcon and fchd) using the multivariate normal SAS macro "mvn" created in Step 8, Steps 9.7 and 9.8 finish
looping over all visits within a subject and all subjects, and Step 9.9 saves the
marginal probabilities in the temporary file "pp" for later reference.

In Step 10, all the marginal probabilities are read and saved as "pp_blsa_MCG"
in the folder "mtemp." Step 11 formats the 15 classification-related quantities to
be summarized into a table from the classification of all subjects. A SAS macro
"ss" is set up in Step 12 to compute the posterior probabilities from the marginal
probabilities using Bayes' theorem with the indifference prior 0.5 for non-CHD
and CHD ranging over the posterior probability cut points of 0.24 to 0.75 by 0.05.
A classification is performed at each of these cut points from which is generated
a receiver operating characteristic (ROC) curve. Note that Step 12.1 combines the
marginal probabilities from the MLME model by CHD status (fcon for a control
or non-CHD case and fchd for a CHD case) and computes the posterior probabilities (postchd) for all subjects.

Using the prior probabilities (priorcon for the non-CHD group and priorchd for
the CHD group), Bayes' theorem or formula for the posterior probability of being in
the CHD group is given by postchd = (priorchd × fchd) / (priorcon × fcon + priorchd
× fchd). Step 12.2 uses the posterior probabilities to create the dataset "predict" for
the classification results, and Step 12.3 computes all of the classification-related
quantities over the entire range of cut points. For example, sensitivity = TPP / (TPP +
FPN) where TPP and FPN are the number of correctly and incorrectly predicted

CHD cases, respectively. Also, specificity = TPN / (TPN + FPP) where TPN and FPP are the number of correctly and incorrectly predicted non-CHD cases, respectively. In addition, the proportion of correctly classified individuals is given by accuracy = (TPP + TPN) / (TPP + FPN + TPN + FPP). Finally, Step 13 prints out or displays all the quantities associated with the classification in the table "Results of Predictions based on posterior prob. for pp_blsa_MCG."

ANALYZING THE DATA

For the case of using the three predictor variables MAP, cholesterol, and glucose to predict CHD, the estimates needed for the individual marginal probabilities related to CHD status are obtained by fitting the MLME model

$$y_{ijgs} = \beta_{0gs} + \beta_{1gs}t_{ij} + \beta_{2gs}t_{ij}^2 + \beta_{3gs}Fage_i + \beta_{4gs}Fage_i t_{ij} + \beta_{5gs}Fage_i t_{ij}^2 +$$
$$b_{0is} + b_{1is}t_{ij} + b_{2is}t_{ij}^2 + \varepsilon_{ijgs} , i = 1, \ldots , N, j = 1, \ldots , n_i, g = 1,2 \text{ and } s = 1,2,3.$$

Note that $Fage_i$ represents the starting age of unit (individual) i, and t_{ij} is the time in years since the start of observation. In addition to the indices i and j representing individuals and time, respectively, the index g represents the diagnostic group (g = 1 for non-CHD, 2 for CHD), and s represents the predictor variable (s = 1 for MAP, 2 for cholesterol, 3 for glucose). Using the individual marginal probabilities from this model, the posterior probabilities of being a CHD case are then calculated from Bayes' theorem as described above in Step 12 of the procedure.

OUTPUT AND ANALYSIS

Coronary heart disease (CHD) is a major health concern in many populations, with CHD occurring in approximately 50% of middle-aged American men during their lifetime. Thus, for the analysis presented in this chapter, the prior probability of CHD for the 892 males examined was taken to be 0.5 (prior = priorcon = priorchd, Step 12.1). In many applications, the user may wish to choose the prior probability of 0.5, since this represents the so-called indifference prior. Also, our experience has shown that the classification results using the posterior probability are relatively insensitive to the choice of the prior. For example, in previous work, prior probabilities were taken on an individual basis, with each person's computed posterior probabilities used as his prior for the next occurring longitudinal measurements. These classification results were similar to those using an indifference prior.

Table 15.3 gives the fixed-effects estimates for the MLME classification or prediction model given above and corresponds to the "betahat" statement of the SAS model described in Step 5 of Table 15.1. For example, using the estimates from the table, the predicted mean levels of MAP (mean arterial pressure), cholesterol, and glucose for a 60-year-old at baseline (Fage = 60 and t = 0) are

Table 15.3	Fixed Effects Estimates for the Trivariate Prediction Model Using Mean Arterial Pressure (MAP), Cholesterol, and Glucose to Predict Coronary Heart Disease (CHD)

		MAP (mm Hg)			Cholesterol (mg/dl)			Glucose (mg/dl)		
Group	Effect	Estimate	Std. Error	P-Value	Estimate	Std. Error	P-Value	Estimate	Std. Error	P-Value
Non-CHD	Intercept	81.501	1.22	<.0001	177.40	4.30	<.0001	86.99	1.61	<.0001
	Time	1.478	0.199	<.0001	0.462	0.301	<0.135	1.351	0.264	<.0001
	Time^2	−0.031	0.0076	<.0001	0.0120	0.0061	0.0486	−0.040	0.0097	<.0001
	Fage	0.269	0.024	<.0001	0.471	0.088	<.0001	0.241	0.0328	<.0001
	Fage×Time	−0.026	0.0041	<.0001	−0.0366	0.0056	<.0001	−0.027	0.0056	<.0001
	Fage×Time^2	0.00047	0.0002	0.0051				0.00082	0.0002	0.0002
CHD	Intercept	84.841	0.798	<.0001	239.61	12.36	<.0001	87.72	1.93	<.0001
	Time	0.175	0.062	0.0049	1.087	0.386	0.005	1.675	0.089	<.0001
	Time^2	−0.031	0.0076	<.0001	−0.052	0.017	0.002	−0.040	0.0097	<.0001
	Fage	0.269	0.024	<.0001	−0.316	0.036	<.0001	0.241	0.0328	<.0001
	Fage×Time	−0.026	0.0041	<.0001	−0.0366	0.0056	<.0001	−0.027	0.0056	<.0001
	Fage×Time^2	0.00047	0.0002	0.0051				0.00082	0.0002	0.0002

97.6 mm Hg, 205.7 mg/dl, and 101.5 mg/dl, respectively, for the non-CHD group and 101.0 mmHg, 220.7 mg/dl, and 102.2 mg/dl, respectively, for the CHD group. (For instance, a 1-unit increase in Fage increases MAP by 0.269 above the intercept baseline, so a 60-year increase augments the baseline by 60 * 0.269 = 16.1, making the estimate 81.5 + 16.1 = 97.6 for mean arterial pressure for a 60-year-old at time 0).

The top portion of Table 15.4 provides all variance and covariance estimates of the nine random effects (b_{0is}, b_{1is} and b_{2is}, s = 1,2,3) for MAP (s = 1), cholesterol (s = 2), and glucose (s = 3) in the MLME model. These estimates are generated as a result of the "output covparms = covb" statement of the SAS model given in Step 5 of Table 15.1. For example, the variance estimates for the three random effects of the intercepts b_{0i1}, b_{0i2}, and b_{0i3}, which represent the between-person variability for MAP, cholesterol, and glucose, are 67.04, 930.78, and 107.25, respectively. Also, for example, the covariance estimate between b_{0i2} (the random effect of intercept for cholesterol) and b_{1i1} (the random effect of time for MAP) is 7.058, and the covariance estimate between b_{0i2} (the random effect of intercept for cholesterol) and b_{2i3} (the random effect of Time^2 for glucose) is 0.0354. In addition, the bottom portion of Table 15.4 gives variance and covariance estimates for the measurement errors corresponding to the three variables used in the classification of CHD. Note that the measurement error variance estimates for MAP, cholesterol, and glucose are $\hat{\sigma}^2_{\varepsilon 1}$ = 77.56,

Table 15.4 The Covariance Matrix (top) of Random Effects for MAP Intercept, MAP Time, MAP Time^2, Cholesterol Intercept, Cholesterol Time, Cholesterol Time^2, Glucose Intercept, Glucose Time, and Glucose Time^2, as Well as the Covariance Matrix (bottom) for the Measurement Errors of MAP, Cholesterol, and Glucose, for the Trivariate Prediction Model Using MAP, Cholesterol, and Glucose

$$
\begin{bmatrix}
67.04 & -2.34 & 0.033 & 3.65 & 1.35 & -0.087 & 22.03 & -1.46 & 0.062 \\
-2.34 & 0.586 & -0.014 & 7.058 & -0.284 & 0.0058 & -2.399 & 0.269 & -0.008 \\
0.033 & -0.014 & 0.0004 & -0.200 & 0.0132 & -0.0003 & 0.0611 & -0.0051 & 0.0002 \\
3.65 & 7.058 & -0.200 & 930.78 & -9.858 & -0.423 & 49.767 & 0.715 & 0.0354 \\
1.35 & -0.284 & 0.0132 & -9.858 & 3.981 & -0.113 & -6.477 & 0.246 & -0.0053 \\
-0.087 & 0.0058 & -0.0003 & -0.423 & -0.113 & 0.0046 & 0.1398 & -0.0104 & 0.0001 \\
22.03 & -2.399 & 0.0611 & 49.767 & -6.477 & 0.1398 & 107.25 & -3.903 & 0.1586 \\
-1.46 & 0.269 & -0.0051 & 0.715 & 0.246 & -0.0104 & -3.903 & 1.261 & -0.0343 \\
0.062 & -0.008 & 0.0002 & 0.0354 & -0.0053 & 0.0001 & 0.1586 & -0.0343 & 0.0011
\end{bmatrix}
$$

$$
\begin{bmatrix}
77.56 & 8.76 & 4.02 \\
8.76 & 451.71 & 8.98 \\
4.02 & 8.98 & 53.41
\end{bmatrix}
$$

$\hat{\sigma}^2_{\varepsilon 2} = 451.71$, and $\hat{\sigma}^2_{\varepsilon 3} = 53.41$, respectively. Also, for example, the estimate of the covariance between ε_{i1} and ε_{i3} (the unexplained error terms for MAP and glucose) for each unit i is 4.02.

The output of the SAS program given in Table 15.1 for the posterior probability estimates that are computed by the macro "ss" given in Step 12 and printed as output in Step 13 is illustrated in Table 15.5. Shown in the table are the classification results for three units or individuals. The first six lines of the table are the results for the first two individuals who are known to be coronary heart disease (CHD = 1) cases. For example, using the simple classification rule of stopping when the individual's posterior probability exceeds the cutoff point of 0.5 (i.e., postchd > 0.5), the first individual (unit ID number 001) is correctly classified as a CHD case at his fourth (row 4) examination visit (postchd = 0.504). Using the same simple rule, the unit ID number 002 is correctly classified as a CHD case at his second visit (postchd = 0.648). Note that the user of this program can devise a classification or stopping rule that best meets his or her needs. Alternatively, the classification rule could be based on results of sensitivity (the proportion of CHD cases correctly classified or the true positive rate) and 1 − specificity (the proportion

	Unit ID Number	CHD	fcon	fchd	priorchd	priorcon	postchd
Table 15.5		Sample Classification Results for Three Different Individuals or Study Units					
1	001	1	2.75E-6	2.65E-6	0.5	0.5	0.491
2	001	1	4.32E-11	4.25E-11	0.5	0.5	0.496
3	001	1	1.06E-15	1.02E-15	0.5	0.5	0.490
4	001	1	1.75E-20	1.78E-20	0.5	0.5	0.504
5	002	1	1.01E-5	7.74E-6	0.5	0.5	0.434
6	002	1	6.95E-12	1.28E-11	0.5	0.5	0.648
⋮	⋮	⋮	⋮	⋮	⋮	⋮	⋮
43	015	0	9.73E-6	5.85E-6	0.5	0.5	0.375
44	015	0	8.88E-11	6.51E-11	0.5	0.5	0.423
45	015	0	8.63E-16	5.86E-16	0.5	0.5	0.404
46	015	0	1.48E-20	8.46E-21	0.5	0.5	0.364
47	015	0	3.13E-25	1.77E-25	0.5	0.5	0.361
48	015	0	5.11E-30	3.73E-30	0.5	0.5	0.422
49	015	0	1.05E-34	9.29E-35	0.5	0.5	0.469

of non-CHD cases incorrectly classified or false positive rate), summarized in a receiver operating characteristic (ROC) curve.

For example, the classification rule could be chosen as the posterior probability cutoff point (CPT) that minimizes the distance between the ROC curve and the point (0,1) on the y-axis of the ROC graph. This minimum distance jointly optimizes the errors in classification represented by sensitivity and 1 – specificity (see below). Additional information on this matter can be obtained from the authors' previous publications (Brant et al., 2003; Sheng & Brant, 2009, 2010). Table 15.5 also shows the classification results based on the simple rule mentioned above for an individual or unit ID number 015 who is a non-CHD case that was correctly classified as a non-CHD case using all of his examination or visit data (postchd <= 0.50 for all visits). It should be noted that the classification procedure presented here is longitudinal in nature, and that by comparing an individual's trends in MAP, cholesterol, and glucose to age-specific population trends for the different classification groups, which in this case is only two (non CHD and CHD), posterior probabilities are computed using Bayes' formula (see Step 12 in the SAS code in Table 15.1), along with the prior and corresponding estimated marginal probability distribution function (pdf) values.

Receiver operating characteristic analysis can be used to evaluate the accuracy of the classification method. A more complete discussion of ROC analysis using SAS can be found at http://pharmasug.org/download/papers/SP09.pdf. Also, in SPSS 19, ROC analysis is a selection under the "Analyze" menu option. The classification results using the posterior probabilities from the MLME model computed at all visits or examinations for each individual or unit needed for the ROC analysis are illustrated in Table 15.5. These results for all individuals are used to construct an ROC curve and are summarized in Table 15.6 where the cutoff points (CTP) for the posterior probabilities of being a CHD case range from 0.24 to 0.74. The corresponding points x = 1 − specificity (One_Spec) and y = sensitivity (Sensitivity) can be plotted using commercially available software such as SigmaPlot® 11 of Systat Software, Inc. The y-axis (Sensitivity, which is the percentage of true positive classifications) represents the true positive rate, and the x-axis (1 − specificity, where specificity is the percentage of true negative classifications) represents the false positive rate of classification for different cutoff points. The x = 0, y = 1 point in the upper left of Figure 15.2 is the point of perfect discrimination in classification, with 100% sensitivity and 100% specificity. The closer the ROC curve is to this (0,1) point, the better the classification model.

Table 15.6	Output of SAS Program for Multivariate Mixed-Model Prediction of CHD Using MAP, Cholesterol, and Glucose

Results of Predictions based on posterior prob. for pp_blsa_MCG
TPP—Corrected predicted positive, TPN—Corrected predicted negative
TOP—True observed positive, TON—True observed negative
CPT—Cutoff point

Obs TPP TPN TOP TON Sensitivity One_Spec Accuracy Distance CPT

Obs	TPP	TPN	TOP	TON	Sensitivity	One_Spec	Accuracy	Distance	CPT
1	163	114	164	728	0.99	0.84	0.31	0.8434	0.24
2	160	165	164	728	0.98	0.77	0.36	0.7737	0.29
3	155	225	164	728	0.95	0.69	0.43	0.6931	0.34
4	146	295	164	728	0.89	0.59	0.49	0.6048	0.39
5	136	366	164	728	0.83	0.50	0.56	0.5257	0.44
6	121	438	164	728	0.74	0.40	0.63	0.4769	0.49
7	103	505	164	728	0.63	0.31	0.68	0.4818	0.54
8	86	559	164	728	0.52	0.23	0.72	0.5292	0.59
9	66	613	164	728	0.40	0.16	0.76	0.6181	0.64
10	49	636	164	728	0.30	0.13	0.77	0.7125	0.69
11	36	669	164	728	0.22	0.08	0.79	0.7847	0.74

Figure 15.2	Receiver operating characteristic curve for the prediction of coronary heart disease using longitudinal measurements of mean arterial pressure (MAP), cholesterol, and glucose

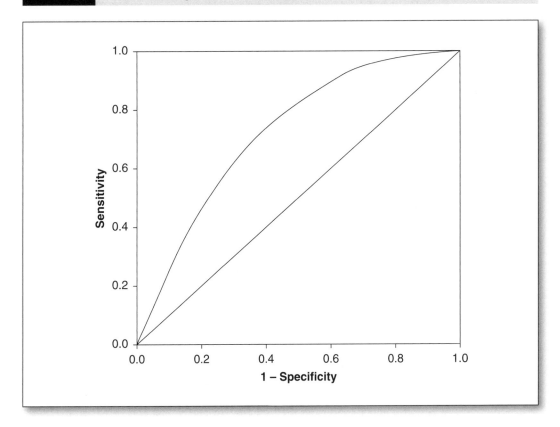

Likewise, the greater the area under the ROC curve, above and beyond the 0.50 level represented by the 45-degree line in Figure 15.2, the better the classification model.

From the resulting plot of the ROC graph shown in Figure 15.2, the minimum distance from the curve to the point (0,1) on the y-axis mentioned above represents approximately a sensitivity of 0.70 and a specificity of 0.65 (1 – specificity = 0.35 on the x-axis), which occurs for the posterior probability CTP = 0.52 (Distance = 0.4653). This refined value of the CTP between lines 6 and 7 in Table 15.6 can be found by running the "ss" macro and changing the last line of Step 12.2 to be "%ss(pp_blsa_MCG_post, 0.5, 49, 54, 1, 100)," which will generate results for cutoff values 0.49, 0.50, 0.51, 0.52, 0.53, and 0.54. Note that the distance between the ROC curve value (0.35, 0.70) corresponding to cutoff 0.52 and the (0,1) point of perfect discrimination is obtained by using the distance formula between two points in the x-y plane and is given by the statement "Distance = sqrt((1 − Sensitivity)*(1 − Sensitivity)+(1 − Specificity)*(1 − Specificity));" in Step 12.2 of Table 15.1.

In a good classification model, the area under the curve (AUC) should be larger than the area under the 45-degree line representing reference area due to chance (0.50). One can compute the AUC using a mathematical procedure such as the trapezoidal rule, which can be found in most introductory calculus books (e.g., *Calculus,* eighth edition, 2005, by Larson, Hostetler, & Edwards). For the CHD classification example using the MLME model, the AUC was computed to be 0.73, which is considerably larger than the reference area of 0.50, representing a classification rule with results that are no better than those obtained by chance alone.

CONCLUSION

This chapter has illustrated the application of multivariate hierarchical or linear mixed-effects (MLME) models to predict the occurrence of future events. The multivariate procedure presented is accomplished using the statistical package SAS and is illustrated with an example of predicting preclinical disease in a longitudinal study of normal human aging. The MLME prediction method is based on the simultaneous estimation of longitudinal trends in the chosen predictor variables observed over a longitudinal period of observation. In the example presented here, longitudinal trends in mean arterial blood pressure (MAP), serum cholesterol, and glucose are utilized to predict the future occurrence of coronary heart disease (CHD).

The MLME procedure has three main components. In the first part of the SAS program, a multivariate mixed-effects model is developed to statistically fit the longitudinal data for the three variables chosen for the prediction. This part alone is useful in that it provides the methodology and computer code necessary to create a model based on the multivariate regression of several longitudinally observed variables. The second part of the program generates the marginal probabilities based on the mixed-model assumptions and the parameter estimates for the model representing all observation times for all experimental units or individuals in the dataset. Finally, the third part computes the individual posterior probabilities of the event at every visit for each individual using Bayes' formula along with selected prior probabilities and the individual's marginal probability values of being in each classification state. These posterior probabilities are then used in the classification of the individuals into classification groups, and an ROC curve is created, which can be used to evaluate the discrimination or classification ability of the method as well as to help decide on a classification or stopping rule that optimizes the sensitivity and specificity of the approach.

Note that usually a cross-validation of the classification procedure is implemented whereby the data for the individual to be classified is omitted and the entire procedure is carried out for the individual using the chosen stopping rule.

Ideally, in practice, the researcher would develop a prediction method based on a training dataset consisting of enough units with a sufficient number of repeated measurements in each classification group in order to obtain good estimates of all the MLME parameters. This prediction method would then be applied to the longitudinal data from some other experimental unit or individual not in the training dataset but appropriately similar, and then used to make a prediction of the future event occurring for that unit.

In addition to obtaining measures of the true positive rate (sensitivity) and the false positive rate (1 – specificity) and the area under the ROC curve to evaluate the discrimination of the prediction approach, the mean lead time between being identified into a specific classification group and the occurrence of the actual event for the unit or individual can be reported when evaluating the overall results from a prediction or classification method. Another aspect of evaluating the prediction approach is to measure the calibration, or how well the observed proportions agree with the predicted probabilities from the classification (Brant et al., 2010). Pepe, James, and Gu (2007) caution that present statistical methods for evaluating risk predictors are not satisfactory, and the researcher should carefully consider all the different tools available when evaluating any prediction or classification procedure.

A prediction or classification method based on longitudinal data to model the trends of several predictor variables in a multivariate fashion over time provides a valuable statistical tool for application in the health and social sciences. In addition to the classification groups and a measure of time, these independent predictor variables are usually modeled as functions of important identifying characteristics of the unit or individual, such as their initial age or year and other variables related to the classification outcome. These might include measures of diet and habits in a health study or household composition and consumer measures in a study of the need for services offered by a political entity.

ACKNOWLEDGMENT

This research was supported entirely by the Intramural Research Program of NIH, the National Institute on Aging.

REFERENCES

Brant, L. J., Ferrucci, L., Sheng, S. L., Concin, H., Zonderman, A. B., Kelleher, C. C., et al. (2010). Gender differences in the accuracy of time-dependent blood pressure indices for predicting coronary heart disease: A random-effects modeling approach. *Gender Medicine, 7,* 616–627.

Brant, L. J., Sheng, S. L., Morrell, C. H., Verbeke, G. N., Carter, H. B., & Lesaffre, E. (2003). Screening for prostate cancer using random-effects models. *Journal of the Royal Statistical Society: Series A, 166,* 51–62.

Brant, L. J., Sheng, S. L., Morrell, C. H., & Zonderman, A. B. (2005). Data from a longitudinal study provided measurements of cognition to screen for Alzheimer's disease. *Journal of Clinical Epidemiology, 58,* 701–707.

Larson, R., Hostetler, R. P., & Edwards, B. H. (2005). *Calculus* (8th ed.). Florence, KY: Brooks Cole.

Pepe, M. S., James, H., & Gu, J. W. (2007). Letter by Pepe et al. regarding article, "Use and misuse of receiver operating characteristic curve in risk prediction." *Circulation, 116,* 132.

Sheng, S. L., & Brant, L. J. (2009). Predicting preclinical disease using the mixed-effects regression model. In N. Balakrishnan (Ed.), *Methods and applications of statistics in the life and health sciences* (pp. 613–633). New York: Wiley.

Sheng, S. L., & Brant, L. J. (2010). Predicting preclinical disease using the mixed-effects regression model. In S. Kotz, N. Balakrishnan, C. B. Read, B. Vidakovic, & N. L. Johnson (Eds.), *Encyclopedia of statistical sciences* (2nd ed., pp. 1–17). New York: Wiley.

AUTHOR INDEX

Note: Page numbers in italics indicate tables and figures.

SUBJECT INDEX

Note: Page numbers in italics *indicate tables and figures.*

SAGE research**methods**
The Essential Online Tool for Researchers

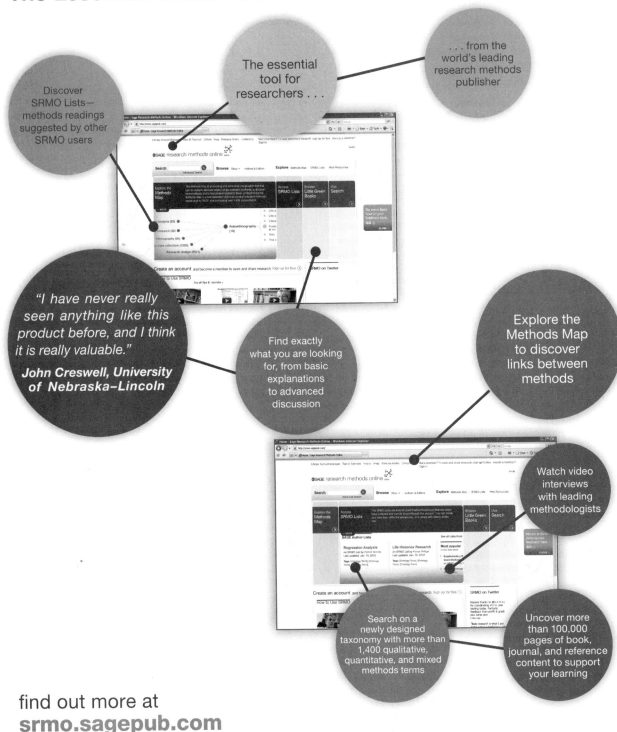

The essential tool for researchers . . .

. . . from the world's leading research methods publisher

Discover SRMO Lists—methods readings suggested by other SRMO users

"I have never really seen anything like this product before, and I think it is really valuable."

John Creswell, University of Nebraska–Lincoln

Find exactly what you are looking for, from basic explanations to advanced discussion

Explore the Methods Map to discover links between methods

Watch video interviews with leading methodologists

Search on a newly designed taxonomy with more than 1,400 qualitative, quantitative, and mixed methods terms

Uncover more than 100,000 pages of book, journal, and reference content to support your learning

find out more at
srmo.sagepub.com